THE HUSBAND BOOK

A Job Description for the Married Man

Dean Merrill

ZONDERVAN
PUBLISHING HOUSE
OF THE ZONDERVAN CORPORATION | GRAND RAPIDS, MICHIGAN 49506

THE HUSBAND BOOK

© 1977 by The Zondervan Corporation
Grand Rapids, Michigan

Second printing September 1977

Library of Congress Cataloging in Publication Data

Merrill, Dean.
    The Husband Book.

    1. Husbands.   I.   Title.
HQ756.M47   301.42'72'041   77-22826

ISBN 0-310-35320-3

Printed in the United States of America

Contents

1 Husbanding Is Not a Natural Talent *9*

2 Leading by Enabling *23*

3 People Who Need People *37*

4 The Dance of the Dollars *53*

5 A Master, a Mistress, and Two Slaves *75*

6 It's a Job *87*

7 The Household of Faith *105*

8 What's a Christian Home? *117*

9 Beyond Anatomy *131*

10 Take It Easy *149*

11 Sickness (What a Pain) *163*

12 The Rest of the Clan *175*

13 The Big Picture *189*

1

Husbanding Is Not a Natural Talent

1

Husbanding
Is Not a
Natural Talent

If you're a carpenter, you haven't forgotten your five long years of apprenticeship.

If you're an attorney, you'll always remember the rigors of law school.

If you're a salesman, you recall the break-in period (all the mistakes you made), and you're still taking time for periodic seminars and training sessions on sales techniques.

If you're a minister, hardly a week goes by without you telling (or retelling) someone a story about your seminary days.

Some of us have spent four — or five, or six, or seven — long years in colleges and graduate schools, getting ready to make a living. Others of us have learned on the job as we've watched, questioned, and imitated a master craftsman of our trade. Some of us are still going to night school, qualifying for the next promotion, honing our skills, learning a better way to lock up that year-end bonus.

We have a second job. Its hours are more irregular, and it pays in a wide range of intangibles rather than cash. Nevertheless, it carries a good deal of responsibility and a lot of challenge. We can succeed at it, we can do a mediocre job, or we can fail. In fact, we can fail so badly that we lose the job and all it means to us.

It's called husbanding. Being the head of our house.

Who trained us for this job?

Most of us have to answer, "No one" — and that's a tragedy. It's not our fault. It's just the way things have worked out. We've been so busy learning how to read profit margin reports and how to rebuild carburetors that we've had no time to study husbanding. And even if we'd asked, there was no one to teach us.

Who ever heard of a college course on how to be a successful household head?

There have been scores of seminars and books on marriage and family life in general, and scores more on parenting — but let's face it: far too many of us have brushed these aside as basically feminine. We've told ourselves, *Yeah, that's good stuff — my wife really needs to keep up on all that.*

We've never really taken a direct look at *our* job from *our* perspective.

What we have done is plunge right on into marriage regardless. We signed up for the job the night we proposed, amid restaurant candlelight or lakeside moonlight or wherever. We said, "I'd like to take on the responsibility of being a husband." (We phrased it a bit more romantically, of course, but the meaning was the same.)

And our sweethearts responded: "Okay, you're hired." (Again, the verbiage was generally altered to fit the occasion.)

We reported for work some months later, with considerable pomp and ceremony in front of a minister and all that. Since then, we've been on the job, for better or for worse. Still no training. Still not much thought about role and responsibility. In the years since the wedding, we've plunged along doing what comes naturally, or what we and our wives have discovered by accident. Sort of like learning to swim Marine-style. We've jumped in the deep water and tried to survive.

It's not our fault that we've made such a haphazard start. It's not our fault that the culture has commonly assumed we know what we're doing. It's just the way things have turned out.

This book is an attempt to help you think about your job as the head of your household. It is, quite simply, a husband's job description.

So far, so good?

Come to think of it — how *have* we survived so far? What accounts for the way we have husbanded up to this point?

More than any of us realize, we have imitated our own fathers. If your dad took out the garbage when you were a kid, you're probably doing it now. If he refused to do it, you've probably done the same. If your dad wrote the checks and watchdogged the money in your home, you're probably doing it too. If your dad said "I love you" to your mother more than once a month, you're probably behaving similarly. (Even though as a kid you weren't within earshot of most of your father's intimate comments, you still picked up his general tone of affection or aloofness and are probably reflecting the same.)

Take the following quiz to see just how closely you're following your father's model.

DID YOUR FATHER...			DO YOU?	
	Yes	No	Yes	No
make time for frequent adult-level communication with his wife?	☐	☐	☐	☐
have a joint checking account?	☐	☐	☐	☐
object to his wife working outside the home?	☐	☐	☐	☐
miss church more than five Sundays in a year?	☐	☐	☐	☐
pray alone with any frequency?	☐	☐	☐	☐
cope well when his wife was pregnant?	☐	☐	☐	☐
change diapers?	☐	☐	☐	☐
play table games with his wife and kids?	☐	☐	☐	☐
become frustrated when his wife got sick?	☐	☐	☐	☐
get along with his in-laws?	☐	☐	☐	☐
plan vacations?	☐	☐	☐	☐

How parallel are your answers?

It's not surprising that you are in many ways a chip off the old block. After all, you started life with his genes. You are biologically similar to him. None of us know how profound and far-reaching are the influences of fundamental heredity.

And you spent the first eighteen or so years of your life — the most impressionable years — watching him.

It would be highly unusual if you *didn't* copy him — subconsciously — in the many details and decisions of being a husband. The points where the two of you differ are probably points about which you've thought a great deal and made a decision *not* to do things like your dad.

Model No. 1

Many of us have grown up under one of two rather unfortunate models. The more common in recent years is *the Abdicator.* His name is on the mailbox, and he is the legal head-of-household, but on a day-to-day basis he serves one — and only one — major purpose: to bring home a paycheck. Every Friday he walks in with the cash necessary to keep things afloat for another week, and having done so, he has pretty well made his contribution.

Did you ever wonder why a husband is commonly called a *breadwinner?* It says something about our priorities.

The rest of the time he spends like any other warm body under the same roof — eating, sleeping, reading, watching TV, and doing whatever he enjoys doing in his spare time. He's not mad at anyone (unless they get in his way); he hasn't resigned from the family. He is indeed one of the bunch. Having financed the enterprise, he now sees it as his right to enjoy the heat, electricity, and refrigerator along with everyone else.

Who is the actual head of this household? Who's in charge?

There are two possible answers:

(1) *The wife.* In many cases, she is the real manager. Once the financial wheels have been greased, she can take it from there. She controls the buying of groceries, clothing, and furniture. She decides the menus and when the family will eat out. She administers discipline to the children, settles arguments, participates in the PTA, and makes sure everyone sees the dentist on time. She sets the spiritual tone of the household as well as how often church is attended. Having worked this hard, she is in a good position to control what happens in the bedroom as well, unless she chooses to surrender this right in exchange for the continued domination of everything else. She is the power behind the throne, the neck that turns the figurehead.

(2) The other possibility, somewhat less frequent, is that *nobody* is in control of the household. A few basic jobs may have been passed out, but beyond that, it's every person for himself. Fix your own meals when you like, go where you want, stay out of trouble, help the other person if it's to your advantage to do so, but otherwise forget it. Laissez faire is the rule.

This is actually more of a hotel than a home. People come and go as they please, encountering one another only by chance and contributing to one another only the minimum necessary to prevent anarchy.

Model No. 2

The second unfortunate model that many of us have seen in our fathers and may be trying, half-heartedly or wholeheartedly, to imitate is *the Autocrat*. Dad is the Boss around here, and don't you forget it. The Resident Caliph, King-of-the-Mountain . . . in stressful moments sometimes even known as Dictator, Tyrant, and other pejorative titles.

Actually, that's pushing it a bit too far, because most Autocrats do love their loyal subjects. They are not wanting to play Attila the Hun; they simply want to do a thorough job of taking care of their wives and children, and that means calling the shots. Almost all the shots. After all, it's their name on the mailbox, and they are not going to let their family suffer for lack of leadership.

This requires a good deal of effort on their part. Setting the budget . . . choosing the apartment or home . . . allowing or denying various activities, especially as they relate to discretionary income . . . setting standards on any number of things from school grades to church attendance to length of hair and hemlines to choice of music.

Add all this to the rigors of an eight-hour day at the office or plant, and you can see why some dads just aren't up to it.

But others are. They have a keen sense of answerability to the community, to God, and to themselves for the state of their household. Also, there is often family pride at stake. *We Johnsons do things a certain way* — the right way, and that's that.

Most families run very smoothly with a strong patriarch. That's one of the advantages of the system. I have a friend now nearing forty who, at a recent all-day family reunion, was directly ordered by his father not to begin washing his car because the noon meal would be ready within half an hour. My friend followed his deeply ingrained habit and promptly obeyed. The father wasn't trying to put down his son, now fully grown with a wife and three children of his own. He was just taking charge as he always had, ensuring that this family would continue to function smoothly!

Maybe your father was an Autocrat. Maybe he was an Abdicator. Maybe he was a variation of one or the other.

Maybe your father was the greatest. Maybe he tried hard but was preoccupied with other things and left a lot of gaps as a result. Maybe, to be honest, he was a downright flop.

Or maybe you grew up without a dad, and thus the preceding section has little relevance to you. In that case, your image of the male adult in the home is especially blurry.

Whatever — it's not likely that any one man can exemplify everything we need to know about husbanding. Our fathers made mistakes. And even when they handled things right, we weren't paying attention or couldn't appreciate the wisdom of their moves much of the time. We need help. We need a clearer understanding of our job in order not to perpetuate the sins of the fathers upon the third and fourth generations.

The Invisible Province

Remember your wedding gifts? That mountain of exquisite paper and ribbon filled with all manner of towels, dishes, and wall hangings that sent your bride into ecstasy?

You stood at her side, smiling and oohing appropriately as she opened each one. People had been most generous to the two of you. Yet . . . their generosity seemed rather slanted, didn't it? The gifts tended toward the housewifely side. Nobody had the common sense to give you a hacksaw, or a quarter-inch drill for putting up those curtain rods in a couple of weeks. Just toasters and queen-size sheets.

The greatest gift of that day, however, was not wrapped in metallic paper and two-tone ribbon. It was an intangible, as masculine as it is feminine, and intended to outlast both toasters and hacksaws. Without meaning to be melodramatic, let me state it clearly: *God has given you and your wife a unique, irreplaceable gift — your home.* The sum total of your togetherness. The atmosphere created by the two of you. The union, the entity created by the merger of your life and hers.

That entity may be housed in a one-bedroom apartment, a suburban split-level, or a fifty-year-old farmhouse with high ceilings and drafty windows. It may or may not have been extended by now to include one, two, or more children. It may have a solid financial base, or it may be severely pinched to make ends meet. The externals that surround the gift of your home are important, but not as important as the gift itself, the special thing God brought into being — your common life and relationship.

It's your base of operations. It's your foundation. It's your shelter from all the nasty people in the world. It's your arena for creativity, for expression, for mutual fulfillment. It is a divine work of art — "what God hath joined together."

It's not yours alone. Neither is it exclusively hers. It belongs to both of you. The apostle Peter calls you "joint heirs of the grace of life" (1 Peter 3:7 RSV). He's talking about procreation, yes. He's saying that it takes both of you to create new life. You are joint heirs of that particular miracle. But in a broader sense, I believe he's saying that married life . . . the home . . . the household . . . is something that belongs to both of you, that both of you create and enjoy, and that neither of you can usurp as your own private possession.

This gift is both glorious and fragile, enduring yet not automatic. And here is where we make our mistake. We start taking our home, our province, for granted. We assume it will always be there. Because it is so fundamental, we think it will hold up on its own. We can always go home, and home will always be home.

Not so. The unattended household has a way of degenerating and coming back to haunt us. We go steaming along our way, climbing our corporation ladders, pushing and getting pushed around in the modern bedlam — then we come home to collapse and recuperate. . . .

And it's not home. Something's wrong. Things are just as ragged here as they were out there. The relationship with our wife has deteriorated, and we hadn't even noticed. And now we desperately need the solace of that relationship, and it's gone, or at least rather seriously dissipated.

Meanwhile, she's hurting as badly as we are. Whether she spends her daytime hours in the house or away at an office, store, hospital, or school, she still needs many of the same things we need — togetherness, understanding, communication, lack of pressure, a place and a mate to facilitate recycling.

That's why husbanding requires *time* and *attention*. A lot of married men weren't thinking about that the night they proposed. They were thinking only about romance and sex and peer expectations and how to get out of doing laundry. Michael Novak, writing in *Harper's* magazine, says rather caustically:

> The central idea of our foggy way of life . . . is that life is solitary and brief, and that its aim is self-fulfillment. Next come beliefs in establishing the imperium of the self. . . . Autonomy we understand to mean protection of our inner kingdom — protection around the self from intrusions of chance, irrationality, necessity, and other persons. ("My self, my castle.") In such a vision of the self, marriage is merely an alliance. It entails as minimal an abridgment of inner privacy as one partner or the other may allow. Children are not a welcome responsibility, for to have children is, plainly, to cease being a child oneself.[1]

In contrast, the household God intends is a kingdom of two or more persons, and no medieval prince was ever so richly endowed. It is a fortress for the protection of love and Christian growth. The drawbridges are down to all who share the values of the kingdom, but they are fast shut against those who would destroy it.

Novak continues his analysis of modern marriage:

> People say of marriage that it is boring, when what they mean is that it terrifies them: too many and too deep are its searing revelations, its angers, its rages, its hates, and its loves. They say of marriage that it is deadening, when what they mean is that it drives us beyond adolescent fantasies and romantic dreams. They say of children that they are

piranhas, eels, brats, snots, when what they mean is that the importance of parents with respect to the future of their children is now known with greater clarity and exactitude than ever before.[2]

The more we value our home, the province God has given us, the more concerned we are that it thrive. It becomes apparent that the realm must come under some sort of organization, some kind of management to enable the people on the inside to reach their full potential while the enemies on the outside are held at bay.

God thought of that. He thought of it right at the beginning when he bequeathed to Adam and Eve the first home. He asked them both to "be fruitful and multiply, and fill the earth and subdue it" (Gen. 1:28). This magnificent task began with Adam being asked to name each animal (2:19). As for Eve, God called her Adam's "helper" (2:18).

Two roles thus begin to emerge at this early time, even before the Temptation and Fall recorded in Genesis 3. The roles are reinforced in the New Testament, where husbands are explicitly called "the head" (Eph. 5:23).

If you're a woman reading this (why are you reading this book?!), or if you're a man who's at all conscious of the current push for female equality, you're probably starting to tense up right now. Is God a male chauvinist? Why the man? And what's a "head"? How do "heads" relate to "helpers"? Is one better than the other?

I think I can answer those questions without being chauvinistic and without twisting Scripture. But it will take all of chapter 2 (and maybe more!) to do so. I'll say this much right here: Headship is not what you're probably thinking. It's a fairly radical idea.

[1]Michael Novak, "The Family Out of Favor," *Harper's*, 252, no. 1511 (April 1976), p. 39.

[2]Ibid., p. 42.

2

Leading
by Enabling

2

Leading
by Enabling

I was in San Francisco on a business trip during their somewhat notorious 1976 strike by municipal workers. Bus drivers, museum guards, trash collectors, and maintenance people at various city buildings had been off their jobs for about three weeks, and things were getting a little ugly.

There had been some pushing and shoving at several City Hall demonstrations as the public servants insisted on more money while the city council insisted it was broke. The situation had deteriorated to the level of bomb scares at the airport — which is what accounted for the rather strange announcement I heard as I walked up the concourse toward the baggage claim: "The restrooms have now been cleared and are again available for use," or some such words.

I didn't know enough about the local issues at stake to side with either the union or the city. But while waiting for my suitcase, I began musing about the rather curious term *public servant*. Obviously a misnomer. Servants don't haggle over wages, demand certain working hours and holidays, or walk off and quit in order to get their way. At least not the servants I've read about, especially in New Testament times.

I suppose that was part of the point of the strike: The "public servants" were tired of being treated like servants (according to their view of the facts) and wanted to be treated like something considerably higher.

Jesus once faced a situation in which a couple of his disciples initiated what might be called a bargaining session on their future working conditions. Actually, their designated negotiator was their mother (how can a boss get rough with anybody's mother, huh?), and the rhetoric was cordial as Mrs. Zebedee presented her case.

But Jesus took the occasion to make some startling statements about roles and relationships in the kingdom of God. He said:

> You know that the rulers of the Gentiles lord it over them, and their high officials exercise authority over them. Not so with you. Instead, whoever wants to become great among you must be your servant, and whoever wants to be first must be your slave — just as the Son of Man did not come to be served, but to serve, and to give his life a ransom for many (Matt. 20:25–28).

I don't think George Meany would like that. Neither, for that matter, would the American Management Association. Jesus is making a scramble of a whole set of preconceptions here, and he admits that the Gentiles aren't on his wavelength at all. That's right; we're not.

But what he is saying is that in *his* set of values, the Big Man is the slave. If you want to get to the top, stop trying to climb and start serving. The quest for power, he says, is all backwards; the only route to fulfillment is to abandon your rights.

The truth is that in our civilized society we've all but forgotten what a servant is and does. That's why we can call unionized municipal workers public servants and not realize the absurdity. A real servant is a human being who has lost everything — his freedom, his power, his prestige, and in ancient cultures, sometimes even his name. He was known commonly as "the slave of _____," symbolizing his total ownership by his master. Whatever the master ordered, he did, no matter how difficult, at what hour of the day or night, or with what hazards. He served, period.

Jesus told the ambitious James and John that the road to greatness in God's scheme of things was a road of serving. He didn't even let himself off the hook. "The Son of man . . . came to serve," he said.

The Bible doesn't say how the two brothers (and mama) reacted to that rather deflating news. But I know how we in the modern church have reacted. We have done our best to avoid the call to servanthood.

One thing we've done is to switch words. The King James Version generally does not say "serving." It says "ministry" instead. "Whosoever will be great among you, let him be your minister" (Matt. 20:26). Ah, that has a little more class to it. Any Christian parent is proud when his or her offspring announces, "I think I'm going to study for the ministry." How nice. He's on his way toward respectability.

Another King James word for *servant* is *deacon*. Again, we've institutionalized something that in the beginning was meant to be plain, honest, hard work for the benefit of the rest of the body of Christ. The first deacons were chosen in Acts 6 to be cooks and waiters for a group of elderly women. (Talk about Women's Liberation!) Read it for yourself. The name *deacon* comes to us straight from the Greek *diakoneō* — to serve.

About this time you're starting to think, *This makes no sense at all. If the leaders of the church — and even Jesus himself — are nothing more than servants, who's in charge of things?! Somebody's got to be the leader.*

You're right. Someone has to lead. And that someone is the servant.

Perhaps the most extraordinary thing Jesus ever did was what he did after they'd finished eating the Last Supper. Everyone was sitting around enjoying a second cup of coffee (or whatever came last in the meal) when all of a sudden the Son of God "got up . . . took off his outer clothing, and wrapped a towel around his waist" (John 13:4).

What's going on?

"After that, he poured water into a basin and began to wash his disciples' feet, drying them with the towel that was wrapped around him" (13:5).

Crazy!

Washing guests' feet was a scum job if there ever was one, a drudgery even slaves did not greet with enthusiasm. Peter's brain was reeling with the incongruity of it all, and he said so. But Jesus was not going to stop.

Finally, the washing was finished. "He put on his clothes and returned to his place. 'Do you understand what I have done for you?' he asked them" (13:12).

A simple question.

NO. They didn't have the slightest notion. (Neither do we. We've read this story dozens of times, and most of us still don't get it.)

So he explained.

> You call me "Teacher" and "Lord," and rightly so,
> for that is what I am. Now that I, your Lord and

Teacher, have washed your feet, you also should wash one another's feet. I have set you an example that you should do as I have done for you. I tell you the truth, no servant is greater than his master, nor is a messenger greater than the one who sent him. Once you know these things, you will be blessed if you do them (13:13–17).

Jesus thus created a new, seemingly schizophrenic role: the leader/servant. The chief/Indian. The honcho/peon. He acknowledged the need for leadership. Jesus was not an anarchist. But neither was he willing to tolerate the all-too-frequent abuses of power. Leadership, he said, is earned, is indeed made possible only by serving.

We have a long way to go to implement this in the church. We have a long way to go to implement it in many of our homes as well.

We are rather adept at pretending to serve while doing the opposite. As I write this, the current television commercials have fresh-faced teen-age employees of a certain fast-food empire smiling into the camera and singing, "We do it all for you!" I happen to live about fifteen miles from that empire's international headquarters, and I must say it's a rather impressive piece of architecture on a rather valuable piece of real estate right beside the tollway. They're obviously not doing it *all* for me. The language is the language of servanthood, but the facts are something else.

We Christians play the same games. Juan Carlos Ortiz, the insightful Buenos Aires pastor, tells in his book *Disciple:*

> Once I was in a meeting where someone was introduced with great fanfare. The organ played and the spotlights came on as someone announced, "And

now, the great servant of God, _____."

If he was great, he was not a servant. And if he was a servant, he was not great. Servants are people who understand that they are worthy of nothing.
. . .

May God help us to do with joy what servants in His Kingdom do.[1]

What is a husband?

It is with this understanding that we must now begin to define what Paul meant when he called the husband "the head." We must not allow secularist management consultants or family psychologists to write our definitions. We must not succumb to the prevailing haphazard opinions of our society.

We must not be swayed even by what we perceive to be "efficient." Efficiency is a great god in most of our lives, and students of human relationships have done much research to find the best ways for the average stubborn bunch of people to get along with each other, to get something accomplished instead of spending nine-to-five at one another's throats. Without modern efficiency methods, this country wouldn't be half as productive as it is.

But certain things are different in the kingdom ruled by love. When the Lord of the kingdom has succeeded in purging us of our basic hostilities toward one another, we are then freed to become one another's servants and not get up-tight about it. Our egos do not have to be pampered. We have chosen a radical, paradoxical road to greatness.

And the place where all this must begin is at home. The head of a Christian household is the man who has given himself to serve his wife and his children, if any. Why? Because he loves them. He is the guy who enables things to succeed. He is the guy who plans ahead so schedules mesh. He is the guy who figures out what's causing tension and then moves to relieve it. He is solution-oriented.

And if the solution involves getting his hands dirty, so be it. He's not on a pedestal. He's not hung up about washing feet . . . or windows, or little boys' elbows. He is not worried about being respected. He is not concerned about prestige. He is concerned only about serving his God-given province.

Do you know any husbands like that?

The greatest challenge (so far) to my leader/servant-hood began on March 3, 1975, at about nine o'clock at night. Our 2½-year-old son was soundly asleep in his crib, and I was enjoying *Time* magazine in the living room. Outside, the Illinois winter was finishing its last gusts. It was one of those nice, quiet evenings that would be even nicer if they'd stay that way.

I was getting back toward the business section when the front door opened and my very pregnant wife came in from her biweekly visit to the obstetrician. She said not a word — she didn't even take off her coat — but walked straight to a chair across from me and slumped. There was shock on her face, but it was her special kind of mock-shock that she puts on whenever she wants to make sure I'm paying attention before she speaks.

I went along with the drama. I waited. Finally, I grinned and said, "Okay — what happened?"

"Heitzler thinks he hears two heartbeats."

"You're kidding."

"No."

A set of X-rays at the hospital tomorrow morning would tell for sure, but suddenly we already knew we were having twins. This weird pregnancy now made sense — the nausea that wouldn't go away, all the urgent rushes to the bathroom during supper (Grace's morning sickness

always struck around 5:00 P.M.), the rather sudden inflation of her middle starting at about the fifth month, and
more recently the mysterious swelling of her feet and
ankles, which had seemed for all the world like diabetes
until the tests turned out negative.

We sat there talking, staring, and crying. She gave me
a second-by-second replay of how the nurse had first
discovered the two heartbeats and then how excited Dr.
Heitzler had gotten, pushing with his stethoscope here
and there in search of thump-thumps until she thought
her abdomen was going to split open on the spot.

After another dozen exclamations ("Wow!" "This is
unbelievable." "Wow!"), we started tracing the family
trees in search of other cases of multiple births. None.
We were unique.

Finally we snapped back to reality. We had approximately six weeks to get ready for two new people in our
lives. Nathan would have to be shifted immediately to a
regular bed so his crib could be added to the one we'd
already bought at a garage sale. Grace would have to drop
her Sunday school teaching immediately instead of later,
since the doctor had ordered complete bed rest from here
on. Our minds were swimming at all the adjustments to be
made in six short weeks, provided the twins didn't arrive
early, as twins often do.

On March 14 — eleven days later — Rhonda Joy and
Tricia Dawn made their entrance.

My memories of that first year are pretty much a blur.
Any parent of twins will tell you that if you can survive the
first year, you're probably going to make it the rest of the
way. We got to the place where Grace would handle the
first nighttime feeding — whichever baby awakened first
— and I would take the second. The weary breakfast
conversation the next morning would invariably go,
"Well, 'my' baby lasted till 3:45 — how long did 'yours'

go?" Throughout the day, of course, simultaneous feedings were necessary to preserve sanity.

The rewards for all this came whenever we mustered the energy to take the family out in public. People would swarm around, ooh and ahh, and ask dumb questions like "Are they twins?" At such times Grace and I would forget about all the work and stand back to appreciate the beauty of God's double gift.

However, the simple process of getting the family ready to go anywhere made these times precarious at best. Long after most procedures of the week had been tamed, Sunday morning remained my nemesis. Getting five people fed, dressed, and in the car on time without two or three episodes of tears (children) or frustrated anger (adults) seemed virtually impossible.

I remember in particular one Sunday not long before the twins' first birthday. It wasn't one of the worst, but it was not the best either. My difficulty was internal; I was feeling that the entire weekend so far had been nothing but children, children, children, and I had been trying to give each of them time and give Grace some relief — but underneath, I really wanted to get at some house jobs and reorganize my makeshift office in the basement and do what *I* wanted to do. I wanted to make efficient use of my time.

Children, you may have noticed, are not particularly geared to that abstraction known as efficiency.

By Sunday morning my inner tendons were getting tighter and tighter. I gritted my way through the breakfast hour and the dressing process, helping Nathan get ready while Grace dressed the girls. A last-minute messy diaper was changed without too much trauma. We even managed to get all three into snowsuits and out to the car with only minor skirmishes.

But I was in no shape for church. I felt like I had done

my duty in spite of myself. We dropped the girls at the nursery, took Nathan to his toddler group, and Grace went on to one of the adult elective classes. I seriously considered finding something else to do until the worship hour. I mainly wanted just to sit and do a little silent fuming. I was not particularly interested in the pronouncements of any Sunday school teacher.

I indulged in my private little muddle for a few minutes, but it didn't feel as good as I had hoped. I finally made a late entrance into the class and found a seat beside Grace.

The text for the morning was Philippians 2. I listened as the Scripture was read:

> Do nothing out of selfish ambition or vain conceit, but in humility consider others better than yourselves. Each of you should not look only to your own interests, but also to the interests of others. Your attitude should be the same as that of Christ Jesus: Who, being in very nature God, did not consider equality with God something to be grasped, but made himself nothing, *taking the very nature of a servant*, being made in human likeness. And being found in appearance as a man, he humbled himself and became obedient to death — even death on a cross! (2:3–8).

The teacher didn't need to say a word. The apostle had already shot me down. *Servanthood, Dean! All weekend you've been refusing to be a servant, and that's why you're so tight. You've forgotten that God has made you the servant of Nathan and Rhonda and Tricia, and Grace as well. No wonder the household is about to explode.*

A friend of mine, Dick Foth, who leads/serves a church near the University of Illinois campus in Urbana, says, "What are the true signs of spiritual maturity? If a poll were taken of Christians, how would they answer? I have a feeling they would cite such things as the ability to pray, to expound Scripture, to witness, to manifest dramatic gifts of the Holy Spirit — healings, miracles, that sort of thing."

Dick doesn't object to those, and neither do I. But in his opinion, "The acid test of spiritual maturity is *relationships*. If my Christianity does not profoundly affect my relationship with my wife, with my children, with the board of my church, with the members of my congregation — then I'm not as mature as I might like to think."

The Jesus Movement of the early seventies generated a lot of slogans — some corny, others pretty good. The one I liked best was SERVE THE LORD, SERVE THE PEOPLE.

The second half is but a practical translation of the first. Both amount to the same thing. In my role as a Christian husband, as head of the unique gift I call home, SERVE THE LORD, SERVE THE HOUSEHOLD is not a bad definition of my job.

[1]Juan Carlos Ortiz, *Disciple* (Carol Stream, Ill.: Creation House, 1975), p. 39.

3

People
Who Need
People

3

People
Who Need
People

You've heard the following sentence so often you've gotten numb to it. It's become a cliche. But God said it, and it's profound. Perhaps some meaning can be injected into it.

Here it is:

"It is not good that the man should be alone" (Gen. 2:18).

Run it through your brain a couple more times. *It is not good that the man should be alone.*

I believe this is something more than just an excuse for getting married. I believe God is making a fundamental observation about the nature of human beings. He is saying something like this: "I could have made people any number of different ways, but I happen to have chosen to make people so that they need other people. A human being by himself — whether he admits it or not — is going to have a tougher time of it."

It becomes fairly clear after a few moments of thought

that God is talking about something more than physical proximity. Simply being in the presence of other people is not the answer. We have all had the experience of being intensely lonely at a crowded party. In fact, some sociologists have observed that the more compacted we become geographically, the more distant we are interpersonally. Most farmers know and relate to the family a mile down the gravel road better than most high-rise apartment dwellers do to the couple behind the next door.

So Genesis 2:18 cannot mean that the simple act of living with your wife under the same roof takes care of the disadvantages of aloneness.

Neither, for that matter, can it mean that the single person who lives by himself is automatically shut out from the blessings of relationship.

What God is saying is that people — men, women, marrieds, singles, everybody — are in need of interaction with other people, and to deny ourselves that interaction is "not good."

There are a lot of single adults who understand this very deeply and have gone out of their way to establish solid, meaningful lines of communication with others.

And there are a lot of husbands (and wives) who, physical proximity notwithstanding, are living alone.

Why is aloneness "not good"?

The need for togetherness implanted by God into the human race there in Eden runs all through our existence from bottom to top. We obviously need each other for physical reasons, to help each other acquire food, clothing, and shelter. The man who gets married essentially to have a cook and seamstress is operating on this low level.

Our greater needs lie in the intangibles. We can cook our own meals and iron our own shirts far easier than we can effectively criticize our own ideas or plan our own futures. Another way of saying this is that we all need *feedback*, someone to bounce things back to us, someone to encourage us when we need it — and deflate us when we need it. Someone to say things like:

"That's a fantastic idea. You're brilliant."

Or: "Yes, but what about————?"

Or: "I was reading something about that the other day; did you know ————?"

Or: "You've got to be kidding!"

At the same time, we husbands can make a contribution by listening to and interacting with our wives' thoughts, ideas, brainstorms, and dreams. It's true not only on the job but also at home: Two heads really are better than one.

All of this is not to deny the value of solitude. The Scriptures are all in favor of times for reflection, for getting away from other people to regain one's perspective. Moses, for example, spent several forty-day spells alone with his God.

But was that really aloneness? Perhaps it was the greatest form of encounter possible. Moses was not really alone. He was face-to-face with another Being, and all his powers of concentration were undoubtedly focused on the dialogue.

We put aloneness furthest from us when we are locked in serious encounter with just one other person, divine or human. This is the wonder of prayer. It is also the wonder of Christian marriage. The more persons we try to relate to simultaneously, the more the bonds begin to break up and the more we slip off toward aloneness again, e.g., the crowded party.

"What'd you do today?"

What if we were to take a poll of our wives and ask them to complete this sentence:

The greatest evidence that my husband loves me is that:

- ☐ he spends money on me.
- ☐ he gives great sex.
- ☐ he talks.

I think we know what the answer would be. Number three would win by a landslide.

Wives seek conversation. They're frustrated when they don't get it. They can endure tight budgets and headaches at bedtime far easier than suppertime silence.

Why?

If you're thinking, *Because all women are gabby,* shame on you. There are some legitimate reasons.

1. A wife is a human being, just like you. And as we've already noted, God didn't program human beings for aloneness. He programed us, male and female, for togetherness, companionship, interaction.

2. A wife is understandably curious about the goings-on of her leader/servant. Assuming she subscribes to the scriptural roles described in the previous chapter, she views you as fairly strategic to the Invisible Province with which the two of you have been gifted. She's looking to you for direction — not in the form of commands or policy statements, but in the subtleties of open conversation and, even more importantly, the actions of servanthood.

Perhaps the whole modern controversy among many Christians about the submission of wives to husbands would not be so heated if we paid more attention to the *oneness* God intends in marriage. It seems to me that the submission passage of Ephesians 5 is perhaps God's emergency provision, a backup measure for those times when a decision's got to be made and we haven't come to consensus with our wives. In cases of deadlock, yes, the husband has to call the shot. But was the deadlock really necessary?

Managers in business give high priority to generating a team atmosphere among workers, a sense of common task, so that problems are approached from a basis of "We ought to . . ." instead of "The boss says. . . ." If in our marriages the goals of *union, oneness, concurrence,* and *consensus* were more central, perhaps we wouldn't need to talk so much about submission. If we truly believed that God intends for two people to become one, there wouldn't be so many confrontations to negotiate. Because if we and our wives are of one mind on a question, no one has to submit. We move ahead in agreement.

And the merger of two sets of opinions takes place largely through conversation.

3. If your wife is the kind who's home all day, she doesn't encounter many adults. She's probably a mother; she lives in the world of children for a major portion of each week. Most of the adults she's with for any length of time are *very* similar to her — namely, other mothers at home with children.

So here you come at five o'clock. You're sort of a novelty. You're male instead of female. And you've been in an adult world all day. You've been in the world of ideas, machines, money, and all sorts of interesting things. You make for a nice change of pace in her day. You're her window to a lot of places, people, and events that otherwise are inaccessible to her.

"But I'm *tired* when I get home from work," you say. "I've been fighting the expressway traffic for forty-five minutes, and the pressures of my job are still swirling through my head, and I'm just not in the mood to walk in and be an instantly charming conversationalist."

That's probably true. A lot of us work in jobs that won't turn off with a switch. It takes us a while to come down, to remember that there's always tomorrow and that the work will still be there.

Thus the evening meal may not be the best communication time for you and your wife. There's no rule that says it has to be. There are lots of other options. I know one couple who get up at 4:30 A.M. every day so they can exercise and then enjoy a long, leisurely breakfast together before heading for work!

What is important is that you and your wife not live your lives in aloneness. The details are up to you.

Actually, your communication goes far deeper than "What'd you do today?" The everyday places you've been, people you've seen, and catastrophes you've avoided are starting points, of course. But they're not enough. In fact, they can get rather boring unless you both can place all this minutiae against the backdrop of a deeper sharing of plans, feelings, wishes, hopes, fears, aspirations, and dreams. A lot of husbands yawn through their wives' descriptions of the morning coffee klatsch, not because the klatsch itself was a bore but because the husband has no feeling for why this might be important to his wife. He hardly knows the other families in the neighborhood; maybe he can't even connect faces with the names his wife is mentioning. They're nonpersons to him. So no wonder he's out of sync with the klatsch discussion of vacation spots or fancy restaurants, because he's not really aware of his wife's secret wishes, likes, and dislikes on those topics.

The New Testament even hints in 1 Corinthians 14:35 that husbands and wives should get into Christian belief and doctrine together. Paul (for whatever reason) asked the first-century women to keep silent in the church meetings — but not to bury their questions. "They should ask their own husbands at home," he wrote.

When was the last time you and your wife had a theological discussion?

Finding the time

The most unfortunate thing about husband-wife communication is that its absence doesn't cause immediate repercussions. Your stomach doesn't growl as it does when you miss a meal. You don't go stumbling through the next day as you do after getting to bed at three or three-thirty in the morning. Therefore, it's fairly easy to stay busy with more mundane things and never get around to genuine meeting of minds.

But if you're convinced that you *need* her and she *needs* you, that it is not good to live alone, then you'll find the time. In addition to the two options already mentioned — evening mealtime and early morning — here are some others:

• *Late at night,* as you're going to sleep (unless you're the type who's "out" the minute you hit the bed). Naturally, some nights you're going to be engaged in nonverbal communication (more about that in chapter 9), but what about the other nights?

• *Driving time* — a beautiful set-up for talking about all kinds of things. You're sitting there together, you can't do much else — why not get in some quality time with each other? Long trips are great, but even the short runs to shopping centers, to church, to friends' houses are good opportunities to talk.

• *Restaurants.* The big, splashy ones, yes, but also the corner coffee shops where you can get two pecan rolls and two cups of coffee for two bucks or less . . . and sit for an hour if you like.

• *Vacations.* The point of a vacation is not only to *do* some neat things and *avoid* the old grind, but also to *be with* each other for greater chunks of time than is possible in the normal week. Vacations are great for getting into those heavy topics that otherwise take too long.

● *"Appointments."* If the above situations aren't enough, there's nothing wrong with blocking out a certain hour each week simply to sit down together in the living room, turn off the TV, and talk. You think that sounds artificial and awkward? Not if you believe that communicating with your wife is at least as important as seeing your doctor. One is as easy to postpone as the other, but in both cases, you'll eventually wish you hadn't.

Finding the time becomes at least 100 percent more difficult as soon as children arrive on the scene. Grace and I'd been married four years when we concluded that the Lord wanted us to help resolve a particular situation in my family by inviting my thirteen-year-old niece to come live with us. We'd been used to totally free and open times of conversation during two meals each day, plus hours and hours of additional time on the weekends.

All of a sudden there were three plates at the table, not two. All of a sudden there was a thirteen-year-old mind listening to everything we said. We immediately shifted, of course, from Dean/Grace conversation to Dean/Vickie and Grace/Vickie conversation: school, swimming, the youth group at church, guys, clothes . . . all important parts of her world. We knew we needed to build a lot of bridges toward her, and mealtimes were natural for working at this.

But when were Grace and I to talk about family finances?

When were we to talk about the pressures of my job (which were considerable that particular year)?

When were we to talk about how we both felt about Vickie? Whether we'd made the right decision on her most recent request? Whether she was feeling wanted and loved? What we ought to be doing differently?

Obviously, not at the supper table.

We simply had to carve out times to be alone and communicate, let our hair down, get used to being the instant parents of a teen-ager, coordinate our decision-making, and reassure each other of our love and gratitude for what the other person was contributing to this venture.

When a newborn baby comes into your home, of course, it's not such a shock to your communication patterns at the beginning. You're super-busy, of course, but you can talk *while* you're taking care of an infant.

In less than a year, though, your son or daughter is in a high chair at the table. He still doesn't understand what you're saying, but it's getting a bit more difficult to bare your soul to your wife while you're also trying to con Li'l Punkin' into downing his strained spinach. Somehow there's a distraction factor in there somewhere.

Between ages two and three, your youngster begins picking up the simple parts of table conversation. At our house there are rather hilarious efforts to talk past our kids either by spelling out the key words ("Keep the c-o-o-k-i-e-s out of sight until she's finished her mashed potatoes.") or by using Parent Double-talk ("The eldest will need to participate in a cleansing soon after the conclusion of this repast." Translation: "Nathan's taking a bath after supper.").

Eventually, of course, your kids learn how to spell and also how to translate, and mom and dad have to find other times and places for saying what needs to be said to each other. The danger here is that, due to children or any number of other reasons (work schedules, for example), you and your wife don't manage to find enough time for strictly adult-level communication. That is a tragedy.

Blessed are the peacemakers

Even with adequate time and the best of intentions, there will be times when the communication lines get snarled. The two of you simply aren't going to be in harmony every moment of your married lives. We have all experienced disagreement and conflict; we know how rotten it feels. I can stand a difference of opinion or even a simple misunderstanding with anyone in the world easier than with Grace. When the two of us have gotten crosswise on an issue, regardless of what it is, I'm miserable.

An important question I ask myself whenever faced with a marital misunderstanding is, "Is this whole problem real or imagined? Did she really intend to cause me this grief? Or was it an accident?"

The majority of times, it was an accident. Either —

• We hadn't taken time to talk things through thoroughly; we were in a hurry, so we cut the conversation short, or maybe we didn't talk at all. We just *assumed* we knew what was in the other person's head.

• Or we fell into blurring the distinction between idea and person. We started wrapping up our ego with the position we were defending. It was no longer a question of whether the bedroom would look better in blue or beige; it was a question of whose will was stronger. In such a moment, we both have forgotten about our calling to be servants of each other.

Sven Wahlroos, in his book *Family Communication*, lists a number of what he calls "unfair techniques" that husbands and wives often employ. How many of the following sound vaguely familiar?

• *"Am I supposed to jump up and down and lick your boots?"* Unfair Technique I: Pretending that the other person has made an unreasonable statement or demand.

• *"You did it only because you feel guilty."* Unfair Technique II: Mind reading, psychologizing, jumping to conclusions; pretending that one single motive constitutes complete motivation; divination.

- *"Anyway, look how filthy this room is!"* Unfair Technique III: Switching the subject; using counter-accusations.
- *"And furthermore. . . ."* Unfair Technique IV: Bringing up more than one accusation at a time; the kitchen sink attack.
- *"I try much harder than you."* Unfair Technique V: Bragging, or playing the numbers game.
- *"Why make a big deal out of nothing?"* Unfair Technique VI: Using logic to hide from emotional reality.
- *"But that's not true. I didn't. . . ."* Unfair Technique VII: Interrupting.
- *"All right, we'll see what you say when I divorce you!"* Unfair Technique VIII: Using the atom bomb, the bull in the china shop; intimidating, yelling, screaming, and "exploding."
- *"You're just like your father, that no-good bum."* Unfair Technique IX: Blaming the partner for something he cannot help or cannot do anything about now, or for something you do yourself; refusing to forgive.
- *"How can you be so stupid?"* Unfair Technique X: Humiliating the partner; using insults and epithets, rubbing in; exposing dirty linen in public, comparing unfavorably.
- *"That's all in your mind."* Unfair Technique XI: Crazy-making; "bugging"; unpredictability.
- *"Boo-hoo, boo-hoo."* Unfair Technique XII: Having one's feelings hurt at the drop of a hat; guilt induction; the destructive use of crying.
- *"Sure, sure, I'll bet."* Unfair Technique XIII: The use of sarcasm and ridicule.
- *"————"* Unfair Technique XIV: Silence, ignoring, sulking, pouting; "cold-shoulder treatment."[1]

The amazing thing to me is that we unleash such comments on the one person whom we love most in all the world — when our sense of common courtesy would prevent us from doing the same to a secretary, a store clerk, or a fellow worker. Any foreman or manager worth his salt knows that there's a right and a wrong way to deal with someone who disagrees with him. Why is it that we can come home and let our mouths say things we'd never dare say to casual acquaintances?

What is *really* interesting is to watch what happens when we put the two together — when we're with our wives and other people in a social situation. A tremendous amount of classified information can be learned just by listening to how husbands and wives talk to and about each other in public. I have, in the course of a single evening, heard apparently happily married spouses cut each other down four, five, and six times. Things like:

"Wow, I didn't think George was ever going to find this place tonight — he went around and around the block; he even forgot the paper where I'd written the directions."

"Oh, look at these hors d'oeuvres. Hey, Joyce, wanna see some good food for a change?'

"How d'ya like my wife's $40 hairdo?"

The American brand of humor, in fact, is built largely upon sarcasm and making the other person look foolish. (In contrast, humor in other parts of the world is more often based on things like word plays and the preposterous, with the result that American jokes often seem crude and mean by comparison.)

The Christian husband is the guy who resists the temptation to use a wife joke to get a laugh. If he has a bone to pick with his wife, he does it straightforwardly and in private. As Paul wrote in Ephesians 5:29,33, "After all, no one ever hated" (shall we add "or embarrassed"?) "his own body, but he feeds and cares for it, just as Christ does the church — for we are members of his body. . . . Each one of you also must love his wife as he loves himself."

I imagine Christ could crack quite a lot of very funny jokes about the imperfections of the church. But he doesn't. He loves us too much.

The evidence of love is often contained in words. Public words, private words. Words *to* our wives, words *about* our wives. Words — the right kind of honest and affirming words — are the stepping stones that lead us from the tragedy of aloneness. They are the stones with which we build the castle of marriage.

[1]Sven Wahlroos, *Family Communication* (New York: Macmillan, 1974).

4

The Dance
of the
Dollars

4

The Dance
of the
Dollars

The first twenty-five years of our lives, according to an old sage whose name I've forgotten, our major shortage is *money*.

The next twenty-five years, our major shortage is *time*.

And the last twenty-five years, we're fighting hardest for *energy*.

There's a good chunk of truth in that — but I've got news for the wise man: the money problems don't evaporate on the twenty-fifth birthday. (And the time squeeze starts several years earlier, right?)

A shortage is a natural breeder of tension. We all know how easily our marriages can sputter, fume, and sizzle over the lack — real or imagined — of enough money to do what we and/or our wives want. Long after our sexual lives have been harmonized, our major career choices have been agreed upon, and the size of our family has been determined, we can still be hassling over money, with no solution in sight.

Our difficulty is usually a classic example of worrying about individual trees instead of the forest. How come groceries are so high? Why did she buy that new coat when she *knew* things were tight this month? A hefty six-month insurance premium is due, and there's no nest egg to take care of it.

And we react. We shoot from the hip. We launch into a harangue about holding down expenses. We bemoan the rising cost of living. We curse the Democrats, or the Republicans, as the case may be. To handle the current brushfire, we write a hot check and hope for the best. Or we run out to the friendly household finance corporation for a quick loan — at highway-robbery interest rates.

There has to be a better way.

Whose money?

The Bible, as you know, does not say that money is the root of all evil. (What it says in 1 Timothy 6:10 is that "the love of money is a root of all kinds of evil.") Money itself ought not to be a headache. It ought not to be a source of contention. Instead, it is one of our resources (along with time, energy, air, water, etc.), part of the raw material with which we build our lives. Money, I happen to believe, is another "good and perfect gift . . . from above, coming down from the Father of the heavenly lights" (James 1:17).

Don't think of God as too holy to touch the stuff. The Scriptures often speak of him as the Creator and Owner of the entire cosmos. His barrage of questions in Job 38–41 is essentially a litany of all that he controls.

And he has chosen to assign a few of his resources to you and your wife to administrate. He has given the two of you a combination of energy and intelligence, which you convert for forty hours or so each week into earnings.

You do a number of other things with your allotment of

energy and intelligence, of course, which don't translate into cash, e.g., mowing the lawn, fixing breakfast, playing racquetball, doing the laundry, etc. Each has its place.

Thus, we come to some premises:

1. Money is a good thing — it's one of God's gifts to us.

2. Since it's one of God's gifts, it needs to be used with care and thoughtfulness.

3. The gift of money is a *joint* gift, a joint asset. It belongs to the household, the unified life that you and your wife have set up.

And the practical question for the two of you boils down to:

What shall *we* do with *our* money?

I'm not just talking about whether you file a joint income tax return each year. And it's more than a matter of both of you signing the house mortgage papers. It is of strategic importance that at the very core of your two brains you *think* and *feel* in terms of common money. It belongs to both of you, and you're answerable to each other as well as to the Giver for how it's used or abused.

You don't have trouble thinking *our refrigerator*.

Or *our TV*.

Or *our children*.

Why not *our money?*

True, it implies that you and your wife have given up your independence. You're totally vulnerable to each other. She can run the household straight into bankruptcy. And so can you. But you love each other . . . you're committed to each other . . . you're watching out for each other's good . . . and that makes the crucial difference.

Lurking in the back of everyone's mind, of course, is *who actually earned the money*. Whose name was on the paycheck? Who actually invested his blood, sweat, and tears to generate that income? I have not only my energy but, unfortunately, a piece of my ego in those dollars. *I* did it. Other people may have been loafing the past two weeks, but *I* was getting things done, and here's the proof. I am a productive person. I'm carrying my own weight in this world.

So what's this bit about *our* money?!

If you are the sole wage earner of the household, you and your wife have simply made a decision that you will venture into the world of commerce and invest a major portion of yourself earning dollars while she invests a major portion of herself on other nonremunerative but equally important tasks. This arrangement, my friend, does *not* make you better than her. It says absolutely nothing about your value to the household or society at large in comparison with hers.

Your neighbors, friends, and business associates may *think* it does. Ours is such a money-hungry culture that the ability to earn money has become a popular gauge of one's worth. The more you earn, the more you're esteemed.

That is a particularly demeaning as well as non-Christian concept. If my value as a person rises or falls solely on my commercial value in this world, I'm in deep trouble. What happens if I get fired . . . or sick . . . or past sixty-five? I'm suddenly a nonperson.

We Christians have trouble resisting this pagan value-system. My wife continues to fret occasionally about the fact that she currently isn't generating any dollars. She was a teacher the first six years of our marriage, including a year when I was in graduate school and she was the sole dollar-producer. She may well return to the classroom in a few years when our children are in school, but for now, she's a full-time mother. We keep reminding each other that mothering is an extremely important and valuable part of our life together — more important that earning dollars, in fact. We'd give up my job and try to subsist off the land before we'd ever give up our kids. But Grace still keeps thinking about the days when she used to bring home a paycheck. So she has a ways to go to make her feelings match her Christian values.

I shouldn't talk — not until I've put myself to the test by turning the tables again as we did in graduate-school days, only on a permanent basis. Mike McGrady, a Long Island newspaper columnist, tells about such a life in his delightful book *The Kitchen Sink Papers*. After reaching a fairly high plateau in his profession, McGrady decided to shake things up and trade places with his wife, whose growing home furnishings business had the potential of supporting the family. Mike became the househusband, caring for their three children, while Corinne became the breadwinner. He describes how it felt to be handed his first weekly "allowance" of a hundred dollars for groceries and etcetera.

> It is an unpracticed exchange, accomplished awkwardly. I don't know which of us has more difficulty, which of us is more embarrassed. I guess Corinne handles her side of the exchange more smoothly than I do. . . .
>
> It is the easiest hundred dollars I've ever made. But the reversal feels strange. . . . This ritual, the giving of allowance by one human being to another, bespeaks whole planets of meaning; it has to do with independence, gratification, reward, punishment, resentment. The feelings are so intertwined that I doubt whether they can be fully understood until the situation is reversed. . . .
>
> My own reaction on receiving money — this first day and every week since then — has not been what I anticipated. It is not a pleasurable experience, not in the least. In fact, there is on my part

inevitably an effort to minimize the transaction, to snatch up the check and stuff it into my wallet as rapidly as possible, to pretend that the transaction doesn't really matter. I can see, in Corinne, opposite tendencies, an effort to ceremonialize the offering, to announce it in advance — "Ah, today is the day you get your allowance" — to make a production number out of locating the checkbook and the pen, to sign it with a flourish, to hand it over with a kiss.

I know her feeling all too well.[1]

Throughout the book, the McGradys (who do not pretend to be Christians) can be seen edging toward an *our-money* concept, although at the end they are still not to the point of a joint checking account, except for certain house expenses.

If both you and your wife work, you may be trapped all the more in the rut of "My dollars are mine and hers are hers." In such a mindset, money often equals clout. And if a highly motivated, successful wife starts bringing home the larger paycheck of the two (which is entirely possible in these times), a threatened husband can go into all manner of traumas.

The leader/servant of a Christian household is the person who refuses to use his or her earning power as a club, or even a small lever. He steadfastly resists the culture's belief that money is power. He thanks God for this gift, along with all others, and works with his spouse to use it responsibly.

Now, back to the question: What shall *we* do with *our* money?

A sizable pile of change

The biggest difficulty for most of us is not that we come up with bad answers to that question. It's that we don't take time to answer it at all. We don't plan; we just spend.

And when we don't have money to spend, we call it a cash flow problem and proceed to borrow so we can keep on spending.

A family exchequer is a larger, more complicated thing than we often realize. Many of us are running through the equivalent of a new Rolls Royce every year. We're spending money in twenty-five to thirty different categories, from housing to utilities to restaurants to gasoline.

The key to keeping control over that rather sizable pile of change . . . the key not only to staying out of financial trouble but *enjoying* God's gift to you as well . . . is for you and your wife to *agree in advance* how you're going to spend it. That process of saying "Here's what we have to work with, and here's what we're going to do with it" is called budgeting. If the word has a nasty odor to it, call it *planning your money* or whatever you like. Just do it.

You begin by finding out your monthly income. If you're on a regular payroll, it's easy. All it takes is a little arithmetic to convert your regular paycheck(s) to a monthly basis. If you're paid biweekly, for example, you simply multiply by twenty-six (the number of paychecks you get each year) and then divide by twelve.

(You had a small excuse for not budgeting before the invention of electronic calculators. But now, the old complaint about "doing all that figuring" is dead.)

Be sure to add any little extra sources of income you've got going on the side. Is your wife tutoring? Do you have a part-time or sometime job? Are there investment dividends to add on?

It gets a little messier if your income is not regular — if you're in business for yourself or if you're a salesman on commission. I know more than one such husband who uses this as an excuse not to budget. "I never know when the money's coming or how much. So I just have to fly by instinct."

Nonsense. If giant corporations can estimate their income on the basis of past records, you can too. You told the IRS what you made last year, didn't you? Take that figure and divide by twelve. Even if your money comes unevenly throughout the year, find the average monthly figure. (There are some tricks you can play in arranging the due-dates of certain bills to compensate for those variances in income. More about that later.)

Before you and your wife go any further — stop and thank the Lord for his gift. Think about all the people in the world making less than you are (there are probably billions of them). Tell the Lord how much you appreciate having this much money to work with, and that you're going to try to use it as responsibly as possible, and that you'd appreciate his guidance as you proceed.

Your first decision is how much you're going to return to the Lord directly. In Old Testament times, as you know, Jehovah set that figure for you: 10 percent. The New Testament doesn't lay down any hard quotas; instead, in keeping with its spiritual nature, it rather cheerfully urges us to "excel in this grace of giving" (2 Cor. 8:7). A little further on, Paul says, "Remember this: Whoever sows sparingly will also reap sparingly, and whoever sows generously will also reap generously. Each man should give what he has decided in his heart to give, not reluctantly or under compulsion . . ." (2 Cor. 9:6,7).

It was during my year of graduate school that Grace and I finally came to an understanding of this concept. We were on a rather stringent budget, and we had dutifully written a tithe into it — a 10 percent contribution to our church each payday. It was an automatic thing, the result of years of indoctrination, a bill to be paid along with Standard Oil, Master Charge, and the telephone company.

It wasn't a whole lot of fun, we finally admitted. We could hardly be classified as "cheerful givers." We were conscientiously doing our religious duty, and that was about it.

But we began noticing what the New Testament said about giving. And we began thinking about the word *giving* itself. Giving — the Christmas/birthday kind — was a neat experience. It was a joyful, even emotional exchange. It generated lots of smiles.

So Grace and I decided to play a little semantic game with ourselves. We declared a revolt against any further tithing. "We quit!" we said. "Instead, we're going to begin giving to the Lord. We're going to think of it as giving, and we're going to enjoy it."

We set a minimum size for our gifts of 10 percent of each paycheck. We decided we didn't ever want to go lower than that, but would go higher whenever we wanted to.

To make us remember, we established a routine of praying together over the Lord's check each time, usually at Sunday morning breakfast. The envelope would be sitting there between the salt and pepper shakers, and we'd say, "Lord, here's a gift for you. We're going to put it in the offering at church this morning, and we want you to know how much we appreciate you."

You may think this is foolishness, but I can tell you that it has totally changed our feelings about giving. We think it's put things into proper perspective.

We're currently away from the 10 percent figure altogether. We've set a different percentage and, with the aid of the handy calculator, it's just as easy to compute every time we plan a new budget.

However you choose to figure it, give the Lord the first slice out of the pie. And smile when you do it.

Groceries, gasoline, and garbage

If you're a budgeting pro, feel free to skip this section. But if you're often coming up short or finding yourself in a financial squeeze, keep going.

Certain expenses are rather unavoidable:

You have to live in some kind of housing.

You're probably making a car payment.

You're probably paying one or more insurance premiums.

You have to heat/cool your home, pay for electricity, water, garbage pick-up, and a telephone.

And you're stashing something away in savings and/or investments. (You aren't? Well, you've heard lots of sermons about how it never gets easier to save, so do it now, and make it an automatic thing. Take heed.)

You may need to be stockpiling for some taxes, if these aren't already withheld from your check.

Somebody in the family may be requiring tuition.

And you may have some loans to keep whittling away.

All these are what the accountants call *fixed expenses*. Once you've committed yourself, there's not a whole lot you can do about them. They're the same amount every month (except for heating bills, for which you need to find an average, and long-distance phone calls, for which you need to set a quota).

Write down each of these figures. They form a big block of your disbursements.

The remaining money goes toward *flexible expenses:* groceries, home furnishings, home maintenance, restaurants, clothing, laundry and dry cleaning, gas and oil, car repair, tolls, parking, fares, haircuts, trips to the beauty shop, drugstore items, postage, magazines, books, records and tapes, "nights out," sports, baby-sitters, doctors, dentists, prescriptions, gifts, and general messing around — wow! Hopefully you won't have too many more categories than those.

What's the tab for all of that?

If you haven't kept records up to now, you don't really know. You're going to have to make some educated guesses. Your guesses can be greatly improved six or even three months down the road if you head now for the nearest stationery store and pick up a family expense record booklet. They cost less than two dollars. My favorite is the kind put out by the Ideal System Company, but you choose your own.

The more accurate records you keep, the better you can see your spending patterns. And the more accurate your budget planning can become.

Now comes the fun of adding up your expenditures — your gifts to the Lord, your fixed expenses, and your flexible expenses — and seeing how far you've exceeded your monthly income! It is at this point that you *cannot* afford to throw up your hands and say, "Oh, well, it'll work out somehow." No, it won't. In fact, things will work out a little worse than you've projected, because you've no doubt forgotten some routine expenditures. And some unexpected surprises will be hitting you — perhaps a major illness, or a valve job on your car. You have no choice but to cut expenses down to your income or a little below. If God has given you $900 of take-home pay a month, it is simply wrong to keep cruising at a $1,000 or $1,100 life style. Make the budget balance, no matter how painful.

Actually, a good feeling comes over you when you've marked out a place for every dollar and when every dollar's in its place. You get rid of that vague uneasiness about whether to spend or not. You *know* whether you can afford an item or event. Some of the best feelings I've had have been taking Grace out to dinner, even when some other column of our budget was in excruciating pain. We had allocated a certain amount of money for restaurant dining, and we could go ahead and enjoy it regardless.

You are not finished with budgeting until both you and your wife can look at the figures and say, "That's good. I'm committed to making that plan work." So long as either of you have reservations about the wisdom or the equity of the various allocations, keep talking. Keep figuring. Keep adjusting. Eventually, copy it onto a clean sheet of paper, and keep it where you both can refer to it as often as necessary.

How to obey a budget

Right away, you have a couple of procedural matters to care for. How are you going to implement your budget on a daily basis? You obviously can't keep mental track of how much has been spent for what. You and your wife must look each other in the eye and solemnly swear that you'll both begin using the expense record booklet mentioned earlier. That way, for the first time in your life you'll have an answer to the periodic wail, "How come we're broke?!" It's right there in black and white.

The discipline of writing down what you spend has a couple of other benefits. It makes you face each expenditure twice — the moment when you shell out the cash, and the moment when you record it in the book. Grace and I have found that this acts as a subtle brake on our spending. (One time we decided we were tired of writing; we were mature adults now, and we didn't need to be so picky-picky. Within *four months*, we were in a serious financial hole, unable to tell how or why we'd gotten there — and eager to get back to record-keeping.)

The other benefit of this procedure is that it partially

solves the classic question of who shall be the family bookkeeper. If one person is charged with *all* the paperwork, it can get to be a grind as well as an irritant trying to keep track of what the other person is spending. But if the expense record book is always in a handy location — the kitchen, for example — and both you and your wife are constantly jotting down cash outlays, neither of you has to play the role of cross-examiner.

Naturally, somebody has to write the checks every payday. I don't know that it makes a great deal of difference whether it's you or your wife, assuming you both know how to add, subtract, and spell. Whichever of you takes on this responsibility is merely following through on the *jointly* planned budget anyway. So it's no great position of power and glory. Whenever there's not enough to cover the bills due, and hence some bills have to be postponed, the two of you can together decide which ones.

The family check-writer also has the responsibility of keeping the bills and other financial papers organized. Many households have gotten in trouble simply because their payables were scattered in three different rooms of the house. A few years ago my ingenious mother gave me an odd but wonderful Christmas gift: a nicely repainted metal lunchbucket, not for lunches but for household records. It has cardboard dividers inside for "Bills Due," "Charge Slips Waiting," "Bills Paid," "Paycheck Stubs," "Checking Account Statements," and a couple of other things. The checkbook rests in front. It's fantastic! In case of a fire, Grace and I would probably grab our kids and that lunchbucket ahead of anything else, because it has everything we ever want to know about our budget.

Which items are paid by check and which in cash? (Your decision may depend on whether or not you're charged for each check you write.) Here's one workable breakdown:

Checks	Cash
The Lord	Groceries
House mortgage or rent	Home supplies
Utilities	Restaurants
Insurance premiums	Clothing
Car payments	Laundry/dry cleaning
Savings	Tolls, parking
Gas, oil, repairs (through charge cards)	Barber, beauty shop
Tuition	Drugstore Items
Subscriptions, books, and records (some through charge cards)	Miscellaneous
	Postage
	"Special events," baby-sitting
	Gifts
Medical	

The check items, as you can see, are a mixture of fixed and flexible expenses. That makes it nice, in that the checking money becomes a sort of pool in which the big bills and little bills can slosh back and forth. If there's a big car repair bill one month, the medical bills can be postponed slightly, and vice versa. This takes place without bothering the day-to-day activity in the cash columns.

I've deliberately arranged for the car and life insurance premiums to come due at the end of the year, when there's a Christmas bonus to cover them. That way they don't play havoc with our month-to-month flow. If you're "richer" at certain times of the year, you might consider jockeying your annual and semiannual bills toward those times.

When it comes to cash, Grace is responsible for certain funds, such as groceries, while I'm responsible for others, such as restaurants. You're going to laugh at this, but I'll tell you anyway: We've even gone so far as to set some of the funds aside in separate little plastic boxes so we *know* whether there's any cash in that fund or not. "Clothing" is one of these; "nights out" is another. We've found that we simply can't trust ourselves to keep either of these in line without an actual, visible "kitty." If the greenbacks are there, okay; if they aren't, we don't spend.

This reflects a basic premise of sound financial operation: *Don't spend it until you've got it. Don't jump the gun.* We laugh at little children who bounce up and down and say they can't wait until Christmas; we discipline them for sneaking cookies a half-hour before dinner. Yet we are sometimes just as guilty when it comes to money. We *just can't wait* until we actually have the money in hand. We can see it coming toward us, and so we go ahead and spend early. Before long, we're going ahead and spending without asking whether the money is soon to come or not — and down that road lies big trouble.

The most enticing form of jumping the gun, of course, is the charge card. I've proven to myself over the years that I can use the convenience of charging gasoline without torpedoing the budget. The monthly total is fairly constant, and there's not much temptation to splurge in this particular area. But we would never put a fund like clothing on a charge basis. The result, we know from experience, would be swift disaster.

Charge cards facilitate the store manager's dream: impulse buying. And impulse buying is what ruins the well-laid plans of a budget. Hence, another rule of sound finances: *When in doubt — wait.* You may miss an occasional hot deal, but it's worth it. Grace and I are still growling about the encyclopedia salesman whose special price was available *only that week* back in 1970. We told ourselves Vickie needed encyclopedias for school (false). We told ourselves all kinds of things as we took the plunge, withdrawing a life insurance dividend to pay for the set.

By the time Nathan and the twins will be old enough to use them, they'll be ten years out of date. The rotten part is that I *knew* that evening we didn't really need a set of encyclopedias right then; I just couldn't muster the courage to tell the guy no and would he please get out of my living room.

A bargain is not a bargain unless you need it.

Of all the areas of a budget that call for maturity on the part of the husband, the greatest is the car. In most households, car expenses are to the husband what groceries are to the wife: a major category about which one spouse knows quite a lot and the other knows next to nothing. You can walk in the door after paying a $78 repair bill, lay three or four sentences of mechanical jargon on her — and she's helpless. She doesn't know what you're talking about, let alone whether the repair was essential or not.

But she does know that you just dropped another $78 on the car. And that hurts, no matter how unavoidable it was.

Our household records show that for the past three years I have sunk 16 percent of the family fortune each year into automobiles — gas, oil, repairs, payments, insurance, license plates, and municipal vehicle taxes. In the same period, Grace has shelled out no higher than 13 percent for groceries. These two categories, along with housing and our gifts to the Lord, make up the Big Four of our budget. Everything else is minor by comparison.

I have a responsibility to Grace and the children to hold the automobile area in line, even though they don't have the mechanical know-how to question my decisions. This means choosing dependable cars in the first place, finding honest and competent repairmen (which can be quite a trick sometimes), and changing oil and getting lube jobs on schedule.

In my case, I have come to believe that it means something even more basic — and more sizable in terms of dollars. It means controlling my attitude toward cars in general, viewing them as the pieces of machinery they are rather than extensions of my own ego or self-image. It means resisting Detroit's media blitzes every fall that tempt me to trade for the newest, biggest, and best. It means getting rid of the myth that cars are an investment. They are *not;* they do *not* appreciate in value or pay returns on the initial capital. They *cost* money — lots of it. Some of them can be resold for more than others, but never for the full amount of what you've spent on them.

Like most men, I remember with considerable sentiment my first car during high-school days: a black 1950 Mercury coupe. I paid $100 for it. My self-image was tremendously bound up in that car . . . those rear-wheel covers . . . the deep-throated rumble that turned heads in the school parking lot . . . well, you know what I mean.

Next came a long black '48 Dodge limo I bought from a funeral director for whom I worked one summer; it was a campus conversation piece that fall. But its charm was soon lost, and in its place came a flashy '56 Olds Holiday two-door hardtop (with a cracked head, I might add, and poorly patched rocker panels that disintegrated in the salted streets of the first Chicago winter). No matter. I was a taller-than-average guy who needed a big car, right? Next, a pink '56 Cadillac Coupe de Ville, followed by a '63 Mercury Monterey with that classy reverse-slant window in the back.

Suddenly, I realized something: I was spending an awful lot of money on cars, and there was no end in sight. It took a while, but Grace and I finally came to the conclusion that what we needed was a basic means of transportation, not a status symbol. We dumped the ailing Mercury for a used Volvo and drove it for the next 6½ years.

I remember the first year I didn't go to drool and dream

at the Chicago Auto Show. It was like giving up an old friend. But I decided I'd be better off without the bombardment. I haven't been back since.

Not that there's anything immoral about an auto show. I'm just saying that for me, it was my annual orgy of automobile covetousness, and I eventually had to deal with that problem, for my own sake as well as for my family's.

How to revise a budget

Obviously, every time you get a raise you need a new budget. But there are other reasons as well. Perhaps your expenses change — a son or daughter starts college, for example. Perhaps your long-range goals change. There was a point early in our marriage at which Grace and I decided to stop using her teaching pay for stereo components and bedroom suites and start socking it away toward a down payment on a house. We knew we'd eventually be living on one income instead of two, so why not now?

Again, we had to trick ourselves into it. We dubbed the salad days of the past the Era of Elasticity. Now we were beginning the Era of Rigidity. (To tell you the truth, I think we've been in Rigidity ever since.) Our goals had changed, and we restructured our spending patterns to match.

The other time when a budget needs revision is when it's just not working. You haven't allocated enough money for utilities, or gifts, or nights out, and you're getting thoroughly frustrated. It's not that you're unwilling to abide by the budget; it's just that the thing is out of whack. Okay; change it. Face the problem. Don't go on gnashing your teeth. Shift some dollars from one of the other accounts. Or find a way to raise income. Naturally, you have to keep the bottom line in balance whatever you do, but if you're in an intolerable situation, sit down with your wife and take a good, hard look at your priorities as expressed by your budget.

What to do when the budget's been blown

For all your care and discipline, there will be times when you — or she — will simply blow it. You'll misplace a $20 bill somewhere. You'll get a traffic ticket. A repair service will rip you off. You'll succumb to the allure of a new sport coat and whip out a charge card before you think.

Well, it's not the end of the world. After all, some things in life are more important than money. Confession, for example. It's *her* money that's been squandered as well as yours, remember? So don't keep her in the dark. Tell her what happened, and how you feel about it . . . and don't be surprised if the whole ordeal draws the two of you closer to each other. You may face a tough month or two recovering from the financial loss, but you'll face it together, and out of such ordeals comes the deepening of love and trust.

The Scriptures direct "those who are rich in this present world [e.g., the majority of us North Americans, compared to the rest of the world] not to be arrogant nor to put their hope in wealth, which is so uncertain, but to put their hope in God, who richly provides us with everything for our enjoyment" (1 Tim. 6:17).

Your household and mine need a leader with that kind of attitude.

[1]Mike McGrady, *The Kitchen Sink Papers* (Garden City, N.Y.: Doubleday, 1975), pp. 26, 27.

5

A Master,
a Mistress,
and Two Slaves

5

A Master,
a Mistress,
and Two Slaves

Having dealt with the shortage of money, we turn now to the remaining two shortages, time and energy. They too can breed considerable tension.

Time and energy are gifts from God just as money is. Especially *discretionary* time and energy — the leftovers after we've finished working, sleeping, and eating. The question may again be posed:

What shall *we* (husband and wife) do with *our* time and energy?

Sounds pretty wide-open, doesn't it? But the fact is that society and tradition have rather thoroughly programed us with a set of answers. Husbands do certain things around the house. Wives do certain things around the house. Each has his/her "place."

How valid are the traditions we've been handed? Before you read on, find a pencil and mark this check list according to the actual nature of eash task, not according to what happens to be the usual at your house.

	Basically a husband's job	Basically a wife's job	Doesn't really matter
1. Opening pickle jars	☐	☐	☐
2. Having babies	☐	☐	☐
3. Changing the car's oil	☐	☐	☐
4. Changing the baby's diapers	☐	☐	☐
5. Mowing the yard	☐	☐	☐
6. Vacuuming the carpet	☐	☐	☐
7. Waxing the car	☐	☐	☐
8. Waxing the kitchen floor	☐	☐	☐
9. Painting a ceiling	☐	☐	☐
10. Getting kids to bed	☐	☐	☐

Women's Liberation, of course, has forced all of us to think twice about these things. It's had the net effect of moving more and more items into the "doesn't really matter" column.

Tasks related to basic anatomy, of course (such as numbers 1 and 2 on the list), are not going to get bumped around. In terms of brute physical strength, men are estimated to be 50 percent stronger than women, and that's simply not going to change. Women, on the other hand, have been found to have a somewhat greater tolerance for extreme heat.

But when it comes to the overwhelming majority of tasks that really have nothing to do with anatomy, a lot of things are up for grabs. Some of us are cheering the current reassessment. Others of us are disturbed by it. Some of us are worried that the ultimate goal is to completely obliterate *la différence*, to create a unisex world. Many of us are confused about the new definitions of masculinity and femininity and whether they're improvements or setbacks.

And while we're philosophizing about the state of the culture at large, we're overlooking the nearest and most relevant situation: our own households. It's much easier to critique Barbara Walters as a TV news anchorperson or to expound the merits and flaws of the Equal Rights Amendment than it is to look at what's happening under our own roof.

We might as well face it: it takes a fair chunk of work to run a house. Work on the outside that brings in a paycheck, yes, but also work right there on the premises. And it's not all fun work. A certain percentage of it is outright drudgery. Servant-type work.

Who's going to do it?

Tradition says, "If it's anything to do with the kitchen, laundry room, bathroom, bedroom, or living areas — the wife. If it's anything to do with the garage, basement, or yard — the husband."

Now you may have altered that tradition to a greater or lesser degree. You and your wife may not have come to the marriage in the first place with identical traditions. Grace's father, a minister and former denominational executive, happens also to be a rather happy vacuumer as well as grocery shopper. I don't remember my dad doing either, unless it was a special occasion. So I naturally don't think about volunteering to vacuum or go to the supermarket — which sometimes, even after eleven years, Grace still finds herself expecting more or less from habit.

But these are minor wrinkles in the overall pattern of traditional husband and wife roles. None of us are free from them. And if someone were to follow any of our wives around with a stopwatch, chances are she'd pile up a greater number of drudgery minutes than we could any week of the year.

Mike McGrady, the newspaperman mentioned in the

last chapter who traded places with his wife for a year, realized this rather powerfully one night as he stood ironing clothes while his kids watched TV.

> I have known little in life more depressing than that experience, standing there ironing my daughter's massive wardrobe, listening to Bob Hope and actor Burt Reynolds trading tacky little jokes about the actor's affair with an older woman.
>
> On second thought, it might have seemed as depressing without the television set on. Any job requiring the constant repetition of a simple act is going to seem dumb. No assembly-line worker in Detroit, no person tightening the same bolt on the same door of every sedan coming out of a factory, ever put in more dummy time than a normal house-wife.[1]

Granted, life at McGrady's old newspaper office had not always been a lark. There had been cranky people and unreliable machinery and all of the normal irritants of any job. But there had also been some significant and applaudable goals in spite of the obstacles. It had its rewards.

Mike's wife Corinne was a person of considerable talent. Nevertheless, from almost the beginning of the marriage, Corinne had

> played Female. That is to say, she stayed home with the children and did the cleaning and cooking. It is, in retrospect, incredible that she did all this routinely and without complaint. . . .
>
> And since she was an artist, since she was gifted and creative, she not unnaturally attempted to apply her skills to her new life as housewife. It was a little like asking a nuclear physicist to apply his talents to sweeping public streets. She did well at the most mundane tasks, very well indeed, but who can measure the toll? Not just the toll in years — for these could have been her most productive

years — but a toll in spirit. There were rough times, times when in the middle of the night she would flee family and house, get in the car and drive for hours along shore roads. There were other times when her patience would be worn thin as gauze and that normally well-modulated voice turned into something out of a low-budget horror movie.[2]

It was out of a desire to change some of that that the McGrady experiment was born.

The question for us husbands is not whether our wives are willing to be the servants of the household. The question is, *are we?* Here is one of the places where the high-flying concepts of chapter 2 hit the road. *Do we really want to be servants in our own homes on a day-to-day basis?* There is a certain irreducible amount of work to a household, requiring a certain amount of human time and human energy, modern conveniences notwithstanding. Whose time and energy shall be expended to do the work?

If you are committed to the idea of one common life, and if you are determined before God to be the leader/servant of that common life, then you face the practical need to take your place along with your wife (and your children, as they're able) in doing the work. The fun work. The drudgery. The so-so kind of work. You also share in the enjoyment of leisure time when the work's done. Whatever's happening, whatever is to be endured or enjoyed, you're in it together.

Here are some specifics to remember:

She's not dumb

Your wife has a brain. She spent a number of years in school cultivating her mind. She's lived approximately as long as you have — maybe longer. She's no dumb kid.

And her mind is probably as flexible and as capable of adapting to various challenges as yours is. It is never very smart to assume that she couldn't understand or comprehend this or that.

Harold and Jeanette Myra are close friends of ours; he and I worked together for several years at *Campus Life* magazine. One January night the four of us were at their place. The temperature hadn't gotten above zero all day. I can't remember the details, but for some reason one of their cars had been left sitting outdoors in a parking lot since the day before, and Jeanette said, "Would you two mind dropping me off on your way home so I can pick up the car and bring it back here?"

"Fine," I said. Then I made a terrible mistake. I temporarily forgot that Jeanette was a farmer's daughter from Wisconsin. "But don't you want Harold to come along to get it started?" I asked.

She looked at me as if I'd just questioned her ability to make a decent pot of coffee.

"Why do I need Harold?" she shot back. "If I can't start it, he sure can't start it!"

Harold duly agreed with that, I duly apologized, and we drove her to the dark, icy parking lot. She hopped in the car, turned the key, kicked the accelerator the way it needed to be kicked, and started the engine on the first try just like it was her father's old John Deere.

There's no biological reason why women shouldn't be allowed to touch the mechanical side of life. There's no reason of any kind to shield wives from the higher disciplines of the mind: politics, economics, law, theology, mass communication, international affairs, and the other supposedly masculine domains. Indeed, to do so is criminal. It is a denial of divine gifts and aptitudes.

You're not privileged

So long as there are certain understandings, spoken or unspoken, that you are "above" having to do certain grundy jobs, you are not a servant. It's sometimes hard to realize where the pockets of privilege still lie. The traditions are so strong. They may never come out into the open unless you get up the courage to ask your wife directly, "Are there some things that you 'just know' not to ask me to do? In what ways am I still playing the role of the big cheese without realizing it?" She'll tell you!

I think every father who's ever changed a diaper can remember his first clumsy attempt. I recall thinking that somebody sure botched the engineering design along the way; how was that big, square piece of cloth supposed to fit this little, tiny, rounded bottom?

And, of course, the smell and the mess are not exactly pleasant. Especially at the beginning, when you're getting used to it.

But since when is a grown man afraid to get his hands dirty? That's the first thing you learn on your first after-school job as a teen-ager — sometimes you just have to get in there and do the job and clean up later. I will always remember a particular chicken coop on a certain widow's farm four miles north of Whitewater, Kansas, where I as a high school sophomore learned that lesson. We'd just moved into the community, and this woman offered me half a Saturday's work using a pitchfork and shovel on about a ten-inch layer of manure. Well, I survived. You can probably tell a similar tale yourself.

So what's so bad about diapers?

After the twins arrived (180 diapers a week to start), I even did something about the engineering problem. Grace was gone for several hours, and I said to myself, *There's got to be a better way.* So I put my masculine mind to work and figured out a tighter way to fold and pin.

I realize that not all my readers have kids, and many of you who do are past the diaper stage. I'm just using this as an illustration of the servanthood motif in a very practical area for husbands.

Find a need and fill it

The more we reexamine our male and female roles in Western society and the more we question the old stereotypes, the more we have to face the necessity for a new order. Some couples engage in writing marriage contracts, in which they spell out precisely who shall pay for what and who shall be responsible for the less exciting parts of running a household. It's all there in black and white. The contracts are rewritten from time to time as needs and feelings change.

Such an approach is probably an improvement over the old silent assumptions — but I think we Christians can do even better. We can, if we really want to, create a miniature of God's kingdom of love right here and now in our own homes. Instead of worrying about the protection of egos, instead of searching for the perfectly just and equitable division of labor, instead of safeguarding against infringement of rights — we can surrender our rights and our lives to each other. This results in a *flow* of service unhindered by union rules; both husband and wife jump in and do whatever needs to be done at the moment. If a child's nose needs to be wiped or a flower patch needs to be weeded, either spouse responds without reference to a contracted list of duties.

There are times — not as many as I would like — when I sense Grace and myself flowing as a work team in an effective and strangely rewarding way. Walking in from an evening church service with three cranky children who need to get to bed, we both sort of spring into action.

There's almost no conversation between us; we know the fifty-nine things that need to be done, and in what order, and we go at it. About twenty minutes later, when all three are down and the lights have been turned off, we meet each other in the hall, sigh, and usually say something inane like, "Hello — how are you?" Our work is done — notice, *our* work — and now we're ready to enjoy some adult time together.

I don't mean to imply that all things can be handled by instinct. Some parts of household life are complicated enough — menu planning, for example — that an administrator is needed. Somebody has to accept it as a responsibility and follow through more or less by himself or herself. But there are probably not as many of these as we think. The sensitive husband and wife can in most areas develop a synergistic approach that lightens the load and deepens the love of both.

As Ambrose Bierce, an American journalist of three generations ago, said, "Marriage is a community consisting of a master, a mistress, and two slaves, making in all, two."

[1]Mike McGrady, *The Kitchen Sink Papers* (Garden City, N.Y.: Doubleday, 1975), p. 82.
[2]Ibid., pp. 30, 31.

6

It's
a Job

6

It's
a Job

This is not a book about how to succeed in business, with or without really trying. That is a science all its own.

But it's impossible to talk about the job of being a husband without taking into account our occupations. After all, work consumes half or more of our waking hours, if we add the work we sometimes bring home at night and the miscellaneous time we spend thinking about work problems.

That constitutes a rather major chunk of our lives. No wonder we men are more often identified and categorized by occupation than any other kind of label. In social situations we make small talk with each other by asking, "And what do you do?" We expect the guy to say, "I'm an electrician (or state senator, or supermarket manager, or whatever)." We would be rather surprised if he said instead, "I'm an avid reader," or "I'm a Little League coach," or "I'm a husband."

There are some good reasons why work predominates,

of course. (1) We like to eat. (2) We've been programed since childhood to grow up and be gainfully employed. (3) What else is there to do all day? Working for money is one of the presuppositions about what a husband does; it's part of our responsibility. Even the Scripture says, "If anyone does not provide . . . especially for his immediate family, he has denied the faith and is worse than an unbeliever" (1 Tim. 5:8).

A lot of us work for an additional reason: the challenge of it. We've been fortunate enough to find our way into an occupation that we find intriguing, that pits us against a set of obstacles, that dares us to wage battle and overcome. The proof of success may be any number of things — the year-end profit on the bottom line, or the number of students whom we successfully prepare for the next level of education, or the score on the stadium scoreboard at the end of the game. We find it psychologically rewarding to see what we can achieve, aside from the pay.

Not all of us, however, are in a challenging job. Some of us are bored to death. Either there's no place to go in our chosen field, or we're not qualified for a promotion or change. The only reward is the paycheck. Management people know that such a situation is not the best for either the worker or the company, and in many cases they are trying to adjust things, to instill some challenge into the work, whether in the form of bonuses for extra output or by rewriting job descriptions.

Even a boring job, of course, is usually preferable to no job at all. Some of us know the anxiety and inner pain of being unemployed. Men in this situation are the most keenly aware of the centrality of work in a man's life.

Our wives are venturing into the world of work in ever increasing numbers and are facing the same challenges (or lack thereof). Either to gain a higher standard of living for the family or to diversify their lives, or both, women are on the payroll.

The question each couple has to face is whether, in the long run, the household is helped or hurt by this. There is no question that the New Testament instructs wives to "guide the house" (1 Tim. 5:14 KJV) and to be "keepers at home" (Titus 2:5 KJV). But it's also rather obvious that if there are no children, or the children are in school throughout the day, most women can do an adequate job of guiding the house and still have a number of hours left over each week, thanks in part to modern conveniences. The use of that leftover time is a matter of Christian stewardship, and the Lord is obviously happier with a wife who uses those hours for productive wage-earning or volunteer ministry than for deadening her mind with soap operas at home.

Whether the wife is employed or not, work is un-doubtedly the biggest thing we do *apart* from each other. No other item on our schedule pulls us away from each other for such long stretches of time. Work therefore has the capacity to drive a giant wedge between us. By its very nature it leads to two separate lives instead of one com-mon one. Thus, it is important for us to consider how work can harmonize with a marriage and, specifically, with our role as husbands.

Containing the camel

Most of us push pretty hard at our jobs. We know it's a competitive world out there, and if we don't produce, there are lots of other guys just waiting for the chance to replace us. Part of the genius of free-enterprise capitalism is its ability to motivate, to crank us up, to draw from us the last full measure of energy and de-votion.

Some of us push so hard that the job, in a curious sort of way, *becomes* us. We are the job, and it is us. If we meet our sales projection, we see ourselves not only as successful salesmen but as successful and worthwhile persons. If we don't make it, we're flops, and not just in the occupational sense. We *ourselves* are plagued with feelings of failure.

These are powerful feelings, and there's no way to shut them off when we come home. The genius of capitalism thus becomes a great danger as well, in that the rush of competition obscures the fact that we are human beings, made in the image of God, worthwhile in and of ourselves whether we make the sales projection or not. We are still, among other things, husbands who have been gifted with wives and households that need us — not just our money, but *us*.

I remember a bull session one night a few years ago with seven other editors. We were talking about the priority of our work. We were all young, bright-eyed, ambitious types, eager to prove ourselves to our bosses and our readers and to continue to climb to greater responsibility and prestige.

We lectured each other on how leadership and excellence demands sacrifice, about how we had to rid ourselves of the clock mentality and commit ourselves to doing the job, whether it required forty hours or seventy. "Anybody who's not willing to make a total commitment to this thing, to go all out," it was said, "is just not going to come up with the award winners. Anything less means mediocrity for the product, and it also means putting a lid on one's own advancement."

It was at about this point that a couple of us began asking, "Yeah, but what about the other parts of one's life — you know, those incidental things out on the periphery, like wife, kids, church, neighbors, physical fitness? Don't they get at least a little piece of the action?"

No one exactly mounted an attack against these, but the drift persisted heavily in favor of work being paramount. As the evening wore on, I found myself increasingly in the role of odd man out as I tried to defend the validity of turning off editing and turning on some other things at certain points of the week. I wasn't really clear in my own mind, but I kept fumbling around saying things like, "Look, I'm committed to excellence. I want to be the best editor in the field. But I'm not sure I have to dismiss everything else from my frame of consciousness in order to reach that goal."

That was in June. By the next January, three of the people at that jam session had resigned their positions and altered their life styles dramatically. One of the three stopped by my office a couple of months later to say, "Hey, remember that night when we were all talking about commitment to the job and how important it was?"

"Yeah, I remember."

He shook his head with a grin. "That sure was a bunch of garbage."

Not everyone would agree with his assessment, but more and more businessmen and managers of all kinds are coming to understand that it is neither smart nor possible to try to *own* people. President Carter demonstrated this in one of his first cabinet meetings when he stated that he didn't want any marriages breaking up because of loyalty to himself.

Our jobs are somewhat like the proverbial camel asking to warm its nose inside the Arab's tent. There's nothing wrong with being nice to camels, but they don't make good house guests. A job that is allowed to take over the entire life of a family is a job out of control.

And if it eventually wrecks the tent, everybody's out in the cold, including the camel. What has been gained? Many of us have known super-achievers on the job whose personal lives were such a shambles that eventually even their careers were destroyed.

But I'm not that bad, you say. *I'm not a workaholic.*

The truth of that claim may depend in part upon your way of thinking about your schedule. Do you have a priority list in your head? Have you said to yourself, "X is the number one priority as far as I'm concerned; Y is number two; Z is number three," and so forth?

If you function on that basis, you have created some built-in problems. (1) You've set up your wife as the opponent of your job, your church as the opponent of your wife, etc. Each is competing for as high a placement as possible, and when one wins, the other loses. (2) The items at the bottom of the list don't stand a chance. There will never be enough time to get to them.

An alternate approach is to state that there are *a number* of important "top-priority" items in your life, and each gets a share. Not long ago I sat down and wrote out a weekly time budget. I had no idea how many of the 168 hours of my week I could account for, but I thought it would be fun to try.

I came up with the following categories. You may want to use them for your own analysis.

	Hours per week	% of total
CHURCH		
Regular meetings	___	
Other groups, committees, boards, etc.	___	
Travel time	___	
Preparation for teaching, music, etc.	___	
Subtotal	___	___

	Hours per week	% of total
PHYSICAL		
Sleep	___	
Meals	___	
Dressing, shaving, etc.	___	
Exercise, sports	___	
Subtotal	___	___
WORK		
On-the-job time	___	
Travel time	___	
Extra work at home	___	
Subtotal	___	___
FAMILY		
Wife communication (home as well as "out")	___	
Children time	___	
Parents and in-laws	___	
Budgeting, bookkeeping, bill-paying	___	
House maintenance	___	
Yard maintenance/snow removal	___	
Auto maintenance	___	
Subtotal	___	___
SELF		
Devotional life	___	
Reading	___	
TV	___	
Subtotal	___	___
COMMUNITY INVOLVEMENT	___	___

I was amazed that I could actually account for 165 hours. That told me that my schedule is more packed than I thought, that there's not much time for general loafing. (If you're wondering how this book ever got written, the answer is vacation time!)

But this little exercise enabled me to look at the percentages and ask myself: Is my week in balance? Am I giving the right amount of hours to each of these areas? Am I being a responsible steward of God's gift of time?

As with money, we often fail to get the big picture. We are taken up with individual trees instead of the forest.

And work is a very aggressive species; it can spread and choke out some of the less sturdy trees that also deserve a place in the sun.

Some special dilemmas

The tradesman whose work is carefully governed by the clock and union rules does not face as many time decisions as the executive, the self-employed businessman, or the professional. Those who are judged not by numbers of hours but by intangibles are the ones who fight with the camel most often.

The problem is especially acute for people in the ministry. Here the motivation is not so much financial as theological. What can be more important than doing the work of God? There are billions of people who haven't heard a decent presentation of the gospel . . . there are swarms of needy, confused, and/or questioning people right at the doorstep . . . how can a pastor or missionary take time even for a cup of coffee with his wife?

For most clergy, the breakdown of activities on pages 92 and 93 has to be altered, since church and work are synonymous. And it's deadly serious work. A guy can turn off the lights and lock the doors of his hot-dog stand and know that the world won't suffer greatly without his services. Even an insurance salesman or a university professor knows that his work is not totally indispensable.

But what if a potential suicide can't get through to the minister? Doctors can at least relax in the knowledge that their patients can always head for the local hospital. The pastor, in contrast, is often the one and only source of help in some extreme situations.

There is no denying that all of this drives ministers, missionaries, church executives, and other clergy to unhealthy and even dangerous life styles. The toll is often most apparent in their wives and children. They find themselves with all kinds of feelings of resentment, isolation, and disillusionment not only against the man of the house, but against the God and the institution he serves. This immediately triggers guilt feelings: *How terrible of me to want him home when he's out serving the Lord.*

So the wife keeps quiet. I know of one man who in the earlier years of his ministry kept such a schedule that he found himself out of town during the births of each of his three children. I am glad to report that more recently he's come to see (and preach to his colleagues) that it makes no sense to try to build the kingdom of God at the expense of another, even more basic divine institution: the home. The Scriptures give no basis for such madness. In fact, among the qualifications for overseers in 1 Timothy 3 is the following: "He must manage his own family well and see that his children obey him with proper respect. (If anyone does not know how to manage his own family, how can he take care of God's church?)" (vv. 4,5).

That . . . takes time. There is no way a minister can put in fourteen-hour days seven days a week and do any kind of a job of leading/serving his own household. It's impossible.

It takes discipline for such a person to apportion his time responsibly. It's all the harder because the work of the church is, among other things, a nights-and-weekends situation. That's when people are available for appointments, classes, committee meetings, and public worship services. The pastorate is actually a swing-shift job! So when does that leave for fixing leaky faucets and taking one's wife shopping? Somehow, it doesn't feel right doing those things on Tuesday mornings when the rest of the world is hard at work. But why not?

The peculiar nature of the ministry calls for some peculiar and rather forceful solutions. I remember seeing one church calendar that included, along with the Sunday school sessions and choir rehearsals and women's groups, a notation of "Pastor's Day Off" each week. Just in case the members forget . . . or are so dense as to assume that Sunday is *his* day of rest . . . it's right there on the calendar in black and white for them to read.

In search of sanity

It's a shame, in a way, that for most of us, work has to be sealed in an airtight set of hours with no allowances for family. There's a lot to be said for the work schedule of such countries as Italy, Spain, and Portugal, where people start early and work straight through to 1:00 P.M. — and then go home for a leisurely lunch and siesta. The shops and offices open up again at 5:00 P.M. for another three-hour stretch.

Granted, the cities are smaller, and commuting time is not so great. But we Americans would do well to consider how we might blend work and family life through some creative scheduling. One of the beautiful assets of farming is that it offers so many tasks that family members can do *together*.

Dr. Charlie Shedd, in his book *Smart Dads I Know*, tells about one bank president who decided to stop doing evening business with out-of-town guests in fancy restaurants. Instead, he began inviting them home for hamburgers around the pool with his wife and kids. "At first I wondered if it would hurt my business," he says. "Funny — things actually went better. As a matter of fact, I've made some awfully big deals by this pool over the hamburgers."

Another man, a small-town doctor, told his two sons that whenever they needed him, they could come and rap three times on the back door of his office, and he'd be there. It's interesting that one of those sons grew up to be Dr. Eugene Nida, executive secretary of the American Bible Society.

A third father faced the tough job of raising his daughter by himself. She remembers one very special thing about those years:

> When I started to school, my father gave me ten cents, and . . . he said, "Patty, I want you always to keep this dime in your purse. Any time you need me, you call me at the plant. Tell them you want to talk to your dad, and I guarantee they'll let you right through." There is no way I could tell you what that ten cent piece from my father meant. Even when I didn't need him, just to know I had it in my purse made me feel secure.[1]

Actually, there are a lot of little things that all of us can do to give our families glimpses into our work. Plant or office tours can be fascinating for them; suddenly the places and situations we talk about at home become real. We can also arrange for our wives to meet our work associates — not only during a walk-through but in evening social situations. That way when we come home and growl, "The boss has got to be out of his mind," she's in a better position to sympathize with us!

Seriously, the more she knows about what we do, the more she can respond to this major part of our lives, the better she can brainstorm with us on ways to solve work problems, and the greater her own sense of security will be. I make it a habit to bring home issues of the company newspaper, new catalogs, company advertisements and public-relations brochures, even some of the trade journals, just so Grace can feel what I'm involved in, ask questions, and participate in my life on the job.

The containment of one's work within a proper balance is not the only occupational dilemma. We also run into problems such as stagnation, when we feel we're not growing in our work and need a change of some kind. Or our employer asks us to move into a new and different responsibility. Or a job offer from the outside comes along, and we wonder whether to switch or not.

All of these call for careful consideration, prayer, and discussion with our wives. It is important to remember, as we said before, that the work is not us; it is only something we do. To change our work is not to change our basic identity. In fact, it may even stretch the real us to a new and better shape.

Dr. Anthony Campolo, a Philadelphia professor of sociology, tells about a colleague of his who finally decided he'd had it with teaching. The daily grind of lecturing and grading papers seemed pointless to him, so he resigned his post at Trenton State College and got a job as a mailman.

His mother was understandably worried. "He's got a Ph.D.!" she told Campolo. "Why don't you go see him and try to get him straightened out?"

Dr. Campolo obliged, but didn't make much progress. The man said, "I know it's a bit strange, but I really enjoy what I'm doing far more than the classroom." All arguments to the contrary were brushed aside.

Finally, Campolo said something like, "Well, I guess that's fine, as long as one does a good job in whatever field he chooses."

"Oh, no," the man objected. "I'm a terrible mailman."

"How is that?"

"It takes me forever. Most guys are finished by one o'clock in the afternoon. I seldom get back before five."

"Why?" Campolo wondered.

"I visit!" he announced with a flourish. "You've no idea how many lonely senior citizens there are on my mail route. So I stop and talk. I must be having twenty cups of coffee a day — I can't even get to sleep at night for all the visiting I'm doing."

The man had taken some occupational risk — and found fulfillment.

Dead end

The biggest occupational change of all, of course, is the change nobody wants — the loss of a job. To be a healthy adult male who's out of work is a trauma we'd all like to avoid. But that's not always possible.

Among the never-to-be-forgotten days of my life is one hot Friday afternoon in June a few years ago when I was asked to come to the office of my supervisor. Rumors had been flying that the financial squeeze was on and that some clerical people were going to have to be cut, but nothing had been said about anyone else.

I sat there listening to an obviously uncomfortable man trying to tell me as gently as possible that certain departments and functions had, regrettably, been chosen for elimination in order to bring the budget into line. He began naming off the victims . . . and suddenly my years of service to the organization had come to an abrupt end.

He insisted, of course, that this was no reflection on my abilities, etc., etc., but that it was a necessary move by management to . . . I forget the rest. All I remember from there on is going out to my car, driving toward home, and pulling off to the side of the road to try and figure out how to tell Grace.

I couldn't escape the fact that no matter what he'd said about how this was solely a financial pruning — when the chips were down, I was one of the guys they could afford to get along without. There was no way to whitewash that fact. My self-esteem was crumbling fast.

Somehow now, with the perspective that comes with

the passing years, I believe that every highly charged, self-confident type like myself needs the experience of such a blow. To walk in your front door, to look at the wife who loves you, to swallow a couple of times and then say, "Well, uh, guess what — come Monday morning, I won't be going anywhere" . . . somehow, the pain of that confession cuts you down to size, confronts you with your inadequacies, humbles you, makes you vulnerable. And in your helplessness, the two of you are drawn closer together.

You find yourselves leaning on each other, praying desperately for divine help, and at the same time counting the blessings that remain. The future is terrifying, and yet at the same time you can view it as a clean slate upon which God may write all sorts of interesting things. In our case, we had to wait five weeks before I went to work again, whereas others have hung in limbo much longer. But even in that amount of time we were made deeply aware of where our truly permanent, reliable resources lay. We were not to trust in organizations or companies or employment agencies or even our own talents or "connections"; we were to rely on the God who had brought us this far and was not about to lose track of us now.

Without this confidence, a marriage can crack under the strain of joblessness. The bills mount up, and so do the questions about whether the husband is really up to the task of leadership in the family. His self-confidence is under tremendous pressure, and the longer he goes without work, the worse it gets. I found myself striving for achievement during those weeks — I dug a trench for a drain tile through the yard while I was waiting, just to demonstrate that I wasn't totally useless. But in the long run, it was the steady confidence of my wife and the knowledge that God was still in control that held the pieces together.

Whether it's the major crisis of unemployment or one of the minor bumps along the road, the sharing of our work with our wives is a tremendously helpful thing to do. She can tell when we've had a bad day, anyway, so she might as well know the specifics! Her support at such times can be beautiful.

She also deserves to know about the good times, the successes, the boss's compliments. To hold back what happens on the job, to assume that "she wouldn't understand" is to impugn her intelligence and also to retreat once again into aloneness. Even though she's not physically present for this major segment of our daily activity, she can share in both its joys and catastrophes if we give her the chance. In this way work becomes another part of the common, unified life together.

[1]Charlie Shedd, *Smart Dads I Know* (New York: Sheed and Ward, 1975), pp. 27-32.

7

The
Household
of Faith

7

The
Household
of Faith

The state of Illinois, where I live, has long been known
for its colorful politics. The late Richard J. Daley, mayor
of Chicago for twenty-one years and undisputed
kingmaker of the Democratic party statewide, was
perhaps the greatest but certainly not the first nor the last
of our public entrepreneurs. The jokes about how Hiz-
zoner used to win elections are legion. (The most popular:
Daley and two others were on Lake Michigan in a yacht
that began to sink. Since only one life buoy was available,
an argument arose over who should get to use it. Finally
the mayor said, "Wait a minute — let's be democratic
about this instead of fighting. Let's take a vote." So each
man cast his ballot, and Daley won 7-2.)

Part of the problem in Illinois, of course, is that the
population is so lopsided. Seven million of the state's
eleven million people are bunched together in the north-
east corner (greater Chicago), while the rest are spread
out on farms and in small and medium-sized communities

all the way to the edge of Kentucky. The state legislature in Springfield is thus a ready-made combat zone, with the Irish, black, Polish, Jewish, and other ethnic representatives from Chicago pitted against the sturdy white Anglo-Saxon Protestants from the farm counties. The farmers don't get terribly excited about spending money to build Chicago's rapid transit system or feed its welfare mothers, while the city slickers aren't exactly turned on by the needs of the hinterlands.

With such a lack of common interests, it's not hard to see how political shenanigans arise.

The state of New York has a similar problem, with similar results. At times it has become so acute that some politicians have seriously asked whether New York City wouldn't be better off on its own as the fifty-first state of the Union. That way it wouldn't have to keep hassling with the upstate "appleknockers," as they are rather contemptuously known.

Yet one wonders whether New York City could survive alone. States are equipped to do some things that would be extremely difficult for cities to handle. And vice versa. Multilevel jurisdictions seem to be a necessity of life, in spite of the problems they cause.

It occurs to me that there's an analogy here. Just as cities and states are bound to each other but sometimes have difficulty interrelating, so do families and churches. The home and the church undeniably overlap — the same people are members of both. The church is clearly made up of husbands, wives, sons, and daughters, who obviously don't drop those identities in the narthex. Thus, the potential exists for tension between the two milieus.

But the potential also exists for common bolstering and reinforcement. In the final analysis, most of us are like New York City; we are not really interested in secession. We recognize that "unless the Lord builds the house, those who build it labor in vain" (Psalm 127 — a very family-oriented psalm, by the way). We suspect that the Lord would like to build and strengthen our various houses through the ministry of his church.

It is up to us — husbands of households as well as men of the church — to figure out how.

How the church enhances the household

The home, of course, can claim seniority as an institution. God started it at the very beginning, whereas the idea of the called-out assembly of worshipers goes back only to the time of the Exodus, around 1480 B.C. So it stands to reason that God intended this larger, more recent unit to synchronize with his smaller, more primary unit.

What is the church? It is perhaps easier to state what it is not.

● It isn't a building (although we spend major amounts of money erecting structures commonly known as churches).

● It isn't a denomination (although most denominations use the word in their formal names).

● It isn't a social arena in which we prove respectability to our friends and neighbors.

● It isn't a museum for the preservation of family tradition ("My grandfather was a Presbyterian minister, and we'll always . . .").

● It isn't a provider of free baby-sitting so you and your wife can enjoy a little peace and quiet each week.

The real essence of the church is far greater than any of these. And far more exciting. The church is meant to be a living, breathing community of Christ-followers who love and support each other to such an extent that they might be called . . .

. . . a family! A household!

At least that's what the New Testament often called it. "You are no longer foreigners and aliens," Paul wrote to the Ephesian church, "but fellow citizens with God's people and members of God's household" (2:19).

A chapter later he said, "I kneel before the Father, from whom the whole family of believers in heaven and on earth derives its name" (3:14,15).

The church is a group of people who have a great deal in common with one another because of their common Father. I ask you: what better definition of a family could there be?

The church is thus a magnification of your family and mine, with the rather clear advantage of having a Head who is far more competent than you or I could ever be. Perhaps the idea of the church was not so novel after all; perhaps God simply did an enlargement of his original invention, the home.

If so, perhaps we husbands are best equipped to understand the intended nature and definition of the church for having struggled in everyday life with the nature and definition of our own households.

We can understand how important it is for the church to bring us, our wives, and our children into meaningful relationships with other husbands, wives, children, and single adults.

We can understand how important it is for the church to lead us by the hand and help us confess our shortcomings and failures in order to receive forgiveness and cleansing.

We can understand how important it is for the church to help us clarify our values in the midst of a relativistic world.

We can understand how important it is for the church to nudge us out of our shells into service and outreach in the name of Christ.

We can understand how important it is for the church to give evidence of the supernatural, of God at work, in the midst of a cynical society.

We can understand how important it is for the church to keep reminding us that *God can change us* for the better — that we are not locked forever in our current habits and patterns of selfish behavior.

We can understand how important it is for the church to lift our eyes from our daily problems and confront us with our Lord's love, power, justice, righteousness, and compassion.

More than once I've come home from a tough Wednesday at the office and had the refreshing experience of rejuvenating my mind and soul at the midweek service of our local church. We happen to enjoy a rather loose format on Wednesday nights, a combination of joyous singing, need-centered praying, spontaneous worshiping, fairly honest sharing by members of the audience, and practical teaching from the Word. This potpourri draws a standing-room-only crowd, and I think most of them come for the same reason Grace and I do: it's an oasis in the middle of a demanding week. One goes away feeling restored; life is put back into perspective, and we're ready to go back and face our individual challenges again.

Such an experience is evidence to us that the church of Jesus Christ is indeed a living organism. It is not just an organization. Nor is it some group called *they*. The church is *we*. *We* are the church, the living family of God, and God uses us to provide these mind-stretching, spirit-expanding times for our brothers and sisters as well as ourselves.

We are called to a rhythm of giving and receiving. Galatians 6 reminds us that we reap what we sow, in the church as well as in all of life. That concept has too long been applied only during lectures to wayward teen-agers. It has a powerful positive side as well, as the passage goes on to show. "Let us not become weary in doing good, for at the proper time we will reap a harvest if we do not give up. Therefore, as we have opportunity, let us do good to all people, especially to those who belong" — again, notice the language — "to the family of believers" (6:9,10).

So there are times when we and our wives work hard, whether teaching in the Sunday school, or singing, or playing an instrument, or going to visit someone who's ill, or doing any number of things. There are other times when we are on the receiving end of such blessings. So long as each person is giving and receiving, each is benefited, and the church fulfills its mission.

It doesn't take any special wisdom to see what happens, however, if we refuse to give. Perhaps we don't actually refuse; we just follow custom, warm the pew, keep our mouths shut, and continue being quiet, passive statistics, names on the roll and little more. Whether we do so by intention or by default, the result is the same: we are actually parasites on the life of the church! Everyone else is constantly having to pour in our direction, and we're not reciprocating. In time we become as stagnant spiritually as the Dead Sea, which has the same problem of taking in but never giving out.

There are other people in the church — and you may be one of them — who have the opposite problem. They're compulsive givers. They have to be juggling six different responsibilities at once, and they get very nervous about sitting down to receive from anyone else. It threatens their sense of importance. Unfortunately, their reserves are nearly always depleted because of their constant giving, with the result that their service is not nearly as effective or substantive as they think.

Both of these are aberrations of the intended life of

God's family. As Dr. Reuben Welch says at the end of his book *We Really Do Need Each Other:*

> You know something —
> we're all just people who need each other.
> We're all learning
> and we've all got a long journey
> ahead of us.
> We've got to go together
> and if it takes us till Jesus comes
> we better stay together
> we better help each other. . . .
> Because that's how it is
> in the body of Christ.[1]

For the past couple of years, Grace and I have seen this implemented at the grass roots by participating in a small *koinonia* group — a collection of a dozen or so people who get together every other Friday night in one of our homes to share with and support each other in our spiritual pilgrimages. We've lived through happy times together (the birth of a healthy son to one couple after an extremely troublesome pregnancy) and sad times (the sudden death of one member in a car accident) — and through it all, we've come closer to the Lord and each other.

The small group, in a way, bridges the distance between the large church and the small household; it has a foot in each. We are a subset of the church, subject to its authority; at the same time, we meet in living rooms and are never far from the joys and trials of family life. We give to each other; we receive from each other; we really do need each other.

But what if . . .

I'm aware, of course, that not everyone enjoys such a fulfilling church experience. In fact, I've often been the only person in a group of Christians who could say something positive about his church. For many, the preceding description is wishful thinking. The most common criticisms I hear are that churches are (a) dead, (b) unfriendly, (c) snobbish, (d) culturally irrelevant, (e) pessimistic, (f) theoretical instead of life-oriented, (g) a drain on the energies of their members, (h) too traditional, (i) any combination of the above.

It's true — a lot of Christians belong to churches that don't resemble families, not even a little bit. The form of worship does little to raise people's consciousness of God Almighty. They don't have meaningful relationships with other members, even though they've been in the same congregation for years. They can't point to any real spiritual change in their lives. They feel as if they're turning the wheels of a giant machine week after week with nothing to show for it.

For reasons such as these, many husbands and wives have simply dropped out of church, or have never chosen one in the first place.

The institution of the church survives without them, however, year after year, century after century. Most institutions do; they have amazing powers of self-preservation. It's incredible to stop and think about the tremendous bank of good will and don't-rock-the-boat that bolsters the institutional church in North America. The average guy in the pew does not easily bring himself to declare its faults or decry its lack of authenticity or spiritual life.

Meanwhile, the institution develops a mind of its own; it exists no longer to serve the needs of the people, but to be served *by* the people. The objection is not that members are called upon to serve, but that they are called upon to serve *a thing*, an empire, an abstraction, instead of one another. They find themselves spending major blocks of time on institutional activity rather than on building and enjoying family relationships with the Father and fellow believers.

What do we do about these things? As heads of our households, how do we promote the vitally important ministry of the church as we know it could be? How do we bring the dream alive?

Well, we do lots of things. First, we refine our understanding of the church in light of the Book of Acts and the Epistles. We make sure our dreams are biblical. Then we talk. We let our needs and desires be known. We pay our dues to the institution so that our voices can be heard and trusted. We jump in and work for change whenever the opportunity comes.

If the opportunity never comes, some may relocate, which is a difficult decision to make. All the while, however, whatever happens or doesn't happen, we keep praying — for clearer goals, for purity of motive, for the life of the Spirit to infuse us all.

This quest for the authentic church experience is important, but not so important that it can be allowed to make lousy husbands and fathers of us. There is a point at which committee sessions and prayer meetings can start to infringe upon the rest of our job description. Even more subtly, we can spend so much time *thinking* about the church (especially if we are in positions of leadership) and what we can do to improve its quality of life that there's not enough think-time left for the people closest to us.

Conversely, we cannot sink into an adversary mentality. As was said earlier, the church is *us*. For the good of both the church and our household, we must call the church to its highest and best, i.e., biblical, state "so that the lame may not be disabled, but rather healed" (Heb. 12:13). We, our wives, and our children desperately need to participate in the growth, the encouragement, the lift, and the challenge of the extended family of God. We are an intrinsic part of the household of faith. To the extent to which the church fulfills its true mission, our job is that much easier.

[1]Reuben Welch, *We Really Do Need Each Other* (Nashville: Impact, 1973).

8

What's a Christian Home?

8

What's a Christian Home?

The effectiveness of the church, of course, is not entirely ours to control. We're only individuals within the larger body. We have to work with others, our peers and spiritual leaders, to make the church beneficial in its ministry to our families.

But when we begin to think about our own households in the spiritual dimension — it's a different story. There's no one to blame but us. There are no church boards or synods standing in the way of progress. If my home reflects the nature and love of Christ on ordinary Mondays, Thursdays, and Saturdays, it's because my wife and I have determined to make it so. If the atmosphere at our house is no different from that of a non-Christian household, I can't really pass the buck to anyone else.

We husbands get this laid on us heavily from time to time, especially in Father's Day sermons. "The husband is the spiritual leader of the home," we're told. "He's the pacesetter, the priest, the representative of God for everyone in the family." (We begin slouching down into the pew at about this point.) The biblical prototypes are trotted out: Noah, who inspired his sons to work with him on a God-ordained project that seemed foolish to everyone else; Abraham, who led his family to a new country in response to divine command; Job, who sacrificed every day to atone for his children's sins; Joseph, who carefully guarded the Christ child. (We start reading the bulletin.)

Then come the bad guys, the biblical fathers who blew it: Eli, whose sons turned the tabernacle worship into an extortion-and-sex racket; Samuel, whose sons "did not walk in his ways, but . . . took bribes and perverted justice" (1 Sam. 8:3); David, who totally alienated his son Absalom and indirectly caused his untimely death; the various kings of Israel and Judah. (We check our watches.)

We know it's all true. We know our homes are supposed to be Christian homes. We don't want our kids to have to get everything spiritual from Sunday school and catechism classes. We know that the difference between a Christian family and a non-Christian family is more than just that the one goes to church on Sunday morning while the other sleeps in.

Indeed, the Puritans used to speak about the family as an *ecclesiola* — a "little church." They felt it was as important for God to be welcomed into the midst of individual families as into the larger congregation.

We all salute that. The only questions are *how* questions. How do we integrate our faith with daily living? How do we keep family prayers fresh and alive? How do we find the time? How do we avoid boredom? How much formal ritual do we need? How much spur-of-the-moment interaction?

"Back when I was a kid . . ."

If you come from a Christian heritage, you no doubt can tell impressive tales about how grandpa used to take down the old family Bible (King James Version) every evening after supper, 365 nights a year, and solemnly read a chapter to his wife and eleven children. The slightest giggle or twitch by the smallest toddler was allegedly clamped off by a severe rap on the knuckles with the heavy end of a table knife.

We won't probe the historical accuracy of all that, although it's true that many of our forefathers took family Bible reading and prayer very seriously. They set up the structures they thought necessary to communicate the Christian message in the home.

Many families continue such traditions today, with various modifications. The King James Version may be replaced by a modern paraphrase, and the father may not do all the reading, but there is still an established pattern to bring Scripture and prayer into daily life.

Even the most casual among us preserves such traditions as prayer before meals and usually before children's bedtime as well.

The questions to be asked of all such activity are: *Is it effective? Does it add up to the creating of a Christian home? Is it causing this family to "grow in the grace and knowledge of our Lord and Savior Jesus Christ"* (2 Peter 3:18)?

There are some good things to be said about the "family altar" tradition. Number one, it's regular. You don't find yourself going long stretches of time and forgetting to have spiritual input in the family.

Number two, the regularity of it says it's important. Children can't help but be impressed that this is a priority.

Number three, there's enough time over the long haul to deal in depth with a lot of spiritual concepts. Twenty minutes a day in the home is equivalent to two hours of Sunday school and church on the weekend. Over the years, it adds up.

There are possibly other advantages as well, but there are some disadvantages, too. The most obvious one is the *sameness* of what most husbands do during the family devotional time. Grandpa's children may not have moved a muscle while he read, but the chances are that at least some of the time they weren't listening either. Without variety, kids get bored, and so do adults.

Hence, we come to an important observation:

In making a Christian household, *results are more important than tradition*.

It is not so important that we continue the family practice. It is not so important that we do what we see other Christian husbands doing or advising us to do. It *is* important that we do what works.

And it's been my experience, both in my own devotional life and with Grace and the family, that *nothing works forever*. It seems that techniques and patterns last only so long, serve their purpose, and then go stale. Maybe I just have a low repetition tolerance or something, but what is neat the first week or two has a way of falling flat after a while, and I find that I need to change the structure for bringing myself and my family into meaningful communication with God.

For example: what about a simple thing like table grace? I carry on a running argument with myself over this tradition. I know the Scripture states that food is something "God created to be received with thanksgiving by those who believe and who know the truth" (1 Tim. 4:3). My problem is that the little eighteen-second prayer I often run through is not much of a carrier of thanksgiving.

Sometimes I'm really grateful that God has enabled us to have enough money to put the food on the table. At other times, I'm too hungry, or the kids are impatient, and all I want to do is get on with the eating. We utter a prayer anyway, but the effect is minimal, as evidenced by the question sometimes asked later in the meal: "Did we pray?" (You will understand why, in our particular family, we don't say, "Did we say grace?")

Once we tried shifting the prayer to *after* the meal. It was somewhat easier to put meaning into the words, "Thank you, Lord, for the food we've just enjoyed." But the tradition of decades is not easily broken, and more than once we found ourselves getting up from the table without remembering to give thanks. We eventually went back to the standard practice.

Perhaps we need to keep experimenting, finding different ways to remind ourselves that the daily food really is a gift from above and that God deserves to hear our appreciation for it. And maybe 1 Timothy 4:3 doesn't insist on prayer at every meal (heresy!), if we could be more genuinely grateful at longer intervals.

When it comes to the devotional life, Grace and I have had some exciting periods of studying the Bible and praying together. We don't do it continuously, but a couple of times each year it seems like one says to the other, "Hey, let's have devotions together for a while." At times we've gone through books of the Bible, making applications to our own lives along the way. At other times we've taken a topical approach to see what the Scripture tells us about a certain area of concern. Sometimes we've used an additional study guide or commentary; more often we've gone it alone.

When we've moved on to pray together, the synergism has been even more beneficial. Grace knows me pretty well, and I know her, so it's no use trying to be pious in front of each other. We just sort of let it all come out before the Lord. It sounds more like a three-way conversation than anything else, except that one side (the Lord's) is inaudible. Grace prays, I pray, she prays again, we wait and listen, I respond . . . sometimes we go whole paragraphs, sometimes just a sentence or two, or even a fragment, the same way a normal conversation runs. No speechmaking is allowed, or even desired.

Sometimes we kneel, sometimes we sit, and sometimes we keep our eyes open (as when praying while driving, for example!). Inevitably, we come away sensing that our heads have been cleared, that we understand a lot more about the various topics and needs we've discussed with the Lord than we did before. (We usually end up kicking ourselves for not making time to do this more often.)

I remember one particular time when our joint devotional life was crucial. The time I was in graduate school at Syracuse University was especially trying for Grace. We lived in a 2½-room efficiency apartment near the campus, and her teaching job required a 32-mile drive each day to a grade school in a small town called Elbridge. Driving is not one of Grace's favorite pastimes, so she was less than excited about commuting.

It began snowing that year on October 22, and by the time the last flakes came down on May 7, Syracuse had racked up a total of 160 inches for the winter. The terrain was hilly and the sky perpetually gray, and all in all, Grace found it depressing.

She'd come in through the drifts at the end of a school day, fix dinner, then spend the evening grading papers while I studied . . . and then, just as we were ready for sleep around eleven o'clock, the woman in the downstairs apartment would begin practicing her classical music. It wouldn't have been so bad if she'd been a good pianist, but her timing was atrocious, and Grace would spend the next couple of hours staring at the ceiling while listening to the massacre of Brahms or whoever. (Being a morning-type person, I had no trouble going on to sleep.)

There wasn't a whole lot we could do to change any of these factors. But I could sense that Grace was really having difficulty; things were piling up on her, and she was tired and worried about getting enough rest to keep functioning the next day and the next and the next.

It was then that I suggested we do a joint exploration of what the Bible has to say about peace. We knew some individual verses, of course, but for the first time we sat down with a concordance and began to pull together the whole of the scriptural message. We started a sheet of paper entitled, "Things We Want to Remember About Peace," and began making notations such as:

Phil. 4:4-7	Peace is the opposite of worry.
John 14:23-31	Peace is a real *something* that Christ deposits in us.
Gal. 5:22-25	The Holy Spirit produces peace in us.
Ps. 28:1-9	Peace is a state of mind *within* action.
2 Tim. 2:22	Follow after, aim at peace. (The human
Rom. 14:19	initiative is needed, too.)

Grace clung to these verses and others for the rest of the school year. They became cords of hope to pull her through the snowy days and the discordant nights. And the change in her outlook was perceptible.

This experience is fresh in my memory because we dug out that sheet of paper a few months ago — six years later — when the person feeling harassed and in knots was not Grace but me. The combination of work responsibilities and my lack of patience with the children was getting to me, and I asked her if she'd mind a rerun of that peace study to help me get some bearings again.

Yes, it's tough to find time for this kind of interaction. It gets considerably tougher once children come into the home. You're busier, and so many of the things on your "To Do" list can't be done while the kids are awake, unless you stop parenting and just insist that they stay out of your way. You know that's not right, so you keep parenting, and wait with eagerness for the later evening hours when they're in bed so you can read and do the other things in quietness. Can you afford to give some of this precious time to a spiritual rendezvous with your wife?

Can you afford not to?

If a husband can't find the time and motivation to come with his wife into the presence of God, how is God to give guidance or input to the affairs of the household? The couple who think they can chart their own course without the help of divine direction are — in this regard — a non-Christian couple. There is no difference between their approach to marriage and that of the others on their block who admit no need of God.

Couples have to work out their own time of day and frequency. Better to get together only once or twice a week than not at all.

The serendipity times

Perhaps the best timing of all — not only for us adults but for our children as well — is the timing that happens spontaneously. While you're lying on the beach, a conversation springs up about prayer and how God answers it. Or, your son wants to know, "Who made squirrels?" Or, you're putting up Christmas decorations, and you get started talking about how to make the whole season reflect its spiritual roots.

The difference is this: you can sit everybody down and

say, "Now I'm going to tell (or read) you the story of the children of Israel crossing the Red Sea. They had just left Egypt, and the Pharaoh had changed his mind about whether to let them go, so he sent his army. . . ." Depending upon your talents as a storyteller, the response can range from medium to absolute zero.

On the other hand, let's say you're driving home from a relative's house late on New Year's Day, and your alternator goes out. You're 150 miles from home, the garages and gas stations are all closed, and it's cold and dark.

You're pretty upset, and a little worried about your limited number of options. You can drive the car on battery power only a few more miles, but you're in strange country and . . . let's face it, you don't know what to do.

If, in such a predicament, you were to say, "Well, uh . . . I don't know how we're going to get home, but I suggest we pray about it. In a way, I guess this is kind of like the jam Moses and the people were in beside the Red Sea — unless God did something, they weren't going anywhere. But the Lord showed that he could pull off a surprise, and I guess that's what we need to ask him for right now."

And suppose God does answer prayer in a dramatic way. Suppose a Good Samaritan pulls up behind you who "happens" to be the brother of the manager of an auto parts store in the next town. Within an hour, you're on your way again.

Your kids will have learned the meaning of Exodus 14 so thoroughly they'll never forget it.

Perhaps our job as Christian fathers does not depend so much on rigid traditions as it does on seizing what educators call "the teachable moment" — the time when a child is ripe for impression. I remember Nathan's fascination last summer when he was up close to a bonfire for the first time during one of our weekend trips to Wisconsin. As we sat there in the evening darkness watching the flames, I told him three fire stories from the Bible: Moses' burning bush, the three Hebrews in Babylon, and Paul on the island of Malta. The reason I know it sunk in is that he still talks about that night and the storytelling session.

God seems even to have instructed the Israelite fathers to "set up" these kinds of situations. Joshua 4:1–7 tells about the men building a huge rockpile alongside the Jordan River as they went into the Promised Land. Why? To elicit questions from their children and thus open the conversation for an account of God's power. The rockpile was intended as "a sign among you, when your children ask in time to come, 'What do those stones mean to you?' Then you shall tell them that the waters of the Jordan were cut off before the ark of the covenant of the Lord" (vv. 6,7).

A few years later, the tribes of Reuben, Gad, and Manasseh did something similar on *their* side of the river; they built "an altar of great size" (Josh. 22:10). The other tribes wanted to know why. So they explained, "We did it from fear that in time to come your children might say to our children, 'What have you to do with the Lord, the God of Israel?' . . . If this should be said . . . we should say, 'Behold the copy of the altar of the Lord, which our fathers made, not for burnt offerings, nor for sacrifice, but to be a witness between us and you ' " (vv. 24,28).

There's nothing wrong with scheduled times of Bible reading and instruction. There's nothing wrong with programs of Bible memory — at age four my parents started me memorizing verses and reviewing them from handwritten three-by-five cards, until by high-school days I'd mastered more than six hundred. But at the same time they knew how to be alert for serendipity. They could point out the hand of God in the most ordinary happenings. They were never taken off guard. It was my father who, while tucking his first grader into bed one April Tuesday night, responded clearly and simply to my question about salvation. The standard bedtime prayer had already been said, but after he'd explained the meaning of confessing my sin and placing my trust in Christ, I crawled out again and knelt beside him to ask entrance into the family of God.

I hope I have the privilege of doing the same with my own son.

A child cannot help but doubt the alleged importance of something that never gets talked about except at pre-scheduled times. If God is noticeable only on Sundays and for fifteen minutes after dinner each evening, then maybe he's not all the grownups claim he is.

Too often we husbands have classified the spiritual training of our children, along with mopping and dish-washing, as "women's work." Either we've been too busy or felt too inept to try to communicate the essence of the gospel to a child. Why? We don't shrink from teaching a child how to tie his shoes or change a bicycle tire or shoot free throws. The Scriptures exhort us to impart a man's touch to the spiritual area as well. Paul, in recounting his ministry in Thessalonica, writes, "We dealt with each of you as a father deals with his own children, encouraging, comforting and urging you to live lives worthy of God, who calls you into his kingdom and glory" (1 Thess. 2:11,12). It is specifically fathers who are directed to "provoke not your children to wrath: but bring them up in the nurture and admonition of the Lord" (Eph. 6:4 KJV).

Actually, the family is the perfect size for such learning and interaction. Both the public schoolteacher with a classroom of thirty and the minister with a congregation of three hundred would give a lot to be able to work with people in such small groupings as we enjoy every day in our homes.

The only valid reason I can think of for backing away from leadership in this area — and perhaps this is the real cause in many cases — is if the husband himself has no thriving relationship with the Lord. If we ourselves are not on familiar terms with God, then no wonder we hesitate to try to set the pace for our wives and/or children.

To cultivate our own rapport with God may mean getting out of bed before the rest of the family, or chopping a hole in our schedules at some point throughout the day, or making some other adjustment. The same battle for time and the same need for creative approaches that we've mentioned above apply on the individual level, too.

But as leaders who are servants, it's worth it. If God can get through to me individually, and to my wife individually, and to us as a couple, we will grow as adults, and we'll also be prepared to nurture the spiritual growth of our children. And that's what you call a Christian home.

9

Beyond
Anatomy

9

Beyond Anatomy

There was an awesome day — at least as Susan Brownmiller tells it in her book *Against Our Will: Men, Women and Rape* — when the cave people first discovered that males could take sexual advantage of females, but not vice versa. In Brownmiller's feminist view, the dawning of that fact of life was as portentous as the discovery of fire or the invention of the wheel. "By anatomical fiat — the inescapable construction of their genital organs — the human male was a natural predator and the human female served as his natural prey."

And that's not all. The privilege of rape led inevitably, the author says, to a desperate female proposal for relief: a proposal called *marriage*. The prehistoric woman was glad to submit to regular rape by one man if he would, in turn, protect her from all the others. Brownmiller explains it this way:

One possibility, and one possibility alone, was available to woman. . . . Among those creatures who were her predators, some might serve as her chosen protectors. Perhaps it was thus that the risky bargain was struck. Female fear of an open season of rape, and not a natural inclination toward monogamy, motherhood or love, was probably the single causative factor in the original subjugation of woman by man, the most important key to her historic dependence, her domestication by protective mating.

. . . But the price of woman's protection *by some men* against an abuse *by others* was steep. . . . Those who did assume the historic burden of her protection — later formalized as husband, father, brother, clan — extracted more than a pound of flesh. They reduced her status to that of chattel. The historic price of woman's protection by man against man was the imposition of chastity and monogamy.[1]

So there you have it, folks — one angry woman's scenario of how the world got to be the way it is. The rest of her book is a catalog of rape across the centuries and cultures. As for the biblical account of how God instituted marriage in the Garden of Eden, as for our society's abundance of sentiments about love and sharing and commitment between husbands and wives, as for Valentine's Day and brides in white dresses holding bouquets — it's all a male chauvinist cover-up of a dastardly evil contract.

Fascinating. Also disgusting. I, for one, am not quite ready to concede that the love, warmth, devotion, and charm that emanate from my wife toward me are nothing more than payoffs for keeping the rest of the male population away from her. I would like to believe that she loves me as a complete person, that our marriage is not a case of making the best of a bad situation but rather a joint adventure toward fulfillment and joy. I believe that marriage was created by God, not by a frantic cave woman.

But having said that, I must go on to say that I can see how Susan Brownmiller came to her thesis. There's a glimmer of reality in her dismal fantasy, a glimmer that most of us would like to ignore but need to face. We must ask ourselves the question: "Do I view my marriage, in part, as a free ticket for sex?" Or, to phrase it another way, "If sex were not part of the package, would I still want to be married?"

The point is not that sex is unimportant. There's no need to disparage the fact that sexual relations with one's wife are neat experiences that feel good.

The point is that sex is a joint dimension in which both husbands and wives give pleasure to each other, thereby communicating their love in a largely nonverbal way. It is an experience in giving. It is another situation for being the servants of our wives. In fact, it may be one of the more difficult situations in which we are called upon to serve, given our Western macho traditions of sexual conquest. From boyhood on, we men have been programed in a thousand different ways to view sex as an area where we *get*, where we *take*, where we *use*. The culture is thoroughly saturated with the image of Don Juan.

But in recent years, a curious thing has happened. Women have decided to follow our example; they've realized there are some rather nice sensations for *them* to get as well. The bookstores are filled with manuals on female orgasm. The result is that many marriages are now composed of two takers, two seekers of the ultimate personal high, who may or may not happen to provide what the other person wants and needs during the process of their own quest. The traditional setup of one taker and one willing or reluctant giver is indeed a form of rape.

The newer setup of two takers is not much better, is it?

When, in contrast, we apply the model of servanthood to this area, all the dynamics change. The goal becomes the provision of her needs rather than our own. And we find, as we've noticed before, that our own needs are met along the way rather automatically. We husbands need to understand the ways and means of female orgasm. We also need to learn more about the psychological, non-physical aspects of a woman's participation in intercourse. Especially since anatomy has given us the role it has, it is all the more our responsibility to set the pattern of true sexual union, not rape.

Warm-ups and turn-ons

Granted, it can be tough sometimes to implement this lofty ideal on a practical basis. After all, what's a guy supposed to do when he slides into bed with his internal turbines already moving, and the first thing his wife says is, "Man, am I exhausted!" Surveys show that one of the most common sexual problems among couples, especially young couples, is the frequency of intercourse.

Well, there are a number of options in such a situation.

● You can argue about it. You can say, "How come? You got more sleep than I did last night."

And she'll say, "Yes, but . . ." and proceed to recount the day's various ordeals.

And you'll respond, "Gee, it'd be nice to have you save a little energy for me once in a while."

"Oh, honey, come on. . . ."

And from there on, the conversation deteriorates until you're no longer in the mood, and both of you are feeling put upon. You go to sleep reciting 1 Corinthians 7:5 to yourself ("Do not cheat each other of normal sexual intercourse" — Phillips) and wondering why your wife won't obey the Word of God!

• You can go ahead and rape her. Not by the legal definition, of course, but that's what it amounts to if you insist against her will. She may have learned over the years to keep her feelings subsurface in such situations, to "submit," to play the role pretty well, but the chances are you both know what's going on.

• You can play the martyr, with or without her knowing about it. You can say, "Well, okay — I thought we could have a little fun tonight, but if you need your sleep . . ." and you deliberately leave the sentence hanging. Such a line may manipulate her into warming up or may earn you a disgusted groan, depending upon how tired she is. You can also just roll over and say nothing and feel sorry for yourself for being married to such an iceberg. Either way, you don't go to sleep happy.

• You can start scheming a better way to turn her on next time. You begin making plans to bring home flowers tomorrow night, or be more cordial throughout the evening, or forego Monday night football, or do a few sexy things before bedtime to get her started.

Such plans are not evil in themselves; in fact, most men don't pay enough attention to the warm-up period that women seem to delight in. But the question is one of motive: are we doing such things in order to get what *we* want in the end or for the purpose of giving her pleasure and the excitement of anticipation?

This brings us to the fifth option:

• You can decide to be her servant. You can force yourself to appreciate the fact that she really is tired and that what she probably needs at the moment is not what you had in mind. You sincerely wanted to provide her with steak and lobster, but all she feels like having is a glass of milk. So that's what you give her — a gentle kiss on the forehead and a quiet "Good night."

I'm assuming in all of this that "Man, am I exhausted!" is to be taken at face value — that it's not code language for "Leave me alone, fella." If it *is* code language for some other problem of sexual adjustment, then that's another matter that needs consideration.

And as we all know, there are dozens of other adjustments to be made in a sexual relationship. We spend a lifetime working through them; frequency is just one of the pack. But many of the others — the need for gentleness on the part of the husband throughout the whole experience, the timing of releases, the place of variety, what you enjoy and don't enjoy, what she enjoys and doesn't enjoy, even ignorance about basic anatomical facts — are resolved much more easily by two people intent on serving each other than by two people out for what they can get.

Husbands and wives who are genuinely interested in pleasing their spouses have got to be willing to *talk* about sex with each other. This goes against the traditional grain — we have the assumption that if everything were going right, we wouldn't have to discuss it. We don't want to admit the existence of any problems, so we keep quiet.

How can you give your wife a greater sexual experience if you don't know how to change what you're doing? After all, you're not a mind reader. So don't pretend to be. Dr. Clifford Penner and his wife Joyce, a psychiatrist/nurse team from Pasadena who conduct seminars on sexual fulfillment, have written:

> Each of us is the best authority on what we need and like sexually. I cannot assume that I know what my partner likes. Thus it is my partner's responsibility to let me know what is pleasurable for him or her.

The Penners openly admit that everyone isn't willing to be this forthright.

> This is a slightly different approach than most of us are used to hearing from popular Christian writers. The emphasis has been much more on it being my responsibility to find out, through whatever method happens to work, what will cause my partner to respond. This approach of playing guessing games to please the other person just has not worked well when dealing with couples who are having sexual problems or wish to enhance their sexual relationship. There is a great release of tension when the couple makes and really believes the agreement that each will be responsible to let the other know what each one needs, what feels good, and what does not.[2]

Naturally, this kind of communication is a little heavy to undertake right in the middle of intercourse. It works better to discuss such things at separate times, when we're not caught up in the sweep of our emotions. The trouble is, we often don't think of it except in bed. It's like fixing a leaky roof; we keep forgetting about it until it actually rains, and at that moment it's rather awkward to try to resolve the problem.

But talk we must. We must also read. In this enlightened age, there's no excuse for being ignorant of the basic physiological facts of how our bodies work. I'm not talking about reading trashy or erotic pseudoscientific material. Every book with "M.D." after its author's name is not necessarily a sober or responsible piece of writing. I'm talking about the straightforward, nonsalacious treatments of sexual anatomy and psychology that can help us understand the way God has put us together.

There's another thing we must do, and that's get professional help if we need it. Again, the field is fraught with all manner of voyeurs and incompetents who've hung out their shingles as marriage counselors. But this cannot be allowed to prevent us from finding the bona fide specialists and listening to what they have to say.

It's interesting that such serious people as Masters and Johnson and Graber and Kline-Graber proposed a particular kind of activity that is amazingly consonant with the idea of Christian servanthood. They call it "nondemand pleasuring," in which one spouse undertakes to do whatever the other finds enjoyable, receiving no stroking or affection in return. The communication is entirely one way. The ground rule for this particular time is: no intercourse. For example, the wife lies in her husband's lap with his legs on either side, a position in which coitus is virtually impossible. He proceeds to "pleasure" her without thought of getting anything back — except the satisfaction of giving her enjoyment. He knows from earlier conversations what she likes, and he presents it to her as a gift of love.

Some of our wives would bet we'd never be able to do that; we'd have to "get ours" at some point along the way. Are they right or wrong? It may depend in part upon our willingness to obey Ephesians 5:28, where it says that "husbands ought to love their wives as their own bodies. He who loves his wife loves himself."

Periods and pregnancies

Our willingness to bend, to be flexible, and to think in terms of her needs instead of our own receives a monthly test of sorts known as The Period. For one thing, it's a test of our forbearance; for a span of up to seven days, she simply "isn't available."

That can be frustrating for us, because our sexual motors don't exactly shut down during that time. We get tired of waiting. One solution, of course, if the wife is so inclined, is to engage in a little nondemand pleasuring as described above, only in reverse. However, the initiative obviously has to be hers.

Our desires, of course, are rather minor compared to the stresses and discomfort our wives are enduring. And we keep forgetting, even though we've been told all the medical facts, how the hormone levels rise and fall to create fretfulness and depression at certain times of the month. We hear phrases like, "There's just no way for you to know what this is like" — and she's right. There isn't.

But we can learn how to make life easier for her. Whether it's fixing our own breakfast so she can sleep in, giving backrubs, or postponing our remarks about the state of the checking account, we can do a lot to accommodate the monthly period, especially in the first couple of days.

And a little wait for loving won't kill us.

There's a much greater test of our willingness to adapt and wait, of course, and that's called pregnancy. As Fitzhugh Dodson mentions in his popular book *How to Father*, the various

> physiological changes trigger drastic psychological changes in her as well. She may become moody, or irrational, or suddenly demanding. She may burst into tears over what seems to you nothing at all. Her behavior may confuse and bewilder you. It is important for you to realize that *all these things are quite normal for a pregnant woman.*
>
> In the same way that you need to make allowances for psychological changes in your wife during her monthly period, you need to make allowances for psychological changes during pregnancy.[3]

Again, there's no way for you and me to know what it's really like. Gaining twenty to thirty pounds, having to switch to a more limited, less fashionable wardrobe, being tired a lot of the time, running out of breath on a single flight of stairs, searching in vain during the later months for a comfortable sleep position, going to the bathroom fifteen times a day (and night) — it's not entirely a picnic being pregnant. Many of these limitations impinge on us as husbands; she just can't do as much as she used to, go with us all the places she'd like to. And as the months wear on, it gets frustrating for both.

At such times we need to remind ourselves whose sperm started all this. Hopefully, the decision to have a child was a joint decision, but even if it was a surprise, it didn't happen without you. You can be glad that the physical burden of carrying a fetus is not equally divided between its parents.

Eventually you find yourself facing a moratorium on sexual relations for approximately three months — the last six weeks of pregnancy and the first six weeks of recovery. Again, you don't turn into a eunuch during that time. You face the need to subjugate your desires to the greater goal of seeing this wonderful woman go through the most dramatic experience of her life — the birth of a child.

Rather than withdrawing from her, you can participate with her in this special miracle. I shall always be grateful for the Lamaze natural-childbirth training that enabled me to help Grace through her two deliveries. It took Nathan twenty-seven hours to get here, and without Lamaze, I don't know if he'd have made it or not. As I sat there in the labor room throughout the afternoon and on into the long night, timing contractions and giving the breathing instructions that would enable Grace to stay in control of the pain, I had never felt closer to her. When it all paid off at 7:20 the next morning, I was as enraptured as she. I eventually found time to write down an account of that day:

I drove home from the hospital in the bright but windy morning. It seemed like a very long time since the Volvo had last been started and I had been in the "outside world." The house was quiet when I arrived. . . . After a half-hour of telephoning, I left the house and drove toward Wheaton's Golden Bear Restaurant for pancakes.

The light turned red as I approached Gary Avenue on Jewell Road. A police car with red lights flashing stopped in the intersection to clear the way for a funeral procession. I sat watching the shiny hearse, the black limousine, the twenty or more cars of mourners, all with headlights on — and thought about birth and death, all on the same day. Little Nathan, barely three hours into life — and someone else, three days into eternity. All the rest of us stand somewhere in between those extremes. . . .

Golden Bear at 10:30 A.M. is not busy. I sat in a booth near the back, by myself. I watched the assortment of humanity before me: 195 lb. businessmen in suits, 160 lb. busboys in jeans, 125 lb. waitresses in uniforms, all so mundane. I wondered at the thought of each one of them having a special day of birth, of emerging tiny and bloody and innocent from their mothers, of sending a set of parents and a family into ecstasy. And now — how had they become so ordinary?

The pancakes finished, I went shopping for a *Chicago Tribune* (to keep) at Walgreen's, a card for Nathan at Sentiments & Sweets, three orders of flowers at Scheffler's, a car wash at Arco. Then I headed home for an unusual midday nap, setting the alarm for 1:30 P.M. in order to be back for hospital visiting an hour later.

In those hours, the inconveniences of pregnancy were a million miles from my thoughts, and Grace's as well. We were indeed "joint heirs of the grace of life" (1 Peter 3:7 RSV), and it was enchanting.

In control

A husband comes down from such mountaintops, of course, by the time the baby comes home from the hospital to launch the reality of 2:00 A.M. feedings. The infant seems a little less cherubic than he did when three shifts of nurses were doing all the dirty work.

And in a similar sort of way, there are times throughout the course of marriage when we are less thrilled with our wives than at other times. It is an ugly but undeniable fact of life that all of us have to cope with temptation outside the marriage bond. *All* of us.

A friend of mine was once gazing out the front window of his house at a neighbor's new Corvette. "Look at that!" he exclaimed to his eight-year-old son Tommy. "Isn't that a beautiful machine? Man, wouldn't I love to have a car like that!"

Tommy, whose recent Sunday school lessons had apparently been taken from the Book of Exodus, was disturbed. "Daddy," he scolded, "you're not supposed to commit adultery!"

His confusion of the seventh and the tenth commandments is perhaps excusable. "Thou shalt not covet" can apply to women as well as sports cars. Either way, most of us don't have trouble knowing where the boundaries are; the difficulty lies in making our drives and desires conform to our moral values.

One of the most common alibis, of course, is, "I deserve to do a little messing around because my wife is such a klutz. If she'd only sharpen up, I wouldn't notice the secretaries at work so much."

You might as well face the fact that in this world there will always be younger, sharper, more shapely women than your wife. That's unavoidable. You, of course, have no way of knowing what *they* look like at 6:30 A.M., but you do know what your own wife is like at that hour, and to compare the two is unfair.

Come to think of it, there are a number of Hollywood actors who can't seem to stay satisfied with the most gorgeous 38-24-36s in the world; their infidelity and divorce problems are scandalous. It serves only to illustrate the fact that a marriage is glued together not so much by sex appeal as by the intangibles of love and commitment.

Those intangibles are intended to be permanent things that stand throughout the years, regardless of the temptations. They stand no matter where a business trip may take me; my wife may be on the other side of the continent, but her commitment to me and mine to her are right there at my side. A violation of that commitment — vicariously through film or print, or in actuality — keeps echoing in the brain for days and weeks afterward, even if it's kept totally secret.

The Scripture has some fairly heavy passages of warning that we'd do well to read periodically. First Thessalonians 4:3–6 is one of them:

> It is God's will that you should be holy; that you should avoid sexual immorality; that each of you should learn to control his own body in a way that is holy and honorable, not in passionate lust like the heathen, who do not know God; and that in this matter no one should wrong his brother or take advantage of him. The Lord will punish men for all such sins. . . .

Paul told Timothy to "flee the evil desires of youth" (2 Tim. 2:22). Don't even stand there thinking about it for a minute — run!

The really big artillery is in Proverbs 2:16–19, all of chapter 5, then 6:20 on through the end of chapter 7, and 9:13–18 — more than 75 verses in all. It seems ironic, but perhaps significant, that the world-champion polygamist should be so concerned about a clean sex life! Solomon was no prude, but even he knew that an extramarital affair is nothing but trouble.

All at once he follows her,
    as an ox goes to the slaughter,
or as a stag is caught fast
    till an arrow pierces its entrails;
as a bird rushes into a snare;
    he does not know that it will cost him his life.
(Prov. 7:22,23)

We've all known men, perhaps even close friends or colleagues, who have tragically proven the truth of those verses. We've seen careers wrecked, mental health shattered, and children devastated. And the scary part is we've known that we ourselves were vulnerable to the same downfall.

Maybe what we need to do is go ahead and admit that, by Jesus' definition, we are all adulterers. Who among us never "looks at a woman lustfully" (Matt. 5:28)? We all know good and well that our imaginations take off at times, and we do little or nothing to stop them. I'm not recommending that we pray, "Lord, forgive me for my adultery" each evening in front of our wives, but it is a sin that does need confession. Jesus was smart enough to know that we don't engage in acts we haven't first thought about. That's why he urged us to deal seriously with the thought level. It calls for unending vigilance.

If the love act is indeed an experience of giving, what can we hope to give to anyone other than our wives? We can give tension, guilt feelings, uncertainties, and apprehensions.

But to our wives we can give security, love, relaxation, affirmation, and pleasure that lasts. We can also give the experience of motherhood within an aura of joy and safety. We can lift her (and ourselves) above the passions of anatomy to the ultimate merger of two persons becoming one flesh . . . as well as one mind and spirit. These are incredible gifts, once you stop to appraise them, and they can be given by no one but husbands.

[1]Susan Brownmiller, *Against Our Will: Men, Women and Rape* (New York: Simon and Schuster, 1975), pp. 16-17.

[2]Clifford and Joyce Penner, *Sexual Fulfillment in Marriage* (Omaha: Family Concern, 1977), p. 9.

[3]Fitzhugh Dodson, *How to Father* (Los Angeles: Nash, 1974), pp. 8-9.

10

Take It
Easy

10

Take It
Easy

Sometimes a guy just has to relax. A man needs time to
unwind, forget about responsibilities, do what feels good
— golfing, fishing, hunting, reading a good book, raising
sunflowers, making furniture, restoring a Model A, playing racquetball with a buddy . . . whatever.
   End of chapter. What else needs to be said?

   Let's not drop the subject quite yet. It's true that one
individual adult with a chunk of unscheduled time can
take care of himself very well. It's also true that every
individual adult *needs* chunks of down-time in order to
recycle, to re-create his physical and mental energies.
That's one of the reasons God instituted the sabbath.
   We North Americans recognize this need so well that
we spend billions of dollars each year on recreation.
We've managed to reduce the work week to forty hours or
less to create more and more leisure time. The fastest
developing region of the United States is the Sunbelt from

Florida across to California, where more and more of us are moving in order to do more relaxing outside.

But the more we take it easy, the more we realize that taking it easy is not a cure-all. Have you ever had *more* leisure time than you wanted? I've talked to men who've gone on three-week vacations, only to be climbing the walls after ten days. They realized they really didn't like to sit around and sit around and keep sitting around. They rather sheepishly ended up going back to the office ahead of schedule.

Leisure is not nirvana. Leisure is meaningful only against the backdrop of other parts of life. And for those of us who have opted to blend ourselves into a larger common life called the household, leisure is inescapably a household matter. As we are the leader/servants of so many other areas, we are the leader/servants of this one, too.

Which doesn't mean we never do things alone. We ought not to feel guilty for indulging in purely personal enjoyments at least some of the time. But since we do have wives and, in some cases, children, we need to think about balance. At the top of the next page is a chart to help you analyze how you take it easy. List ten of your common things-to-do, not necessarily in any order of preference. Just jot them down quickly as they come to mind; by the time you finish listing ten, you'll be sure to have included all the favorites.

Now go back and check off a box for each entry.

If it's a *solitary* activity — working on your car, for example, or reading a magazine — mark the S column.

If it's something you do with one or more members of your *family* — playing softball with your kids or going out to dinner with your wife — use the F column.

If it's something you do with *outside* people — such as Monday night basketball in the YMCA league or playing

HOW I TAKE IT EASY

		S	F	O
1.	_____	☐	☐	☐
2.	_____	☐	☐	☐
3.	_____	☐	☐	☐
4.	_____	☐	☐	☐
5.	_____	☐	☐	☐
6.	_____	☐	☐	☐
7.	_____	☐	☐	☐
8.	_____	☐	☐	☐
9.	_____	☐	☐	☐
10.	_____	☐	☐	☐

your tuba in the community orchestra — mark the box in the O column.

How does it look? With whom are you doing most of your relaxing? If you don't have many checks in the middle column, what does that tell you?

In many marriages, there is indeed a great wall between husbanding/fathering and leisure. Both spouses have an understanding that the husband is entitled to a certain amount of "off-duty" time, as if with a switch he could turn off his regular identity and turn into a man-about-town. Sometimes this is formally scheduled as a weekly "night out with the boys."

Let me repeat: there's nothing particularly evil about a man relaxing by himself or with nonfamily individuals. But it *is* a problem if he so divides his life into two parts that the one is considered fun and the other drudgery. This is neither helpful nor fair. True husbanding is not a drag. A man can have some of the most pleasurable and rewarding times of his life with his family. A lot depends on his own perspective.

TV and other pursuits of pleasure

You're a rare breed if you didn't list TV as one of your ten relaxation activities. But how did you classify it — solitary or family?

The social critics of our time have rather convincingly pointed out that TV watching is rarely a shared experience. The fact that other family members may be in the same room, even sitting on the same couch with you and digging into the same sack of potato chips, doesn't alter the fact that the communication is pretty unidirectional. The tube is the sender of messages to you, a receiver, and also to your wife and/or child, other receivers — but that's the end. You don't interact with each other beyond a common laugh or groan once in a while. You don't even have a medium for giving feedback to the people on the screen (which may partially explain the quality of programing these days).

And if the messages being emitted happen to be messages about the progress of the Oakland Raiders against the defensive unit of the Pittsburgh Steelers, chances are your wife isn't even in the room to share your groans. Only when we go to the bother of looking for a program of interest to both and following it up with some dialogue can TV watching be called a shared form of leisure activity.

This problem is most inflamed on New Year's Day, when football games run nonstop for around eleven hours of what is commonly assumed to be a family holiday. Many husbands and wives are never so near and yet so far from each other as on January 1. I'm not saying that football should be *verboten* on holidays; I'm simply saying that all of us need to be aware year-round of TV's great power to isolate us right under our own roofs.

My current battle happens to be with the six o'clock news. If I had my way, I'd choose to come home from work, sit down to eat with Grace and the kids, then take my dessert into the family room for a half-hour of watching Chancellor and Brinkley. It's a relaxing thing for me to do, and it's also a free source of up-to-the-minute information.

The only trouble is, it doesn't mesh with what has come to be known at our house as the Grizzly Hour — that period from about four-thirty in the afternoon on through to bedtime when young children are tiredest and crankiest. Parents need to be at their best during the Grizzly Hour, inventing creative things to do and heading off potential conflicts. Grace has already spent a good deal of her creativity throughout the day and is looking forward to the charms of a fresh, new voice. When all that new voice can come up with is, "Nathan, go play in your room — I'm watching the news," the scene has a way of deteriorating.

There *are* ways for me to relax with Nathan and Rhonda and Tricia instead of apart from them. And there are ways for me to get the news during less critical times of the day, too. It all comes down to whether I'm willing to be a servant or not.

One of the tougher skills we husbands have to acquire is the ability to genuinely enjoy playing with young children. Playing is not a waste of time; it's the primary learning activity for kids, and if their dads are willing to participate enthusiastically, an invaluable bond is formed between parent and child.

I remember in the early months of fathering how frustrated I got trying to spend time with my son and accomplish some adult task at the same time. My conscience told me I needed to sit on the floor and stack blocks with Nathan, that I shouldn't wait until he could hit a baseball to start playing with him. But what inefficiency! Surely I could redeem the time by reading a news magazine *while* I stacked blocks.

Wrong. Nathan could tell I wasn't really interested, and I could tell I wasn't comprehending a third of what I was trying to read. It took a while to convince myself that spending time with a child, even an infant or a toddler, is *worthwhile in itself,* an activity worthy of my full attention. Better to spend twenty minutes playing — and enjoying it — followed by twenty minutes of reading, than to attempt forty minutes of trying both and doing neither well.

Heaven help the preschooler whose father thinks puzzles and dot-to-dot books are dumb. Heaven help the grade schooler whose dad can't be bothered with bugs and Barbie dolls. The same man will be hard-pressed to build any kind of relationship once his kids reach the teen-age years. As Maureen Green says in her book *Fathering,* "The biggest deprivation children suffer is not having been enjoyed by both parents."[1]

And the beautiful thing is that if our values are in the right places, our time spent with children doesn't have to be a chore. It can be genuine fun, which makes it good for us as well as for them. Mrs. Ethylene Nowicki, mother of the famous ice skater Janet Lynn, told me once during an interview while I was ghostwriting her daughter's book, "My husband and I made a decision early in our marriage: we decided that for the first twenty years or so we'd do things *with* our kids. We said there would be enough time later on for us, but while the kids were growing up, we'd invest the time in their lives."

By the looks of the awards and trophies that festoon the Nowicki home — not only Janet's but the other three children's as well — it's obvious that their decision was a brilliant one. Little did this parent realize that "doing things with the kids" would take her from Rockford, Illinois, to points as diverse as Davos, Switzerland, and

Sapporo, Japan, en route to her daughter becoming an Olympic bronze medalist.

Games we play

There's a lot to be said for sports and games as a way for couples and families to have fun together. It can be as vigorous as football on the lawn or as quiet as a father-son chess match; the options are more numerous than you'll ever have time for. Games make it easy for us to get in touch with each other, to interact, even to stretch each other's abilities. My family happens to be fanatical about word games, everything from Probe to Scrabble to a corny but funny thing called the Dictionary Game. Other families generate more of their togetherness with athletics. Both are effective in helping parents and children as well as husbands and wives to relate and recreate together.

But something else needs to be said about games: they're a little dangerous. They have the potential of harming the household and ripping up relationships if competition gets out of hand. Competition is a powerful motivator so long as it's in harness, but left to run wild, it can devastate. If we join in the combat of a game to give the other person a challenge to try and overcome, we have done him a service. But if we join in combat for the thrill of humiliating the other person, of proving how much better we are, of grinding him into the dirt, we've degraded both him and ourselves.

A lot of gung-ho husbands and fathers don't understand that distinction. (Neither, for that matter, do a lot of coaches and managers.) I was fortunate enough to have a father who once forbade me and my foster brother to keep score after the Ping-Pong rivalry between us had gotten raw. He said, "For the next couple of weeks, you guys can practice all you want — but no scorekeeping. You both need to cool down." It worked.

Competition may be even tougher to handle between husbands and wives. Everything's fine, of course, so long as we keep winning, and some of our wives have been programed by social custom to make sure that happens. But more and more women are rejecting such nonsense. We do, too — in theory. Yet when we actually lose a game, especially one that requires brawn as well as brains, some of us can't take it.

You can tell a lot about a marriage by watching and listening to its partners play a game together. All kinds of repressed hostilities can come to the surface. The opportunities for vengeance, for embarrassment, and for reprisal are just waiting to be seized by a mate with an ax to grind or a grievance to air. The husband and wife don't necessarily have to be opponents in the game. In fact, it is often even more revealing when they have to cooperate with each other as members of the same team.

In a cover story entitled "Sex & Tennis: The New Battleground," *Time* magazine outlined the pitfalls of mixed doubles:

> If there is one serpent most easily discernible in the Garden of Eden togetherness that Americans hope for from tennis, it is the American husband. . . . He is found guilty of coaching and poaching — *i.e.*, taking shots from his wife's side of the court. Of preaching and reaching and teaching. Of cheating and bleating. Of serving too fast. Of serving too slow. Of hitting the ball right at his female opponent. Of not hitting the ball right at his female opponent. Of bad tennis, bad sportsmanship and, above all, a bad mouth. . . . "Run! Run!" "Hit the ball. *Hit* the ball." "Up! Up!" and, maddeningly above all for women partners, "Outta the way! I got it! I got it!"[2]

The same article reprinted a cartoon from Bil Keane's *Deuce and Don'ts of Tennis* showing a husband and wife in bed, facing opposite directions, both as far to the outside edge as possible. The husband is saying, "Cripes! You don't think I double-faulted on the final point of the tie breaker *on purpose,* do you?"

Games can be a delightful unifying factor in a household; they can also be a wedge that divides and destroys. The choice is ours.

The hassle-free vacation

One particular time of year, of course, is given almost entirely to recreation and leisure: the vacation. At no other time do we have so many free hours in a row to take it easy.

Yet vacations can be mixed blessings. Psychologists tell us that husbands and wives are more likely to argue on vacation than at almost any other time. It's not hard to see why. The most frequent disputes are about:

● *Money.* The splurge mentality takes over . . . forget the budget . . . we've been saving all year for this . . . we're going to have a good time or else! There is, of course, a limit to the amount that can be spent, and not everyone's wishes can always be accommodated. So some hard decisions have to be made, and no one wants to lose.

The financial squeeze is undoubtedly the cause of the rise of camping in recent years. What's neat about camping is that it allows you to relax and do a lot of different things together as a family without spending money every time you turn around. Granted, the equipment costs something, but once you own it, that's it, and the nightly fees aren't much. In some cases, even the equipment can be borrowed or rented. Meanwhile, camping offers dozens of built-in opportunities for husbands to get reacquainted with their wives and kids — everything from gathering firewood to riding bikes to staying dry during rainstorms. Even the housekeeping tasks of dishwashing and bedmaking can be profitably shared.

• *Discipline of children.* The other fifty weeks of the year, we're not home during the day to observe how our wives handle things. Suddenly the reality of round-the-clock child care hits us. We discover that our reserves of patience are not as great as we thought.

And the demand for patience is greater when you have kids cooped up in a car all day than when you're at home. On a long trip, the car can become a pressure cooker of tension if the husband isn't sensitive to the need for —

1. Frequent stops. Some of us cherish our reputations, established during college days, for marathon driving — Nashville-to-Los Angeles in twenty-seven hours straight through, and all that. We've always prided ourselves on our ability to get to a place faster than anyone else. But with kids who need to stretch and run off excess energy every hour and a half — forget it. To keep pushing only puts the entire family on edge.

2. Games and activities while driving. Grace and I have some friends who each year before vacation assign their five children to collect their own "fun-paks" of things to do in the car. Parents are wise to bring along some extras themselves.

3. Simple conversation. Why do so many of us seem to clam up once we're behind the wheel? Driving time is great time for talking about ordinary things, special things, spiritual things, anything. It beats watching the mileposts in silence.

• *Choice of activities/location.* If your idea of a vacation is a fishing/canoeing trip in northern Ontario, while hers is a Sheraton hotel next to three shopping centers, and the kids are thinking of Disneyland . . . you've got some work to do before you pull out of the driveway. The task is to reconcile the desires of each and somehow create an experience that will be fun for everyone. What you *don't* want to do is promise features that probably aren't going to happen once you start.

You may have to do one person's favorite one year and someone else's the next. Or you may split up, letting a teen-ager go to a camp or to a friend's or relative's house while you and your wife head a different direction. If your children are very young, the difference between Six Flags Over Texas and the local amusement park is minimal — and if it would take three days to drive to Six Flags, you're far better off hitting the local spot on a Saturday and planning a strictly adult vacation for yourself and your wife. If you don't want to be away from the children that long, why not a series of weekends at a nearby hotel or resort?

But having said that, let's be careful not to forfeit the togetherness that a family vacation can engender. Some parents are all too happy to dump their kids summer after summer. There are many things we can do together, and the benefits are significant.

Vacations are probably more strategic for our wives than for either the kids or ourselves. Why? Because wives carry the major responsibility for the work of the household . . . seven days a week. We enjoy a day or two of "vacation" at the end of each week during which we temporarily forget about our jobs. Not so the housewife. Thus, in terms of pure recycling and change of scenery, she is the neediest.

As a matter of fact, vacations are but part of the relief she needs. Weekend dinners and excursions are even more refreshing for her than for us. They don't have to be expensive. Grace and I once spent a delightful day on my birthday taking in free things of Chicago — the Museum of Science and Industry, a photography exhibit in the lobby of a downtown bank, the Chicago Board of Trade, a historical museum, State Street window-shopping. You might want to sit down with your wife sometime and make a list of all the things the two of you could do for less than five dollars. Keep adding to the list as things come to your mind, as you read the Sunday paper, and as friends happen to mention places they've gone and evenings they've enjoyed.

In the final analysis, taking it easy is not as dependent upon externals — money, travel, sports equipment, electronic gadgetry — as it is on our internal capacity to find enjoyment not only in Hawaiian scuba diving but in rainy Saturdays at home as well. If we can give leisure its proper place in our lives and strike the right balance with the other more serious ingredients, we'll not only live longer ourselves, but we'll have a happier, more relaxed, more integrated household along the way.

[1]Maureen Green, *Fathering* (New York: McGraw-Hill, 1976), p. 180.
[2]"Sex & Tennis," *Time*, Vol. 108, No. 10 (Sept. 6, 1976), p. 42.

11

Sickness
(What a Pain)

11

Sickness
(What a Pain)

What causes stress?

Not long ago a couple of doctors at the University of Washington Medical School set out to answer that question. They studied the most common causes, the things that upset us, and tried to rank them on a numerical scale.

What they came up with was the Holmes-Rahe Stress Test, a list of forty-two events that range from the death of a spouse (100 points) to a minor violation of the law (11 points). By going down the list and checking off what's happened to you in the past year, you can get an idea of how much stress has been accumulating inside you, whether you're aware of it or not.

It is significant that, based on their research, the two professors ranked personal injury or illness near the top of the list — 53 points. The only things more upsetting than getting hurt or getting sick were marital separation or divorce, a jail term, and the death of a close family member. It's *less* of a jolt to get married (50 points), to get fired from your job (47 points), to be reconciled to an estranged spouse, or to retire (45 points each).

And very next in the hierarchy of stress-causing events comes change in a family member's health (44 points).

. . . We already knew all that, didn't we? We hate being sick ourselves, and we hate what happens to the household when anyone in it is sick. We hate the bills that sickness brings. We hate everything about it.

We hate it enough that we go to considerable effort to prevent it — everything from taking vitamins, to insisting that our kids wear coats when they don't want to, to installing humidifiers to cut down on wintertime sore throats, to about anything else we can think of. Still, it's not enough. We continue to get sick. Not as often as people did in the past, or as often as we would if we didn't take precautions, but it still happens. And it's hard on us.

Why it's tough

When somebody at your house comes down with the flu, or when a more serious illness invades, some rather deep-running things happen to the equilibrium of the household. Often we don't recognize them; we're too busy feeling awful (if we're the person who's sick), or worrying (if it's our wives or children), or trying to keep the household going — getting meals on the table, etc. We don't stop to observe the scene as a whole.

But what's going on is that one member of the family is no longer able to make his or her normal contribution to the life of the household. If the household is composed of only two persons, that means a loss of 50 percent! Even if you have several children, it still means you're missing a major chunk of the life and energy that in normal times make up your family.

The rest have to pick up the slack. If your wife's in bed,

someone else — probably you — has to cook. If you're in bed, someone else has to make sure the car has gas. If your son's sick, someone else has to do his paper route. All this switching around causes pressures that we don't normally face. It creates a special test of our willingness to "serve one another in love" (Gal. 5:13).

And as if that weren't enough — the overall work load of the household is increased above its normal level by the need to take care of the sick person himself. He may need peace and quiet so he can sleep, even when it's daytime and the kids are accustomed to playing their kazoos. He may need special kinds of food. He may need help eating the food. He may need help with certain kinds of therapy or exercise. He probably needs medication or, in some cases, even injections.

In other words, there is more than the average amount of work to be done, and there's one less person in the household to do it. No wonder we get uptight.

Many of us men have particular difficulty coping with sickness because, of all the family members, we're the most efficiency-minded. Our jobs have done it to us. We think in terms of accomplishing certain blocks of work within certain time-frames; we're constantly thinking about ways to get more done faster. Efficiency is a key word in our vocabulary.

In contrast, our kids enjoy the prerogatives of childhood, one of which is to fritter away hours upon hours as they wish. Even our wives, at least most of them, are not as clock-conscious as we are. As the old saying goes, "A mother's work is never done" — and since that is true, mothers usually take a somewhat less intense attitude toward their work. There's always tomorrow.

Thus, it's not hard to see that sickness is more disrupting to our life style than to any other member of the family. If we get sick, it means staying home in the daytime — and that's a major shock all by itself. We've never seen what happens around the house at ten-thirty and noon and three o'clock. We don't know how to act. At least when our wives or children get sick, they remain on familiar turf. We're out of our element, and we can't help but wonder what's going on at the office or the plant or the construction site, where we'd prefer to be at this hour.

Factors such as these lead women to say that men don't cope well with sickness, are "big babies," etc. They're often correct. Part of it definitely has to do with our efficiency mindset. But another part has to do with the traditional masculine self-image of toughness and independence. Many of us can't stand to be weak or vulnerable. So when sickness does precisely that to us, we turn cranky. We know we don't look like big, strong he-men any more, and that makes us mad. Our ego has been bruised.

Remember the story of Nebuchadnezzar in the Old Testament? There was a point at which God sent him into severe mental and physical trauma "until you have learned that the Most High rules the kingdom of men and gives it to whom he will" (Dan. 4:32). Is it not possible that God sometimes does the same to us in order to cut us down to size?

"I'm all right, Jack" vs. "Must be cancer"

The more we face illnesses — both our own and those of our household — the more we come to realize the importance of the mental or attitudinal battle that accompanies the physical. The doctor does his thing against the germs and viruses; concurrently, we must do ours against the despondency and discouragement that is an intrinsic part of being sick.

After all, there's a limit to what we can do on the physical front. But there's a great deal we can do to control our minds. The story is told of Bill Klem, famous National League umpire who sometimes used to wait a bit before announcing his decision after a pitch.

One day a young, impetuous rookie was on the mound, and Klem's delays started to irritate him. After unloading one pitch, he hollered in, "Come on, Bill — what is it?"

Klem took off his face mask and glared back. Then he drawled, "Son — it ain't nothin' till I call it somethin'."

We husbands have a choice as to what the curve balls of illness are to be called in our homes. Most of our wives take the cue from us. And from that point, the two of us can set the atmosphere for the rest of the household. We can call a situation a major tragedy, or a moderate difficulty that is quite surmountable. We can call it a big fake on the part of the person in bed, or we can pronounce it legitimate. We can call it a torpedo to the family budget, or we can call it another one of those unexpected challenges that we'll get through somehow. We can call it a sadistic slap from a capricious God, or we can admit that we human beings don't always understand the reasons why — and don't have to. In the realm of attitudes, sickness ain't nothin' till we call it somethin'.

As with Bill Klem's balls and strikes, of course, the call has to bear some resemblance to reality. We cannot pretend that a doctor's diagnosis of leukemia is trivial. But neither should we act like appendicitis is the end of the world. My wife and I have a good deal of adjusting to do in this area, since I tend to underplay sickness and she tends to overplay it. When I was growing up, we seldom went to the doctor; the assumption was that the less spotlight given to illness, the less it would be around. In her family, health discussions seemed to get more air time.

So we've had more than one disagreement about what to call various sets of symptoms. We haven't completely resolved the problem yet, but we're working on it. On two or three different occasions I've brushed off a baby's crying in the night as simply teething or bad dreams; finally, Grace has persuaded me that it ought to be checked by the pediatrician, and it has turned out to be an ear infection that definitely needed medication.

On the other hand: as I write this chapter, two-year-old Rhonda is wearing a cast, having broken her right arm while playing last Thursday. The doctor warned us to keep watching the fingers until the swelling recedes to make sure the cast isn't cutting off circulation, especially during sleep. Grace spent most of the weekend stewing over whether Rhonda's right fingers were exactly as warm and as pink as her left ones, while I saw almost no difference. As of yesterday and today, the swelling is gone and the danger is past.

It's hard at such times for a lot of us men not to turn sarcastic ("Good grief — what a hypochondriac!") or to accuse the other person of malingering. Such biting remarks may feel good as we unleash them, but they don't do much for the atmosphere of the household in general. Instead, we must find ways to be constructive; we must ask ourselves, "What can I do and say that will help my wife (or child) get over this as soon as possible?"

So many of us feel awkward in the face of sickness. Especially when our children are ill, we automatically think, *Well, my wife will take care of it. She's good at that.* Not any better than we can be. Serious research into the differences between males and females has found that "the two sexes appear to be equally 'empathic,' in the sense of understanding the emotional reactions of others."[1] We can respond in a loving way to pain, to nausea, and to fever as well as our wives can — if we will.

But along with our empathy, we must also look toward recovery. There has to be a balance between "You poor darling" and "It's not so bad." It is a great ministry to let the sick person know he's not alone, that we care deeply and hurt deeply along with him. It is also a ministry to establish a climate of hope, an expectancy of getting well, in the midst of a sickroom.

And the neat thing is that God has so many different ways of bringing about healing. He's built into our bodies an amazing recuperative power, from white corpuscles in the blood that kill off harmful bacteria to the ability to grow new skin and tissue wherever needed. He's given all kinds of natural and synthetic substances for the medical profession to use. He's also reserved for himself the right to intervene directly and correct problems that baffle laymen and doctors alike. He is a God of many options. And since he's a loving Father who — all other things being equal — prefers not to see his children suffer, he uses his options continuously.

It is only natural, then, that we as earthly husbands and fathers present our needs to him and ask for his healing. A lot of the flap over divine healing in this century has arisen over methodology — how God restores our health. I grew up in a culture that considered it righteous to call for divine intervention and a lapse of faith to solicit a doctor's help. Other Christians have erred in the opposite direction; they've said that in our modern, enlightened era, God heals through doctors only, and any prayer for healing is quackery. Well, God is not to be put into a box. He can — and does — restore the human body however he pleases. Scriptures such as James 5:14–18 most clearly exhort us to pray when we're sick and to ask others to pray for us. Nowhere in Scripture, however, are we told that this is the only method, or that medical help is a believer's cop-out.

Practically speaking, the prayer of faith is a major factor in controlling the atmosphere of our homes when sickness strikes. It is a symbol of hope. It is a positive voice in the midst of negativsm. Through it, we remind ourselves that all is not lost, that the supernatural is entirely possible, and that God our Father is still in control.

As a husband, I sometimes find myself waiting far too long before I pray about some of the minor illnesses that come along. I keep thinking that they'll go away by themselves, and sometimes it's several days before I wake up and say, "Hmmm, the Bible told us to pray about things like this." We've had some rather quick recoveries (I prefer to believe they were direct healings) at our house once I took hold of my responsibility as the leader/servant of the household and had a definite time of prayer. Grace and I have then asked each other, "What took us so long?"

I'm not saying that God will heal every time we ask him. In fact, the evidence shows that he doesn't. We have to face the fact that sometimes a family member doesn't naturally recuperate, and medicine is unable to help, and God doesn't intervene supernaturally — and the person dies. Such an event has to be the worst shock a household experiences. Drs. Holmes and Rahe put the death of a spouse at the top of their stress list, and they didn't even try to rank the death of a child. It would probably have been 300 stress units or more. Whole books have been written on the subject, and all of us need to become more realistic about these possibilities. It's not good to be morbid, but neither is it wise to assume that we and the members of our household are immortal.

Nevertheless, until death becomes unavoidable, we must remain on the side of life and health. We must refuse to live in fear. We must do all that we can to be healthy, and ask God to do the rest. John Donne, the famous English poet and clergyman, was stricken with a devastating illness that kept him down throughout the winter of 1623. In spite of his suffering, he managed to record his thoughts during that time, which were published the next year as *Devotions upon Emergent Occasions*. One passage summarizes well his hope and ours in the face of sickness:

> Pray in thy bed at midnight, and God will not say, "I will hear thee tomorrow upon thy knees at thy bedside"; pray upon thy knees there then, and God will not say, "I will hear thee on Sunday at church." God is no tardy God, no presumptuous God; prayer is never unseasonable; God is never asleep, nor absent.[2]

---

[1]Eleanor E. Jaccoby, *The Psychology of Sex Differences* (Stanford, Calif.: Stanford University Press, 1974), p. 351.
[2]John J. Pollock, comp., *We Lie Down in Hope: Selections from John Donne's Meditations on Sickness* (Elgin, Ill.: David C. Cook, 1977).

12

The Rest
of the Clan

12

The Rest of the Clan

If a pollster came to your front door with the following questions, how would you answer? Take a pencil and mark your responses.

1. Please think for a moment about the way things operate at your house compared to that of your parents. Would you say the two are —
   ☐ very similar?
   ☐ generally similar?
   ☐ only partly similar?
   ☐ generally different?
   ☐ very different?

2. Now please think for a moment about the way things operate at your house compared to that of your parents-in-law. Would you say the two are —
   ☐ very similar?
   ☐ generally similar?
   ☐ only partly similar?
   ☐ generally different?
   ☐ very different?

Very similar? You're probably among a minority. The continuous changing and shifting that's going on in twentieth-century society means a lot of people conduct their households differently from their parents. The extent of those differences — and how the younger and older generations choose to view them — are often the determining factor between compatibility and open warfare.

All through this book we've been developing a concept, a set of values and definitions, of what a household is. We've talked about a particular perspective on communication, money, spiritual life, and a number of other things.

But we don't happen to live in airtight bubbles where we can work out our life styles by ourselves. Our parents and parents-in-law have been thinking about how we ought to live, too. In fact, they've had the jump on us — they've been thinking, planning, dreaming, wishing, and churning all this over for twenty years or more before we even started! Long ago, while we were engrossed with bubble gum cards and Little League, their minds were at work: *Someday, when they get married and set up a home, it'll be like this. . . .*

And now, we've done it.

And in at least some ways, it's not at all what they were expecting.

That's a tough break for any fifty-year-old. Our parents were counting on us to think so highly of their values and the example they set that we would go out and produce a carbon copy. And we didn't do it. *Why not? Don't they appreciate all that we tried to instill? Why aren't they using their heads? Are they going to have to learn everything the hard way?*

Such traumas can affect everything from the flow of conversation to the condition of their blood pressure. In a way, their side is understandable. At their age, they don't deserve any more hassles or worries. We love our parents and want to please them.

But on the other hand, we cannot afford to perpetuate their marital mistakes and weaknesses for the sake of family unity. We have a vision of the caring, serving, loving, Christian household, and the crucial questions are:

1. Does the rest of the clan (parents, parents-in-law, siblings on both sides) comprehend our vision? Do they understand what we have in mind? Do they grasp the dynamics at work?

2. If they do comprehend "where we're at," does this mesh with their long-cherished expectations?

If their definitions are our definitions, a beautiful synchronization is the result. The disagreements of childhood, especially adolescence, are past; we and our parents can finally get in step with one another on a permanent basis. We see so much of the logic they wanted us to see in earlier years. At the same time, they see the reward of two decades of work and sacrifice as we take our place in adult life and become productive. The need for authoritative direction is gone; we can be friends, equals, comrades.

Our children cannot help but sense the solidity of this relationship. A great continuity is formed as they find themselves surrounded not only by parents but grandparents and uncles and aunts, all of whom share the same set of family values and priorities. The child gradually realizes that he is part of a lasting, ongoing, tried and tested unit.

If, however, the rest of the clan does not define the household as we do, there *will* be conflicts. It's unavoidable. Any time two groups of people with differing philosophies make contact with each other in an area of vital interest to both, an extra measure of Christian grace and flexibility is needed.

Hot spots

Some of the common difficulties are:

● *Allocations of time.* You and I are busy people. In chapters 5, 6, and 10, we discussed how to dispense the time available among all the things we need to do. We've got a lot going.

Maybe your parents don't agree with your allotments. They think you ought to be carving out more time for them. Maybe her parents think you're too job-oriented, and their sweet little darling is virtually a widow.

Stop and think a minute. They're most likely in one of two stages of adult life: (1) the "empty nest" stage (approximately 50-65), when you and your brothers and sisters have left home and their responsibilities are suddenly much lighter, or (2) outright retirement. In either case, they're slowing down, taking life easier, and trying to cope with more leisure hours than they've had since their own school days. Meanwhile, you're charging around as busy as you've ever been. Your pace may leave them breathless — as well as envious of the fact that your productivity is still high while theirs is tapering.

It's not unusual, is it, that they should express themselves about your use of time?

● *Allocations of money.* While you and your wife are still in the process of fine-tuning your approach to fiscal management, your parents are heading into an adjustment that can be just as rugged: how to keep from starving in old age. Their earning power only has a few more years to go, or else it has already dropped to zero — no wonder they're suddenly very aware of financial reserves. Meanwhile, you're buying houses, cars, and clothes like there was no tomorrow — sometimes wisely, sometimes foolishly.

They remember hard times, especially the 1930s

(when today's retirees were starting married life), and they would do anything to spare you a similar ordeal. Unfortunately, their good intentions can sometimes degenerate into meddling.

The situation can get even stickier if you and your wife borrow some of their money. Now they occupy the role of creditor as well as parent. And you are a debtor as well as a son. It takes a great deal of discipline to keep the two separate. If, on a strictly business basis, it makes good sense for them to invest in your project, and they can refrain from using the debt, however subtly, as a psychological lever in other areas, a parent-child loan can be all right. Otherwise, see your local banker.

• *Number of children.* I've never been a grandparent, so I'm sure I can't fully describe the emotional thrill it brings. But it's understandable that older people would get rather excited about their children starting or enlarging the family. The third generation is, to them, a symbol of hope, new life, almost a reincarnation; their name is preserved and extended; the dynasty lives on.

So if you and your wife seem not to be cooperating in this noble cause — if, for example, you're preoccupied for several years with finishing an education or accumulating a down payment *in order* to create a more stable household in which to raise children — you'll just have to endure the various little hints and suggestions. You've got to march to the beat of your own drummer.

• *Discipline of children.* Grandparents can run a wide gamut. On the one end are those who see it as their gleeful privilege to spoil your kids rotten. On the other end are those who are sure your kids are going to the dogs, and they've been given back-up responsibility to straighten them out since you won't.

Hopefully, your parents and your wife's are somewhere in between. Grandparents can make a tremendously positive contribution if they remember that these are *your* kids and are willing to follow and reinforce your leads.

• *Politics.* It's highly possible — even probable — that you and your parents and in-laws don't see eye-to-eye on public affairs. You probably never will. It becomes even tougher when someone mounts a soapbox and tries to convert the rest of the family to his side. Some families are skilled at discussing political issues at the conceptual level and can learn a great deal from one another in the process. Others, however, can't seem to keep the discussion from turning into a verbal brawl.

• *Reunions and holidays.* It took me a while to realize why I'm occasionally frustrated at a family gathering. We'll drive 300 miles to be together, and then it sometimes seems like we're not having a good time. Why? It's no one's fault in particular; the problem arises from the fact that family get-togethers take a good deal of logistical planning, not only for meals and sleeping accommodations, but in terms of how to fill the time. We've got a day or a whole weekend together — what shall we do besides sit around and talk?

The restlessness results because this particular situation has *no designated leader*. My dad long ago stopped telling us what to do, now that we're grown. But it seems presumptuous for any of the rest of us to take charge — especially me, being the youngest of the siblings. (Birth order is a very real factor even in adulthood.) What time shall we eat? What games shall we play? Who shall pay for what?

The answers to these questions have to be reached by *consensus*, which is always tricky for people who aren't with one another on a day-to-day basis. I'll say something like, "Well, uh, maybe we could do such-and-such," and then timidly wait to see if anyone endorses my idea. It can be a clumsy, time-consuming process!

Full-scale family reunions that involve large numbers cannot help but throw together people who hardly know one another. It's almost like getting together all the left-handed people on your block; they don't really have that much in common. It takes more than a common surname to make the day enjoyable.

One part of our clan heritage that most of us want to preserve, however, are our holiday traditions, especially Christmas. All newlyweds face the task of merging their two sets of ritual. Grace comes from a gifts-on-Christmas-Eve family while I come from a gifts-on-Christmas-morning family. She was accustomed to placing gifts under the tree, while my parents had made a point of drawing our young eyes to the Nativity crèche by placing gifts there. Such relatively "minor" things are laden with great emotional and sentimental freight built up over twenty or more Christmases. They can be the makings of real conflicts.

The obvious solution is to blend the best of both and create a new, original family tradition. This past year Grace and I chanced onto an innovation that we're both eager to try again. Her parents were with us for the traditional Scandinavian Christmas Eve dinner, and as we opened their gifts afterward, the kids were very wound up and the whole scene seemed more like bedlam than anything else. What blew my fuse was when Nathan, having torn through several nice presents in less than fifteen minutes, looked up and whined, "Is that all I get?"

I reprimanded him, apologized to his grandparents, and made a silent resolution that Gift Time No. 2, scheduled for the next morning, would be different. Late that night, after everything had calmed down and the wrappings and ribbons had been squashed into the trash can, I went to the basement and got six cardboard boxes. I sorted out the remaining gifts as follows:

The Rest of the Clan | *181*

- Gifts *from* Nathan
- Gifts *from* Rhonda
- Gifts *from* Tricia
- Gifts *from* Mom and Dad
- Gifts *from* Grandma and Grandpa Merrill
- Gifts *from* our friends.

The next morning when everyone got up, the boxes with signs attached were sitting on a high table. I explained that each of us would take turns getting a gift from his box and *giving* it to someone else in the room, and that we'd all watch to see what had been given before going on to the next gift. By shifting the spotlight from getting to giving, I hoped to restore some of the meaning we'd lost.

It worked. Even the twins at twenty-one months of age seemed to catch the idea as they toddled around placing gifts in other people's hands. Since my parents weren't with us, the children were allowed to make their presentations too. The whole experience was quieter, not at all frenzied, and reflected the symbolism of God giving us his Son. When, later in the day, I asked Nathan, "What did you *give* for Christmas?" he was able to list a number of things, and the pride that showed on his face told me he was pleased.

Christmases as well as birthdays are times when *my* traditions and *her* traditions need to be merged and redeveloped into *our* traditions. They can be important cords that bind the household together.

- *Spiritual life*. A final area that is sometimes a focus of tension between the generations is the spiritual dimension. If your parents and/or hers are not Christians, you know all too well that what's important to you is not always important to them, and vice versa. Your commitment of time and money to the church as well as your entire life style of serving may draw objections — anything from the silent treatment to open tirade.

However, anything you endure is probably mild compared to what happens in less tolerant cultures, where outraged parents, with the help of the law, can back up their religious preferences with violence. Jesus warned us that at times his message might "turn 'a man against his father, a daughter against her mother, and a daughter-in-law against her mother-in-law. A man's enemies will be the members of his own household' " (Matt. 10:35,36).

But he continued with a strong statement about where our ultimate allegiance lies: "Anyone who loves his father or mother more than me is not worthy of me . . . and anyone who does not take his cross and follow me is not worthy of me" (vv. 37,38).

We know from experience that the faithful carrying of the cross in our daily lives can sometimes have a dramatic effect on non-Christian parents. The words that we say and, even more importantly, the lives that we live can be the means of spiritual awakening. The joy of seeing one's own parents surrender to Christ has to be one of life's greatest moments.

Some guidelines

As we thread our way through the above areas of potential conflict — and others like them that we haven't mentioned — here are some watchwords to pin to the front wall of our minds:

1. *The household is not for sale.* As much as we want to please our parents, we must not give up the identity or the integrity of God's gift to *us*, our homes. We must fulfill our mission; we must do and be what God has directed us to do and be, regardless. As Jesus said, "Haven't you read . . . 'For this reason a man will leave his father and mother and be united to his wife'? . . . Therefore what God has joined together, let man not separate" (Matt. 19:4–6).

Leaving our father and mother may mean geographical separation. It almost certainly means psychological detachment. Your household must never be in bondage — emotionally, financially, or any other way — to someone else in the clan.

But . . . let's temper this with a second guideline:

2. *Diplomacy is better than confrontation.* You know your parents pretty well, and by now you've discovered the right and wrong ways to resolve conflicts with them. You know what causes a major blow-up. You know what helps to defuse a situation. As often as possible, without compromising your integrity, you're wise to adjust and bend.

If your father-in-law feels like maligning your favorite senator over dinner, it won't kill you to keep still. If your mother persists in nagging you about taking care of your health as if you were still twelve years old — what difference does it make? Just smile, and keep moving.

People who have lived to their age are not likely to do a lot of changing in the remaining years. Any campaign of yours to improve them or change their basic values or habits is unlikely to get far. About the only thing you'll accomplish is to irritate the relationship between the two of you. So save your energy. Be a nice guy, huh?

Which brings us to number three:

3. *Keep your mouth shut about the sins of other people's relatives — especially your wife's.* Let her do the criticizing. If she feels like saying, "My mother is absolutely unreasonable," that's her business, but don't *you* say it, even if it's true. Yankees don't go to Arkansas and tell hillbilly jokes; they leave that to the Arkansans.

After all, most of us have the common courtesy not to make negative remarks about a family member of someone such as our boss or a colleague at work. Why should you sound off about your in-laws? No matter how perceptive your comments, they will raise your wife's defenses and serve no useful purpose. Even humor is likely to backfire in this case; mother-in-law jokes are usually troublemakers.

You and your wife may come to a point where you can talk openly about her family's weaknesses without tensing up. She may need to work through some of the hurts of the past by verbalizing them. Even so, wait for her to lead you throughout the conversation. Never go further than she has already gone. And keep looking for ways to balance her perspective, to help her remember the strong points as well as the problems.

Virtually every father-in-law has something a son-in-law can relate to and appreciate. Virtually every mother-in-law is good at something. The sooner we learn to relax with them, let our hair down, and enjoy the areas of common interest, the better for all concerned. We don't have to impress them any more. We're not back in the courting days. For better or worse, they're stuck with us, and we with them, and we all might as well enjoy it.

As the years go by, parents — both our wives' and our own — need more and more of our patience and understanding as they may become less and less able to care for themselves. In time, the relationship turns upside down as we find ourselves making many of their major decisions and "parenting" them through the final years. Many husbands and wives in our society aren't willing to be the servants of their parents when they get old and sick. It takes time and a great deal of wisdom.

The Scripture is clear that "if a widow has children or grandchildren, these should learn first of all to put their religion into practice by caring for their own family and so repaying their parents and grandparents, for this is pleasing to God" (1 Tim. 5:4). Some Christians seek to obey this verse by bringing the aged parent into their own homes, even though this means a major adjustment in the family life. Others provide institutional care — but are diligent at the same time to find ways to keep the parent alive mentally and spiritually, not just physically.

Eventually, each of us will experience the loss of our parents and parents-in-law. From that vantage point, their idiosyncrasies won't seem so important after all. What will stick in our memories, though, is the quality of the relationship that we maintained while they were with us. That quality deserves our attention now.

I know one young husband who recently adjusted his work responsibilities and moved his family from San Diego to the Seattle area essentially to be close to the grandparents. He and his wife considered it important enough for their two children to know and participate in the extended family that they made a 1,300-mile relocation.

The generation that gave us birth can contribute a great deal to the life of our households. Instead of tension and frustration, we can have the benefits of their maturity and wisdom in a healthy, mutually respectful relationship. It depends in part upon them. It also depends upon us.

13

The Big Picture

13

The Big
Picture

Have you heard of the Fifth Spiritual Law?
5. God loves you and has a wonderful plan for your household.

With due apologies to the people who promulgated the first four, I'd like to suggest that God is indeed concerned with the overall development of the Invisible Province he's given us. He has called us to serve our wives and children day by day; he also has some things in mind for the long haul that deserve our attention.

The business world talks a lot about goal-setting, management by objective, five-year plans, career progress. Businessmen have to look to the future; they hire consultants and forecasters to help lay out projections; they listen to the witty and sometimes corny slogans of motivation experts urging us all to set our sights on brighter, preplanned tomorrows.

This push for *goals* sometimes becomes so strong that we forget about *process*, with some rather dehumanizing

189

results. A company division not making a fat enough contribution to the corporate profit gets shut down, throwing several hundred people out of work and perhaps upsetting the life of an entire community. Bright prospects in another product line may cause executives to demand unreasonable overtime from their people.

So in our quieter moments, we know that goals ought not to be lord and master of our lives. They are important, but not all-important. We were created to *be* as well as to *do*, and neither ought to be allowed to overpower the other.

The magnificent thing about God's planning is that it is totally wise and good, and it never compromises personhood. Thus, when we turn to the future of our families, the question is not: What goals shall we set? It is: *What is God's will for our household?*

This is not meant as a pious dodge of responsibility. God's planning is more than just platitudinous; it comes down to specifics. If we're listening, we can hear his very specific input from time to time, especially when we find ourselves facing major decisions. For example, an opportunity comes to change jobs. What shall we do? If we make up our minds solely on the basis of which firm is offering the better financial package, we've short-circuited the whole process. What would a change mean to the household in terms of moving, of different working hours, of happiness and fulfillment in the job once the new wears off, and a number of other things?

Younger couples tend to face these decisions more frequently, simply because there are more low and middle-level positions in the job market to be filled. Over a year's time, any company is out looking for more trainees and assistant supervisors than vice-presidents. During our first few years of marriage Grace and I began noticing a pattern: it seemed like every spring we had one or more job offers to think through. It got to the place that when March would roll around, we'd say, "Well, I wonder what it'll be this year."

Job decisions are tough ones; in spite of all your research, you're almost always left with a stack of unknowns. Even the counsel of trusted advisors is sometimes conflicting. Thus it is crucial that you and your wife turn to the only source of omniscience, the God who has planned that this question come into your life in the first place. What is his will for your future?

The wisdom of his answer may not be immediately apparent. Only now do I see how the work experiences of my earlier years were pieces of a puzzle that together form the background for what I'm currently doing. God was in those moves, even though sometimes we wondered. His strategy has become apparent only with time.

Another major part of the will of God for the household has to do with children. To have or not to have? If to have, how many? When? Modern contraception has given us control over all these questions. How should we decide?

Most of our wives, of course, start from an entirely different point than we do. They have a vested interest; after all, their bodies are rather directly involved in the process! Furthermore, the society (and, some would say, biology as well) has programed them to want to be mothers. First there were years of playing with dolls; then more years of baby-sitting. As a result, it's not uncommon to find a wife considerably more psyched up for parenting than her husband.

There are exceptions, of course. More and more women today want to do a number of other things *along with* mothering. Some want to do their things *instead of* mothering. And some modern husbands think having six kids would be just great.

Once again we're faced with a complex question. We

can debate the wisdom of Zero Population Growth. We can analyze the decline of the birth rate in the United States from 3.76 children per woman to 1.75 in just the last twenty years. We can count the financial cost. Indeed, we ought to examine our own motives: are we hesitating simply because we don't want to be bothered? Is it a matter of not wanting to serve another human life in the household? Face it: parenting is primarily an experience of giving, not getting. There are rewards, but there's a lot more that's mostly serving.

God calls us and our wives to think deeply about these things and to discuss them as long as necessary. They have tremendous import; the decision to have a child or not has ramifications for years to come. Some couples give more thought to the purchase of new stereo components than they do to starting or enlarging a family. It is imperative that we make time for prayer and meditation until we are sure we have the mind of Christ. We dare not plan by default.

The tough decisions never stop coming. How shall a child be educated? Is it more important that he get the spiritual nurturing of a Christian school? But shouldn't Christians be the salt of the earth; if we abandon the public school system, are we neglecting a potential influence in the community?

What about long-range financial priorities? Can we handle this big a mortgage? How much insurance do we really need? If we trade cars now, will the next couple of years be a constant squeeze? The motto of America is buy now, pay later; one man in Los Altos, California, has been able to accumulate over eight hundred credit cards in his own name as a hobby. There's no shortage of credit for most of us, but there's a dire shortage of sense in knowing how to use — or refuse — it. And often only God can give us the fortitude to say no to a tempting expenditure or investment that, in the long run, is not the best for the household. Again, it comes down to whether we ask for his input.

Should I go back to school? Should she go back to school? Should I run for a public office? Should she? In all of these areas, and others like them, God reveals the big picture as we wait before him. He reveals it to us husbands, since we are the ones whom he has designated the head of the household. He reveals it to us and our wives together, since we are joint recipients of his gifts. And God may reveal his plan to the wife alone if her husband isn't listening to the divine voice. God is possibly less concerned than we are with the routing of his communication; what he desperately wants is for us to have the benefit of his wisdom. But we, the leader/servants of the household, should be the most eager to receive it.

God made an interesting comment about one husband in Genesis 18:19 — "I have chosen him, that he may charge his children and his household after him to keep the way of the Lord by doing righteousness and justice; so that the Lord may bring to Abraham what he has promised him." Abraham was apparently a pacesetter in his home. He established "the way of the Lord" as the family pattern. And that diligence at home, where few others could see, apparently unleashed the remarkable public aspects of God's plan for his household throughout his life and even after he was gone.

I believe God has great things in mind for my household and yours. We must not block their coming. We must be what God has called us to be, do what he has asked us to do, serve where he has placed us to serve — and watch what happens. The apostle Paul was "confident of this, that he who began a good work in you will carry it on to completion" (Phil. 1:6). We are all on the way. We're not yet the husbands God wants to make us. But we're coming along.

"Finally, brothers, whatever is true, whatever is noble, whatever is right. . . . Whatever you have learned or received or heard . . . put it into practice. And the God of peace will be with you" (Phil. 4:8,9).

Scotland's Future:
The Economics of Constitutional Change

Scotland's Future:
The Economics of Constitutional Change
Andrew Goudie

Dundee
University
Press

First published in Great Britain in 2013
by Dundee University Press

University of Dundee
Dundee DD1 4HN

www.dup.dundee.ac.uk

ISBN: 9781 84586 1629

British Library
Cataloguing-in-Publication Data

A catalogue record for this book
is available on request from the
British Library

Typeset and designed by Freight

Printed and bound by
TJ International, Cornwall

CONTENTS

List of contributors   8
Preface   13

INTRODUCTION

1 Scotland's Future: The Economics of Constitutional Change   19
   Professor Andrew Goudie
2 An Approach to the Economic Assessment of
   Constitutional Change   85
   Professor Andrew Goudie

PART I: MACROECONOMIC THEMES

3 Currency and Monetary Policy Options for an
   Independent Scotland   105
   Professor John Kay
4 Fiscal Policy and Constitutional Change   119
   Lord Gus O'Donnell
5 The Scottish Financial Structure   133
   Professor Charles Goodhart

PART II: MICROECONOMIC THEMES

6 The Impact of Greater Autonomy on the Growth of the
   Scottish Economy   153
   Professor Peter McGregor and Professor Kim Swales
7 The Impact of Greater Autonomy on Scottish Climate
   Change Policy   177
   Professor Peter McGregor and Professor Kim Swales
8 Economic Development and Skills for the Knowledge Economy:
   Contribution of Higher Education and R&D   203
   Professor Sir Jim McDonald and Simon Jennings
9 Energy and Constitutional Change   223
   Jamie Carstairs
10 North Sea Oil and Gas   243
   Professor Alex Kemp

PART III: GOVERNANCE

11 Governance and the Institutional Framework   267
   Sir John Elvidge

APPENDIX

A Note on Welfare Policy and the Distributional Objectives
of Economic Policy   287
Compiled by Professor Andrew Goudie

Jamie Carstairs
Jamie Carstairs currently heads up
his own consultancy vehicle, Linnfall
Consulting. After studying economics
(PPE) at Oxford, he worked in the UK
Overseas Development Administration
before moving into energy consultancy
with London Economics. In 1997 he
joined the Cabinet Office in Victoria,
Australia, assisting with an A\$30
billion energy privatisation, including
the market design and regulatory
institutions. In 2001 he established
Firecone, an Australian boutique
providing policy advice and transaction
support in energy and transport. He
was also a non-executive director of the
National Electricity Code Administrator
in Australia, which set and enforced the
rules for the National Electricity Market.
He returned to the UK in 2009, working
initially for KPMG prior to setting up his
consultancy.

Sir John Elvidge
John Elvidge was Permanent
Secretary to the Scottish Government,
2003–10. This followed roles in the
post-devolution period as Head of
the Scottish Executive Finance and
Central Services Department (2002–3)
and Head of the Scottish Executive
Education Department (1999–2002).
Prior to that he was a senior member
of the UK Government's Cabinet
Secretariat (1998–9) and had a varied
Civil Service career, beginning in 1973.
He is now an Associate of the Institute
for Government and a Fellow of the
Carnegie UK Trust and works in an
advisory capacity with several overseas
governments. He is Chairman of
Edinburgh Airport Limited and holds
several other non-executive roles in
the private, academic and charitable
sectors within the UK. His publications
include Northern Exposure: Lessons
from the First Twelve Years of Devolved
Government in Scotland, published by
the Institute for Government (2011) and
The Enabling State, published by the
Carnegie UK Trust (2012).

Professor Charles Goodhart
Charles Goodhart is Emeritus
Professor of Banking and Finance
with the Financial Markets Group
at the London School of Economics,
having previously, from 1987 to 2005,
been its Deputy Director. From 1985
until his retirement in 2002 he was the
Norman Sosnow Professor of Banking
and Finance at LSE. Before then, he
had worked at the Bank of England for
seventeen years as a Monetary Adviser,
becoming a Chief Adviser in 1980.
In 1997 he was appointed one of the
outside independent members of the
Bank of England's new Monetary Policy
Committee until May 2000. Earlier, he
taught at Cambridge and LSE.

Professor Andrew Goudie
Andrew Goudie is currently Visiting
Professor and Special Adviser to the
Principal at the University of Strathclyde
in Glasgow. He is the former Chief
Economic Adviser to the Scottish
Government and a former Chief
Economist at the UK Department for
International Development. He was a
Research Fellow of Queens' College,
Cambridge, and Research Officer at
the Department of Applied Economics,
University of Cambridge, prior to
becoming Senior Economist at the World
Bank and subsequently at the OECD.
He is a Fellow of the Royal Society of
Edinburgh.

Simon Jennings
Simon Jennings is Director of Strategy
and Policy for the University of
Strathclyde. He has over ten years'
experience in the higher education sector
having previously worked at Universities
Scotland, the University of Edinburgh
and the Joint Information Systems
Committee. Simon holds a BA (Hons)
from the University of Oxford, an MA
from the University of Sheffield and is
currently completing a part-time MSc at
Queen Margaret University, Edinburgh.

Professor John Kay

John Kay is a Visiting Professor of Economics at the London School of Economics and a Fellow of St John's College, Oxford. He is a Fellow of the British Academy and a Fellow of the Royal Society of Edinburgh. He is a director of several public companies and contributes a weekly column to the Financial Times. He is the author of many books, including The Truth about Markets (2003), The Long and the Short of It: Finance and Investment for Normally Intelligent People Who Are Not in the Industry (2009) and Obliquity (2010). He chaired the Review of UK Equity Markets and Long-Term Decision-Making, which reported to the UK Secretary of State for Business, Innovation and Skills in July 2012.

Professor Alex Kemp

Alex Kemp is Professor of Petroleum Economics and Director of the Aberdeen Centre for Research in Energy Economics and Finance (ACREEF) at the University of Aberdeen. He previously worked for Shell, the University of Strathclyde and the University of Nairobi. He has been a consultant on petroleum contracts and legislation to a large number of governments, the World Bank, the United Nations, various oil companies, the European Commission, the UK Know-How Fund and the Commonwealth Secretariat. He was a Specialist Adviser to the UK House of Commons Select Committee on Energy from 1980 to 1992, and also in 2004 and 2009. His book, The Official History of North Sea Oil and Gas, was published in 2011. In March 2012 he received the Lifetime Achievement Award at the Society of Petroleum Engineers Offshore Achievements Awards ceremony. Professor Kemp is a Fellow of the Royal Society of Edinburgh.

Professor Sir Jim McDonald

Professor Sir Jim McDonald has been Principal and Vice-Chancellor of the University of Strathclyde since March 2009 and has held the Rolls-Royce Chair in Electrical Power Systems since 1993. In October 2012 he was appointed Vice-President of the UK's Institution of Engineering and Technology. He co-chairs, with the First Minister of Scotland, the Energy Advisory Board in Scotland. He is Chairman of the Independent Glasgow Economic Leadership Board for the City of Glasgow and Chairman of the Board of the Glasgow Science Centre. He is a member of the Scottish Enterprise Board. He is also Chairman of the Scottish Research Partnership in Engineering and chairs the Scottish Energy Technology Partnership. Professor McDonald joined the University of Strathclyde in 1984, following seven years in the UK electricity supply industry, having worked for SSEB and Scottish Hydro Electric. He is a Fellow of the Royal Academy of Engineering, the Royal Society of Edinburgh, the Institution of Engineering and Technology and the Institute of Physics.

9

Professor Peter McGregor

Peter McGregor is currently Professor and Head of the Department of Economics, University of Strathclyde, and Director of the Strathclyde International Public Policy Institute. He was formerly Director of the Fraser of Allander Institute, University of Strathclyde. Peter is, or recently has been, a co-investigator on four EPSRC Supergen Research Consortia (Marine, Wind, HiDEF, UKSHEC) and on EPSRC-funded Desimax. He is also a co-investigator in two EU-funded energy projects (BioMara and TROPOS), and the Scottish Government-funded ClimateXChange, a centre of expertise in climate change. He has been a visiting Research Professor at the Regional Economics Application Laboratory (REAL), University of Illinois, a member of the Advisory Board of the Regional Research Institute, West Virginia, and has also held visiting academic posts in Germany, Japan and Sweden. He has published extensively on energy issues. He is a past Editor of Regional Studies.

Lord Gus O'Donnell

Gus O'Donnell is currently a cross-bench member of the House of Lords and a Visiting Professor at the London School of Economics and University College, London. He is also a Senior Fellow at the Institute for Government, Strategic Adviser to the Toronto Dominion Bank (a Canadian AAA-rated bank) and a consultant with Frontier Economics. Gus was Cabinet Secretary and Head of the UK Civil Service from 2005 to 2011, before being appointed to the House of Lords in January 2012. Prior to his role as Cabinet Secretary, he served as Permanent Secretary of the UK Treasury from 2002 to 2005. In 1999 he was appointed Managing Director of Macroeconomic Policy and International Finance, and was responsible for fiscal policy, international development and European Union Economic and Monetary Union. From 1997 to 1998 he was the UK Executive Director on the boards of the IMF and the World Bank. Early in his career Gus lectured in political economy at the University of Glasgow.

Professor Kim Swales

Kim Swales is currently Professor and Director of the Fraser of Allander Institute (FAI), University of Strathclyde. He is a graduate of Queens' College, Cambridge. In 1989 he joined the FAI to be part of an ESRC-funded project to develop a macro-micro model of the Scottish economy (AMOS). He became Research Director of the FAI in 1999 and Director in 2007. He has published widely in the field of regional economics, regional modelling, regional policy and energy and environmental modelling.

Will there be constitutional change?

What would it mean for our economic potential?

How would this impact on our vision of Scotland's future?

OBJECTIVES

The primary objective of this book is to bring a greater focus to the proposals for constitutional change. It aims to highlight the principal questions and challenges that bear on the potential transfer of more economic powers and governance to the Scottish Parliament. Any politically charged environment – as the debate over the future governance of Scotland inevitably will create – can easily obscure the most important issues. It equally tends to conclude debate prematurely, thereby losing the benefit of considered analysis.

In this publication, the goal is to sharpen the focus in an accessible document, written by colleagues of globally recognised reputation and wisdom. While some of the analysis and the supporting evidence may be seen to lead towards a particular conclusion, the emphasis is first and foremost on the framing of the challenge and on the nature of the options and choices that must be tackled, and certainly not on the identification of a single solution.

Of utmost importance here is the professional objectivity and integrity of the contributors and their explicit commitment to the production of a politically non-aligned document. I am confident that that commitment has been upheld. The book is intended to assist all those who have an interest in designing the best possible economic framework for Scotland.

The book has two primary foci: the first being the key economic questions that should form the centre of this debate; the second being the questions of governance and government that underpin the economic policy environment. If we leave aside the attention that will always be accorded to the process by which constitutional change may or may not be effected – important as it inevitably will be to the integrity and legitimacy of both the process and the outcome – the economic issues will tend to dominate discussion, but the institutional infrastructure and the governance of those institutions are an integral part of any proposed constitutional transformation.

What the book does not do is cover the full breadth of the constitutional debate. It may occasionally touch on other elements of policy, but it is fundamentally concerned with the future of economic powers. It makes no claims to consider other areas of government powers and their associated policies. Equally, it does not claim to address the legal issues that impinge at various points, for example those relating to Scotland's future relationship with the European Union.

The book is structured around the primary economic and governance themes that should shape the debate around the constitutional future of Scotland. Such is the complexity and the degree of interrelationship between the themes that it necessarily imposes a degree of fragmentation to what should be a coherent analysis. This is, however, purely to be pragmatic and is a means of structuring such a complex subject. To compensate for this, all the contributors have sought to make the linkages between themes from their own perspective. In addition, the two introductory chapters similarly look to make these linkages sharper and consider the coherence of the economic system as a whole.

The book has four sections:

» Introduction
  › The constitutional and economic context for the contributions set out in the following three parts
  › An approach to the economic assessment of constitutional change: the Six Tests

» Part I: Macroeconomic themes
  › Currency options and monetary policy
  › Fiscal policy and constitutional change
  › The Scottish financial structure

» Part II: Microeconomic themes
  › The objectives of policy:
    — The impact of greater autonomy on the growth of the
      Scottish economy
    — Welfare policy and the distributional objectives of
      economic policy[1]
    — The impact of greater autonomy on climate change policy

  › Key elements of the Scottish economy:
    — Economic development and skills for the knowledge
      economy: the contribution of higher education and R&D
    — Energy and constitutional change
    — North Sea oil and gas

» Part III: Governance and the institutional framework
  › Central government and the wider public sector and local
    government

As the introductory chapters make clear, while there are many proposals for constitutional change, there are of course fundamentally
two distinct models, defined largely by either the continuance of the
United Kingdom, with increased economic powers being transferred
to the Scottish Parliament, or the establishment of an independent
Scotland. The book does not mechanistically assess these propositions – or, indeed, their many variants – but does consider the themes
in the light of these distinct constitutional arrangements.

SOME KEY PRINCIPLES

In addition to the contributors seeking to sharpen the focus and
objectivity around the constitutional debate, several other principles
are broadly promoted here.
  The time horizon. Firstly, the contributions aim to look at constitutional change with a long-term outcome in mind. Whichever new
constitutional arrangement might emerge from the political process,
it is reasonable to assume that it should be seen as one that would be
in place for many decades. Naturally, there is no reason why waves
of political opinion over coming years and decades should not seek
to refine Scotland's constitutional status, but, as regards the most
fundamental decisions – such as the degree of self-determination
or the nature of the relationship with the United Kingdom and the
European Union – it might be assumed that a degree of stability

---

1   This theme is included in the Appendix to the book.

would be sought. It is therefore important that, when addressing the various constitutional proposals, the discussion focuses well beyond the immediate economic and political perspectives and events. Rather, it needs to seek to understand the value of each constitutional proposition within a longer-term context in which the precise nature of the challenges may not be known.

It might also be noted that much of the focus has been on the configuration of powers that might most appropriately be transferred to the Scottish Parliament and on which policies would be selected with those additional powers, whether within the UK or as an independent state. It should be self-evident that any initial agreements or treaties with any external party will survive only as long as the parties wish that to be the case. Over time, it would appear obvious that different governments may well seek refinements or, indeed, more substantive changes to any such agreements. It is therefore a major mistake to see any initial settlement as reflecting anything other than one of many positions that might be adopted by governments within a new constitution, if the time horizon is many decades.

Of far greater importance is which choices are made possible by any new powers. A focus simply on one or two options, that might be advocated by current interest groups, within this set of choices, will miss the potential opportunities and risks of any new settlement.

Risk, uncertainty and opportunity. Indeed, arguably one of the key goals of the analysis is to understand how future risk and uncertainty would be managed within any particular constitutional framework. Recent history powerfully demonstrates the limitations both in our capacity to identify and provide forewarning of global shocks and in our preparedness and adaptability to respond to unanticipated events. One conclusion is therefore that we might place greater value in seeking to understand the development of the global economy, but another – and particularly relevant to the objectives of this publication – would be that we should understand how different constitutional forms and different international interdependencies might be used to manage such uncertainty, risk and new opportunities. While this inevitably implies a greater element of speculation, the capacity to respond flexibly and rapidly to future global trends and global events is probably the most important characteristic of any proposition.

Clarity and answers. Third, a further observation on the constitutional debate relates to the somewhat simplistic desire on the part of some participants for ready-made solutions and answers to every potential economic question. While, as is noted later, there is indeed a need for far greater clarity around the various constitutional propositions that are being advanced and, equally, around the likely interpretation of some of the legal questions that have been raised, there are also many areas in which precision will not be possible. Clarity and clear-cut answers to many questions may simply be unachievable in the immediate future, and specifically in advance of any referendum on future constitutional status.

In particular, those legitimate questions that have been raised for which the answer – and, equally importantly, the process towards a resolution – is dependent on the engagement of the authorities in other jurisdictions may well remain unanswered till the post-referendum period. Only then, once the constitutional future is at least clarified in principle, might the relevant authorities wish to engage meaningfully with a Scottish Government. Any process of negotiation to clarify the transfer of economic powers and, much more significantly, of political powers could not be allowed by either party to jeopardise the desired outcome of the political process itself.

Experience and knowledge. Finally, this book is not concerned with unsubstantiated and subjective assertion. Its goal is to ensure a grounding in experience and knowledge. It rests only on well-established theory and evidence to support the thinking and insights.

THE POLITICAL CONTEXT

Throughout 2012 there was considerable discussion about the nature of the referendum that would be held and notably about the formulation of the question that would be put to the Scottish people. In essence, it focused on whether it would embrace a single question asking whether the Scottish people wished Scotland to be an independent country or remain within the United Kingdom, or, whether the referendum would additionally ask whether the people wished to have greater devolution for Scotland within the UK. The precise wording was itself, of course, a critical issue. With the signing of the Edinburgh Agreement in October 2012, it was agreed that there would be a single question focusing solely on the choice between an independent Scotland and a Scotland remaining within the United Kingdom.

This political outcome has two important implications for this publication. First, within the immediate time horizon, while it might have been decided that the referendum question itself would now exclude any mention of further devolution within the Union, it is arguable that such an enhancement of devolution powers remains centre stage. As noted elsewhere, opinion polls continue to suggest that a significant proportion of the electorate sees this as an important – and, for many, their preferred – proposition. In consequence, both sides in the debate in the run up to the referendum are likely to seek to exploit this preference to their own advantage. In particular, are there promises of greater devolution powers, short of independence, and what is the nature and credibility of those promises? The impact on the debate of those promises is necessarily unknown at this time. In any event, the propositions for enhanced devolution are likely to continue to play a critical role in the debate.

Second, over the longer term, looking to the post-referendum period and irrespective of the outcome of that referendum, we might anticipate a continuing period of intense debate around Scotland's constitutional position. Whether it be around the further development of devolution within the UK or around precisely how an independent Scotland might be designed, the questions and challenges that are articulated within this publication will remain highly pertinent. Indeed, the reality of actually needing to design a future constitutional state would no doubt sharply focus the thinking.

CONTRIBUTORS

This book benefits immensely from including the work of some of the most distinguished and pre-eminent writers in their field of expertise. Indeed, all of them have deservedly built world-class reputations for their past work, and it is a great privilege to be able to bring their collective thinking together into one succinct document. I remain most grateful to them for agreeing to contribute both their time and their insights to the debate in this manner.

I would also acknowledge the immensely valuable support that I have received in this project from friends and colleagues, some of whom have contributed very significantly to this work. Finally, I would like to recognise the role played by Professor Sir Jim McDonald, Principal of the University of Strathclyde, for his enthusiastic support for this project and for seeing the potential value of such a contribution.

Andrew Goudie
University of Strathclyde
Glasgow
February 2013

CHAPTER 1

Scotland's Future:
The Economics of Constitutional Change
Professor Andrew Goudie[1]

This chapter provides a context for the array of constitutional propositions that have been advanced. It looks at five key areas of context:

» the basic constitutional models that have been set out, together with the nature of the economic powers they embrace and their distinctive elements;

» the macroeconomic framework within which the detail of economic policy will be focused. The chapter considers the degree to which any framework is subject to the interdependencies of the real world, whether they derive from economic partnership or from the interrelationships between different areas of economic policy. It looks at the nature of the key choices, together with the hierarchy of those choices and the limitations upon them;

» the nature of policy dependence and constraint within the different constitutional models that arise from economic partnerships and interdependencies;

» the primary elements of economic policy and particularly the centrality of the choice of currency in this regard.

» the value of constitutional change.

The objective of this introductory chapter is therefore to offer a context for the detailed chapters that form the focus of this book. These contributions are thematically based and one goal of this chapter is to demonstrate the interrelationships among these key themes and the coherence of the economic system as a whole. The analysis and discussion of the specific propositions for future constitutional arrangements need to encompass the detail of each policy area and interrogate the range of policy propositions that are advanced. Ultimately, however, it is the integrity of the entire proposed system

---

1 Visiting Professor and Special Adviser to the Principal, University of Strathclyde; former Chief Economic Adviser to the Scottish Government.

and its prospective benefits, weaknesses and overall potential value that are important.

While much of the literature has previously focused on fiscal autonomy and has rightly looked closely at the microeconomic opportunities and risks that enhanced autonomy might bring, this chapter places a greater emphasis on the broader macroeconomic perspective. It is widely accepted that a sustainable and supportive macroeconomic environment is a prerequisite for the effectiveness of microeconomic policy and for the securing of the fundamental outcome objectives of government. Consequently, while the detailed analysis of the microeconomic drivers of these outcomes is indeed crucial, together with the manner in which constitutional change might have implications for their efficacy, the macroeconomic framework provides the fundamental underpinning. Later chapters focus, therefore, both on the macroeconomic framework for constitutional thinking and on the key microeconomic determinants in delivering chosen outcome objectives.

1.1 BASIC CONSTITUTIONAL MODELS AND ECONOMIC POWERS

1.1.1 *The basic constitutional models*

From the political perspective, the key defining characteristic of the alternative constitutional settlements that might be adopted in the United Kingdom and Scotland is self-evidently the establishment of Scottish political independence or the continuation of Scotland as a part of the United Kingdom. In this sense, the distinctiveness of the economic model that is subsequently established would be rooted in the choice of political system. Just how distinctive would be the new economic environment in any particular political context, however, would depend on the precise economic arrangements agreed within that new constitutional arrangement.

The participants in the current debate have offered a wide array of alternative models for constitutional change. While many are only minor variants on other models that have been proposed, some are radically different. In principle, five sets of constitutional arrangement might be distinguished, namely, those broadly identified as:

» the revised devolution settlement: Scotland Act (2012)[2]
» the Devo plus[3] proposals within the United Kingdom

---

2   Scotland Act (2012): www.legislation.gov.uk/ukpga/2012/11/contents/enacted.
3   The Devo plus proposal is drawn together in: www.devoplus.com.
    See A New Union: The Third Report of the Devo Plus Group, November 2012.

» the Devo max[4] proposals within the United Kingdom
» the Independence[5] models within a monetary union
» the Independence models with Scotland's own currency

FIGURE 1. THE CHOICE OF CONSTITUTIONAL STRUCTURE

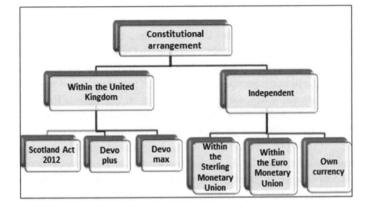

The first model represents the *status quo* following the coming into force of the 2012 Scotland Act. It superseded the initial Devolution Settlement enshrined in the Scotland Act (1998)[6] that formed the constitutional basis for the first phase of devolution between 1999 and 2012.

Of the remaining models that have been articulated over recent years, there are broadly two groups that are rooted in the assumption of a continuance of the United Kingdom in its current form: Devo plus and Devo max. Both terms have been used loosely at times and have often lacked precision, thereby not only making analysis of the propositions problematic but also leading to many varying interpretations of what each might mean.

Within the group of models that are established on the assumption of an independent Scotland, two variants might be defined that broadly capture the primary distinctive feature: namely, one with an economic system founded upon the joining of a monetary union and one founded upon the adoption of the nation's own currency. Within

4 Few coherent accounts of Devo max have been compiled and much of the debate has been conducted through the media. One such example of Devo max was provided by the Scottish Government: Fiscal Autonomy in Scotland: The Case for Change and Options for Reform, 23 February 2009. www.scotland.gov.uk/Publications/2009/02/23092643/6. For a second description, see: www.bbc.co.uk/news/uk-scotland-scotland-politics-17094333.

5 Your Scotland, Your Voice: A National Conversation, Scottish Government White Paper, November 2009: www.scotland.gov.uk/Publications/2009/11/26155932/0.

6 Scotland Act (1998): www.legislation.gov.uk/ukpga/1998/46/contents.

the first of these, the option of joining a sterling monetary union or joining the European Union's Economic and Monetary Union (EMU) – and thus adopting the euro – have been the primary alternatives under discussion.

1.1.2 *The nature of economic power*

This characterisation is not intended to limit the range of constitutional frameworks that might be considered but, rather, is aimed at crystallising the key elements upon which the debate should focus. From the political perspective, there is, in principle, a spectrum of constitutional states, ranging from one in which there is the total absence of the devolution of economic powers to a nation or region within the United Kingdom, to one of full independence for that nation or region. While there may be a significant number of political options within the Union that represent ever increasing degrees of economic self-determination for the recipient nation or region, the spectrum contains one specific and critical discontinuity: the point where total self-determination or political independence is attained. This is not to suggest that total self-determination is, or could be, a state in which the newly independent nation could literally determine any economic direction through its own political process. Rather, the realities of the global economy, in which there are substantive interdependencies and dependencies between economies, are widely acknowledged to have imposed significant constraints on self-determination in this sense.

However, the key point with respect to economic self-determination is that, in principle, the independent nation would have the political and legal freedom to define its choices within this constrained global economy. Like most comparable countries, many elements of the global economic environment would be completely outwith the control of any independent Scottish Government and its influence over these elements would be strictly limited or indeed negligible. Other elements of the Scottish economic context would, on the other hand, be explicitly within the power of the Government to determine. There would be an array of complex choices to be made, but they would not be resolved through the imposition of policy decisions by another jurisdiction unless – and only unless – the Scottish political leadership chose to allow this external jurisdiction to play that role. There would, therefore, be a real political independence and the exercising of economic self-determination, albeit one that would ultimately be limited by the reality of interaction and participation in global or regional institutions and with global economic agents. It would be a constrained self-determination.

An independent Scotland with constrained self-determination may be seen by some as a major step forward compared to the *status quo*, even if the limitations are substantive. Others may see this as the illusion of self-determination and independence, or as a relatively modest gain in autonomy but at a significant cost. This is essentially what this book seeks to explore.

There is similarly a spectrum of possible macroeconomic frameworks that might be identified. It ranges from one in which no economic powers reside within the nation or region within the UK and the macroeconomic framework is entirely defined at the UK level, to one in which full economic powers over the determination of the macroeconomic framework not only reside within the independent nation but those powers are not, by choice, passed by statute or less formally to the control of another jurisdiction for all operational purposes. It is also a spectrum that displays a greater degree of continuity than the constitutional spectrum above. Indeed, despite a sharp discontinuity in the political spectrum of the type described in the previous paragraphs, similar macroeconomic frameworks can be defined that are economically coherent and sustainable, whether underpinned by a political union or by an independent nation. Whether, in reality, such a framework might emerge clearly hinges on the distinctive political process that might lead to this similar outcome.

One specific illustration of this potential similarity is the macroeconomic framework in which Scotland continues to utilise sterling within a monetary union with the determination of monetary policy, together with its implementation, remaining within the existing UK institutional framework and UK mechanisms. While the precise frameworks would no doubt differ in some respects, the fundamental model could be very similar as regards many critical elements whether Scotland remained within or were outwith the existing political union of the UK. A similar macroeconomic framework might, of course, conceal a different set of behaviours brought about by the move to a different constitutional arrangement or, indeed, the establishment of a different set of channels of influence for the partners in that arrangement. Thus, while the technical definition of a macroeconomic framework might appear broadly common – or, at least, share many key characteristics – to two very distinct political states, the mechanisms for decision-making might differ markedly and thereby lead to potentially highly distinct policy decision-making.

There is a further aspect of economic power which, though exceptionally basic, tends not to be accorded the importance that it deserves. Economic power does not necessarily imply the determination of good economic strategy and good economic policy or, conversely, of poor strategy and policy. Indeed, it is perhaps surprising how much of the debate has focused either on why constitutional change is a good thing because of the (allegedly) ill-founded and misguided economic policies of the UK Government over past decades and notably throughout the post-2008 economic and financial crisis, or, similarly, on why constitutional change is a bad thing because the current proposed policies of the groupings that support an independence-based model are (allegedly) deemed deficient. Both perspectives appear deeply flawed. For example, unless it is argued that the UK as presently constituted will always – or typically – have administrations that are deemed to pursue poor policy, and, with an independent Scotland, future Scottish administrations are assumed to always – or typically – pursue policy that will be deemed good, the argument for constitutional change, on this count, is weak. Similarly, unless it is argued that the present UK will typically have administrations that are deemed to pursue good policy, and, with an independent Scotland, future Scottish administrations are assumed to typically pursue policy that will be deemed poor, the argument against constitutional change, on this count, is equally weak.

In one important respect, however, UK policy may of course not be optimal for Scotland or, indeed, other regions of the UK, even though it may be broadly seen as optimal – or even simply good – policy for the UK as a single economic area. Certainly, from a theoretical point of view, optimal economic policy at the UK level might not be optimal at the Scottish level if the collective benefit at the UK level is at the expense of a negative impact on Scotland. A different UK policy, while less beneficial for the UK as a whole, might be preferable for Scotland, or, alternatively, a distinct Scottish approach might be better for Scotland. Strong evidence that Scotland has been consistently disadvantaged by good UK policy, and that distinctive Scottish policy could bring a substantive benefit, would be a key element in the argument for greater autonomy of some degree. In other words, it can be argued that UK economic policy could be sub-optimal for Scotland, not because it is flawed, but because *one size doesn't fit all*. It does, however, also need to be established that a distinctive Scottish policy would not weaken the benefits that the rest of the UK gain from the UK policy in such a way as to impact adversely, albeit more indirectly, on Scotland.

In addition, it should be noted that good and poor policy may have another dimension: for example, policy that is considered good by the majority of the UK might, of course, be regarded otherwise by Scots purely because they might have a different set of preferences. Attitudes to the welfare state and to welfare reform are often cited here as examples of this. The issue here is again the degree to which these different views are held by the vast majority of the peoples in both countries and whether these differential preferences are long-standing and seen as permanent rather than transient.

Certainly, different configurations of economic power can facilitate and permit better or more appropriate policy for particular jurisdictions but, while the securing of specific economic powers may be deemed necessary for good policy, they are undoubtedly insufficient. It is, therefore, important not to confuse the poor use of economic power within an existing constitutional arrangement as necessarily implying the weakness of that constitution, just as the poor use of new powers within an alternative constitutional arrangement does not necessarily imply an inherent failing of that new arrangement.

The interest here should presumably be in the potential benefits and potential losses that a specific constitutional arrangement might bring[7] when the exercising of these powers is seen to be optimal and most appropriate for the national economy as it evolves through an array of global environments. But, of course, ultimately, this hinges on the critical and highly problematic political and economic question of what constitutes 'optimal' and 'most appropriate'.

1.1.3 The distinctiveness of the constitutional models

It is, therefore, helpful to ask what fundamentally defines the distinctiveness of the constitutional model and what differentiates it from other options for change or, similarly, what are the natural groupings for the possible options based on their defining characteristics. In principle, distinctiveness flows from three perspectives: the nominal powers embodied in the model; the reality of those powers, taking account of both the external and internal constraints and interdependencies; and the institutional structures through which the powers are exercised.

---

7   The economic theory of fiscal federalism, often summarised in Oates's decentralisation theorem has relevance here. It is further discussed in section 1.5.2, footnote 33.

Table 1 sets out the basic constitutional models that have dominated the debate, together with a simplified summary of the degree to which responsibility for the primary economic powers would rest with the Scottish Parliament. It incorporates an interpretation of both Devo plus and Devo max, although it should be stressed that their definition is far from clear,[8] together with that of independence. Apart from the obvious political distinction, the Table highlights the economic elements that potentially differentiate most importantly between the different proposed models. These can be captured in the following key questions:

Currency and exchange rate management; monetary policy powers

» in which jurisdiction does the choice of currency – and the associated monetary policy powers – reside?
» what currency underpins the macroeconomic framework: a distinct national currency or a permanently fixed exchange rate within a wider monetary union?

Fiscal powers; debt issuance powers

» is the transfer of economic powers, as defined within the proposed constitutional arrangement, confined – or limited primarily – to fiscal policy powers?
» how extensive is that transfer of fiscal policy powers, with respect both to the scope of any new powers and to the quality of those new powers?
  › does it transfer *all* revenue-raising powers?
  › to what extent is there fiscal devolution, fiscal assignment or the full transfer of powers?
  › is the transfer such that the beneficiary is responsible for the future costs of all expenditure incurred on behalf of Scotland?
» does it embody the transfer of powers over the fiscal aggregates and fiscal financing, including the deficit-determining powers

---

8   For example, in Reform Scotland's evidence to the Scottish Parliament's Scotland Bill Committee, September 2011 (see www.devoplus.com/downloads/), setting out the Devo plus model, several key elements remained ill defined. For instance, it asserted that the model removed the need for any fiscal transfer from the UK Government, but it was unclear how this shortfall of revenues would be managed and what deficit financing assumptions were being made. Similarly, the nature of the extension of tax powers as between greater fiscal autonomy, devolution or assignment was not set out. More generally, it was unclear what ongoing UK Government role there would be in setting the parameters within which a Scottish Government would work.

and the associated debt policy powers?

» is the deployment of those fiscal powers subject to any actual or potential external limitation or constraint, formally or informally, by another jurisdiction?

Fiscal transfers

» to what extent is the Budget financially self-supporting?
» does the transfer of powers entail the continuation of an accompanying and complementary fiscal transfer from another jurisdiction? And a mechanism for the annual revaluation of those transfers?

Institutional infrastructure

» in which jurisdiction do the primary economic institutions sit and where does the accountability and control of these institutions lie?
» how significant is the capacity to influence the determination of economic policy?

As will be considered in greater detail later in this chapter, the uncertainty surrounding the various proposed models is such to make the analysis problematic. In part, this is attributable to the lack of clarity with which some of the proposals have been advanced. In addition, it derives from the fact that the definition of many elements of the models will remain indeterminate until such time as the two governments of the UK and Scotland – and, as necessary, the European Union – specifically negotiate a settlement that will set these parameters.

The current set of constitutional proposals, that take the continuance of the United Kingdom in its current form as their fundamental political basis, share a common thread and are broadly distinctive in that they restrict the potential transfer of economic powers to fiscal policy and, to a lesser extent, to the determination of deficit and debt policy. These models range from being very radical in the proposed degree of transfer of fiscal power, as with the Devo max model, to being less so, as with the Devo plus model. Other models are self-evidently not at all radical as, of course, with the neo-*status quo* models founded around the Scotland Act (2012). Equally, some of these models entail a relatively minor extension of powers to determine the fiscal deficit and the associated debt policy, while other models embody a more substantive – though, in all likelihood, not full – transfer of deficit-determination and debt powers. There is also an important distinction that relates to the quality of the fiscal autonomy that is granted, as reflected not simply in the range of devolved taxes that are transferred, but also to the extent that full powers or only limited powers over the specification of any particular tax are accorded. In the latter case there is a very substantive difference, both in terms of the accountability that is associated with the taxation powers and in terms of the potential to impact on economic behaviour and performance, if the powers are limited to tax devolution or tax assignment.

The key distinction between the Devo plus and Devo max proposals ultimately focuses on the degree of fiscal revenue-raising power. With Devo plus, it remains relatively constrained and, importantly, small enough to necessitate the retention of fiscal transfers from the UK Government, assuming that the principle of equalisation is upheld. There would, therefore, continue to be an ongoing need for a transfer mechanism and for an agreement of how transfers would be revalued over time. In principle, the current mechanism focused on the Barnett formula, which in effect simply adjusts the transfer at the margin each year to reflect changes in comparable expenditure in the rest of the UK,[9] might continue, but it might also be seen as an opportunity to reintroduce a mechanism rooted more specifically in an understanding of relative needs. Whatever agreement were reached, it would presumably be premised on the view that, within the UK, there were a continuing case for some form of equalisation across the regions and nations.

---

9   The calculations each year do, of course, also reflect the updating of the population weights for that year.

In contrast, with Devo max, the full revenue-raising powers are transferred to the Scottish Parliament and no further fiscal transfers from the UK would take place. Instead, Scotland would be empowered to finance expenditure through its own revenues and its own debt issuance mechanisms. Under these proposals, the Scottish Government would be responsible for all expenditure costs incurred on behalf of Scotland, whether provided directly by the Scottish Government or not. For those areas of UK expenditure policy that remained reserved, it appears to be envisaged that Scotland would make annual payments to the UK Government for the reserved services that are provided by the UK for the benefit of Scotland. It is unclear through what process these payments would be determined and agreed but, presumably, they could have a prior claim over Scotland's revenues.[10]

All the models based on the constitutional premise of independence are distinctive in that they entail full economic self-determination in the sense set out above. Possible macroeconomic frameworks in the context of constitutional independence are differentiated most sharply by the choice of currency. This is considered in detail elsewhere, but, once made, that decision dictates the nature of monetary policy and, increasingly, financial regulation and fiscal policy. In the event of seeking entry into a monetary union, as noted elsewhere, the nature of the possible agreements that could be negotiated with the relevant partners could vary widely. In this context, the capacity to influence both the entry negotiations and the long-term policy-making of any monetary union is a central issue that underlies the prospect of any preference being actually achievable. The political and economic reality will be that size and the relative economic significance of the partners would matter. It seems inevitable that the dominant partners would exercise the greatest influence over the potential outcomes, although it is, of course, always open to the applicant to reject the terms and, with them, the option of monetary union.

One fundamental difference between Scotland adopting independence and remaining within the United Kingdom is worth highlighting. Within the UK, any decision on future constitutional and economic powers can only be ultimately determined by the

---

10 Whether this is a workable practical arrangement is beyond the scope of this introductory chapter. Some have highlighted the potential for disagreement if payments were made to finance reserved policies with which the Scottish Government and/or the majority of the Scottish people did not agree. Others have, in contrast, suggested that, in one sense, this is not dissimilar to the present constitutional arrangement, but, with the more explicit determination of the Scottish payment being necessary, Scotland would, in fact, have a greater voice in the determination of reserved policy.

UK Government. The transference of powers may be the subject of intensive discussion and apparent negotiation, but, ultimately, it will be for the UK Government to determine what powers are transferred and upon what terms and conditions. Strictly speaking, this is not something the Scottish Government can negotiate with the UK Government. This, of course, contrasts with independence, for which the decision-making processes are quite different.

All of these issues are taken up in further detail later in this chapter and in the thematic chapters that form the core of this book.

1.2 THE MACROECONOMIC FRAMEWORK AND HIERARCHIES OF CHOICE

1.2.1 The macroeconomic framework

The selection of a constitutional model is necessarily the dominant political decision, but it does not define the macroeconomic framework within which economic strategy, economic policy and the economic institutions will operate.

Table 2 sets out the broad strands of the macroeconomic framework and its key constituent components; including the monetary framework, the fiscal framework, the public spending framework and the financial stability framework. Irrespective of the specific form of constitutional arrangement that Scotland ultimately adopts, all of the components that are applicable to that chosen model would need to be addressed. Within the independence-based models, each framework would ultimately require definition by the Scottish Parliament and would necessarily depend on the initial choice of currency arrangement. With the UK-based models, only the fiscal and public spending frameworks would be expected to be the responsibility of the Scottish Parliament.

Within the set of UK-based constitutional models, even though the fundamental currency and monetary policy frameworks are predetermined or, more precisely, their determination sits outwith the powers of the Scottish Parliament, there are other key elements that would be for a future Scottish Government to determine. The fiscal framework – and its associated deficit and debt policy framework – would be crucial and would be anticipated to vary substantially over the decades, reflecting the political and economic thinking of the time. The key elements of the fiscal framework, together with the public expenditure framework that it necessarily constrains, are summarised in Table 2.

Within the set of independence-based models, the powers to determine the macroeconomic framework rest fully with the Scottish

Parliament, and it can, therefore, be shaped across the full range of currency, monetary and fiscal policy. There are, in consequence, more fundamental questions to address in defining the framework. Foremost are two central and closely interrelated choices:

» the choice of currency system and the intimately associated choice of monetary policy framework; and
» the choices with respect to potential membership of the key global economic institutions.[11]

Both are fundamental to the macroeconomic framework under which the economy will operate over the long term and therefore deeply relevant to the choice of long-term constitutional model. Professor John Kay's chapter on *Currency and Monetary Policy* is, for this reason, a pivotal chapter in this whole debate.

Indeed, the choice of currency and monetary framework are arguably prerequisites for defining the broader macroeconomic framework: particularly, the fiscal framework, which then forms the focus of Lord Gus O'Donnell's chapter on *Fiscal Policy*, and the management of official finance and the monetary institutions, which are covered in detail in Professor Charles Goodhart's chapter, *The Scottish Financial Structure*.

In addition, there are two further critical factors that immediately impinge on these choices:

» the extent to which these choices are a unilateral decision or are subject to the thinking and approach of other jurisdictions; and
» the degree to which these choices can and should be isolated from other policy choices.

In the sections that follow, these two challenges are considered further.

---

11 This factor is not fully reflected in Table 2: for example, with the decision to choose EU membership.

TABLE 2. THE MACROECONOMIC FRAMEWORK

The key elements of the macroeconomic framework, which are intended to work in an integrated manner, may be summarily identified as:

» the monetary framework
» the fiscal framework
» the public spending framework
» the financial stability framework

Within the independence-based models, each framework would ultimately require definition by the Scottish Parliament and would necessarily depend on the initial choice of currency arrangement. With the UK-based models, the first and, probably, the last would be established at the UK level, with only the fiscal and public spending frameworks being the responsibility of the Scottish Parliament.

The primary elements within each framework would be determined by the appropriate Parliament, with the relevant implementing institutions being accountable to that Parliament. Here, the fundamental elements that typically are captured within each framework are briefly summarised.

At the outset, most governments make specific commitments to the principles that they see as underpinning the entire macroeconomic framework: namely, to values such as the need to uphold transparency, accountability, responsibility and fairness; and to broad goals such as efficiency, stability and sustainability.

The monetary framework. Several strands to the monetary framework may be identified:

» *the monetary objectives* focused broadly on the inflationary objectives – typically of low and stable inflation – and on broader objectives of economic stability, growth and employment;
» *the specific institutional framework* within which monetary policy would be implemented, including the degree of independence that the key agencies of government will have in the implementation of government policy,[12] and the accountability and reporting processes;
» *the specific instruments* at the disposal of the government and its

---

12 As seen in the UK with the establishment of the Monetary Policy Committee in 1998 (see the Bank of England Act 1998).

operational arms;

» *the precise parameters* against which monetary policy would be taken forward – typically, focused on an inflation rate target or band, which may embrace a symmetric element;

» *the flexibility of response* that would be accepted within the fundamental operating framework.

The fiscal framework. Five strands to the fiscal framework may be identified:

» *the fiscal objectives:* typically including, at a high strategic level, supporting the achievement of long-term macroeconomic stability through ensuring that (i) over the medium term, there are sound and sustainable public finances, a stable underlying economic environment and that spending and taxation impact fairly across society and between generations; and (ii) over the short term, fiscal policy is complementary to, and supportive of, the effectiveness of monetary policy in securing economic stabilisation;

» *the overall stance of fiscal policy:* including, for example, the fundamental questions relating to whether the economy pursues a relatively high tax and high expenditure regime, or a low one;

» *specific limitations or rules imposed on policy* limiting the definition of the policy over the medium term, primarily to build the credibility of the framework and ensure sustainability. They have variously been seen as part of a Fiscal Mandate[13] or similarly as a Set of Fiscal Rules;[14]

» *the flexibility of policy* establishing the manner in which fiscal policy can respond with discretion to short-term economic events without destabilising the medium-term strategic objectives and undermining the credibility of government policy; and allowing the automatic stabilisers to help smooth the path of the economy;

» *the presentational issues* aiming to maximise the credibility of fiscal policy-making, fiscal budgeting and fiscal forecasting through enhanced transparency; supported by a more independent fiscal institutional structure,[15] by greater clarity and

---

13 See the Coalition Government approach in Budget 2010, HMT, June 2010.

14 See the Labour Government approach in The Government's Fiscal Framework, HMT, November 2008.

15 As with the establishment of the Office for Budgetary Responsibility in 2010. See The Budget Responsibility and National Audit Act, March 2011, which established the OBR as part of a reformed fiscal framework, with a statutory duty to examine and report on the sustainability of the public finances.

transparency around the objectives of policy, and by enhancing the quality of accountability and basic annual reporting.

The public spending framework. The framework sets out how, within the macroeconomic framework and fiscal expenditure envelope, public expenditure resources over the long term will address:

» *the outcome objectives* that reflect the primary goals of government;
» *the allocation amongst the competing demands* of government and through what processes this is achieved;
» *the balance between capital and recurrent expenditure,* and how this will affect the decisions regarding the appropriate source of finance;
» *flexibility,* conducted through an approach that enhances the quality and efficiency of expenditure, as well as the effectiveness with which desired outcomes are achieved.

The financial stability framework. In essence, this framework establishes the regulations and parameters within which the financial system will operate:

» *the roles and responsibilities:* it establishes the different bodies accountable to the Parliament for the supervision and regulation of the financial system;
» *supervision and regulation:* it seeks to ensure the stability of the financial system as a whole, together with the supervision and regulation of each individual financial institution, financial market or other body;
» *resolution and deposit guarantee:* it determines the nature of resolution and associated questions relating to deposit guarantee; and
» *regulatory policy:* it identifies where regulatory policy will be determined and the statutory framework which is required to support it.

1.2.2 *Interdependence of economic partners*

In this section two different perspectives on external partnership are considered: first, the extent to which the deployment of national economic powers is, in many instances, contingent on the collaboration, or at least acquiescence, of external partners and, second, the trade-off that is inherent in seeking closer economic and political partnerships.

In many respects, the first point is self-evident. It is, however, critical to those constitutional proposals that entail formal monetary union of some kind, whether within or outwith the United Kingdom. Entry into any monetary union, or indeed any international economic body, is contingent on the acceptance of the existing membership and on their seeing it as in their own interest. To this extent, as will be developed later, the process of application is not necessarily straightforward and certainly one of negotiation. It cannot be a unilateral decision on the part of the applicant. Equally, if the monetary union sees an interest in including the applicant, it will need to define any entry conditions such that they are sufficiently favourable not to deter the potential entrant.

The second aspect of external partnership focuses on weighing the trade-off between any constraints on sovereignty that external partnership inevitably entails against the benefits that partnership might bring. While judging the trade-off is immensely difficult, not least over many future decades, which is arguably our interest here, it is possible to consider some of the high-level considerations. Some of the more detailed choices are assessed later in this and subsequent chapters.

In summary, the potential benefits of closer partnership come from several sources and some key ones are illustrated here:

» *a single market*: potential gains flow from easier and uninhibited access to a substantively larger market, albeit accompanied by the improved access to the domestic economy for overseas competitors within the same single market;
» *risk-pooling*: benefits are gained from the agreed mechanisms through which external and domestic shocks are mitigated by the sharing of the costs and of the necessary adjustment. The common fiscal stabilisation processes that operate widely at the level of many national economies are an example of effective risk-pooling across a larger region than the sub-region that is adversely impacted by an unfavourable economic event. Similarly, the prevalence of regular annual intra-national fiscal transfers and other such equalisation mechanisms demonstrate

the sharing of risks and a levelling of circumstances, as do the processes of redistribution embedded in many of the European Union funding mechanisms;

» *the value of collective action*: the potential value of a coordinated global or regional response to both the post-2008 financial crisis and to the subsequent economic recession provides an important example of how collective action has the capacity to be more effective than fragmented national responses. It has, for example, been argued that one key challenge in the current crisis has been that financial companies operating across borders should have been subject to collective global regulation. In reality, the development of the regulatory system had not kept pace with the rapid evolution of the financial system and, particularly, with its massive cross-border growth. This suggests that, if this is the model for financial services in the future, both the regulation of the financial sector and, if required, the financial support for illiquid and insolvent global financial sector companies should be secured through the collaboration of all the relevant economic partners.[16]

Others have similarly suggested that the European Sovereign Debt crisis can only be managed in the short to medium term through international collective action, particularly as the root of the crisis stemmed from a shared framework. This would need, however, to not detract from the critical importance of national reforms which typically remain a prerequisite for the longer-term resolution of underlying structural weaknesses. Equally, the emergence of any single economy from the protracted global recession is arguably impossible – or, at least, considerably more problematic – through the actions of that one economy, but requires the transformation of economic confidence and economic behaviour that only a coordinated response can achieve;

» *the channels of influencing*: the argument rests on the degree to which influence – particularly in a highly globalised world in which many of the key challenges are both global in nature and global in resolution – is more effectively exercised either by acting as a single voice in the global community or by acting as a part of a larger grouping or partnership within the wider global community, assuming that they are in fact mutually exclusive. This is considered later in this chapter in more detail.

---

16 This view is apparently supported by the plans presently under discussion for the EU banking union; with the three pillars for i) common supervision, ii) common resolution and iii) common deposit guarantee.

The common thread here that has the potential to generate significant benefit is the greater certainty of collaboration and support that comes with partnership. The absence of formal, predetermined partnerships is not necessarily an obstacle to benefiting from collaboration in the ways illustrated above, since more *ad hoc* or short-term collaboration is, of course, quite possible and can in principle achieve the same outcome. Nonetheless, many have argued that there are important benefits that derive from greater certainty of collaboration, not least in the incentive signals that this sends to the primary economic interests in the private and personal sectors.

As was concluded above, weighing the anticipated reality of these potential gains from closer partnership against the anticipated reality of the potential gains from greater economic power and the capacity to use those powers more freely is the crux.

1.2.3 *Interdependence of policy areas: hierarchies and policy configurations*

The constitutional debate has often given the impression that key policy decisions can be made independently of each other and without reference to the implications for the overall macroeconomic framework. In reality, the significant interdependence of key policy areas necessitates a more complex analysis in which there is a greater emphasis on the choices between policy configurations or packages of related policy. If, as would seem unexceptionable, there is also a recognition of the primacy of some elements of the macroeconomic framework over other elements, whether for political or economic reasons, there is clearly a hierarchy of decisions interacting with this choice of configuration.

The interlinkage between policies can be demonstrated from several distinct perspectives.

1.2.3.1 Economic interdependencies: the currency policy framework

With an independence-based model, the choice of currency system is broadly agreed to be the most critical choice in the hierarchy of choices. From it flows automatically the nature and primary point of decision-making power for exchange rate policy and the management of monetary policy. Equally, it carries with it an explicit definition of the extent of economic policy interdependence with, and dependence upon, an external jurisdiction and other policy-making bodies. Thus, the future economic system is immediately shaped to a considerable extent by this single choice. Professor Kay develops this point extensively in chapter 3 and looks in detail at the factors that should influence this choice. In chapter 2 there is also a more detailed discussion of the issues surrounding monetary union and optimal currency areas.

The ramifications of this choice are necessarily extensive. For example, the choice to adopt a distinct 'own' Scottish currency leads to a crucial set of questions regarding the management of the currency, both with respect to its valuation and to the possible pegging or otherwise of that currency. Additionally, it raises significant questions relating to the operational management of a currency without the underpinning of a historical record of competent and effective management and with the apparent fragility that derives from being a commodity-based currency. Similarly, it leads immediately to considerations of how monetary and fiscal policy should be conducted given the close interrelationship and sensitivity between these policy areas. In this instance, monetary policy powers would sit unambiguously with the Scottish Government, and the definition of that monetary policy framework would be a critical element in the overall economic policy framework and in the international credibility of the new nation and its currency.

From a different perspective, any fundamental preference, within an independence-based constitutional arrangement, for a currency policy that entails monetary union with either the rest of the UK or with the EU opens up a very different set of issues. As Professor Kay considers, there would be basic decisions within the hierarchy of choices as to whether Scotland wished to form part of an agreed and formally negotiated economic and monetary union or to adopt an informal, more *ad hoc* relationship with another union. Again, this choice carries immediate implications. Most fundamental are the critical questions of precisely what that union entails and what are the rules of the game to which Scotland would need to adhere. This issue is picked up in more detail below.

But, once that first and foremost choice is made – and self-determination has been exercised over the currency system that will be adopted – a new set of issues follows with respect to subsequent and secondary choices of policy. For example, at the macroeconomic level, monetary policy is no longer self-determined, while, at the microeconomic level, the union's strategic approach, for example, to tax policy – and tax harmonisation, in particular – may limit the policy choices around any specific tax. Another example of this point is clearly set out in chapter 7, where Professors McGregor and Swales consider the implications of Scotland being within the EU and therefore being part of the EU Emissions Trading System.

Importantly, the primary currency choice here could have

implications for current policy in the light of preserving the integrity of the monetary union, but will also have an impact on future policy according to the evolution of policy as determined by the collective decision-making of the union.

1.2.3.2 The global economic institutions

Indeed, this conclusion may be generalised further. Membership of any of the primary global and regional economic institutions – and not solely in the context of the membership of a monetary union – would be a key decision within the economic strategy choice hierarchy. For example, membership of the World Trade Organisation, International Monetary Fund and OECD would bring important obligations. Many of these might not be seen to be as demanding or as controversial as those that a monetary union might impose, but, nonetheless, a single institutional choice could bring conditions across the range of possible economic policy configurations that were attainable. The institutional rules are, in many cases, highly significant, as is the obvious recognition that future strategic and policy decisions within the body would be broadly obligatory and carry sanctions in the case of their being breached. The economic choice that any constitutional arrangement would permit may carry key benefits – as, for example, with the WTO and its facilitation of trade access and collective protection – but equally carries important responsibilities with implications for economic self-determination.

1.2.3.3 Political conditionality

One set of interdependencies derives from the political environment in which any prospective Agreement between partners to underpin the future shape of a monetary union might be negotiated and concluded. While the linkages between different elements in the macroeconomic framework might be driven by the fundamental economic relationships, with a compelling economic logic and rationale, the nature of the conditionality embodied in any Agreement would also reflect the political relationship between Scotland and the other partners in any joint political Agreement.

As was discussed earlier, the nature of any negotiation between the Scottish Government and the UK Government will vary substantively, according to whether Scotland remains within the United Kingdom or adopts independence. Within the UK, under all forms of devolution, it was noted that any decision on future constitutional and economic powers would be ultimately determined by the UK Government. While it might be assumed that the UK Government would certainly consult with the Scottish Government, it would be for the UK Government to determine what powers are transferred and upon what terms and conditions.

These aspects are considered further below, but they introduce an important set of issues into the macroeconomic frameworks of all the constitutional models that embrace monetary union.

1.2.3.4 Budgetary interdependence

A final illustration of the key role of policy interdependence is that provided from a budget or affordability perspective. It is a self-evident proposition in a budgetary-constrained environment that the adoption of any policy typically carries with it resource implications that must be accommodated either through the identification of additional resources or through the compensating adjustment to another policy in order to free up the required resource. Partial analysis of policy, without taking account of the system-wide budgetary impact, is of limited value and fails to identify the all-important net impact of moving from one affordable policy configuration to another.

An additional concern here is the capacity to undertake a meaningful complete analysis of the move from one policy configuration to another. There is a basic asymmetry of knowledge that significantly impacts on our level of understanding of such changes for, while the basic costs of a policy can typically be estimated with a degree of confidence, the beneficial impacts are usually highly uncertain and difficult to quantify. Thus, the nature of the change to the overall affordable set of policies and the precise trade-off of policies is hard to define.

This is readily illustrated by one of the primary microeconomic policies advanced in the context of the debate: namely, that relating to corporate tax. In essence, the contention is that reduced corporate tax rates would generate significant increases in corporate investment and corporate growth, and, hence, additional corporate tax revenues would, in time, more than offset the initial losses in tax-take that a lower rate would necessitate. The logic of these Laffer effects is well understood, and, while the time lags involved are hotly debated, the propositions are well respected. What is typically lacking is the analysis of the transitional period, with its unknown duration and ill-determined costings, and of the compensating policy adjustments that are required elsewhere if the policy is to be affordable. Consequently, the economic cost and impact of the compensatory policy changes – both over the short and longer term – are similarly ill considered, implying that the net economic impact of the move from one affordable policy configuration to another is unknown.

Thus, while a corporate tax power may indeed be beneficial, there is little analysis and evidence to clearly support this conclusion.

The key point is that political and economic self-determination are necessarily and unavoidably constrained concepts. Once the primary and initial choice (or group of choices) is determined – or negotiated, if such is necessary – and self-determination has been exercised with respect to this one choice, the subsequent and less important choices relating to the vast array of other policy areas are substantively restricted. In many of these areas of policy, choices may no longer exist.

1.2.4 Key questions

We might identify, therefore, several key questions that are critical to the process by which potential configurations of economic powers, together with their associated macroeconomic frameworks, might be determined:

» *primary choice*: what is deemed to be the primary choice in the hierarchy of choices in the determination of the economic system?
» *constraints consequent on the primary choice*: following the primary choice, what implications would there be for other policy areas as a result of that initial choice or set of choices? Where, in reality, are the degrees of policy freedom in the subsequent set of choices?
» *trade-offs in choice*: what is the trade-off between choosing an economic system with greater self-determination, flexibility and self-reliance and one where any risks and uncertainties are pooled to a greater extent?
» *certainty of external support*: to what extent does the nature of the constitutional arrangement secure greater certainty of economic support, if such need arises, from other partners in that arrangement? And at what cost does that support come?
» *weighing the options*: how is this complex set of considerations weighed in determining an optimal or preferable economic system?

1.3 POLICY DEPENDENCE AND CONSTRAINT

Critical to defining the new economic environment is the extent to which a new Scottish Government is directly and immediately dependent on other parties for its own economic policy. There is a broad understanding and recognition that the interrelationship and degree of interdependence between economies has significantly intensified as the principal elements of globalisation have increasingly taken root over recent decades. From this perspective, it is accepted that the formulation of economic strategy and policy in most, if not all, national economies is necessarily shaped and constrained by wider global economic pressures. Here, though, the interest is in two specific limitations on national policy-making:

» first, the *dependence* on other parties – whether within the same or a different jurisdiction – for the determination of explicit economic policy decisions; and
» second, the degree to which the determination of policy by a Scottish Parliament itself would be *constrained* by limitations externally imposed on Scotland as part of a wider contract or understanding with an external body.

In the context of defining alternative economic models that are feasible for a new constitutional arrangement, these questions of dependence and constraint are, in reality, key to the defining of distinctiveness.

1.3.1 Policy constraint

One perspective on the key role of policy dependence and policy constraint that starts from the premise that the currency choice is the dominant choice in the hierarchy of decision-making is illustrated in the simplified framework below. This starting assumption is, of course, not the only possible one, but a compelling case can be made that it is the critical choice, as was discussed above.

The key conclusion that can be drawn from this analysis is that the potential degree of policy dependence and policy constraint in some of the proposed models is significant. However, since the extent of these limitations is presently undetermined and can only be resolved through a process of discussion or negotiation at some future time, there will remain uncertainty surrounding the precise nature of the various proposed constitutional models. As was noted earlier, the nature of these negotiations will be quite different, depending on whether the new constitutional arrangements embrace independence or the continuance of the United Kingdom in its present form. Moreover, not only is the outcome of those negotiations unknown, but so too is the timing: both will no doubt be the subject of intense political debate. The corollary of this is that, without knowing the nature of any final outcome, the fundamental uncertainty makes analysis highly problematic.

We might also note that, with all the proposed constitutional models, the initial agreed settlement and the shape of the macroeconomic framework, in particular, would not of course represent a permanent, unchangeable state, but it does set the economic framework for the key, first phase of any new constitutional arrangement.

Table 3 below sets out the key areas of economic powers and illustrates – in a simplified and summary form – the degree to which they can be defined at this time for three of the primary constitutional models that have been advanced for Scotland: first, the United Kingdom-based models that extend fiscal and debt powers; second, the independence-based models that adopt membership of the sterling monetary union; and third, the independence-based models that adopt their own currency. It highlights those powers for which a proposed constitutional arrangement would imply no change compared to the prevailing constitutional settlement;[17] those powers which would then be unconstrained; and those powers for which there would be an expectation that the operation of policy might then be limited to some degree through policy dependence or policy constraint.

The latter cases, following a decision in principle of the constitutional model to which Scotland would move, would presumably be the crucial focus of negotiation in which the precise determination of the policy framework would be made.

These are, of course, only three of many feasible constitutional models,[18] but they illustrate the importance of potential policy limitations under each model and of the process by which the dependencies and constraints are defined.

In the cases that embrace a monetary union, it would be the inability of a member-state to unilaterally and freely determine its national policy that would make the negotiating phase so critical. Constraints of this type would be a direct consequence of the requirement of the

---

17 As defined by the Scotland Act (2012).

18 It is, for example, possible to envisage an independence-based model in which Scotland would use sterling as an informal member of the sterling area (such as other nations have chosen with respect to the dollar or the euro). In this model, Scotland would have no direct influence over the redefined UK's currency or monetary policy, and it is unlikely that the Bank of England would play an active role in the Scottish economy. Scotland would arguably be more unconstrained in all aspects of its fiscal policy. As ever, the crucial question is whether the benefits of greater degrees of freedom in fiscal policy outweigh the costs of having no formal Agreement with the redefined UK, and whether the real world constraints on policy in fact circumscribe the operation of those policies that are in principle unconstrained. In particular, external market perceptions of risk may move adversely if the economy were seen to be more vulnerable and the certainty of international support in time of difficulty were markedly reduced, thereby raising the risk premium.

monetary and fiscal authorities of the union that member-states pursue certain objectives and, therefore, adhere to certain policy goals in return for receiving – and as a safeguard against undermining – the benefits of union membership. How severe and how binding these would be on the preferred policy stance of the potential entrant to the union is, of course, the key question.

TABLE 3. THE BASIC CONSTITUTIONAL MODELS:
DEFINING THE POWERS OF THE SCOTTISH PARLIAMENT

	Constitutional arrangement:	Nation within the United Kingdom	Independent Nation	
	Currency arrangement:	Within Sterling Monetary Union		With Own Currency
	Economic model:	Extension of fiscal and debt powers[10]	Agreement negotiated as part of Sterling Monetary Union	Control of all economic powers
Economic power:				
Macro-economic policy	Currency policy and Monetary policy	None	None	Unconstrained
	Role of Central Bank[20]	Unchanged	To be negotiated	Own Central Bank
	Fiscal aggregates and deficit policy; and debt policy	To be negotiated; ultimately determined by the UK Government	To be negotiated, constrained	Unconstrained
	Fiscal transfer mechanism from the Union to Scotland	To be negotiated; ultimately determined by the UK Government	None	None
Regulatory framework	Financial regulation	None	To be negotiated, constrained	Unconstrained
Fiscal Powers (micro)	Revenue-raising Autonomy	Increased autonomy. To be negotiated; ultimately determined by the UK Government	To be negotiated, constrained	Unconstrained
	Expenditure autonomy[21]	Significant, unchanged	Unconstrained	Unconstrained
Powers re. economic objectives	Fiscal policy (micro) for achievement of policy objectives (growth, equity, environmental)	Increased autonomy. To be negotiated; ultimately determined by the UK Government	To be negotiated, constrained	Unconstrained
Influence over economic policy	Influence over UK economic policy	Unchanged	Reduced	None
	Influence over global (and EU) economic policy	Unchanged: through the UK	In own name	In own name

1.3.2 *Illustrating constraint under independence*

Two of the primary areas in which a redefined UK Government might take an active interest in an independent Scottish Government operating within a sterling monetary union would be:

» fiscal policy; and
» the continuing role of the Bank of England.

1.3.2.1 Fiscal constraint within a sterling monetary union

In this case, the UK would have a very direct interest in preserving the integrity of its own macroeconomic policy and specifically in securing its medium-term policy objectives. Within the sterling union, the Scottish economy would not be insignificant, accounting indicatively for around 8 to 10% of total sterling area GDP, markedly greater, for example, than the weight of many of the euro zone economies in the EMU.[22] Thus, its capacity in theory to destabilise UK macroeconomic policy cannot be dismissed. Whether a Scottish Government, in fact, would wish to diverge substantively from UK policy is not self-evident, although the debate that has dominated macroeconomic policy throughout the period since 2008 over the wisdom, or otherwise, of the UK Coalition Government's adjustment programme starkly illustrates the point. It has been fiercely contested by both the Scottish Government and the main opposition party in the Scottish Parliament as being too austere in terms of both the underlying rationale and the adopted speed of adjustment.

What is certainly the case is that any UK Government is likely to seek an Agreement that set limitations on the fiscal aggregates – and the associated fiscal deficit and debt financing – to protect its macroeconomic policy and safeguard it from adverse market reactions,

---

19 As set out earlier, the models here could range from a modest extension to more radical extensions of powers, largely focused on the degree of fiscal and debt-raising chapter.
20 The nature of these potential constraints is considered in more detail later in the chapter.
21 Were Scotland to remain within the European Union, there would of course be constraints as, for example, in the case of those related to the various State Aids provisions. It is similarly possible that, with the sterling monetary union models, there might be attempts to limit some expenditure policy variations within the sterling area as, for example, in the case of the support offered to potential FDI, to reduce perceived expenditure competition.
22 Only four of the seventeen current euro zone economies had a share in total euro zone GDP in 2011 that exceeded 10%. Germany and France together accounted for almost 50%.

notably from an increased risk premium on its debt were the perceived risk allowed to rise.

It should be noted, however, that Scotland would equally have a considerable interest in the constraints on the new UK's macroeconomic policy. Over the time horizon that should be the focus of the constitutional debate, there should be no presumption that one jurisdiction would consistently wish to pursue a more conservative economic policy than the other jurisdiction. The principle underlying an Agreement needs to make no such presumption.

As Table 3 suggests, that breadth of potential conditionality is a critical issue. Just as the UK might seek to protect its macroeconomic programme, it might also seek to introduce clauses within any Agreement that posed limits on the ability of an independent Scottish Government to exercise its microeconomic powers to the perceived detriment of the UK. This point is picked up below, but the perceived threat of *beggar-thy-neighbour* tax competition in pursuit of advantage would be a key concern.

1.3.2.2 The role of the Bank of England within a sterling monetary union

With respect to the second point, Table 4 sets out the critical role of the Bank of England with an independence-based constitutional model within a sterling monetary union, together with the key issues that would arise. This would seem to be one of the most critical elements to be understood were constitutional independence to be adopted.

Foremost are important questions relating to the legal status of the Bank of England and its governance in the event of Scotland deciding to become independent. These have been contested in recent debate and would clearly need to be resolved as a prerequisite to determining the nature of the Bank's roles and responsibilities as regards Scotland.

Within a sterling monetary union, most of the responsibilities of the Bank would continue unaffected by the political transformation. From the Scottish perspective, the single most important question probably relates to whether Scotland enters into a formal Agreement with the redefined UK as part of the sterling monetary union. If it does, the form of that Agreement and the nature of an independent Scottish Government's influence over the monetary strategy and policy of the newly defined UK would be key issues. Equally significant would be an understanding of how, if at all, the Bank would support the Scottish Government and Scottish financial companies, were the need to arise.

Whether the Bank of England would support an independent Scottish Government in financial difficulty depends fundamentally on whether it is in the interest of the redefined UK to do so. Some have argued that, if the external markets do not believe that the UK would not support a Scottish Government in financial difficulty, then, if it were perceived that Scotland were at risk of getting into difficulty, the UK would suffer an additional cost. Only if the markets found the UK position not to assist Scotland to be credible would the UK avoid this cost. It could, of course, face a cost for a different reason: for example, if economic performance in Scotland were seen to threaten the UK's own economic performance. If the UK accepted that it would have to support a Scottish Government *in extremis*, or that others believed this to be the case, then the UK Government would necessarily display a close interest in Scottish economic policy. Whether the two governments wished to reach an *ex ante* Agreement in this regard is, of course, one of the issues to resolve.

Whether the Bank of England would support Scottish financial companies in the event of financial difficulty is equally important. Here, the key point is that the Bank of England's remit is to maintain financial stability in its jurisdiction. It could, therefore, be expected to stand behind any Scottish institution that threatened the stability of the financial system of the redefined UK for which it had a responsibility. Thus, the support of the Bank of England would be provided as and when it saw the need to protect the UK financial system. For example, during the current financial crisis, whenever a bank – be it a UK or overseas bank – threatened the UK's stability and presented any systemic risk to the UK, the Bank of England in principle saw an obligation to intervene: in effect, providing the lender of last resort support to these companies. This conclusion is supported by the comments made to the House of Lords Select Committee by Sir Philip Hampton[23] and also by the research of Bloomberg[24] that found that

---

23 In his Evidence to the House of Lords Select Committee on Economic Affairs in its inquiry on The Economic Implications for the United Kingdom of Scottish Independence, in November 2012, Sir Philip Hampton noted that in "late 2008, because we have substantial operations in the United States, we used the US Federal Reserve as a lender of last resort, providing short-term liquidity when the market completely dried up. That was because we had a US banking licence and we were operating in the United States. A central bank does not want its banking system to collapse, so it acts for all the banks that are operating in that country. We have used many central banks as a lender of last resort for the many operations that we have in the many jurisdictions in which we operate. That is a key part of what central banks do in the jurisdictions that they control." See www.parliament. uk/documents/lords-committees/economic-affairs/ScottishIndependence/ ucEAC20121113Ev15.pdf

24 See: www.bloomberg.com/data-visualization/federal-reserve-emergency-lending/#/ overview/?sort=nomPeakValue&group=none&view=peak&position=0&comparelist =&search=

four of the ten banks to have been in receipt of the largest support from the US Federal Reserve during the 2007–2010 crisis were overseas banks, for whom the US central bank was effectively operating as the lender of last resort. They estimated that RBS was the fourth largest recipient of support.

Whether the Bank of England would be prepared to play a more conventional and principal lender of last resort role to Scottish institutions that were in difficulty, but not threatening to the stability of the redefined UK, would presumably be the subject of negotiation. Were the redefined UK Government, in principle, willing to enter into a formal Agreement in this regard, it would undoubtedly seek to bind Scotland to adhere to certain constraints on policy. Moreover, the UK Government and the Bank might decide to impose strict conditions on Scottish companies, such as regulation by the UK and even incorporation in London.

If an independent Scotland saw major benefit in securing the support of the Bank of England in these various respects and were, therefore, motivated to finalise such an Agreement, the UK would be powerfully positioned to secure the conditionality that it deemed desirable for the stability of its macroeconomic objectives, a desire only reinforced by the recent experience of the euro zone. This would no doubt incorporate the areas of fiscal policy raised above, specifically with regard to the fiscal aggregates and the profile of annual deficits and debt requirement.

For Scotland, understanding the role that the Bank of England might play as a traditional lender of last resort to Scottish financial companies with severe problems of illiquidity would be of immense importance. Similarly, the nature of any support that the Bank of England might offer to an independent Scottish Government would be equally significant. Both roles potentially have a profound importance to an understanding of how the Scottish economy would evolve and perform, and are therefore a primary concern. Indeed, the credibility of Scottish policy would reflect the clarity with which these issues are understood, with important ramifications, for example, for the risk premia that attached to Scottish debt.

TABLE 4. THE ROLE OF THE BANK OF ENGLAND IN THE
INDEPENDENCE-BASED CONSTITUTIONAL MODELS

Within the set of independence-based models, the Central Bank plays a pivotal role: either Scotland establishes its own currency and its own central bank with the full range of traditional central bank powers or, alternatively, it participates as part of another monetary union and establishes its own central bank with a much reduced set of powers and responsibilities. In the latter case, it notably would not have powers over exchange rate management and monetary policy. Instead, the Bank of England – in the case of a sterling monetary union – and the European Central Bank – in the case of the EMU – would exercise those key powers.

Within a sterling monetary union, the role played by the Bank of England would not be self-evident, particularly insofar as it related to an independent Scotland. Some elements might indeed be the subject of complex negotiations once any decision to move to independence had been finalised. In this context, there are a series of critical challenges that would be faced:

» *Current legal status:* the Bank of England is established and regulated under a series of UK Parliamentary Acts and Charters.[25] Its remit and accountability, therefore, are directly determined by the UK Parliament, and any changes to this

---

25 The Constitution of the Bank of England is largely contained in the following documents:
   » the Bank of England Act (1694), which provides for the incorporation of the Bank;
   » the Charter of the Bank of England (1694), insofar as it incorporates the Bank, constitutes its capital stock and authorises it to have a common seal, to hold land and other property, and to sue and be sued;
   » the Bank Charter Act (1844), which provides for the separation of the issue and banking departments;
   » the Bank of England Act (1946), which contains amended provisions relating to the payment of distributions by the Bank to the Treasury;
   » the Charter of the Bank of England (1998), which, apart from continuing the 1694 Charter, contains provisions relating to the transfer of capital stock and the declaration required of Governors and Directors;
   » the Bank of England Act (1998), which deals with the constitution and functions of Court and the MPC, reporting, funding and related matters; and
   » the Banking Act (2009), which amends certain provisions of the 1998 Act regarding the governance of the Bank, introduces a new statutory financial stability objective and confers immunity on the Bank in its capacity as a monetary authority.

Although not part of the Bank's constitution, the Memorandum of Understanding between HM Treasury, the Bank and the Financial Services Authority is also relevant. See: Bank of England, Bank of England Legislation, the Charters of the Bank and Related Documents. www.bankofengland.co.uk

relationship would presumably be made in future by the new UK Parliament.

» *Governance of the Bank*: differing models for the governance of the Bank have been advanced, were an independence-based constitutional model to be adopted. These range from it being transformed into a Central Bank:

> - solely for the redefined UK with no formal Scottish role;
> - solely for the redefined UK with a Scottish observer presence;
> - for the sterling monetary area, but owned and directed by the redefined UK Parliament;
> - for the sterling monetary area with joint shareholdings held by Scotland and the redefined UK, presumably initially reflecting a GDP or population share;
> - based on an European Central Bank model.

The nature of the Bank of England would presumably only be determined through a process of negotiation, but any Agreement between the Scottish and redefined UK Governments would certainly need to provide clarity on several key elements:

> - ownership;
> - lines of accountability;
> - formal decision-making roles and responsibilities;
> - respective financial assets and liabilities;
> - the *de facto* degree of Scottish power and influence over the fundamental remit, operation and strategic and policy decision-making.

» *The operational independence of the Bank*: the Bank is independent in the sense that 'the Treasury has no operational responsibility for the activities of ... the Bank and shall not be involved in [it]'.[26] While, therefore, the Bank has this operational independence, the remit to which it works and its line of accountability are clearly determined by the UK Government of the day. Consequently, the roles and responsibilities of the Bank, insofar as they would relate to any different constitutional arrangement for Scotland, would be revised as deemed necessary by the new UK Government.

---

26 Memorandum of Understanding between HM Treasury, the Bank of England and the Financial Services Authority. Bank of England. 1997.

» *Monetary policy*: with powers over monetary policy – including, for example, the setting of interest rate and quantitative easing policy – resting with the Bank, questions would focus on:

> › the influence that the Scottish Government would have over policy definition;
> › the criteria that would prevail for membership of the Monetary Policy Committee.

» *Lender of last resort/liquidity support role*: considerable attention has focused on whether the Bank of England could and would play a lender of last resort role for the Scottish financial sector for an independent Scotland within a sterling monetary union. Many writers have rightly noted the confusion of roles since the onset of the financial crisis, with central banks playing a role not only in the traditional sense of being a provider of liquidity to a fundamentally solvent bank or banking system, but also supporting bodies whose solvency is at best questionable.[27]

There are an important set of questions relating to the traditional lender of last resort/liquidity support role upon which the focus needs to fall:

> › would the Bank of England continue to support any financial company that it considered threatening to the financial stability of the redefined UK?
> › would Scotland want the Bank of England to play a lender of last resort role in the traditional sense for those Scottish companies that the Bank considered to be no threat to the redefined UK's stability? Or would Scotland have a preference effectively for being without a lender of last resort with regard to these companies?
> › on what terms would the Bank be permitted to play these roles in Scotland by the new UK Government?
> › would those terms be acceptable to the Scottish Government of the day?

---

27 See, for example, Professor John Kay's contribution in Evidence to the Inquiry on The Economic Implications for the UK of Scottish Independence, The House of Lords, Select Committee on Economic Affairs, 22 May 2012: http://www.parliament.uk/documents/lords-committees/economic-affairs/ ScottishIndependence/scottishindev.pdf; or his Evidence to The House of Commons, Scottish Affairs Committee, 14 March 2012: www.publications. parliament.uk/pa/cm201012/cmselect/cmscotaf/1608/120314.htm.

> > what would be the sanctions were there to be breaches to an Agreement?

» *Support to Government*:

Similarly, attention has focused on the support that the Bank of England might provide to a Scottish Government in difficulty:

> > what role would the UK Government wish, in principle, to play in support of the Scottish Government in the event of it experiencing financial difficulty?
> > would a Scottish Government wish to have the assurance of the Bank's support?
> > on what terms and conditions would this support be available?

» *Financial sector solvency*: the financial crisis has clearly raised critical questions relating to the response to the emergence of insolvent financial companies. This response has focused on two strands: first, the nature and structures of the regulatory framework, and, second, the definition and mechanisms of support for insolvent companies. In this context, therefore, key questions arise with respect to :

> > the ownership of the regulatory responsibility and definition of the regulatory framework (not least in the light of EU requirements);
> > the location of responsibility for the support of large internationally diverse companies and the appropriate response;
> > the structure of the sector in the light of concerns about (i) corporate size relative to the scale of the national economy, and the capacity of Government to respond, and (ii) the incentive implications of any response;
> > the role of the Bank of England in resolution and deposit guarantee;
> > the terms and costs of any Bank of England support for insolvent companies.

» *Conditionality and the role of Bank of England*: this is discussed in the main text.

» *Credibility of an Agreement*: two key questions arise in this context:

> first, the degree to which Scotland has certainty of the nature of the Bank support when required; and

> second, the ultimate test of whether the international community and the international markets, in particular, believe that the Agreement would be implemented strictly as set out. The latter point would significantly affect the risk premia on Scottish borrowing for example.

As was observed above, Scotland's greatest interest might well be in the governance of the Bank of England and in the decision-making mechanisms through which it would seek to influence policy. The legal status of the current Bank of England is defined by the various Acts of the UK Parliament noted in Table 4, and any refinements to that status and its roles and responsibilities would, therefore, presumably rest with the redefined UK Parliament. Commentators[28] have debated the possibilities that constitutional change might bring, but, at the centre of this issue, is the key question: to which body would the Bank be accountable and which body would ultimately determine its remit and role. At present, there are no signs that the UK Government has any intentions of changing the existing position, which suggests a redefined UK Parliament would retain its current relationship with the Bank and the Bank would continue to be accountable to the new UK institutions. Scotland's interest would therefore be primarily in the potential refinements to the governance model. Its possible formal shareholding, the channels of communication with the ongoing operational decision-making bodies, its degree of influence over those bodies and its rights to vote would then be of very considerable importance.

As was noted earlier, to the extent that the continuing services of the redefined UK's central bank are deemed very important for Scotland within the sterling zone, the bargaining power of the UK would, of course, increase. Indeed, it is not difficult to envisage the UK Government seeking an Agreement in which wider economic and financial conditionality is determined. For example, from the perspective of microeconomic policy, while Scotland would notionally have full powers over taxation policy, the degree of freedom to exercise those powers might be limited. Many have argued that the UK Government would have a key self-interest in preserving the stability and sustainability of the Scottish economy, and, given

---

28 The evidence that Martin Wolf and Professor John Kay gave to The House of Commons, Scottish Affairs Committee, on 14 March 2012 provides a valuable insight into this debate and the contrasting possibilities that have been put forward: www.publications.parliament.uk/pa/cm201012/cmselect/cmscotaf/1608/120314.htm.

the degree of integration of the two economies, this would seem correct. However, the UK would equally have a major interest, for instance, in preserving the competitiveness of the redefined UK. For this reason, it would seem highly probable that the UK would seek an Agreement that incorporated significant safeguards for the new UK economy. While tax harmonisation throughout the sterling monetary union would not necessarily be sought, it seems improbable that *beggar-thy-neighbour* tax competition would be permitted on any substantive scale. There also exists the potential for conditionality that impinges on other Scottish powers to form part of any negotiations, but the outcome necessarily remains uncertain. Much would depend on the political climate of the day, as much as on the economic and financial argument.

Monetary policy strategy, which notably includes the setting of interest rates or the policy on quantitative easing as in the post-2008 economic crisis, would obviously be important for a Scottish Government, but would not attract the same concerns as *ex ante* conditionality and the *ex ante* constraints over Scottish policy. Rather, Scottish interests would focus on the mechanisms by which Scotland might influence policy on a continuing basis as economic conditions evolved. It would be anticipated that the operational independence of the Bank of England would remain a feature of the redefined UK institutional framework. However, as since its establishment as independent in 1998, the remit and strategic guidance, together with the critical operational parameters, would be determined by the new UK Parliament, even though the operational day-to-day functions would be independent of government. In this context, the Scottish Government would presumably seek to influence the fundamental remit, focused on the inflation rate target that is the primary driver of current monetary policy and the operational decision-making of the Bank. The channels through which this influence might be most effectively conducted would, of course, be critical and would again form part of a negotiation process.

This section has focused on the nature of constraint and conditionality in any Agreement within the context of a potential sterling monetary union, but it could readily be applied to the similar circumstance that would arise within the Economic and Monetary Union in the event of Scotland seeking admission to the euro zone. Similar safeguards and conditions would no doubt be sought by the EU authorities. Indeed, the interesting question in the context of the EU – which would no doubt apply equally to a sterling monetary area – would be the future direction in which the Union wished to evolve. Over decades, this is impossible to predict, but certainly the indications arising from the financial and euro crises is that there will be moves towards greater union across most areas of economic policy and management, including fiscal policy. This would suggest an environment in which member-states would individually have less power at national level to diverge significantly from the centrally determined limits.

1.3.3 *Constraint with increased fiscal autonomy*

Much of the discussion in the previous section in the context of the independence-based models applies equally to the UK-based models characterised by an extension of fiscal powers. Under these models, any new powers would be granted by the UK Government. While the opinion of the Scottish Government would no doubt be sought by a UK Government, and there may be a degree of discussion or apparent negotiation, ultimately the decision on the particular framework would be a decision of the UK Government.

1.3.3.1 Devo plus-type models

While the role of the Bank of England would be anticipated to remain broadly unchanged and, therefore, not the subject of discussion or negotiation,[29] there would certainly be a need to clarify the fiscal parameters within an Agreement. The earlier discussion regarding the potential destabilising effect of Scottish fiscal and debt policy on UK macroeconomic policy remains highly relevant here. The UK's concerns to maintain the stability of the entire UK economy and sustain its macroeconomic programme would suggest that the UK Government would retain a close interest in Scottish borrowing levels and the trends in Scottish debt accumulation. Whether this interest led to an Agreement that focused explicitly on the Scottish fiscal deficit and on the revenue and spending levels, albeit within a climate of increased fiscal responsibility and fiscal power, would only be apparent from the negotiations at the time. To the extent that limitations were, in fact, agreed or imposed on Scottish borrowing and debt policy, it would be important to identify a clear economic and financial rationale, founded on an understanding of Scotland's underlying borrowing and debt capacity.

Equally, and for similar reasons, the exercising of the extended fiscal powers by the Scottish Parliament to secure specific economic objectives would probably be subject to scrutiny at the UK level, not

---

29 It could be argued that negotiations could seek, even with these models, to extend the degree of Scottish participation in the governance of the Bank of England and to enhance the level of Scottish influence over strategic and operational thinking. This is, however, not an issue of powers *per se*.

least to avert tax competition deemed unacceptable to the rest of the UK. This would be particularly likely where it was feared that competition would have adverse consequences for the regions of the UK, and specifically for those in the north of England, where competition would be perceived to be at its most intense. Whether these concerns would ultimately lead to a highly constraining Agreement would only be revealed through negotiation at that time.

1.3.3.2 Devo max-type models

With the more radical models of fiscal autonomy, the constraints on the use of those additional Scottish powers might be expected to be significantly less limiting. However, while, in principle, models of Devo max seem to suggest that there would be unrestricted borrowing powers and full fiscal autonomy within the United Kingdom, it remains to be seen whether, in reality, the UK Government would grant such unrestricted powers. In some other countries, unrestricted powers over borrowing are granted by the central authorities to provinces or sub-national regions – as in the case with California and its relationship within the federal USA – but, in these cases, the federal authorities do not always guarantee the regions debt. The cost of borrowing then reflects the creditworthiness and financial sustainability of the regional government, assuming, of course, that the financial markets are, in fact, convinced that the contract between the federal and regional governments is credible and would indeed be implemented as set out. The first key decision would therefore be to determine whether there would be any UK guarantee of Scottish debt and then, if there were to be such, what would be its nature.

Were Scotland to operate without any such guarantee, the external pressure to establish a credible long-term policy would clearly be significantly greater. In the absence of this form of dissociation by the UK authorities and their acceptance of financial responsibility for the region, it would seem improbable that they would not retain a close interest in the conduct of macroeconomic policy in the region. What form this would take is again inevitably uncertain until a process of negotiation is concluded.

Similarly, as is arguably the case with Devo plus models, it is improbable that the UK Government would not retain an equal interest in the microeconomic policy of a Scottish Government. As before, the potential costs to the rest of the UK of a competitive tax policy would attract attention and only through the negotiation of a UK–Scotland Agreement would the nature of any constraint be clarified.

1.3.4 *The nature of the constraints in a monetary union*

The striking conclusion from this illustrative framework is that, under most proposed constitutional arrangements, there are many policy areas in which the value of the economic powers and the available policy instruments is indeterminate at this time. It is probable that, to a greater or lesser degree, policy would be subject to constraint, thereby impacting on the choice of macroeconomic framework. The degree of that constraint is, however, simply unknown at this time and would only emerge as an outcome of the key negotiation with the other relevant parties.

Some observers would no doubt contest the existence of a constraint at all in some areas of policy; others might see the constraints as both real and prohibitive in the sense of *de facto* removing the value of the economic power. This cannot of course be resolved in the abstract.

There are some specific considerations upon which any negotiations would need to focus and which would be reflected in any Agreement between the two Governments on the operation of the monetary union. These would determine the reality or otherwise of a potential constraint:

» *the nature of the constraint*: over which specific policies would one or more partners wish to impose some limitation or control?
» *the justification for the constraint*: what policy objective would underlie the negotiations for both parties?
» *the degree of potential constraint*: would the constraint be a severe restriction in the application of the economic power transferred to Scotland or relatively minor when judged against the potential value of the power to Scotland?
» *enforceability*: how enforceable would any Agreement be and what would be the associated sanctions and penalties that would be attracted through breach of that Agreement?
» *external credibility*: to the extent that a particular policy area – and the detail of an Agreement that relates to this policy area – has important implications for the relationship with external economic interests, what credibility would the Agreement have? Would it be seen as one that will be adhered to by both parties?

To this set of thoughts we might add a further set of crucial questions that concern the overall negotiations and their outcomes:

» *cross-policy conditionality*: to what extent might there be – indeed, should there be – cross-policy conditionality in any Agreement?

» *trade-offs*: are there meaningful trade-offs that can be made within any negotiation?
» *bargaining strength*: what is the relative power of the parties to the negotiations and the bargaining strength that each can bring at the time of the negotiations?
» *overall outcome of negotiations*: how is the net economic impact of the full breadth of any prospective Agreement valued by each? How is the potential Agreement viewed from a political perspective?
» *timing of negotiations*: what timing for such negotiations would be most appropriate, not least in the context of the political debate and the value that might be attached to the clarity of potential choices that are embedded in that debate? What is the political reality that will determine that timing?
» *life of an Agreement*: what would be the life and sustainability of an Agreement, especially acknowledging the political cycle and political changes that might be anticipated for each jurisdiction?

1.4 PRIMARY ECONOMIC POLICY

It is self-evident that the determination of how Scotland can optimally position itself within the global economic system is highly complex, not least given the array of potential options that are in principle available. As suggested earlier, in practice the options are less numerous than might initially appear, since once the primary choices are made early in the decision-making process, the subsequent choices that are deemed of less strategic importance will be simplified and constrained to a smaller set of possibilities.

This, however, begs the question of how to identify the areas of economic policy that are most critical and which therefore should be accorded primacy in the decision-making hierarchy. Once made, these primary choices might, of course, subsequently reveal a set of secondary options that are unacceptable for political or economic reasons, and it may then be necessary to revisit the primary choices. There may therefore be a degree of iteration about this process.

Nonetheless, the identification of the most critical policy areas and the associated primary choices that must be resolved would appear to be an obvious starting point.

To define the primary policy areas rests on first defining the key objectives of economic policy. In this context we are not concerned with the specific political preferences that different future administrations might have, not least since it is probable that, over many decades, they will span a vast range of possible visions and strategic objectives. Rather, our concern is for the higher-level objectives of government and for the array of economic powers and economic instruments at their disposal to pursue a range of visions.

1.4.1 *The primary economic objectives*

In summary, five key high-level economic objectives of government might be identified which should drive the consideration of the available economic powers and levers. In essence, this entails establishing a configuration of economic powers that supports the national economy and defining the appropriate balance of these powers between those held at the national and those held at the supra-national level. The national government would legitimately seek a configuration of powers that:

» provides an enhanced opportunity to pursue its economic, social and environmental objectives more effectively;
» facilitates a competitive economy and one that is sustainably so;
» provides the capacity to be resilient in the face of serious external shocks;
» provides adaptability and resilience to the other major risks and uncertainties that will inevitably emerge as the global economy develops in unforeseen directions and at an unanticipated rate over the decades; and
» seeks – to the extent that this configuration entails membership of a monetary union – a union with partners that are broadly similar in structure and economic behaviour.

With this set of objectives it is instructive to identify those criteria that arguably should be satisfied by any constitutional arrangement and its associated configuration of economic powers and instruments. Or, perhaps more realistically, the focus might be on those criteria that should shape the thinking around the choice of constitutional arrangement, even when the criteria cannot be satisfied in full or with total certainty over the long term. The discussion returns to these key criteria in detail in chapter 2, where we consider the assessment of the various propositions for constitutional change. In particular, we look at how a more structured approach to that assessment is possible, which can readily be deployed to explore and test the integrity, sustainability and value of the potential outcomes that might be generated by a proposition.

1.4.2 *The primary economic choice*

The primary question in the decision-making hierarchy is arguably that of the choice of currency and the wider policy configuration that is an integral part of that choice. Professor John Kay looks at this question in detail in chapter 3 and at the critical questions that underlie that choice. Here, the focus is on the context for that choice and particularly the definition of the broad options that are available.

1.4.2.1 The Economic and Monetary Union configuration

The present context of the Economic and Monetary Union and, in all probability, the context for many years to come is undoubtedly hugely volatile and uncertain. In the run-up to the introduction of the euro in 1999 there were inevitably significant risks regarding both its operational integrity and efficiency, and its effectiveness in securing the objectives of the EMU but, in some respects, its future was easier to foresee. For example, at the commencement of the euro zone,[30] the commitment of the founding members was unsurprisingly unquestioned and the debate focused on the zone's future potential expansion to embrace additional EU member-states rather than any fears of the fundamental stability of the Union or the imminent departure of any member. In addition, the dominance of the German Central Bank in the establishment of the institutions and policies of the new Union provided significant reassurance to potential participants and the markets that the euro zone would be stable and sustainable. In contrast, in the current context of continuing crisis in both the financial sector and in sovereign accounts across the euro zone – and, indeed, more broadly and to varying degrees within most European economies – the future economic choices are less easy to define.

From one perspective, the uncertainty surrounding the future of the European Union, in general, and the euro zone, in particular, might be seen as unwelcome complications. Any future Scottish constitutional arrangement that embraces a preference for the adoption of the euro faces an EMU that is far from static and highly unstable at present. The strategic direction, together with the policy and institutional environment, of the future euro zone that Scotland might join are continuously evolving and the EMU's future, more stable form is currently undetermined.

---

30 On 1 January 1999, the third and final stage of EMU commenced, with the irrevocable fixing of the exchange rates of the currencies of the eleven member-states initially participating in the Monetary Union and with the conduct of a single monetary policy under the responsibility of the European Central Bank.

At perhaps the most fundamental level, the membership itself of the euro zone remains uncertain as the crisis evolves. Consequently, even in the medium term, it is difficult to determine the policy configuration that joining the euro might entail. A significantly smaller euro zone of those economies seen to have withstood the crisis most successfully would embrace a very different set of economic policies to a euro zone that continues to attempt to reconcile the very different economic performance and characteristics of the present membership.

One illustration of this point is the present discussion over the future degree of integration of members within the EMU. Many argue for both a greater intensity and extensity of the EMU, embracing more rigorous and disciplined moves to consolidate existing policy and strategy and, in addition, extending the scope of union to embrace more comprehensively a fiscal union, a banking union, a regulatory union and indeed wider forms of common policy. The precise nature of the configuration of these policies – and the institutional structures that are designed for the implementation of the policy – are not only difficult to clarify in the short term, but their development over the medium to long term is unknown. In this sense, the context is a moving target.

From a different perspective, however, this volatility within the current euro zone and, more generally, within the global economic system may be seen as a positive contribution to the debate, deflecting the argument from short-term static analysis of current problems and current challenges to considerations of complex and uncertain future challenges. This central point will be considered further.

1.4.2.2 The sterling union configuration

From one perspective defining the sterling union is relatively more straightforward than defining the EMU and euro zone. Notwithstanding the economic turbulence since 2008 and the heated controversy over the appropriate response to the financial crisis and to the protracted recession and under-performance of the UK economy, the fundamental nature of the UK currency area has been more settled and better understood. Certainly, the economic governance and institutional framework within which policy is determined is relatively stable and, while there continue to be refinements in the economic landscape as regards the bodies charged with particular economic and financial responsibilities, together with the nature of those responsibilities, there is no perceived threat to the stability of the union itself, even in the event that Scotland were to withdraw.

Constitutional change would necessarily entail the redefining of the relationships, but, currently, the role and responsibilities of the UK Government and of the UK Central Bank in the financial and economic management of all the constituent parts of the UK are clearly established. The main exception here that is worth highlighting is, of course, the changes incorporated within the Financial Services Act which received Royal Assent in December 2012.[31] This Act gives the Bank of England macroprudential responsibility for oversight of the financial system and, through a new, operationally independent subsidiary, for day-to-day prudential supervision of financial services companies. This reform is expected to significantly redefine the role of the Bank of England. While these changes are very fundamental for the UK as a whole, they do not imply any change in the basic relationship between central government and the regions and nations of the UK. The new arrangements would continue to be applied uniformly across the UK. Thus, while the financial crisis has stimulated intense debate, the present structures are not open to the same uncertainty and questioning as is apparent with the European political administration and the European Central Bank.

Perhaps most significantly within a sterling zone, whether within a UK-based or an independence-based model, it is the nature of any future Agreement between the UK and Scottish Governments that provides the greatest uncertainty. However, in the current environment, this might be seen as a more advantageous position from the Scottish perspective. Whereas the uncertainty within the EMU derives primarily from the profound failure of government at that level to define and implement stable policy – over which Scotland would be expected to have little influence, were it a member of the EMU – within the context of the sterling zone, uncertainty is likely to derive more from the inability to know how influential or otherwise Scotland might be over UK Government policy. In the long term, one key consideration would of course be the relative influence that Scotland might expect to achieve within the two monetary unions.

It is worth noting additionally that there will always be an asymmetry in knowledge, in that the understanding of the *status quo* within the current sterling union is inevitably greater than the knowledge of what benefits and costs a different possible constitutional arrangement might bring. Equally, however, it can, of course, be argued that the risks to any set of desired national outcomes of remaining in what some might see as a sub-optimal *status quo* are no less profound than the risks in moving to a constitutional state where the outcomes may be inherently less certain. Moreover, it can

---

31 See, for example, the UK HM Treasury summary in www.hm-treasury.gov.uk/ fin_financial_services_bill.htm.

be argued that there are equally considerable uncertainties regarding the nature of the 'status quo': for example, it is far from clear that, within the *status quo* models – and, indeed, those that entail relatively modest further extensions of devolution – the Barnett formula will remain the primary mechanism for the annual adjusting of the Scottish Budget beyond the next few years. Many have argued for a comprehensive rethink around the funding of the budget, potentially entailing a new look at both the basic underlying Needs Assessment approach and the Barnett mechanism.

1.4.2.3 A Scottish currency configuration

In principle, the choice to adopt its own currency within an independence-based model would provide Scotland with an immediate degree of clarity, without the need to negotiate an Agreement with the other parties to a monetary union. Equally, it would give the Scottish Parliament the widest choice of policy configuration. While it would potentially offer the greatest flexibility and, in theory, allow an apparently unrestricted choice in subsequent economic policy decision-making, the opportunities for Scotland to pursue a distinct economic path would, as noted earlier, be relatively limited given the importance of its closest and dominant market, the redefined UK. In addition, many see it as also being inherently more risky with the possibility of significant currency volatility, not least due to the economy's degree of dependence on, and vulnerability to, the oil and gas sector. The importance of this exposure would be unpredictable and that, in itself, might increase the risk premia faced in Scotland.

The prospect of increased risk from these forms of uncertainty would, moreover, be in the context of a political arrangement that would leave Scotland less certain of support from other nations in time of difficulty. Within a monetary union it would be anticipated that financial and economic risk-sharing would be a dominant element, with either predetermined or anticipated mechanisms of mutual support operating to mitigate the impact of external or, indeed, self-induced crisis in any one member-state. Outwith a monetary union it would be highly unlikely that the certainty of support and, at least, the cost of any such support would be prearranged, again making the external markets more wary. Thus, the management of these risks would be a key part of economic management alongside the exploitation of the opportunities that the assumption of full economic powers would bring.

The alternative forms of currency management are considered in chapter 3, with each carrying important implications for the conduct of wider economic management. In each basic option, whether freely floating or whether pegged more or less formally to the currency of a larger economic bloc or single currency area, the credibility of the choice would receive serious external scrutiny in the light of the policy configuration adopted to support that choice. To this extent, the primary policy choices take on a greater significance.

It is also noteworthy that our knowledge of the current external balance for Scotland is, at best, very limited. Data are weak in this area, leaving a significant degree of ignorance regarding the starting point from which Scotland might expect to initiate its new currency arrangements. This factor, therefore, injects another level of risk that would need careful management with this arrangement. Within a monetary union, as recent years have graphically demonstrated, the emergence of major external imbalances have not immediately imposed significant pressure on national policy makers and, while playing a major underlying role in the current euro crisis, were not tackled. In consequence, the substantive variance in economic performance of the different member-states was allowed to emerge in other more serious ways, notably through the credit markets and in the accumulation of unsustainable levels of debt. With the adoption of a Scottish currency, external weakness would be expected to be considerably more visible and to impact on policy much more rapidly.

1.5 THE ECONOMIC VALUE OF CONSTITUTIONAL CHANGE

1.5.1 *Accountability*

Since the establishment of the Scottish Parliament in 1999 there has continued to be a strong emphasis in the ongoing constitutional debate on the relationship between the granting of greater powers and the increased degree of perceived and real accountability of the Parliament that might flow from the granting of those powers. Indeed, one of the key factors behind the renewed impetus in the debate has been the strongly held view of some observers that accountability remains fundamentally inadequate. In this regard, accountability has focused particularly on three themes:

» the nature of the financing of Scottish expenditure has been one major theme, with a strong current of thinking suggesting that accountability can only be meaningful when the Parliament is accountable for the revenues – or, at least, a much greater share of the revenues – that finance its expenditure programmes. There has, therefore, been a particular focus on the proportion of total Scottish expenditures approved by the Scottish

Parliament that are financed through tax instruments over which the Parliament has control. Equivalently, given the basic statutory imposition of a balanced budget on the Parliament, the scale of the transfers from the UK Government has been seen by some as a prime concern and a major obstacle to accountability;

» equally, much attention has focused on the extent to which the revenues accruing to the Scottish Parliament would benefit from any enhancement to Scottish economic performance, especially when that improved performance is generated through variations in tax policy which were themselves enabled through the transfer of greater fiscal powers. Depending on the precise nature of the constitutional arrangement, the fiscal benefits would not be fully reflected in the Scottish budgetary position;

» and, related to these themes, is the view that there is little incentive for the Scottish Parliament to deploy its available resources efficiently and to maximum effect when it neither controls, or has little control over, its total pool of available resources, nor benefits to the full extent from the outcomes of its economic strategy and policy. To the extent that, under the present constitutional arrangement and some of the models that propose more modest extensions of fiscal power, some significant proportion of the fiscal benefit to Scotland of accelerated economic growth would indeed fall to the UK Government, at least in the first instance, there is clearly a disincentive here.

On the other hand, the non-fiscal benefits that flow to Scotland from accelerated growth are potentially still highly significant. For example, crucial benefits may be seen to derive in the form of a stronger labour market, with greater and higher quality employment, or, similarly, from the establishment of a more powerful reputation for economic dynamism with all that that implies for the attraction of foreign direct investment and for domestic Scottish and UK investment. Indeed, even in the absence of the full fiscal benefits, the economic – and arguably the political – incentives to maximise growth and employment remain substantive and thus a powerful driver of behaviour.

It should be noted, however, that, while there may be an incentive to be efficient in the above sense, any system that provides a fixed transfer or grant, which accounts for the vast majority of the available resource to a government, takes away the key decision relating to the aggregate revenues that should be raised. This critical choice should be driven by a clear understanding of the use to which those revenues might be put and the value they would generate, notably at the margin. In this sense, any block grant arrangement – that would operate with all the proposed UK-based models, with the exception of Devo max – would not provide any incentive to question whether the size of the grant was optimal or too large or small.[32]

1.5.2 *Economic outcomes*

While the debate has entailed considerable discussion of the specific fiscal powers that might be transferred to Scotland, there has generally been far less emphasis placed on defining how those powers might be best deployed[33] and upon what outcomes the new powers might be expected to focus – albeit with some notable exceptions, such as the use of potential corporate tax powers. In general, the value of economic powers, particularly in the sense of the achievability of the critical outcomes that motivate government, has arguably been significantly under-emphasised. Indeed, there has been little to demonstrate either the improved outcomes that might flow from these greater powers or the threat to the desired outcomes that these extended powers might bring. Where these questions have been addressed, the responses have typically suffered from a paucity of evidence to support specific propositions and, instead, have often lapsed into cavalier assertions with little or no foundation.

One example from the recent past makes the point. Within the

---

32 See, for example, C. P. Hallwood and Ronald MacDonald (2009) on this point in The Political Economy of Financing Scottish Government: Considering a New Constitutional Settlement for Scotland.

33 The economic theory of fiscal federalism, often summarised in Oates's decentralisation theorem, has an obvious relevance here, with its focus on 'understanding which functions and instruments are best centralised and which are best placed in the sphere of decentralised levels of government' (Oates, 1972, 1999). It provides a theory of the appropriate allocation of powers to different levels of government, including the allocation of both expenditure and revenue powers and instruments. While much of the literature was developed in the context of local public finance, it could equally be seen as relevant to the distribution of powers between the UK and Scottish levels of government. Fiscal federalism concerns both horizontal and vertical fiscal relationships: horizontal relations relate to regional imbalances and horizontal competition; and vertical relations relate to relations between two levels of government, a centre and a more local level.

Much of Oates's work focused on the trade-off between autonomy and accountability, and on the potential value of decentralisation. Any conclusions did, however, rest on the crucial underlying economic conditions, regarding the degree of homogeneity across regions in their preferences for public goods, the existence of interregional externalities, and the economies of scale from central provision.

We are not aware of any explicit attempts to apply this thinking to the current debate about constitutional change and the benefits and costs of the different options, with their associated allocation of economic powers between the different levels of government.

context of the Scotland Act (2012) that, most notably, extended greater powers over income tax to the Scottish Parliament, there were many contributions during its development, from all parts of the political spectrum, asserting the value of the new powers,[34] but a notable absence of discussion of how the new powers would be utilised. Indeed, some very fundamental questions were barely touched upon:

» would the economic benefit be greatest from an increase, a reduction or an unchanged[35] income tax rate in Scotland, compared to that prevailing in the rest of the UK and the EU?
» through what economic channels and mechanisms would these benefits or costs flow?
» upon what evidence were these conclusions founded?

An important question is therefore to ask what we can say about the potential opportunities and risks that a new constitutional arrangement might bring in the context of the vision and outcomes of any particular government.

An obvious starting point is to note that no two governments, of course, have the same vision, and, therefore, from one perspective, there is an infinite array of possible desirable outcomes to consider in this context of a new constitutional arrangement. With this in mind, and at a higher level of analysis, however, the key question is whether the transfer of greater economic powers provides significant new economic opportunities that would facilitate the achievement of any economic set of outcomes. Or whether extended powers are seen to carry greater risks and uncertainties that would counter the identified opportunities. We return to this issue in detail in chapter 2.

In reality, the challenge is less daunting since there is a strong case that there has been considerable convergence in the economic visions and growth strategies that are pursued across the globe today. The core elements of most strategies are common to many economies, based as they are on a similar understanding of the theoretical economic underpinning. They do, of course, differ substantively in the detail of strategy and policy.

Closer to home, the economic strategy of successive Scottish

---

34 As, for example, in the evidence provided to the various Scotland Bill Committees: see The 1st Report, 2011 (Session 4), Report on the Scotland Bill, Scotland Bill Committee, Scottish Parliament, 15 December 2011. Similarly, see the work of Kenneth Calman reported in Serving Scotland Better: Scotland and the United Kingdom in the 21st Century, Final Report, Commission on Scottish Devolution, June 2009.

35 In the light of the experience with the Single Variable Rate (SVR) since 1999, it would also be legitimate to ask whether the power would be used at all.

Governments since the establishment of devolution in 1999 has reflected significant convergence of thinking across Scotland. The primary determinants that have been identified in a succession of strategies[36] as central to the driving of an enhanced economic growth performance in Scotland have, at a high level, shared many common elements. Certainly, there have been distinctive policy solutions advanced in order to stimulate these key economic drivers, not least, of course, those that have related to the use of, and access to, the reserved economic powers. However, the understanding of the primary drivers of economic growth and, in addition, the current understanding of Scotland's comparative advantage – and perhaps more importantly its potential comparative advantage – are widely shared.

Comparative advantage is by no means a static concept or a static reality, and, equally, the primary economic drivers would be anticipated to evolve over time, but it is, nonetheless, reasonable to consider constitutional change here in the context of our current understanding.

1.5.3 Specific objectives and constitutional change

In Part II of this publication, the focus is upon the potential significance of constitutional change to the primary outcome perspectives and to some of their associated key drivers.

The earlier chapters, specifically chapters 6 and 7, look at the broadest outcome objectives: Professors Peter McGregor and Kim Swales consider *The Impact of Greater Autonomy on the Growth of the Scottish Economy* and then look at *The Impact of Greater Autonomy on Climate Change Policy*. In the Appendix to this book there is a further look at *Welfare Policy and the Distributional Objectives of Economic Policy*.

Chapters 8 and 9 then look in greater detail at two specific themes, both of which are broadly agreed to be critical drivers of economic development: Professor Sir Jim McDonald and Simon Jennings look at *Economic Development and Skills for the Knowledge Economy: Contribution of Higher Education and R&D*; and Jamie Carstairs considers *Energy and Constitutional Change*.

Analysis of Scotland's comparative advantage in recent decades has focused on these elements as two of the primary drivers. The

---

36 As with the Scottish Executive's economic strategy from 2000 to 2007, the Framework for Economic Development in Scotland (FEDS), Scottish Executive (June 2000), and the post-2007 Scottish Government's strategy, the Government Economic Strategy (GES), Scottish Government (November 2007) and the recent update of the GES in September 2011.

pursuit of the highest possible quality in our human capital has long been a goal of successive Scottish Governments and there is a broad consensus that this goal would remain dominant for the foreseeable future. Higher education and the generation of an excellent research base have been the foundation of one key part of the long-term economic development strategy, and most observers would agree that, were there to be constitutional change, it must certainly not damage that comparative advantage and should, in principle, provide an impetus to greater advantage. In the case of energy, the emphasis has not been static but has moved from the dominance of North Sea oil and gas production to the broader comparative advantage of both the non-renewable and the renewable sub-sectors. While the former is an established and mature industry, there still remain, in the latter case, important challenges to overcome at both the technical and financial levels in converting the strong fundamental renewable asset base into a powerful comparative advantage.

More generally, does the prospect of new powers under a new constitutional arrangement have the potential to establish stronger and more effective incentives to the development of the key sectors or does it carry important risks and uncertainties that could hinder their development? At the microeconomic level, there have been an array of studies[37] that have sought to identify the impact of specific fiscal instruments on economic growth as, for example, with those that have looked at the potential impact of varying corporation tax rates.[38] These issues are considered further in chapters 6 to 9. All of the studies have shortcomings and none have provided clear-cut evidence of the type that would be most instructive. Inevitably, none relate to the Scottish economy specifically, leaving the reader with the task of discerning the degree to which results are relevant to the domestic economy with its own behavioural characteristics.

Perhaps most problematic is that the impact of the immense shock of the post-2008 period – rooted in the financial crisis but now far wider in its causes and impact – is unknown. Previously, relatively stable relationships between fiscal policy and their intended targets were able to convey significant information about potential future behaviour and future impacts. The economic context is

---

37 For example, see the paper of the Organisation for Economic Cooperation and Development, Tax and Economic Growth, Economics Department Working Paper No. 620, Åsa Johansson et al, 11 July 2008.

38 For example, regarding corporation tax and its implications for economic growth, see Peter McGregor and Kim Swales (2012), The Impact of a Devolved Corporation Tax to Scotland, a paper presented at the British and Irish Regional Science Association meeting in Galway, August 2012; or see Young Lee and Roger H. Gordon, Tax Structure and Economic Growth, Journal of Public Economics, 89, 2005.

now substantively different with behaviours that are yet to stabilise and attain an equilibrium. Inferring impact from any economic change has therefore become a significantly more complex challenge. Moreover, and particularly given the long-term nature of the fiscal adjustment programmes that are required in most economies, affordability of policy has taken on a more immediate importance. The opportunity cost of any, more generous, tax policy, for example, in terms of the lost benefits from finding the necessary resources from elsewhere, is as difficult to determine as the value of the policy itself. The net benefits are therefore an elusive value.

There is arguably a more profound point here that relates directly to the claimed implications – for good or for ill – of major constitutional change and, particularly, of independence. In principle, a transformation of this type is not simply about minor changes to the parameters within the existing economic model. It is presumably about seeking to change expectations, behaviours and incentives. The step-change that is sought is explicitly intended to create a clear discontinuity in economic impact. It is therefore about transforming the economic model itself. In which case, a reliance on past evidence or traditional economic techniques (for example, macro forecasting models) to 'test' whether independence is a good or a bad thing (or whether a particular policy is a good or a bad thing) is not only misplaced but potentially highly misleading: unless, that is, the change is anticipated to be relatively minor in its impact on the primary economic behaviours.

The debate around the value of the Scottish Government publication, *Government Expenditure and Revenue, Scotland* (GERS)[39] sharply illustrates the point. GERS provides an estimate of the total revenues raised in Scotland and the total expenditures incurred for the benefit of Scotland. It seeks to capture the actual flows in a particular year that result from the economic activity of both the private and public sector in that year: it reflects the behaviours and choices with the constitutional arrangement and the economic policy that prevail at that time. It, therefore, reveals little, if anything, about the state of the public accounts were a radically different constitutional arrangement to be put in place, assuming that such a change did, indeed, create a substantively different economic model of behaviour and incentives. It would offer considerable insight into the Scottish Government accounts on Day 1 with a new constitution but, thereafter, would provide little value. It is, therefore, a very good example of the serious – if not, fatal – limitations of forecasting

---

39 See, for example, Government Expenditure and Revenue, Scotland, 2010-11,
    Scottish Government, March 2012.

or producing shadow budgets or green budgets for a new regime for anything except the very short term indeed. Given the importance of a long-term perspective to constitutional change, this transitional information falls well short of its intended objective.

Finally, at present, the North Sea sector clearly continues to dominate the energy economy and provides one key perspective on the constitutional debate, both in its implications for the real economy and for the public accounts. In chapter 10 Professor Alex Kemp offers an analysis of the medium and long-term prospects for *North Sea Oil and Gas*, looking at the production prospects for the sector and the implications for the broader economy of its future evolution. He identifies the relevant economic powers and provides an insightful look at the challenges and opportunities that the alternative constitutional arrangements might pose.

1.5.4 *Macroeconomic outcomes*

Academic studies have tended not to look at the overall macroeconomic impact of increasing degrees of economic autonomy, but many have focused on the impact of greater fiscal autonomy. Indeed, the question of what change in economic performance and in the underlying long-term growth trends might be anticipated from the enhancement to a nation's fiscal powers has at times been both high-profile and hotly contested. Unfortunately, the evidence[40] remains largely inconclusive, irrespective of the earlier points made in relation to the relevance of the evidence to the Scottish context and the relevance of historical analysis in a period following a very major shock to the economic system.

From the theoretical perspective, as is explored further in chapter 6 by Professors McGregor and Swales, there are strong arguments that support the conclusion that increasing fiscal autonomy can, through distinct mechanisms, both stimulate and hinder the growth process. Where the balance lies between these two opposing forces is theoretically uncertain and would be anticipated in reality to vary substantively between different economies. Empirical study could potentially shed light here, but these studies have produced evidence that has been both hard to interpret and often contradictory in its findings.

---

40 Several academic pieces have provided valuable reviews of the evidence: see, for example, Feld et al (2007) and Roy (2006).

One recent example of this inconclusiveness was the exchange between Professors Andrew Hughes Hallett and Drew Scott and Professor David Ulph,[41] within the context of the work of the Scottish Parliament's Committee on the Scotland Bill[42] during the period 2010 to 2011. Much of the exchange drew on the work of Feld cited earlier and, if nothing else, it demonstrated the magnitude of the challenge in identifying meaningful evidence with which to enlighten the critical question of whether greater fiscal powers have the capacity to enhance economic growth.

The literature has broadly highlighted several key elements that have made conclusive findings so difficult to discern. First, it has identified the important distinction between the level of government at which economic powers might reside and the manner in which those powers are in fact deployed. It is impossible to argue that powers alone will or will not lead to a specific outcome: it will always be the way in which the powers are utilised that is key. Second, the distinction between whether economic powers and economic policies can stimulate a higher level of output or a higher long-term trend growth rate has often been confused, but this is a critical error in understanding the value of economic policy. Third, most empirical studies make no attempt to investigate the primary channels and mechanisms through which greater fiscal powers might indeed stimulate or hinder economic growth. They have been largely[43] conducted without reference to these mechanisms, focusing solely on relating autonomy to the aggregate growth out-turn data. We are therefore none the wiser about how these systems might operate to good or ill effect and, perhaps, most importantly, are therefore seriously hampered in our understanding of whether the experience and evidence is meaningful in the Scottish context. Fourth, as this chapter and this book amply demonstrate, fiscal autonomy is, at its simplest, a complex set of expenditure, revenue and borrowing powers, and the definition and quantitative measurement are exceptionally difficult if the nature of autonomy is to be accurately reflected in any study. There has been a wide variation in the definitions that past studies have deployed and few have captured the subtlety and detail of autonomy satisfactorily. Fifth, no studies make any serious attempt to analyse the relevance of non-Scottish evidence.

---

41 For example, see Andrew Hughes Hallett and Drew Scott (2010) and David Ulph (2011).

42 See, for example, the Scottish Parliament website on the work of the Committee: www.scottish.parliament.uk/parliamentarybusiness/PreviousCommittees/27025.aspx.

43 Thieβen (2003) is one exception that looked at the impact of greater fiscal autonomy on capital formation and productivity.

These observations could be extended but they are certainly not intended to disparage an exceptionally difficult area of study or indeed discredit any attempts to understand the subject. They simply demonstrate how problematic are the findings and the value of those studies. This is a disappointing conclusion and suggests the urgent need for better evidence and understanding, as well as the acceptance of the limitations of our current knowledge.

1.5.5 *Institutional structures and governance*

While the debate over constitutional change tends to focus heavily on the powers that might ultimately lie with one jurisdiction or another, there is a critical dimension that relates to the institutional framework in each jurisdiction and the systems of governance that are established, within which those powers are exercised and policy is determined. Any redistribution of powers between the United Kingdom Parliament and the Scottish Parliament – and notably any redistribution that would entail Scottish independence – has implications for the manner in which those powers are deployed. This consideration is of course relevant across the entire range of powers, with its implications for economic powers being but one – albeit crucial – element. These issues are looked at in detail in chapter 11, where Sir John Elvidge considers *Governance and the Institutional Framework*.

These issues raise questions relating not only to the processes for the development of statute and for the exercise of existing powers, but also to the checks and balances within any level of government, and for the relationships between different levels of government. Above all, these processes and systems of challenge have historically focused on the objective of enhancing the quality and broad acceptability of the use of powers. Sir John Elvidge considers many of these issues and their significance for the constitutional debate.

One other perspective on the institutional structure is of particular importance: namely, the relationship between Scotland and the European Union. Though beyond the remit of this book, the relationship is relevant to all of the chapters, with several options for change embracing a continuing link with the EU.

Independence would give Scotland, as a Member State, a seat at the table in the Council of the EU and potentially a doubling of its representation in the European Parliament. The question is how this would change the nature of Scotland's power and influence in EU decision-making: in terms of advancing Scotland's political and policy goals, is it better to be an independent small state or an influential part of a large Member State? Small states in the EU suffer from structural disadvantages – less political power and fewer administrative resources – compared to larger Member States, and many have argued that the trend has been for smaller states to have less influence in areas like foreign and security policy, and economic and monetary policy[44]. Nevertheless, countries like Finland and Ireland have shown that small states can effectively advance their national interests, albeit selectively, by exploiting the intergovernmental bargaining process through coordination or alliances with other small countries and partnerships with larger Member States.

A more immediate issue is the accession process for Scotland to become a Member State, a situation for which there is no precedent. The current opinion of the European Commission President is that an independent Scotland would need formally to apply for and negotiate EU membership: Scotland would not inherit membership.[45] If so, Scotland could face a period of uncertainty of unknown duration as the application process proceeded, and there is the question of the terms and conditions on which Scotland would join. Problematic issues would include whether and when Scotland would be required to join the euro, its participation in the Schengen Agreement on borderless travel, and its contribution to the EU budget (probably without the rebate currently enjoyed by the UK).

The application process is, therefore, necessarily uncertain at this time. Some have argued that, after being members of the EU for 40 years, Scots could not have citizenship withdrawn were they to vote for independence, requiring some form of transition arrangement until membership is settled[46]. Others have pointed to the need for every existing Member State to approve Scotland's accession and the concern that several countries have about their own regions seeking independence may lead some to put obstacles in the path of ratifying Scotland's membership. This could certainly delay the process, albeit not necessarily de-railing it.

---

44 See Panke, D. (2010). Small states in the European Union: coping with structural disadvantages, Farnham, Ashgate; and Thorhallsson B and Wivel A (2006) Small States in the European Union: What do we know and what would we like to know? Cambridge Review of International Affairs, 19(4), 651-668.

45 The position of the European Commission, stated by the Commission President to the European Parliament in 2004, and restated by the current President Barroso in 2012 is that: "when a part of the territory of a Member State ceases to be part of that state, for example because that territory becomes an independent state, the treaties will no longer apply to that territory. In other words, a newly independent region would, by the fact of its independence, become a third country with respect to the Union and the treaties would, from the day of its independence, not apply any more on its territory."

46 See Graham Avery's evidence to the House of Commons Select Committee on Foreign Affairs, 17 October 2012, www.publications.parliament.uk/pa/cm201213/cmselect/cmfaff/writev/643/m05.htm

Self-evidently, with the options that propose Scotland continuing within the UK with varying degrees of increased autonomy, the institutional relationship with the EU would not be expected to change significantly unless, of course, there were to be a substantive change in the overarching UK relation with the European Union[47]. Within the current arrangements or under variants of further devolution, however, it would be open to Scotland to argue for a more formalised role in the UK's decision-making process on EU matters, similar to the rights of the German *Länder*, for example.

1.6 GLOBAL ECONOMIC INFLUENCE

The preoccupation with performance at the national economic level and with the economic powers and levers at the disposal of a Scottish Parliament is unsurprising in view of the politically charged atmosphere in which constitutional debate is inevitably conducted. Similarly, the concern with the primary decision-making institutions – whether within Scotland itself or within a broader grouping of an economic and monetary union – and their direct and immediate role in Scottish economic policy is to be expected.

It is, nonetheless, the case that, as is widely recognised now, many of the critical global challenges that face this and coming generations will only be resolved through global collaboration and global action. Indeed, to the extent that there is a common global vision for the long term, it is to the global community that we must look for global solutions. To date, with some notable exceptions, success at this level in effectively addressing these challenges has been limited, with rhetoric and posturing often overwhelming evidence-based global decision-making. This somewhat depressing observation does not, in itself, negate the fundamental view that it will still need to be at this level that solutions are found.

If this basic premise is accepted, one key dimension of the constitutional debate should focus on the capacity of Scotland to influence these global debates and inject insight and hard-edged programmes of action onto the appropriate stage, typically global but sometimes at a more regional level. Even from a more parochial perspective, future Scottish economic performance is closely related to many of

---

47 The recent proposal by the UK Government to call a referendum on UK membership of the EU in the next UK Parliament does, of course, raise this issue more starkly. Were the UK to leave the EU, it would raise important questions for Scotland, whether Scotland remained within the UK or sought independence. Within the independence-based models, the currency question would of course take on an added complexity, as would all issues relating to the border between the two nations.

these global challenges and by no means immune should they remain unresolved.

Immediate concerns illustrate the need for the global community to play the lead role in addressing global economic challenges. The nature of the financial sector and the dominance of global corporations, and particularly the extensive interlinkages that now permeate the entire sector, demonstrate the necessity of a global approach to financial sector regulation and monitoring. The common refrain that national governments cannot act alone, without fear of losing competitive advantage in some respect, provides compelling evidence that a collective decision-making process is critical.

Perhaps less critical to global economic stability and sustainability, but arguably equally crucial to the integrity of the global economy, is the future of many other global economic policies. One excellent illustration of considerable relevance to the current constitutional discussions proves the general point. Considerable attention has been devoted to the role of the corporate tax system within any new constitutional arrangement. Some have argued that it is critical to Scotland's future economic performance and therefore a key economic power over which control is of paramount importance. Others have argued that, in practice, the use of the power – were it to be passed to the Scottish Parliament under any future constitutional arrangement – would be severely curtailed by either the UK or the EU authorities, depending on the precise form of economic system adopted. Both perspectives seem to miss a far more important point: namely, that the global corporate tax system itself is widely recognised now as hugely deficient and operationally flawed. While its operation in the case of domestically based companies may be broadly as intended, few global corporations now face tax regimes as intended by the local tax jurisdiction and as notionally set down in statute. The ability of global corporations to direct their profit to low-tax locations and effectively and efficiently avoid tax is well documented. Specific examples that hit the headlines reflect this systemic failure. Some might challenge the ethics of these corporates but, irrespective of these questions of morality, it is the systemic failure which permits this behaviour that is the key underlying problem. The need for a global solution to an intrinsically global challenge in terms of corporate taxation and the legitimate and systematic taxation of corporate profit is self-evident. Attempts at resolving the question at the level of the national government seem doomed to fail and merely reinforce the value of global influence in global policy determination.

We can, however, take a broader perspective on the critical importance of global collaboration and global influence. We might look, for example, at the contribution that Scotland does, and increasingly can, make to the advance of global knowledge and understanding in the field of science and technology and the contribution that these, in turn, make to economic progress. Global collaboration in research and innovation is already far advanced with joint research teams from different international universities, research centres, governments and global corporates having undertaken cutting-edge work for decades. In the light of the huge gains from such collaboration, any debate should presumably embrace a consideration of how any new constitutional arrangement might impinge on this work, beneficially or otherwise.

A global perspective arguably has an even greater contribution to make that goes well beyond the more immediate needs of the global economy. It is strikingly illustrated by what many argue is the key current global challenge: namely that of environmental sustainability in all its dimensions, including the addressing of climate change, climate justice, climate mitigation and adaptation. Here, both economic strategy and economic policy need to play a crucial role. Indeed, there are broader dimensions to sustainability. The challenge presented by the pressure on key resources impinges not only on the economic performance of every nation but equally on the social fabric of many societies, and increasingly on the political stability and sustainability of many regions of the world, bringing the prospect of conflict over resources to the fore. Global water supplies and security, along with global energy supplies and security, are emerging as key in this respect.

Indeed, challenges from the unequal global distribution of assets, wealth and incomes are increasingly likely to bear on the more local economic performance of the Scottish economy. Some of these concerns over distribution and equity relate to the advanced economies and have been increasingly highlighted as the global financial crisis has evolved, impacting directly on the long-term performance of many economies. Other concerns relate to the developing world where severe poverty continues to dominate in many economies and undermine the political and economic stability of those regions.

While issues of equity and poverty within advanced economies are typically regarded as the concern and responsibility of those countries themselves, given the obvious political sensitivity and judgement that these questions raise, the concerns in relation to the developing world are quite different in nature. Most observers would question whether many developing countries are able to pull themselves out of extreme poverty – certainly within an acceptable time horizon – without collective international support. Such support may range, for example, from the provision of time-limited preferential access to highly competitive and sophisticated developed economy markets or the removal of historic debt burdens to the advanced economies and the international organisations, accumulated in the past by corrupt or misguided political regimes. Again, the crucial point is that a key global problem is unlikely to be successfully addressed in the absence of the global community combining in a unified strategic approach.

Within the context of the constitutional debate, the primary question must, therefore, be how can the Scottish people make their contribution to these critical global challenges in the most effective way, and through what channels would their voice be best heard. The crux is whether the Scot's economic voice is more effectively raised when intermediated by a larger institutional organisation, be it a government or economic bloc or international organisation, or when raised in its own name as an independent national government. Are the big global economic questions resolved or, more realistically, are small but important steps taken most effectively in discussions between the largest economic blocs and, if so, how are they best influenced? Or does the intrinsic value of the insight or the proposition, whatever its origin and originator, bring advances to global policy? In which case, we might argue that it is the individual, or the individual university or some other body or grouping that is our key asset, and constitutional configurations are of far less significance.

Of great relevance and importance to the current constitutional debate, therefore, is the analysis of how Scottish economic thinking does and could evolve to influence UK Government, European Union and global economic thinking. How effectively do Scots' ideas and insights get communicated to the points of real decision-making power? And how does the voice of a very small economy fare when it stands in its own name: does it achieve a voice disproportionate to its size? Some of these questions can be better informed by an enhanced understanding of the institutional structures that would be expected to dominate global economic thinking over the coming decades and the role that Scotland might be anticipated to play in these under different constitutional arrangements. What, for example, would be Scotland's standing, participation, involvement and influence within the dominant international economic organisations of the International Monetary Fund, the World Bank, the World Trade Organisation, the Organisation for Economic Cooperation and Development, and the United Nations or, indeed, its influence upon the G7, G8, G20 communities to name but some? Or, in reality, do these structures play a small role in defining future directions?

Avery, Graham. (2012). Evidence to the House of Commons Select Committee on Foreign Affairs, 17 October 2012, www.publications. parliament.uk/pa/cm201213/ cmselect/cmfaff/writev/643/m05.htm

Bank of England, *Bank of England Legislation: The Charters of the Bank and Related Documents*. www. bankofengland.co.uk.

Bank of England. 1998. Bank of England Act (1998). www.legislation.gov.uk/ ukpga/1998/11/contents.

Bank of England. 1997. *Memorandum of Understanding between HM Treasury, the Bank of England and the Financial Services Authority*.

Commission on Scottish Devolution. 2009. *Serving Scotland Better: Scotland and the United Kingdom in the 21st Century: Final Report*. June.

Devo max illustration: www.bbc. co.uk/news/uk-scotland-scotland-politics-17094333.

Devo Plus Group. 2012. *A New Union: The Third Report of the Devo Plus Group*, November 2012. www. devoplus.com.

Feld, L.P., Zimmerman, H. & Doring, T. 2007. 'Fiscal federalism, decentralisation and economic growth', *in Public Economics and Public Choice*, (eds) Baake, P. & Borck, R.

Hallwood, C.P. & MacDonald, R. 2009. *The Political Economy of Financing Scottish Government: Considering a New Constitutional Settlement for Scotland*.

HM Treasury. 2010. *Budget 2010*. HMT. June.

HM Treasury. 2008. *The Government's Fiscal Framework*. HMT. November.

HM Treasury. 2012. Financial Services Bill 2012. http://www.hm-treasury. gov.uk/fin_financial_services_bill. htm.

House of Lords. 2012. Evidence of Sir Philip Hampton to the House of Lords Select Committee on Economic Affairs in its Inquiry on *The Economic Implications for the United Kingdom of Scottish Independence*. Evidence Session No. 15, 13 November 2012. www.parliament.uk/documents/ lords-committees/economic-affairs/ScottishIndependence/ ucEAC20121113Ev15.pdf.

Hughes Hallett, A. & Scott, D. 2010. *Scotland: A New Fiscal Settlement*, Centre for Dynamic Macroeconomic Analysis Working Paper Series. University of St Andrews. March.

Kay, J. 2012. *Minutes of Evidence*, The House of Commons, Scottish Affairs Committee. 14 March 2012: www.publications.parliament. uk/pa/cm201012/cmselect/ cmscotaf/1608/120314.htm.

Kay, J. 2012. *Evidence to the Inquiry on The Economic Implications for the UK of Scottish Independence*. The House of Lords, Select Committee on Economic Affairs. 22 May 2012. www.parliament.uk/documents/ lords-committees/economic-affairs/ ScottishIndependence/scottishindev. pdf.

Lee, Y. & Gordon, R.H. 2005. 'Tax structure and economic growth', *Journal of Public Economics*, 89.

Organisation for Economic Cooperation and Development. 2008. *Tax and Economic Growth*, Economics Department Working Paper No. 620, Åsa Johansson *et al*, July.

Panke, D (2010). *Small states in the European Union: coping with structural disadvantages*, Farnham, Ashgate.

Reform Scotland. 2011. *Evidence to the Scottish Parliament's Scotland Bill Committee*, September. www. devoplus.com/downloads/.

Roy, G. 2006. *Is Fiscal Decentralisation Good for Growth?* Fraser of Allander Institute Quarterly Economic Commentary, October.

Scotland Act (1998): www.legislation.gov. uk/ukpga/1998/46/contents.

Scotland Act (2012): www.legislation.gov.
uk/ukpga/2012/11/contents/enacted.

Scottish Executive. 2000. *The Way
Forward: Framework for Economic
Development in Scotland.* June.

Scottish Government. 2007. *The
Government Economic Strategy.*
November.

Scottish Government. 2009. *Fiscal
Autonomy in Scotland: The Case
for Change and Options for Reform.*
23 February 2009. www.scotland.gov.
uk/Publications/2009/02/23092643/6.

Scottish Government. 2009. *Your
Scotland, Your Voice: A National
Conversation, Scottish Government*
White Paper. November
2009. www.scotland.gov.uk/
Publications/2009/11/26155932/0.

Scottish Government. 2011. *The
Government Economic Strategy,*
September.

Scottish Government. 2012. *Government
Expenditure and Revenue, Scotland,
2010–11.* March.

Scottish Parliament, website on the work
of the Scotland Bill Committee,
2010–11. www.scottish.parliament.
uk/parliamentarybusiness/
PreviousCommittees/27025.aspx.

Scottish Parliament. 2011. *The 1st
Report, 2011 (Session 4), Report
on the Scotland Bill,* Scotland Bill
Committee. 15 December 2011.

Thießen, U. 2003. *Fiscal Decentralisation
and Economic Growth in High-Income
Countries,* Fiscal Studies, vol. 24,
no. 3.

Thorhallsson, B. & Wivel, A, 2006. Small
States in the European Union: What
do we know and what would we
like to know? *Cambridge Review of
International Affairs,* 19(4), 651-668

Ulph, D. 2011. *The Impact of Greater
Fiscal Autonomy,* mimeo. February.

UK Government. 2011. *The Budget
Responsibility and National Audit Act
2011.* March. www.legislation.gov.uk/
uksi/2011/2576/made.

CHAPTER 2

An Approach to the Economic Assessment of Constitutional Change
Professor Andrew Goudie[1]

2.1 THE SIX TESTS

This chapter looks at how a more structured approach to the assessment of the various constitutional proposals is possible, which can readily be deployed to explore and test the integrity, sustainability and value of the potential outcomes that might be generated by a proposition.

Importantly, the approach facilitates the testing of any constitutional proposition, whether the *status quo*, one of enhanced devolution within the United Kingdom, or one based upon political independence, although clearly some elements are more relevant to particular constitutional propositions than others. While the constitutional debate tends naturally to focus on the new propositions that are advanced, it is equally important to assess the present constitutional arrangement to allow the weaknesses and strengths of all the propositions to be understood in this comparative setting. This approach focuses only on the economic dimension of the constitutional propositions: it specifically takes no account of an array of other factors, whether political or social in nature, for example. There are, of course, many instances of different peoples legitimately choosing self-determination and an independence model irrespective of any economic arguments that were advanced at the time.

---

1 Visiting Professor and Special Adviser to the Principal, University of Strathclyde; former Chief Economic Adviser to the Scottish Government.

In the run-up to the establishment of the euro zone in 1999, there was an intensive debate in the UK focused on the appropriateness or not of the UK joining the European Union's new Economic and Monetary Union (EMU) and adopting the new common currency. Scotland faces a very different context and, in some ways, a more complex choice. Most strikingly, it is not faced by such a binary question but by a significantly wider set of fundamental choices[2].

Six Tests are set out here to crystallise the key challenges for Scotland in its economic analysis of potential constitutional change. The objective is not to simplistically see which constitutional arrangement would allow us to put a tick by each test, or, less demandingly, to have no strongly negative conclusions for any of the tests. Instead, the Six Tests are designed to answer the questions:

» how does any proposed constitutional arrangement[3] bear up when evaluated against these Tests?
» is the long-term economic sustainability of the Scottish economy secured under this constitutional arrangement, given the exceptional uncertainty and risks that most certainly exist when our time horizon is many decades?
» where are the relative strengths and vulnerabilities of the different proposals?

---

2   As a contribution to the debate, the UK Government of the day set out five tests that they considered to be central to the decision-making process and the ultimate choice. The tests were posited to answer a binary question: should the UK join the Economic and Monetary Union with a common currency or retain the *status quo*?

3   One obvious pre-requisite is, of course, that the constitutional option is sufficiently well defined to allow its detailed analysis and assessment. This condition has not always been met, as was noted earlier.

In summary, the Six Tests can be presented as:

Six Tests to evaluate proposals for constitutional change.

1. New Opportunities:
   › Would the proposed political and economic structure bring new economic, social and environmental opportunities that do not currently exist?
2. Cyclical compatibility and stability:
   › Are the business cycles and economic structures of the partners in any proposed monetary union compatible? How would the implications of incompatibility and the need for cyclical stabilisation be managed?
3. Long term competitiveness:
   › How would Scotland promote competitiveness and, if need be, restore competitiveness?
4. Resilience and managing global shocks:
   › Are there well developed means to manage significant global shocks?
5. Risk management and uncertainty:
   › Are the other primary risks and uncertainties of the proposal identified, and are there mechanisms through which they could be effectively managed?
6. Summary Test for proposals for constitutional change:
   a. Is the proposal fundamentally economically and financially stable?
   b. Would the proposal enhance the capacity to promote the primary objectives of economic policy ?

2.3 THE SIX TESTS IN DETAIL

Each of these Tests necessarily encompasses a complex set of underlying issues and here we set out some of the primary ones that they raise.

2.3.1 *New opportunities: would the proposed political and economic structure bring new economic, social and environmental opportunities that do not currently exist?*

» *Macroeconomic opportunities*: would the new constitutional arrangement bring an improved macroeconomic environment: does it, in principle, provide a more stable and more sustainable economic context for the promotion of the key objectives of government?

» *New policy opportunities*: are there policy choices that are more appropriate to Scotland that could be exploited and which would accelerate progress towards the key objectives – whether environmental, social, and sustainable economic growth objectives?

» *Private sector development*: would it generate a more dynamic private sector and facilitate an enhanced contribution from the public sector to these objectives?

» *Accountability and decentralisation*: does it bring greater decentralisation of economic policy and greater political accountability?

» *Constraints to opportunities*: where would the internal and externally imposed limitations on policy constrain these opportunities?

» *Scale*: are the new powers and levers significant in scale and potential effectiveness?

The essence of this Test focuses on the key question of the extent to which the extension of economic powers provides an opportunity to substantively enhance Scotland's performance. If there is one overarching purpose in all the propositions that are advanced for further constitutional development, it is the belief that new opportunities can be created within Scotland, through the adoption of new or different economic powers, that the current constitutional arrangement in some way inhibits. For this reason, this Test is at the core of this debate. It is, moreover, the creation of *real* opportunities that is key: opportunities that are politically, financially and economically feasible and which take full account of their overall impact on the economy and do not merely rest on a partial analysis that abstracts from the wider implications of the policy. These should, in addition, be opportunities for which the weight of evidence and knowledge supports the identified outcome, and not ones that simply rest on assertion or the weakest of evidence. These are powerful conditions for the acceptance of opportunities as both being feasible and having outcomes that are indeed probable.

In this publication, the early chapters look in detail at the macroeconomic considerations that arise with constitutional change and particularly at the stability and sustainability of the possible policy environments. The later chapters consider how new opportunities and risks might arise within these alternative macroeconomic frameworks to address the primary objectives of government.

Within the context of this Test, the specific questions and challenges outlined above form an obvious focus. Self-evidently, a greater set of economic powers brings with it the potential to use a greater array of economic policy instruments that, from a partial perspective, could enhance the capacity to provide an economic environment that is conducive to a significant improvement in performance. Against this must be set the degree to which the extending of those same powers might induce a different, if not more challenging, set of economic problems that policy must then address. The *net* value of any single power transferring to the Scottish Parliament may therefore be indeterminate and, when the consideration focuses on the transfer of a complex configuration of many economic powers, the net impact will be all the more problematic.

A common thread that should run through the analysis of all the constitutional proposals is, therefore, the specific policy opportunities that might be made available by the transference of additional powers. This analysis must, however, take account of questions of affordability and the opportunity cost of any single policy choice, as well as the anticipated net impacts of policy on the outcome objectives, given the existing knowledge and evidence relating to the effectiveness of policy. As discussed in chapter 1, the likely limitations and constraints on policy, both internally- and externally-imposed in the real world, form a key consideration here.

2.3.2 *Cyclical compatibility and stability: are the business cycles and economic structures of the partners in any proposed monetary union compatible? How would the implications of incompatibility and the need for cyclical stabilisation be managed?*

» *Economic fundamentals*: are the economic and financial fundamentals of all the members of any proposed monetary union compatible and stable?
» *Monetary policy*: is the monetary policy of any monetary union (and, especially, the policy interest of the dominant partners) consistently compatible with the monetary needs of the Scottish economy?
» *Compensating mechanisms*: if monetary policy in any monetary union were not always appropriate for the Scottish economy, what are the compensating mechanisms available to Scotland?
» *Stabilisation policy*: how would economic stabilisation be secured?
» *Wider policy context*: how would Scotland manage other policy decisions within any monetary union that are not seen as appropriate for Scotland?

Of the Tests set out in this chapter, this Test explicitly relates to the constitutional options that entail membership of either the sterling or the EMU. These options raise a set of challenges that have taken on a greater significance since the onset of the euro crisis, with more substantive reservations now being expressed with regard to the conditions necessary for the continued stability and sustainability of not only the EMU, but also other possible monetary unions.

The importance of different economies sharing a similar cyclical profile if they are operating within the same monetary union has been asserted for many years. The crisis of the euro zone in recent years has only served to reinforce this point. The severe financial difficulties of many economies have, at least in part, been attributable to the inappropriateness of policy over a protracted period for those particular economies. Policies, determined in response to the economic context and requirements of the more dominant, and typically larger, economies of the euro zone, are seen to have been not benign but positively damaging to the peripheral economies for which the economic pressures were quite different. The example of interest rate determination is one of the best documented for which a common policy was clearly ill suited to a group of economies experiencing significantly different economic cycles and macroeconomic pressures. The experience of the Irish and Spanish economies over the years preceding the crisis is a good case in point. Here, the impact of EMU-wide monetary policy and, notably, of the prevailing levels of interest rates on economic incentives and behaviours were seen to be highly destabilising, with consequent adverse impacts on key national markets.

The convergence of economic performance, and particularly of cyclical performance, has long been seen as a key prerequisite for the successful admission to any monetary union. Indeed, the original five euro-convergence criteria[4], that were established as the Maastricht criteria in the Maastricht Treaty[5] of February 1992, set the conditions for the entry of European Union member-states into the third stage of the Economic and Monetary Union and for the adoption of the euro as their currency. In the light of subsequent events, however, it could be argued that the recent crisis of the euro zone demonstrates the shortcomings of these original Maastricht criteria and indeed, in addition, of the Growth and Stability Pact[6] that sought to maintain stability and convergence after entry into the EMU. Not only were there significant breaches of the Pact even prior to the euro crisis, but it can be advanced that the convergence criteria and the Pact were both inadequate in the degree to which they sought to ensure a continuing process of convergence in economic performance and maintain a union for which macroeconomic policy was broadly appropriate across all the member states of the euro zone.

The UK Government clearly held the view in the late 1990s and early 2000s that not only were the convergence requirements prior to entry of critical importance, but that the Maastricht criteria were too

---

4   The five Maastricht criteria for EMU entry were:
   1. Inflation rates. No more than 1.5 percentage points higher than the average of the three best performing member states of the EU.
   2. Government finance: Annual government deficit. The ratio of the annual government deficit to gross domestic product (GDP) must not exceed 3% at the end of the preceding fiscal year. If not, it is at least required to reach a level close to 3%. Exceptional and temporary excesses would only be granted for exceptional cases.
   3. Government finance: Government debt. The ratio of gross government debt to GDP must not exceed 60% at the end of the preceding fiscal year. Even if the target cannot be achieved due to the specific conditions, the ratio must have sufficiently diminished and must be approaching the reference value at a satisfactory pace.
   4. Exchange rate: Applicant countries should have joined the exchange-rate mechanism (ERM II) under the European Monetary System (EMS) for two consecutive years and should not have devalued its currency during the period.
   5. Long-term interest rates: The nominal long-term interest rate must not be more than 2 percentage points higher than in the three lowest inflation member states.
5   See, for example, the European Commission:
   europa.eu/legislation__summaries/institutional__affairs/treaties/treaties__ maastricht__en.htm
6   The Growth and Stability Pact was adopted in 1997 so that fiscal discipline would be maintained and enforced in the EMU. The actual criteria that member states were required to respect were:
   »   an annual budget deficit no higher than 3% of GDP (this includes the sum of all public budgets, including municipalities, regions etc.)
   »   a national debt lower than 60% of GDP or approaching that value.

narrow in scope, as the UK Government's adoption and monitoring of progress against its five tests demonstrated. Failure to converge prior to admission, or very slow convergence upon admission, were argued to have the capacity to seriously derail the transition process and bring significant costs. Consequently, it was of paramount importance to the UK that convergence was both sustainable and durable.

Interestingly, one strand of the literature on optimal currency areas (OCAs) has accorded less significance to the condition that convergence should precede membership of a monetary union. Instead, it has been argued[7] that entry into the monetary union has itself promoted greater integration and convergence, thereby reducing the asynchronous fluctuations in demand and incomes. In contrast, however, other writers[8] have reached the opposite conclusion, arguing that even a stable monetary union may become less of an optimal currency area if the nations and regions within it become increasingly more specialised and diversified over time. Certainly, the UK Government in 1997 clearly rejected any notion of weakening the condition, arguing that 'it is not safe to assume that the act of joining the monetary union would automatically trigger convergence'.

In practice, these more forward-looking dynamic processes have received less attention, particularly in the political debates that have dominated, with the focus falling typically on the immediate process of convergence and the supposed need to achieve this prior to entry to a monetary union. In this context, the analysis of convergence has focused not only on the point in the economic cycle that a potential entrant might have reached, relative to the existing monetary union in the immediate run-up to entry, but also on the past cyclical patterns, including their degree of synchronisation and the relative volatility and amplitude of the cycles.[9]

Notwithstanding the importance that has been ascribed to the convergence process, it is self-evident that periods of divergence and policy sub-optimality are entirely predictable for any member of the union, if the long term is the time horizon of interest. The key policy challenge is, therefore, how the implications of dissimilarity in performance and divergence in the policy interests of individual members of a monetary union would be managed. How would national stabilisation policy be handled within the union in the

---

7 As, for example, in Frankel and Rose (1998) and Frankel (1999). The latter argues that the OCA criteria may be satisfied *ex post*, even if not *ex ante*.

8 As, for example, has been argued by Eichengreen (1992) and Krugman (1993), where it is suggested that the OCA criteria may not be satisfied *ex post*, even if satisfied *ex ante*.

9 These perspectives on convergence have typically been analysed using GDP, unemployment, inflation and output gap indicators.

absence of exchange rate and monetary policy instruments? And how are policies at the level of the monetary union that are deemed divergent from the cyclical interests of the member state to be mitigated by national policy decisions in order to maintain stability at the level?

An emphasis on not only achieving convergence, but equally on sustainability and – perhaps most importantly in the real world – the rectification of divergent trends is crucial. Differing underlying economic structures and behaviours have long been seen as contributing to the divergence in response across economies to common policies set for a monetary union. Distinctive patterns of behaviour and performance in key markets – as, for instance, in the housing market and with regard to personal savings and corporate funding preferences – have provided good examples of how fundamental structural differences can generate significant questions with respect to policy appropriateness. Recent economic shocks may, indeed, have significantly exacerbated the scale of this problem, if future patterns of underlying economic behaviour and performance have further diverged.

The constitutional choices that embrace monetary union offer different solutions to the management of problems of stabilisation and to compensating mechanisms in the event that union-wide policy diverges from the perceived national need. While membership of a union may bring other significant benefits, many highlight the loss of key powers over the exchange rate and over monetary policy, leaving fiscal policy powers as the primary set of instruments at their disposal to handle these challenges. In contrast, others have highlighted the source of disturbance that the adoption of a Scottish currency might bring and the likelihood of this factor outweighing the potential gains from having an additional instrument with which to manage economic adjustment.

There are therefore two different sets of challenges at the national level here: first, how to bring about greater convergence in the shorter term prior to membership of a monetary union, if this is ultimately the preferred constitutional choice;[10] and, second, how to manage questions of national cyclical variation and stabilisation within a monetary union. To the extent that national cyclical patterns are similar to those of the union as a whole, or shared with the key economies that dominate union policy-making, cyclical variation may be mitigated by the monetary and exchange rate policies of the union

10 One interesting and important question here, with respect to a possible independent Scotland wishing to join the EMU, is how it might satisfy the entry criteria, especially if it were within the sterling monetary union. The fourth criteria (see footnote 4 above) would appear to pose a challenge, unless the criteria were redefined to allow for this circumstance.

as a whole. But the identification of policy options at the national level in the presence of asynchronous cycles within the union is a more challenging question.

Finally, it is worth noting the specific circumstances of the Scottish economy in this context. While the challenges raised above are undoubtedly fundamental to the present problems within the EMU, the nature of a monetary union that might be anticipated between Scotland and a redefined UK post-independence would be quite different to that, for example, between Germany and Greece.

The evidence suggests that Scotland would be substantially more convergent with a redefined UK than are many countries within the EU. Determining whether or not Scotland would form an optimal currency area with the redefined UK may be problematic. However, it would seem that Scotland and a redefined UK are probably closer in reality to the theoretical propositions of an OCA[11] than other areas that are already deemed to be such, because of the existence over three hundred years of an integrated economy. Interestingly, the Netherlands and Germany effectively operated a currency union throughout the period of the European Exchange Rate Mechanism, and Belgium and Luxembourg similarly formed a currency union for over eighty years prior to the establishment of the euro. The key point is whether or not such a high degree of integration would be maintained post-independence.

2.3.3 Long-term competitiveness: how would Scotland promote competitiveness and, if need be, restore competitiveness?

» within a monetary union, in the absence of its own currency and monetary policy, what are the adjustment mechanisms that Scotland could deploy, if required, to restore competitiveness and balanced economic growth?
» with its own currency, how would competitiveness be promoted?
» what are the implications for the sectors with a current comparative advantage (for example, for universities, energy, financial sector) of the UK and EU Single Markets? And what are the implications for capital and labour mobility?

If the underlying motivation for constitutional change is the potential benefits that might accrue over many decades, the primary concern must be with issues of flexibility and responsiveness to longer-term global economic developments. With a preference for Scotland to

---

11   See section 2.5 below.

be within a monetary union, this implies a more complex challenge than seeking convergence to a known, or relatively known, economic performance and cyclical pattern within the existing union, important though this may be. Concerns over convergence and current synchronisation are shorter-term, transitional issues; concerns over flexibility and adaptability in the face of competitive pressures are of critical long-term significance for any future constitutional arrangement. Some of these pressures may emerge inexorably over time and bring only a gradual erosion of national comparative advantage; others may have a more sudden onset, even if foreseen in principle.

Over the long term, challenges to the national economy's existing comparative advantage are entirely predictable, albeit the exact form of that competition may not be known with certainty. The rapid economic development of the newly emerging economies – notably, of China, Brazil, India and Russia[12] – has already led to a significant erosion of developed economies' economic advantage and the expectation must be that this competition will only intensify. It is, moreover, not confined to the mass production of products, which was once seen as the primary source of competition from emerging economies, but, as the educational and research achievements in these economies continue to advance at an immense pace, competition is already being encountered in the most knowledge intensive markets too.

Potential global competition is not confined though to the emerging economies. Indeed, most, if not all, of the constitutional choices incorporate a preference for the membership of international organisations that are committed increasingly to the opening up of markets which raises the prospect of further competitive challenge. The World Trade Organisation is specifically focused in its remit to establishing a global trading system that lowers trade barriers through negotiation and applies the principle of non-discrimination, with the intention of reducing the costs of production and the prices of finished goods and services, and ultimately securing a lower cost of living.

Of more immediate importance to the constitutional debate are the choices that entail membership of a monetary union in which the single market is a primary policy objective, as is evident both for the UK and EU monetary unions. In these contexts, the promotion of a dynamic economic environment that acknowledges the continual need to drive greater competitiveness in the anticipation of an ever intensifying pressure is crucial.

The analysis of the present euro crisis and its origins remains highly contentious at this time, but there is a strong strand of thinking

---

12 In 2012 this set of countries was responsible for about 18% of the world's Gross Domestic Product and around 40% of the global population.

that the monetary union masked many of the underlying problems of competitiveness that both existed at the start and were then allowed to develop further. Comparisons of long-term German economic performance relative to that of Greece and other peripheral economies have been highlighted as demonstrating the increasing disparity in the underlying performance of member states. The emergence of uncompetitiveness in many economies appears to have resulted from a progressive divergence in both macroeconomic and microeconomic performance. Cumulative divergences in inflationary performance and in earnings growth, with consequent disparities emerging in productivity and in unit labour costs, were at the root of the competitive decline. But, in addition, microeconomic stagnation arguably played a central role. Failure to compete on product quality, price and non-price elements, as well as on market reform, were equally corrosive. The reforms in both the public and private sectors were seen to be inadequate to meet the growing competitive pressure of neighbouring economies, as were the weaknesses in the fundamental innovation systems which failed to deliver the necessary dynamic and progressive development that was critical. As noted earlier, these failures were exacerbated by euro zone-wide policies that may have been appropriate to the monetary union as a whole, but were arguably generating increasingly unsustainable economic structures and economic behaviours in some national economies. Far too little attention was focused on the long-term performance and competitiveness of the individual member state within the economic and monetary union and on the substantive imbalances that were cumulating between the different members.

Outwith a monetary union, these imbalances and divergences tend to manifest themselves both more rapidly and more visibly, generating the need for a response, while, within a union – and, particularly, in the case of the smaller partners – they tend to remain relatively obscured and impose less of an immediate pressure on economic management.

It is apparent, therefore, that under each proposed constitutional arrangement, these challenges of long-term competitiveness are critical and the configurations of policy powers are a key element in addressing them.

In all these varied economic environments, the capacity to counter these competitive pressures and maintain areas of economic advantage is crucial. Different constitutional powers bring alternative available instruments, and determining the capacity to respond and manage this key area is a central concern. In the later chapters the implications of the constitutional choice for the securing of long-term economic objectives is considered further, particularly in the light of the need to establish a continual comparative advantage and secure long-term competiveness.

2.3.4 Resilience and managing global shocks: are there well-developed means to manage significant global shocks?

» what capacity is there to manage external shocks and through what mechanisms?
» would the economy be able to demonstrate flexibility, adaptability and responsiveness?
» would the relatively small Scottish economy, with large domestically based (financial) companies, require international support to manage financial shocks?
» how would the implications of being a resource-based and small open economy be managed?

One specific concern relates to global economic developments that are both sudden and powerful in their onset. Such economic shocks might be unforeseen, although they may also be anticipated at some future time, but without any clear understanding of when precisely they will occur.

While over the long term, it is necessarily highly problematic and speculative from where a shock of this type might originate, it is not difficult to identify such shocks over past decades. In the 1970s there were the well-documented oil shocks, most notable of which was that initiated by the decision of Middle Eastern oil producers to introduce an embargo on oil supplies to the USA and other western countries in retaliation for the USA's support for Israel during the Yom Kippur war of October 1973. In consequence, there was a quadrupling of crude oil prices from $3 to $12 per barrel by 1974, with significant impacts on inflation and on demand throughout the global economy. The size of these impacts was clearly driven by the size of the shock, both in terms of the increase in nominal and real oil prices, by the persistence of the shock and by the dependence on oil as a source of energy. They were also related to the policy response of the monetary and fiscal authorities in many countries. Some initial policy responses merely exacerbated the shock. What it did demonstrate was not only the importance of the policy response but the equally important underlying economic structure and the vulnerability to such a shock due to established patterns of energy dependence and consumption.

From this perspective, the significance of the constitutional powers and the associated economic policies of each nation is clear, both with regard to its ability to define appropriate macroeconomic policy to address such shocks and to define longer-term economic strategy that reduces the fundamental vulnerability of the economy to major external shock.

More recently, the financial crisis that erupted in 2008 is now seen as the most dominant shock to the global economic system since at least the 1930s. Once again, the macroeconomic response to the crisis, and equally to the deep and very protracted period of recession and stagnation that has followed, has been highly contentious. It has highlighted both the fundamental divergence in policy thinking and the limitations on nations to respond, depending on their constitutional status and their economic and financial powers. The relative merits or otherwise of the capacity to take advantage of exchange rate flexibility, as compared to benefiting from the stability of a common currency, have surfaced in an extreme form, as have the merits of less austere adjustment paths compared to the more rapid paths adopted in other economies. Indeed, considerable divergence is evident across the euro zone and, more generally, across Europe, where different constitutional models have opened up the possibility of different macro responses.

The more microeconomic dimension of the crisis has equally highlighted the critical interplay between constitutional form and economic management, most notably in the handling of the companies within the financial sector that have experienced severe difficulty and in defining the most appropriate policy response. Considerations around *the too big to fail* challenge, together with the associated questions of, first, how to minimise the moral hazard that is inherent in many policy responses and, second, where the real financial responsibility should lie when massive international financial institutions collapse, have rightly played a critical role in the constitutional debate. As the experiences in Ireland and Iceland, with their specific structural configurations in the banking sector, have demonstrated, for example, small economies undoubtedly face a different set of issues. These are explored further in chapter 1 and subsequent chapters.

Even these few, highly selective examples demonstrate the importance of monetary and fiscal policy at the onset of external shocks and during the management of the repercussions of those shocks. The set of available economic powers that can be brought to bear on both the more immediate macroeconomic challenge and the longer-term challenges that result from an underlying vulnerability to potential external shock is therefore a crucial issue. These necessary powers and the key policy instruments may, of course, reside in more than one jurisdiction, but understanding how they can combine to address the shock is an integral part of the economic risk management.

Moreover, while they have the capacity to mitigate the shocks, it is also clear that there are examples of how inappropriate policy responses can themselves be a factor in the exacerbation of ensuing crisis. This is, therefore, an interesting example of a more general point referred to earlier; namely, that, while the constitutional powers that a state may have at its disposal are crucial to its capacity to respond, it is also the manner in which those powers are deployed that is critical. This may seem an obvious point, but it is highly relevant to any analysis of whether poor past performance is attributable more to the absence of good policy or to the absence of appropriate powers, and why future performance is not simplistically linked to the choice of powers.

2.3.5 Risk management and uncertainty: are the other primary risks and uncertainties of the proposal identified, and are there mechanisms through which they could be effectively managed?

As has been noted repeatedly, and as is apparent in the Tests outlined above, it is impossible to escape from a world of considerable uncertainty. Over the long term, this is scarcely surprising, but it has been demonstrated that even the very short term is highly uncertain. Highlighting the importance of these risks and the imperative to have thought through the management of these risks, insofar as they can be anticipated, is critical: hence the value of identifying a distinct Test from this perspective.

Uncertainty clearly derives from a wide array of sources, not least the global economic environment, including the policy stance of the more proximate economic partners, and the direction and speed with which it evolves. The form of the uncertainty that is the focus of interest here, however, derives from the lack of clarity surrounding the precise form that different constitutional models might take and to the negotiation process that would determine the model. These questions were extensively discussed in chapter 1. Many of these risks are implicit above, but good risk management would suggest the value of sharply identifying the manner in which they are handled. As was observed before, many of these elements not only lie at the heart of the constitutional debate but may well remain highly uncertain throughout the period preceding a referendum on whether to pursue constitutional change. Indeed, they may only be resolved and clarified post-referendum as the hard negotiations take place.

Purely by way of illustration, a few of the key uncertainties that should dominate the thinking over constitutional change are set out below. Many more could be added to this list as was evident from the breadth of the issues raised in chapter 1, but these examples amply indicate the importance of managing the risks that surround the current proposals and of defining alternative contingency strategies.

» *Dependence on other jurisdictions*: what is the dependence on the political and economic institutions and decisions of other jurisdictions?
» *Fiscal conditionality*: is the fiscal conditionality that any monetary union would bring politically acceptable?
» *Lender of last resort role*: would Scotland's financial sector institutions need a lender of last resort? What bodies might, in principle, play that role and upon what terms?
» *Fiscal volatility*: does the change bring greater fiscal volatility and how would it be managed?
» *Debt management*: what role would borrowing play and how would debt policy and market risk be handled?
» *Risk pooling*: what would be the implications for the pooling of risk?
» *Transitional and permanent costs*: would the costs of transition pose a substantive problem and does the proposal imply significant long-term additional costs to Government and business?

2.3.6 *Summary test for potential proposals for reform*

a. is the new proposal fundamentally economically and financially stable?
b. would the proposal enhance the capacity to promote the primary objectives of economic policy?

The final test has the great attribute that it refocuses the thinking back to the two elements that ultimately may be seen as most critical: first, the stability of the economic and financial basis of any proposed constitutional model; and, second, the capacity of that new model to enhance progress towards the objectives of Scottish society.

2.4 THE SIX TESTS: CONCLUDING THOUGHT

This set of Six Tests is central to the constitutional choice and to the macroeconomic framework that is subsequently selected. Weighing the various elements of this complex picture to form an overall perspective is far more complex than is sometimes suggested. As was observed earlier, it would be surprising if any single constitutional proposal uniformly stood up to these Tests, therefore immediately making the question of the relative value of different proposals significantly more problematic.

One example is particularly relevant. As Test 1 suggests, one key motivation for seeking to identify the most supportive constitutional form is to secure the best opportunities to promote economic dynamism over the long term. However, to the extent that any proposed constitutional arrangement increases the likelihood of economic vulnerability and of economic uncertainty, the net benefit of the change becomes substantively harder to identify. For example, would problems of competitiveness be exacerbated or the probability of external shocks be increased by a proposal? And would these economic risks be outweighed by the new opportunities that change presented? And, most importantly, how can these types of conflicting repercussions of constitutional change be analysed?

Finally, we note the fundamental dilemma of determining how we weigh the greater – albeit, in all probability, constrained – ability to self-determine economic policy, both to seek enhanced economic opportunity and to manage economic problems and crises, relative to the greater assurance of international collaboration and support in creating collective economic opportunity and in managing national risk and adversity.

2.5 THE TESTS IN THE CONTEXT OF MONETARY UNION

The Six Tests, and the crucial questions that they stimulate, have relevance across all the constitutional arrangements that might be advanced. However, to the extent that they are focused on the constitutional options that embrace monetary union, either with the sterling or euro areas, they equally reflect the long-standing debate over the conditions that are argued to underpin the sustainability of optimal currency areas (OCAs). The literature in this regard is extensive, as have been the attempts to apply its insights to the question of the appropriateness of the UK seeking membership of the EMU. One study,[13] while primarily focused on the case for UK entry into the EMU, also included some discussion of Scotland's standing as a potential optimal currency area.

---

13 Optimal Currency Areas: Why Does The Exchange Rate Regime Matter? Willem H. Buiter. Sixth Royal Bank of Scotland and Scottish Economic Society Annual Lecture. October 1999.

Much of the OCA debate still focuses around the original two contributions of Robert Mundell;[14] the first in a more static framework with stationary expectations[15] and the second with its explicit incorporation of uncertainty, and particularly that of exchange rate uncertainty, and its insight into the potential benefits of international risk sharing within a monetary union.[16] The two studies have ultimately contributed to a somewhat inconclusive discussion of the sustainability and benefits of the EMU, in particular, and of monetary unions, more generally, with different thinkers reaching contrasting conclusions on the basis of these works.[17] Nonetheless, many of the principal elements of the early thinking have continued to exert a strong influence. For example, the five tests[18] that the UK adopted in 1997 against which to assess the option of EMU entry were clearly rooted in the OCA thinking, although they appear to be a more ad hoc interpretation of that debate. They certainly reflected some, but not all, of the original criteria outlined by Mundell in 1961, although

---

14 (i) 'A Theory of Optimal Currency Areas', Robert A. Mundell. American Economic Review, 51, 1961. (ii) Uncommon Arguments for Common Currencies, Robert A. Mundell. In H.G. Johnson and A.K Swoboda, The Economics of Common Currencies, Allen & Unwin, 1973.

15 The primary conditions in considering the case for a monetary union or for the retention of a national currency have been variously set out (see, for example, Mundell (1961) and Buiter (1999)). They have focused on: the degree of nominal price and cost rigidity; the degree of labour and capital mobility across economies; the likelihood of asymmetric, nation-specific shocks that bring asymmetric impacts; the diversity of national economic structures and transmission mechanisms; the openness of trade; the provision for significant international fiscal transfers; and the degree of diversification in production and demand.

16 Buiter (1999) highlights two weaknesses of the conventional OCA literature, with its roots in the earlier 1961 work of Mundell: the failure to distinguish between the nominal and real exchange rate and the failure to consider the implications of significant international financial integration and the associated disruptive potential of exchange rate flexibility in the modern global economy.

17 Interesting reflections on the debate appear for example in Optimum Currency Areas and the European Experience, Ronald McKinnon, Stanford University, 2001; and in Optimal Currency Areas: Why Does The Exchange Rate Regime Matter? Willem H. Buiter, Sixth Royal Bank of Scotland/Scottish Economic Society Annual Lecture, October 1999.

18 The UK's Five Tests (UK Membership of the Single Currency: An Assessment of the Five Tests. HM Treasury, October 1997) were defined to be:
    1. Cyclical convergence: are business cycles and economic structures compatible, so that we and others could live comfortably with euro interest rates on a permanent basis?
    2. Flexibility: if problems emerge, is there sufficient flexibility to deal with them?
    3. Investment: would joining EMU create better conditions for firms making long-term decisions to invest in Britain?
    4. Financial Services: what impact would entry into EMU have on the competitive position of the UK's financial services industry, particularly the City's wholesale markets?
    5. Employment and growth: in summary, will joining EMU promote higher growth, stability and a lasting increase in jobs?

they, additionally, included more specific conditions, notably with regard to securing the future prosperity of the UK financial services sector and to protecting the contribution of inward investment into the British economy.

The core of the debate has focused on the efficacy of the potential mechanisms of adjustment within a monetary union. In particular, the role of market flexibility and the rapidity and effectiveness of market responses to emerging pressures and imbalances continue to dominate the discussion, both with regard to product and labour markets and the role of foreign exchange markets. In essence, the management of asymmetric shocks remains a central issue, with its focus on the potential value of the exchange rate as a key adjustment mechanism outwith a monetary union and on the other potential adjustment processes within a monetary union, including the sharing of risk and of the adjustment itself.

In contrast to the earlier writings that focused on the potential value of the emerging EMU and the insights that the academic literature could bring to the complex decision-making at that time, the current debate has the benefit of the experience of the operation of the Economic and Monetary Union over the past fourteen years. More specifically, this experience encompasses both the first decade of relative stability and consolidation, together with the period since the financial crisis and, more pertinently, the onset of the subsequent and ongoing euro crisis. This has provided a wealth of new experience against which to test both the previous thinking and any new propositions regarding monetary union or the future development of existing unions. Unsurprisingly, the interpretation of the current crisis is far from conclusive, not least because the crisis has yet to resolve itself and the appropriate policy response is therefore unproven.

2.6 CONCLUSION

As was noted earlier, the Six Tests are designed to answer the questions:

» how does any proposed constitutional arrangement bear up when evaluated against these Tests?
» is the long-term economic sustainability of the Scottish economy secured under this constitutional arrangement, given the exceptional uncertainty and risks that most certainly exist when our time horizon is many decades?
» where are the relative strengths and vulnerabilities of the different proposals?

REFERENCES

Buiter, Willem H. 1999. Optimal Currency Areas: Why Does The Exchange Rate Regime Matter? Sixth Royal Bank of Scotland/Scottish Economic Society Annual Lecture, October.

Eichengreen, Barry. 1992. 'Should the Maastricht Treaty be saved?', Princeton Studies in International Finance, Princeton University, no. 74, December.

European Commission. Detail of the Maastricht Treaty is available on the Commission web site: europa.eu/legislation__summaries/institutional__affairs/treaties/treaties__maastricht__en.htm

Frankel, Jeffrey & Rose, Andrew. 1998. 'The endogeneity of the optimum currency area criterion', Economic Journal, 108, July.

Frankel, Jeffrey. 1999. 'No single currency regime is right for all countries or at all times', Princeton Essays in International Finance, Princeton University, no. 215, August.

HM Treasury. 1997. UK Membership of the Single Currency: An Assessment of the Five Tests. October.

Krugman, Paul. 1993. 'Lessons of Massachusetts for EMU', in Torres, F. & Giavazzi, F. (eds) Adjustment for Growth in the European Monetary Union. Cambridge University Press, New York.

McGregor, Peter & Swales, Kim. 2012. The Impact of a Devolved Corporation Tax to Scotland, paper presented at the British and Irish Regional Science Association meeting in Galway. August.

McKinnon, Ronald. 2001. Optimum Currency Areas and the European Experience, Stanford University.

Mundell, Robert A. 1961. 'A theory of optimal currency areas', American Economic Review, 51.

Mundell, Robert A. 1973. Uncommon Arguments for Common Currencies, in Johnson, H.G. & Swoboda, A.K. The Economics of Common Currencies, Allen & Unwin.

CHAPTER 3

Currency and Monetary Policy Options for an Independent Scotland
Professor John Kay[1]

The choice of currency would be the most important economic decision for an independent Scotland. All aspects of economic policy,
including fiscal and monetary arrangements, are contingent on that
choice, which would have to be made in consultation with the UK
and the European Union, and would require their agreement or at
least acquiescence.

Destabilising speculation would begin as soon as a referendum
vote went in favour with businesses and financial market participants
positioning themselves to benefit from, or at least avoid loss from, the
changes. A decision by the Scottish Government could not therefore
be long delayed, although the final outcome would depend on negotiation. Such a decision would not be irrevocable, but the opportunity
for an independent Scotland to reconsider its currency options poses
problems as well as offering opportunities.

3.1 PRECEDENTS

Ireland achieved legal economic independence from the UK in 1922.
The newly independent country continued to use the pound sterling
as if no change had occurred. Irish commercial banks, like those of
Scotland but unlike those of England, issued their own notes, and
continued to do so. This note issue was completely backed by holdings of UK government securities. The Irish pound came into being
six years later, its value equal to the UK pound. On behalf of the Irish
government Irish pound notes were issued by a currency board, and
that issue was also entirely covered by holdings of UK government
securities.

Only in 1943 did Ireland elevate its currency board to the status
of a Central Bank. Irish pounds continued to trade at parity with
sterling until 1979. Until that date British notes circulated in Ireland,

---

1 Visiting Professor, London School of Economics and Fellow, St John's College,
Oxford.

and notes issued by the Republic of Ireland were widely used in Northern Ireland. After the general move to floating exchange rates in the early 1970s, the maintenance of parity became less certain. In 1979 the link was broken, and the Irish pound became part of the European Monetary System. There was a widespread expectation in Ireland that the Irish pound would trade at a premium to the pound sterling. It did not. Irish pounds fluctuated in value, at a discount to sterling, until in 1999 Ireland became a founder member of the euro zone.

Such a leisurely timescale of economic adaptation to changes in constitutional arrangements is no longer possible. The pace and volume of activity in financial markets has increased beyond the imagination of the bankers and policymakers of the 1920s to 1970s. Any possibility of change in the value of the Scottish currency – whether or not such a change was desired by the Scottish government – would have substantial effects on the value of assets and liabilities held by individuals living in Scotland and businesses operating in Scotland. These individuals and businesses would attempt to position themselves to maximise the resulting gains and minimise the associated losses. The effects would be aggravated by speculative activity by traders and other individuals who might have no other connection with Scotland.

When Czechoslovakia broke up in 1992, negotiators for the new Czech and Slovak republics decided to defer the settlement of currency issues. This arrangement broke down almost immediately. The Czech Republic was perceived as economically stronger than Slovakia, and there were substantial transfers of funds from accounts in the Slovak region to accounts in the Czech region even before the two areas became distinct countries. Less than three weeks after the formal split, the two new states made a secret agreement to introduce separate currencies, and this was in turn implemented three weeks later. The Slovak crown immediately traded at a discount to the Czech crown. (In 2009 Slovakia joined the euro at an exchange rate of about 30 Slovak crowns to the euro. The Czech crown maintains a separate existence, and one euro is currently worth around 25 Czech crowns).

The breakup of Czechoslovakia occurred only three years after the collapse of communism and neither country had a developed or sophisticated financial system. The two successor states were of broadly similar size. The Scottish situation is different in both respects. Scotland has a financial sector which is internationally active but Scotland accounts for less than ten per cent of UK economic activity. The appropriate currency arrangements for an independent or autonomous Scotland would need to be settled well

in advance of the implementation of constitutional changes if destabilising consequences for finance and investment within Scotland
were to be avoided.

An independent Scotland would have three principal currency
options:

1. Scotland could adopt the euro;
2. Scotland could retain the pound sterling either by agreement
   or through unilateral action;
3. Scotland could adopt its own currency.

Each of these three possibilities contains a variety of sub-options.

There are day-to-day practical advantages of adopting a common
currency wherever there is extensive movement of individuals, goods
and capital. A single currency avoids transaction costs for individuals
and for business and the commercial uncertainties that arise from fluc-
tuating exchange rates. But these gains are obtained at a price. If there
are differences in political and economic conditions between parts of
a common currency zone, economic adjustments that might otherwise have taken place through changes in exchange rates will have to
be effected in other ways – through reductions in nominal wages and
prices or by fiscal transfers within the common currency zone.

In the absence of a political union or other basis for subsidy of
weak regions, the desirability of a common currency depends on the
similarity of economic conditions between the potential members of
the currency zone and the extent of trade between them – a subject
which has been for long discussed amongst economists under the
heading of 'optimal currency areas'. Seen in this way, the arrangement that best meets the criteria for an optimal currency area is
the *status quo*. If the decision were purely economic, the desirable
outcome would be that Scotland would continue to use the pound
sterling. But economics mingles here with politics.

3.2 SCOTLAND AND THE EURO

The euro is formally the currency of the European Union and members are required to prepare for its adoption. Unless, implausibly,
Scotland simply inherited the opt-outs from the Maastricht Treaty
obtained by the UK, Scotland would be expected to move towards
euro zone membership. These issues are discussed further in chapter
5 by Charles Goodhart.

If Scotland did join the euro zone, monetary policy, and particularly the level of interest rates in Scotland, would be determined by

the European Central Bank (ECB). There would be a premium, or conceivably a discount, relative to European interest rates reflecting the perceived creditworthiness of the Scottish Government. Scottish financial institutions might be perceived as better, or worse, credit risks than a Scottish Government. Scotland would be entitled to a representative on the governing council of the ECB. Scotland would also participate *pro rata* in the various arrangements, including the stability mechanism, which have been devised in support of the euro.

At an earlier stage of discussion of Scottish independence, there were suggestions that euro membership would represent a powerful declaration of Scotland's economic independence from the UK and an assertion of its place in Europe. But a more hard-headed approach is now appropriate, and generally accepted.

It is evident now – and it should have been evident at a much earlier date – that, from a purely economic perspective, Irish membership of the euro zone was not a sensible decision. Ireland's principal trading partner is the UK. Between 1999 and 2007 interest rates were, generally, significantly lower in Ireland than they would have been if the Irish pound had been linked to the pound sterling: this low level of interest rates in a strong economy contributed substantially to Ireland's spectacular property boom and bust. Irish membership of the euro was in large part a political statement, and while some in Scotland might want to make a similar assertion, the attractions of euro zone membership have fallen significantly as the zone itself has come under pressure.

It is unlikely that the formal obligation to euro membership contained in the Maastricht Treaty and enshrined in the accession criteria poses a real practical problem. Scotland could anticipate initial levels of budget deficit and government debt above those required for accession to the euro zone. The country would fail to meet the Maastricht criteria for membership – conditions which are likely to be more rigorously applied to new members of the euro zone than they were to old ones. More fundamentally, while such accession to the euro makes little sense for Scotland, it also makes little sense for other euro zone members so long as the euro is not the currency of the rest of the UK (RUK).

The sensible currency union for an independent Scotland is with RUK, and Scottish adoption of the euro is not appropriate so long as RUK does not use the euro. A pragmatic acceptance that Scotland might aspire to euro zone membership – at some time in a future so long delayed that no one could foresee a date – would be a sensible arrangement for both Scotland and the EU.

Even such a weak commitment, however, is not without consequence. The euro zone crisis is itself a powerful illustration that the stability of any monetary arrangement is influenced by the perception that it is permanent – or the fear that it is not. The existence of a commitment to change course at some time, even if couched in the vaguest possible terms, is a potential subject of speculative activity.

The probability that financial markets would destabilise political arrangements depends on the resilience and perceived permanence of these arrangements. Both the objective strength of agreements and commitments, and subjective perceptions of their strength, are important. The current debate on the future of the euro zone is a product of both underlying reality and market and political judgements of that reality. The wide perception today, in both political circles and financial markets, is that a common currency arrangement such as the euro area can be maintained only if there is, at a minimum, a trajectory towards banking union, common debt issue and a political union involving substantial transfers between different areas of the currency zone. It should be anticipated that both government and financial markets in London would view the issues posed by a monetary union with RUK in a similar way.

It would be absurd for a newly independent Scotland to adopt a currency arrangement which is sustainable only if it is generally recognised as a prelude to a political union with RUK. The immediate question is therefore whether the implicit premise of the euro zone debate is correct: could there be a monetary union between Scotland and the RUK in the absence of any intention, or expectation, that the arrangement would lead, even in the long run, to comprehensive economic integration, including common fiscal policies and internal transfers?

3.3 A MONETARY UNION WITH RUK

At the centre of the euro zone debate has been an assumption that member states have a degree of responsibility for each other's debts. The origins of this assumption are not altogether clear. The creation of the euro zone in 1999 was followed by rapid convergence of interest rates on sovereign debt across the area. Thus markets appear to have assumed not only that currency risk had been eliminated but that credit risk was negligible. Such an assumption made sense only on the basis either that fiscal disciplines within the euro zone, as reflected in the Maastricht criteria, essentially eliminated the risk of sovereign default, or that sovereign debts had effectively been mutualised. The former belief was implausible; the second, in principle, appeared to be excluded by the terms of the Maastricht Treaty. Nevertheless, by 2007, spreads between Greek and German bonds had fallen to between 20 and 30 basis points, a spread which could hardly be justified by reference to the relative public finances of the two countries.

The implied market assumption that the German government stood behind Greek debt (despite explicit contrary provision in the relevant agreements) proved partly true, and partly false. Greece did ultimately default on its debt, but the European Central Bank and other European agencies assumed a role in underwriting the funding of the debts of euro zone members. Spreads over German interest rates have, however, widened very considerably, and not just for Greece, but for Spain, Italy and even France.

A currency union does not require pooling of the debts of members. The United States is a currency union of unquestioned stability, but most state debt is not underwritten by the Federal Government, and there is no general expectation that the Federal Government would support a state in financial trouble. No American state has defaulted in modern times, and most states do have balanced budget requirements written into their state constitutions. But these provisions represent a choice made by individual states and are not imposed by Congress or the US constitution. The US does, however, have a banking union: although there are regional Federal Reserve Banks, monetary policy is controlled from Washington and there is federal insurance of bank deposits. The debt of states with particularly weak finances, such as California, Illinois and Rhode Island, has traded at a substantial yield premium to federal debt issued by the US Treasury. In the US, the issue of collectivisation of debt is quite separate from the issue of a common currency. No one supposes that if California did default, by no means an unlikely event, the state would not continue to use the dollar.

An independent Scotland would be expected to borrow on its own account – chapter 5 discusses the basis and terms on which it might do so. It does not seem likely that anyone would imagine that Scotland would be an implicit or explicit guarantor of the debts of RUK. It is difficult to imagine any realistic circumstances in which the RUK Treasury might agree to act as explicit guarantor of the debts of an independent Scotland. There might be a market belief in an implicit guarantee: that RUK would not allow Scotland to fail, or that the RUK government might be so concerned by the possible knock-on effect of a Scottish default to the RUK credit rating that RUK would organise a bail-out. But RUK, and perhaps the newly independent Scottish government itself, would naturally seek to distance themselves from any suggestion of this kind.

Even if the arrangements between Scotland and RUK fell short of fiscal union, there would certainly be a requirement for some fiscal coordination between the two countries, since substantially looser or tighter fiscal policies in one country would inevitably have an impact on the other. In the light of the recent euro zone experience, it is hard to imagine RUK countenancing either deficit or debt levels in Scotland significantly in excess of those for the UK as a whole within a currency union.

The original Maastricht Treaty for the euro zone imposed limits on debt and deficit levels (which were not in fact observed). Greece cheated in order to appear to meet membership criteria, so did Italy, and it is disingenuous to suggest that this was not understood at the time. The UK pioneered the use of creative financing arrangements to misrepresent public accounts, and UK-based institutions have developed a substantial export market for such schemes. Both France and Germany quickly and explicitly breached their euro zone deficit obligations.

That EU experience illustrates the problem of enforcement of the detailed provision of agreements between member states. The EU has sought to impose austerity programmes on Greece, Ireland and Portugal, but the incentive for these countries to meet the requirements imposed on them is the, ultimately empty, threat that central support for their borrowing will not be forthcoming. Even so, there have been failures of compliance. The threat to withhold transfers would presumably not be available since a UK monetary union would very explicitly not be a transfer union.

The credibility of the European Stability and Growth Pact was quickly undermined when it was ignored by France and Germany. This defiance by large countries of agreements reached collectively points to a serious difficulty in economic cooperation, and specifically in fiscal coordination, between Scotland and RUK: the asymmetry in the size of the partners. It is easy to see why RUK, representing 91.5% of a monetary union, might seek oversight of the economic affairs of Scotland, representing 8.5% of the same union. It is more difficult to see why RUK, representing 91.5% of a monetary union, should concede oversight over its policies to Scotland, representing 8.5% of the union. But, in the absence of such reciprocity, the degree of autonomy Scotland would enjoy in fiscal policy might differ very little from the modest amount Scotland currently enjoys under the allocation of a block grant within the UK.

Scotland might reasonably ask for a role on the Bank of England's monetary policy committee. Such a demand might be conceded, although there has been firm resistance to the idea of representative, as distinct from individual, members of that committee. If Scotland did achieve representation, one appointment to a nine-person committee would be as much as could reasonably be expected. The choice of members of the committee is intended to exclude direct political influence on decisions, and Scotland would be expected to follow this principle: thus it would be acceptable to choose an economist with Scottish connections, but not one whose brief was to represent the particular interests of Scotland (to the extent that an appropriate monetary policy for Scotland appeared to differ from that appropriate for RUK).

Monetary policy for Scotland would therefore be determined by a mechanism over which Scots and Scottish interests would have at best marginal influence and, by design, no political influence. The management of an over- or under-funding policy such as quantitative easing would be a complex matter. The ECB has operated similar policies, in principle without regard to the national origin of the debt it is buying. It is difficult to imagine the RUK Treasury agreeing to this arrangement in a UK monetary union, just as it is hard to imagine Germany sustaining a policy of indiscriminate purchase of debt in the secondary market in the long run without tight control over the fiscal policies of the beneficiary states.

It would be difficult, though it might not be impossible, to negotiate an agreement on monetary union with RUK which retained a degree of fiscal autonomy consistent with aspirations for Scottish independence. But the problematic nature of such negotiations makes it necessary to consider what the alternatives to such an agreement might be. The negotiating stance of Scottish representatives would be influenced by the attractiveness of these alternatives.

3.4 THE UNILATERAL OPTION

It is not necessary to agree the terms of a monetary union to establish a common currency. Countries can unilaterally choose to use the money of another country. Montenegro, a small Balkan state formed in the breakup of Yugoslavia, has no currency of its own. All trade in Montenegro takes place in euros, even though the country is not a member of the European Union and has no borders with any EU member state.

The European Central Bank does not much like this arrangement, but there is no practical step it can take, or wishes to take, to stop it. Montenegro does not, obviously, print euros or mint euro coins, and, if it did, action to stop the process would follow very quickly.

The option of using another country's money is often called dollarisation, because the dollar is the currency most commonly used in this way. Most of these states are very small countries such as Monaco (euros) and the Turks and Caicos Islands (dollars) for which an independent currency and the apparatus of a central bank implies excessive cost and complexity, and whose economic relations are mostly with the larger country whose currency they use. In some places the history of currency debasement and monetary misman-agement is so dismal that exasperated politicians have decided to hand over monetary policy to a competent institution based else-where. The largest country to have followed this dollarisation route is Ecuador. There is no modern analogue for the adoption of such a pol-icy by a country of the size and economic sophistication of Scotland.

The likely reason is that dollarisation is not a very attractive route. A country following dollarisation not only has no influence over monetary policy (interest rates and the monetary base are essentially under another country's control) it has no access to the resource of the Central Bank which conducts its monetary policy, without having any analogous resources of its own.

The issue of notes and coins yields an immediate profit of the dif-ference between the cost of the paper and metal and the face value of the money. That is why governments monopolise the printing of money. There is a similar benefit obtained from the requirement for commercial banks to hold deposits at the central bank, which is necessary for the monetary system to function. These deposits are, in effect, government obligations which will in aggregate never be repaid and, to the extent they are called, fulfilled by the printing of notes.

The benefit derived by governments issuing currency from their monopoly of the monetary base is known as seigneurage. In the UK the value of notes and coin in issue is around £60bn and the value of the reserve deposits of banks around £250bn. In a monetary union, such as the euro zone, arrangements are made for this seigneurage to be shared between the members, and such an agreement would pre-sumably be negotiated as part of a monetary union between Scotland and RUK. Montenegro, obviously, does not derive any seigneurage benefits, nor does Ecuador. Rather eccentrically, Monaco, which issued Monegasque francs before monetary union, does receive sei-gneurage, along with other European micro-states.

Far from deriving seigneurage benefit, a country unilaterally adopting another country's currency has to import sufficient of that currency to fill the wallets of its population and enable its banking system to function. This can be achieved either by running a trade surplus or by borrowing from the country that runs the currency. In either case, the effect is to impose severe monetary and fiscal disci-pline on the country concerned: if it does not earn sufficient dollars or euros it will have to take steps to establish a trade surplus or resume printing its own currency to pay its soldiers and police. Such firm discipline is, of course, the intention of the scheme. Montenegrin interest rates are at a substantial premium to general euro zone interest rates although the country's finances are relatively sound. The inability of most traders to place Montenegro on a map may be another relevant factor keeping rates high and markets illiquid.

3.5 THE SCOTS POUND

If Scotland chooses not to link its currency to the euro, and cannot secure an appropriate basis for linking its currency to the pound sterling, the only option that remains is an independent Scottish currency.

The Scots pound could be linked to sterling, as the Irish pound was for fifty years. But for most of that period, fixed exchange rates were the international norm. Even in a world of floating exchange rates, however, many countries have chosen to fix the value of their currency, formally or informally, relative to another: or in some cases to a basket of other currencies. A currency peg is another possible unilateral option.

The Hong Kong dollar has been pegged at a rate of 7.8 HK to the $US since 1983. Traders and investors can have a high degree of confidence in the stability of the value of the Hong Kong dollar, and Hong Kong is, in a sense, in monetary union with the US, although it did not seek or receive US agreement to this and plays no part in the determination of US monetary policy. Hong Kong enjoys a degree of freedom in its monetary policy and considerable freedom in its fiscal policy, in both cases considerably more than would be possible in a formal currency union.

Although Denmark is not a member of the euro zone and has refused to participate in the European Financial Stability Fund, its exchange rate has been pegged since the founding of the euro at 7.5 Danish krone to the euro. In contrast to Ecuador and Montenegro, Hong Kong and Denmark are countries with a history of prudent fiscal and monetary management, and in both cases it is likely that if the exchange rate were not pegged the currency would rise in value. In fact, Hong Kong has accumulated very large foreign exchange reserves in the course of maintaining its currency peg.

Such reserves are necessary to maintain a currency peg, since the country adopting a peg must be able to purchase US dollars, or euros, or sterling, if the value of the domestic currency is in danger of falling below the prescribed level. Scotland's pro rata share of the UK's foreign exchange reserve would be around £4bn. This amount is clearly inadequate to balance the rate of speculative flows in modern financial markets. Larger reserves could be built up only, as Hong Kong has done, through the accumulation of trade surpluses.

US dollars can be used in Hong Kong, and euros in Denmark,

but mainly in establishments catering to tourists: most transactions take place in local currency. Hong Kong dollars are not accepted in the United States, nor Danish krone in the rest of Europe. Both individuals and businesses are therefore faced with the costs and inconvenience of currency conversion. If a Scots pound was pegged at a value of one English pound, it is likely that English pounds might circulate widely in Scotland, but less likely that Scottish pounds would be generally accepted in England: that was the experience when the Irish and UK currencies were pegged. Since the euro zone crisis, there would now be more nervousness about such transactions. Banks operating in Scotland would be likely to offer accounts in both Scottish and English pounds.

Danish monetary policy is in practice delivered by the European Central Bank, although Denmark is not represented on the governing board of the ECB. Danish politicians, who have mainly supported Danish membership of the euro zone, have emphasised this absence of voice. But in reality the Danish influence on ECB decisions would not be large in any event: Denmark would represent an even smaller proportion of the euro zone than Scotland would represent of a British monetary union. Public opinion in Denmark, which has twice narrowly rejected Danish adherence to the euro, has moved strongly against membership as the euro zone crisis has deepened.

Sweden has also retained its own currency. The Swedish crown, unlike the Danish, is not formally pegged to the euro. In practice, however, its fluctuations closely follow those of the euro, and Swedish interest rates and monetary policy generally follow the lead set by the European Central Bank. Sweden would find itself experiencing large currency swings, which would cause difficulties for Swedish businesses operating internationally, if it did not do this. Like Denmark, Sweden has no part in ECB decisions.

Although notes and coin are the visible manifestation of separate currencies, what happens in the banking system is of far more importance. When currencies are wholly distinct, as those of Denmark and Sweden, the situation of individuals and businesses is easy to understand, if not as easy to operate. Loans and deposits are either in crowns or euros, and it is obvious which are which. It is also obvious what will happen to the value of any particular loan or deposit if the exchange rate between crowns and euros changes. Since banks in Scotland would offer accounts in both Scottish and English pounds, most businesses operating in Scotland, and many Scottish people, would maintain accounts in both currencies, as many Danes do.

The spreads and charges generally levied by banks on currency exchanges of small size and for personal customers appear far in excess of the costs involved. It would probably be necessary for the

Scottish Government to control the level of these charges, as the EU has done for cross-border transfers within the euro zone.

However, if money can readily and cheaply be transferred between Scottish and English pounds for transaction purposes – and it is essential to the operation of a separate Scottish currency that this should be so – money can also be transferred between Scottish and English pounds for speculative purposes. Investors have judged, plausibly, that Denmark is more likely to break the peg between the krone and the euro than Germany is to leave the euro. The general result has been an inflow of money into Denmark, pushing up Danish asset prices and reducing Danish interest rates below even German ones, so that short-term interest rates have become negative. Over the same period, the Swedish crown, which is free to float, has appreciated moderately against the euro.

It is less likely that Scotland would be able, and much less likely that it would be willing, to revalue a Scottish pound against sterling. It is sometimes suggested that because an independent Scotland would be an oil exporter, and oil exporters tend to have strong currencies, a Scottish currency would be likely to appreciate against the RUK pound, or, conversely, that there would be a large benefit to RUK in attracting Scotland as a member of a monetary union. This argument is based on a misunderstanding.

We do not know what exactly a Scottish balance of payments would look like, but we do know that, taking transfers and capital inflows together, it balances; that is a simple matter of arithmetic. Thus the hypothetical Scottish oil surplus is necessarily matched by a corresponding deficit with RUK. This deficit is, on average, roughly funded by the block grant from Westminster, which would not continue. It is therefore an error to believe that Scotland could anticipate a current account balance of payments surplus which would lead to currency appreciation. There would, however, be some potential for instability if oil price fluctuations affected currency values. It would be sensible for the Scottish government to use reserves to attempt to offset this instability.

The more likely market concern is that in some circumstances the Scottish government would be unable to maintain the peg, or choose to improve competitiveness through devaluation. This creates the danger of an essentially one-sided option – the Scottish pound might decline in value relative to the English pound but could not increase – which would result in either or both higher interest rates in Scotland and a substantial proportion of Scottish businesses being conducted in English pounds.

These issues arise even within the context of monetary union. The common currency of the Czech and Slovak republics proved unsustainable because, even before the final breakup, many businesses and individuals no longer regarded a hypothetical Slovak crown as the equivalent of a hypothetical Czech crown, and transferred funds to Czech banks. Most international businesses, and an increasing number of individuals, no longer regard a Greek euro or a Spanish one as identical to a German or Finnish euro.

The Scandinavian examples illustrate that the option of a distinct Scottish currency, either formally or loosely pegged to a major currency, is an option which can work well, allowing a degree, albeit limited, of economic independence without unacceptable cost and instability for individuals and business. It should be acknowledged, however, that most Swedish and Danish politicians and business people would abandon the currency in favour of the euro if voters in the two countries would agree.

3.6 CONCLUSIONS

An independent Scotland has a number of currency options, none of them altogether satisfactory. Scottish membership of the euro zone makes little economic or political sense in present circumstances. Unilateral retention of the pound sterling, while superficially seeming a low-risk option, would take the country into uncharted territory. The considerable uncertainty which would result might cause significant damage to the Scottish economy and its financial sector in particular.

That leaves three serious possibilities. The best outcome would be a monetary union with the rest of the UK, provided such a union could be negotiated on terms which would be consistent with the expectations of fiscal autonomy implied by independence. That caveat may be impossible to fulfil.

If acceptable terms of monetary union cannot be agreed, then Scotland would introduce its own currency, which might initially be pegged to the pound sterling. Given the modest size of its foreign exchange reserves, Scotland would encounter difficulty in establishing confidence in its ability to make that peg. Scottish interest rates would necessarily follow those set by the Bank of England for RUK, but Scotland would have freedom in fiscal policy subject to the requirements of prudence imposed by capital markets, but it is likely that a well-managed Scottish economy could develop an internationally tradable currency which would fluctuate in value around the pound sterling.

If such an outcome does not seem ideal – and it does not – it reflects the acknowledgement of a central reality. The degree of economic independence available to a small country, like Denmark or

Sweden, close to its major trading partner and associated with a large currency block and customs union is, in a global market for goods, services and capital, inevitably limited. But these examples suggest that such an outcome is entirely feasible.

3.7 QUESTIONS AND CHALLENGES

» Scottish membership of the EU would imply some degree of commitment to the euro zone. Is it accepted that such membership makes little sense in the foreseeable future? If so, would that conclusion be acceptable to other member states?

» Is unilateral retention of the pound sterling, without RUK agreement, a feasible option?

» What conditions would RUK be likely to impose in agreeing to Scottish membership of a sterling currency union? Would these conditions be compatible with the objective of Scottish independence?

» What would be the cost of borrowing to an independent Scottish government, given that Scotland would expect to have little influence over its monetary policy? How would the rest of the world perceive the quality of Scotland's credit?

» What are the implications of a distinct Scottish currency? How serious would be the costs and inconvenience for business and individuals? Could Scotland maintain a peg between its currency and the pound sterling? If feasible, would it be desirable?

CHAPTER 4

Fiscal Policy and Constitutional Change
Lord Gus O'Donnell[1]

A mark of a truly independent country is the ability to manage its own fiscal policy. That means deciding how much the government will spend, how that spending will be allocated and how it will be financed. There are also choices about which taxes to use, how much spending should be met by charges, and whether to run surpluses or deficits. In reality, there are all sorts of checks and balances, even in a completely independent country having its own currency. The US Government can only run big deficits as long as it can find buyers for its funding instruments. The markets will impose disciplines and charge higher interest rates for countries that are deemed to have less sustainable deficit and debt positions. No country can impose taxes on mobile factors of production that are too far out of line with global averages as the tax base will simply migrate to the lower-taxed area. And, of course, the electorate will have strong views on issues like paying charges for entering museums or for receiving certain types of medical care or further education.

4.1 GOOD FISCAL POLICIES

Three requirements of a good fiscal policy may be identified that should underpin any debate regarding the implications of potential constitutional change.

4.1.1 *Sustainability*

The first requirement of a good fiscal policy is that it is sustainable. In other words, the spending should be broadly matched by financing. If this doesn't happen, the level of debt will rise, and, with it, debt interest payments which can lead to an explosive situation. High debt means high debt interest, enhanced by the fact that markets may require a higher interest rate on the debts of highly indebted

---

1   Former UK Cabinet Secretary.

economies. A sustainable fiscal policy is one where the government can continue current spending and tax policies while meeting its debt obligations. Things start to go badly wrong when the interest rate that must be paid on the debt is above the growth rate of the economy (nominal GDP growth). Sustainable policies can be maintained at any level of debt, but the higher the debt level the bigger the primary surplus that must be run to stabilise the debt as a share of GDP.[2]

There are real challenges on both the spending and the revenue sides of the balance sheet. The number of older retired people relative to younger workers is likely to carry on rising. This will be expensive for governments and the current Scottish system is, of course, more generous than that in England. And public expectations of the quality of state provision, in all areas but particularly with regard to the care of the elderly, are on an upward trend.

On the revenue side, it is becoming increasingly difficult to tax mobile factors of production. The use of 'royalty fees' to reduce *taxable* profits by companies earning huge revenues in the UK is already creating large revenue shortfalls. As global competition increases, there is downward pressure on all costs, including taxes and energy costs. The reliance of Scotland and the UK on North Sea revenues is a particular problem given that these natural resources are being depleted every day.

4.1.2 Supportive of the economy

The second requirement of a good fiscal policy is that it should support the economy. The 'macro' side of this involves fiscal policy acting as a stabiliser to the economy, putting money into the system during downturns and reversing that during upturns. This is not without risks as it is difficult to define 'downturns' and 'upturns', but economists can provide rough answers which allow the raw deficit figures to be adjusted for the cyclical state of the economy. UK experience suggests there is a lot to be said for this being done by an independent body like the Office of Budget Responsibility (OBR). In the USA they have the Congressional Budget Office which provides its own fiscal forecasts.

It is important to distinguish between the automatic stabilisers, which kick in without the need for government to do anything, and discretionary fiscal policies. European economies tend to have stronger automatic stabilisers, because of more generous welfare systems and higher income tax rates, than the US and many emerging

---

2   See Balls and O'Donnell (2002), pp. 170–3.

economies. Sadly, many analysts overlook this factor when comparing the size of actions taken by governments to offset downturns. Independent countries can, of course, set the level of their automatic stabilisers to suit their circumstances. Stronger automatic stabilisers tend to reduce work incentives but they take some of the politics out of fiscal policy.

Turning to the longer term, fiscal policy can affect the trend growth rate of an economy. A fiscal system which enhances productivity by, for example, encouraging innovation and research and development is generally thought to be good for productivity. If fiscal policy is used to deliver greater macroeconomic stability which makes planning and investing easier, then it can also raise potential output.

Of course, there are many other factors besides fiscal policy which affect trend growth, such as education and migration policies. An independent Scotland could decide to allow in more migrants, particularly skilled migrants. This could raise Scottish GDP and perhaps GDP *per capita* if the new migrants had high skill levels. Of course, any changes by Scotland might lead to responses by the rest of the UK in order for it not to lose out competitively.

A fiscal regime which encourages the right kind of investment can also raise long-term growth. The difficulty is knowing what is the *right* kind of investment. Improving a country's infrastructure is generally thought to be beneficial, especially in new areas like enhancing broadband speeds and availability. The question is: would an independent Scotland be more prepared to forego current consumption to invest to raise future productivity?

The 'micro' side of a good fiscal policy relates to the impact of particular tax and spend policies on incentives and behaviour and the resulting consequences for growth and wellbeing of the population. In general, economists have found that low tax rates on as broad a base as possible are the most efficient. This is an excellent general rule which is rarely given enough weight by Ministers or legislators. They like to use the tax and spending systems to achieve political goals. For example, there may be an objective to encourage people to spend more on energy-saving materials like loft insulation by lowering its VAT rate.

There is a crucial point to highlight in the attempt by governments to change incentives and behaviours, which can be easily illustrated through, again, analysing the various energy-efficiency schemes that have been adopted. In particular, the experience with trying to persuade people to insulate their lofts carries an important lesson. For years governments have been offering discounts on the price to improve take-up. It was only when the policy was switched to a loft-clearance scheme, which incidentally involved loft insulation, that a real breakthrough was made. The lesson is that policies need to be based on an understanding of how people actually make choices, not on how a model says they should.

One possible advantage of Scotland having control of its own taxes would be that a Scottish Government could decide what special 'tweaks' to give to the system to suit national needs. For example, there might be an objective to establish a different tax rate on goods where the goals were to discourage consumption (for example, fatty foods and alcohol). If these decisions are made wisely, they can bring benefits. The downside is the need to worry about cross-border divergence and the cost that always comes with a more complex tax system. Complexity is great news for lawyers, and those who can avoid extra taxes tend to be the better off, so there is a distributional problem as well.

One particular 'micro' fiscal issue is important when considering Scottish independence: should both countries agree to consult on fiscal issues that could end up in competition that damages both countries? For example, both Scotland and the redefined UK (RUK) might want to have a slightly lower corporation tax rate than the other to encourage firms to locate profits, and hence pay tax, in their countries. Transfer pricing rules are very difficult to police, particularly for UK-wide companies, so where a company earns its profits is a decision that could be driven by tax considerations.

There are also the usual problems concerning different tax rates being charged in two countries when consumers can choose where to buy their goods. Consumers would, of course, want to pay the lower tax, so businesses would lobby both governments to reduce the VAT rates for their products. This kind of tax competition puts downward pressure on rates. Is this such a bad thing? If the amount of revenue to be collected is taken as given, then it means upward pressure on other taxes. The advantage of taxes like VAT, which are taxes on spending, not earnings, is that they do not disincentivise work. The disadvantage is that consumption taxes tend to be more regressive than income taxes.

Different VAT rates could, therefore, cause big distortions, as have already occurred with the Channel Islands. On the other hand, the UK has managed to live within the EU Single Market where there are variations in VAT rates, but within the fairly tight rules policed by the Commission. This suggests that an independent Scotland and RUK would survive in much the same way. However, it is undoubtedly the case that different VAT rates in certain goods between the two countries would lead to problems. Hence, while there may be no need for any further intervention, the high degree of integration between Scotland and the rest of the UK and the shared land border would create some challenges. The situation in Ireland and Northern Ireland demonstrates the kinds of problems that can occur. In general, UK governments have welcomed tax competition between countries, but it will not always be beneficial.

In addition, some of the most serious problems we face, like climate change, require international agreements if they are to be effective. Imposing a different carbon price or say a financial transactions tax might have advantages if imposed by all countries, but they would be generally unattractive and inefficient if imposed at the level of a newly independent Scotland, and, indeed, at the level of the present United Kingdom.

4.1.3 *Supportive of equity*

A third requirement of a good fiscal policy should be the capacity of the system to address issues of equity. Fiscal policy is used in many countries to redistribute income, both between people and between generations. Obviously, these are deeply political questions and different parties will have different objectives. The one group who are likely to be under-represented in these discussions are future generations. By definition, they don't vote and have no voice. Their interests are reflected by the importance that current generations put on creating a sustainable future for their children. We can be fairly certain that future generations will be older, with fewer tax-paying workers living to fund non-working pensioners with expensive health care and medical needs.

There is growing concern at the problem of increasing income inequality and all that goes with that. Richard G. Wilkinson and Kate Pickett[3] set out the problems in their book, *The Spirit Level: Why More Equal Societies Almost Always Do Better*. Many economists would argue with the way this analysis has been done, but they would not dispute the fact that inequality has been rising in the UK. Governments can and do redistribute large amounts of income through the tax and benefit system. This is far from costless and politicians need to decide on the trade-offs they want to make between efficiency and distribution. An independent Scotland might choose to make this trade-off in a different place to the UK, but there are no free lunches here. What you gain in equity you lose in efficiency; at least that is the theory. In practice, our current system has become so complex that there might well be changes that improve both efficiency and equity. These changes should be made by any government,

3   Richard G. Wilkinson & Kate Pickett (2009). The Spirit Level: Why More Equal Societies Almost Always Do Better, published by Allen Lane.

but the power of vested interests and the bias towards the *status quo* – remember, losers always shout and winners keep quiet – mean that we haven't ended up with a perfect system.

4.1.4 *Choice of taxes*

The requirements outlined above have been captured in the work of James Mirrlees, whose Report[4] is probably the most definitive study of how best to set taxes. The study concluded that a 'good' tax system had three attributes: it should be progressive, neutral and a tax *system*. The latter refers to the need for the tax system as a whole to generate enough revenue to meet spending needs. Not all taxes need to meet the multiple objectives of a government. For example, it might be decided to impose VAT on all spending and offset any distributional impact by changing direct personal taxes and benefits.

The case for neutrality, by which the Report means treating similar economic activities in similar ways, is that it is simpler, avoids *unjustifiable* discrimination between people and activities and can minimise economic distortions. Of course, it is necessary to have a large caveat here to emphasise the word *unjustifiable*. Cigarettes, alcohol and activities that damage the environment are all taxed at high rates to offset the problems associated with their consumption. Of course, the principle of tax neutrality, particularly in the international context, needs to refer to tax rates and the tax base. Many countries seek to gain a competitive advantage by applying the internationally agreed tax rate, but to a narrower base.

The third aspect is progressivity. There is an inevitable trade-off between redistribution and work incentives. A well-designed tax system will minimise the efficiency loss associated with the politically desired level of progressivity.

Does the UK have an ideal progressive, neutral tax system? Unfortunately not. In theory, Scotland could do better, but the political forces that have added complexity and inefficiency to the system are likely to be just as prevalent in Scotland as in the UK.

The ideal system, in the view of the authors of the Mirrlees Report, is one that taxes all sources of income at the same rate but also allows all the costs of generating that income to be deducted. So, they would tax income from paid work, self-employment, property, saving, dividends and capital gains at the same rate. Indirect taxes should be largely uniform with limited exceptions on efficiency

---

4   See the two volumes: Dimensions of Tax Design: The Mirrlees Review, J. Mirrlees et al, Oxford University Press: April 2010; and Tax by Design: The Mirrlees Review, J. Mirrlees et al, Oxford University Press: September 2011.

grounds and for harmful goods. There should be no transactions taxes, such as stamp duty on property and shares.

4.1.5 Improving policy

Of course, there are many ways in which Scotland, and the UK, could improve the way fiscal policies are decided. Taking tax first, substantial improvements could be achieved by having the right processes for deciding on which taxes to change and how precisely to change them. Ideally, there should be timely consultation and testing. The gold standard of testing is a randomised control trial (RCT). These trials are increasingly being used in the behavioural area. There is a hierarchy of ways to select policies, including RCTs, pilots and standard cost-benefit analyses. At least, governments should be clear about the level of testing and analysis that has been undertaken. There will be cases where nothing can be said in advance as, otherwise, people will act to avoid the impact of the change: so-called forestalling. This can have huge effects, as was demonstrated by the responses to the pre-announced changes to the top rate of income tax.

Ex post evaluation is also extremely beneficial and used far too rarely. It can help refine policies and show whether they are achieving the intended objective.

Governments should also be transparent about the distributional impact of their fiscal policies. Too often, this job has been left to the Institute of Fiscal Studies. Their role should be to validate, or not, the Government's analysis. In years to come, it should be possible to go further and provide an analysis of the impacts of measures and complete budgets on overall wellbeing. Just giving the monetary impacts, as is done now, implies that £1 going to a billionaire is as valuable as £1 going to someone on the poverty line – a daft assumption.

All of the above ideas can be applied to spending decisions in much the same way.

4.2 BIG STATE OR SMALL STATE?

One critical choice that drives the entire fiscal system relates to the size of the state: should there be a big or a small state? This is an enormous question and has been the subject of discussion amongst philosophers, political scientists and economists. There are many areas where markets have an advantage in efficiently allocating resources. And it is doubtful whether any mainstream political parties would back the renationalisation of companies like BP or Cable & Wireless. However, there are still areas where there are doubts about whether the state or the private sector can run industries more efficiently.[5] Competitive markets, in general, tend to allocate resource efficiently but they are strongly influenced by the starting point. People with more money have more weight. Michael Sandel[6] has argued that there are moral, as opposed to efficiency, considerations that are also relevant. These arguments are about specific issues: do we get a better supply of blood by the donor system or would it be better to pay people to give blood?

But there is also a 'macro' issue. Do countries who choose to have bigger spending and taxes do better or worse than those with a smaller state? Again, it is important to realise that we don't have experiments with a parallel world where everything else is the same, but we try out a different size of government in one of them. Nevertheless, economists have tried to answer this question as best they can. The answers are very inconclusive. The USA has an unusually small government relative to its GDP. The Scandinavians tend to have relatively large governments for the size of GDP. Both appear to do well in terms of GDP per capita or wellbeing measures. The truth is that this is far too large a question to have a simple answer. Governments can be large because they have large welfare states or because they control a lot of production. Well-designed welfare states are good for growth but state companies are often inefficiently run. It cannot be inferred from such general statements that there is a 'right' size for government.

4.3 HOW TO ACHIEVE 'GOOD' FISCAL POLICIES

My first suggestion is that a government should be clear about what it is trying to achieve. This clarity has been achieved in many countries by using targets or rules for debts and/or deficits. Some of these rules are designed to ensure sustainability (usually debt/GDP or deficit targets or ceilings). Others attempt to influence the type of spending as, for example, the so-called golden rule which requires non-capital spending to be matched by revenues. This gives a bias in the system towards capital spending which some economists regard as a necessary incentive to avoid large fluctuations in infrastructure spending which can have damaging effects on growth.

My second suggestion is to set up an independent monitoring body. The OBR in the UK is one example. This enhances the credibility of the fiscal system. An independent national body seems to work better than international surveillance. The IMF and the EU

---

5   David Parker's book, The Official History of Privatisation Vol. I. The Formative Years, 1970-1987, discusses this area in some detail, including the case of North Sea oil which is, of course, highly relevant to the constitutional debate.

6   Michael Sandler (2012). *What Money Can't Buy: The Moral Limits of Markets.*

Commission provide examples of supra-national bodies that have tried to police fiscal policies but, during difficult times when they are most needed, they tend to be ignored.

My third suggestion is to provide electorates with the information they need to make informed voting choices. This could mean, for example, as is done in the Netherlands, having an independent body to explain the fiscal consequences of each party's manifesto.

4.3.1 *Fiscal policy within a monetary union*

All of the above refers to the case of any country with its own currency and specifically to the constitutional option of a newly independent Scotland with its own currency. But what does good fiscal policy entail if you share a currency with one or more other countries? Certainly, the fundamental elements of good fiscal policy, set out above, are broadly still both relevant and hugely important. There is now a living example of this situation in the euro area. The architects of the euro were at pains to explain that the new currency needed all its members to have sustainable fiscal policies. They imposed debt and deficit levels as part of the entrance criteria (the Maastricht rules) and had rules governing debt and deficits for those sharing the euro. The experience of fiscal rules around the world is mixed. However, these rules are particularly necessary in a currency union because the costs of having an unsustainable debt position can be hidden if the markets believe that other countries in the union will bail out the unsustainable member.

In the case of the euro, there is a 'no bail-out' clause and the Stability and Growth Pact contains rules on debt and deficits. The problem in the euro zone was not with the rules, but with the failure to ensure that the rules were enforced. So, in the early days, countries like Greece could borrow at similar rates to Finland, even though the Greek debt position was far worse than the Finnish situation. The euro zone badly needed fiscal rules to stop countries exploiting the market's perception that deficit countries would be bailed out by the richer, in-surplus countries. When the debts reached seriously high levels, the markets started to realise that defaults were much more likely, with the result that the high-debt euro zone countries faced very high borrowing costs – and, of course, these fed back into higher deficits through increased interest payments. The virtuous circles that kept interest rates low in the early days of the euro – and had the unfortunate consequence of delaying needed structural reforms, especially in the public sector – turned into vicious circles. And, in tough times, it is much harder to undertake structural reforms. The key lesson is the need to establish the necessary rules and to ensure the rules are actually followed. Credible surveillance and sanctions regimes are a necessary component of this regime.

So, if Scotland and the rest of the UK (RUK) were to share a currency, both partners would want to ensure that the other does not run unsustainable fiscal policies. This means agreeing some rules, which should not be too difficult, and finding a way to ensure the rules are obeyed, which is likely to be extremely difficult. It would undoubtedly mean each partner surrendering some sovereignty to the body charged with 'rule enforcement'.

But the very high interest rates that countries like Greece and Ireland are having to pay to finance their debt levels demonstrates the risks of running what the markets perceive to be an unsustainable fiscal policy while in a currency union.

However, the analogy with the euro is imperfect. The euro is a brand new currency that was not formerly used by any country. It would certainly be possible to have a currency union between Scotland and the rest of the UK with both agreeing to adopt a new currency, but it is doubtful whether the rest of the UK would want to give up the pound. So, let us consider the implications of fiscal policy if Scotland and the redefined UK were to agree that they would both carry on using the pound. From the RUK's point of view, it would want to be sure that Scotland did not run an unsustainable fiscal policy. Similarly, Scotland would not want the rest of the UK to have an unsustainable policy, as this would considerably push up Scotland's borrowing costs. Just as in the early days of the euro, it is likely that the interest rates on Scottish and RUK government bonds would be very similar at first. This situation would only change if the markets believed that either country was running an unsustainable policy and, in the case of Scotland, that it would not be bailed out by the RUK. Of course, if the RUK were the fiscal 'bad guy', the question would arise as to whether Scotland would or could bail out the RUK.

Enforcement is the key issue. One solution would be an OBRSA (Office of Budget Responsibility for the Sterling Area) for the two countries, which would have the job of assessing the two fiscal policies and, crucially, the power to ensure the rules were followed. In principle, the two countries could have different fiscal rules but they would need to follow at least some 'sustainability rules' that were jointly agreed. For example, two jointly agreed rules could be:

» net debt/GDP ratio must be less than 60%
» deficit/GDP ratio must be less than 3%, cyclically adjusted.

This would not stop either country imposing tighter rules but would stop them having looser ones.

The OBRSA would also need to have rules that were sufficiently flexible to deal with external shocks, like the current deflationary shock from the financial crisis, in which growth and confidence have fallen sharply and deficits have risen automatically. The so-called automatic stabilisers help to dampen the shock. The trick is to have rules that are flexible enough to handle shocks but tough enough to stop the emergence of unsustainable fiscal positions. There could be a process for allowing one or both countries a longer period to get back within the parameters. Such a process might involve a proposal from the OBRSA that had to be agreed by both legislatures. The euro zone is currently rewriting its rules, having determined that the previous ones turned out not to be tough enough in the good times and, in my view, to be excessively tough in the bad times.

What would happen if the OBRSA finds that a country is heading to break one of these rules? Presumably, there would be a requirement in each country to introduce fiscal measures at the next available fiscal event (or, possibly, sooner in a crisis), which in OBRSA's view would get the debt or deficit back within the agreed parameters.

We can learn about precisely how to ensure compliance with these rules from the current work on euro zone rules. The key point is that countries which share a currency cannot have complete fiscal autonomy. The European Monetary Union intends to make it a requirement that the fiscal rules are embedded in each country's constitution. How might this work for Scotland and the RUK? One possibility would be to allow each country to have a veto over the other country's budget if, in the eyes of OBRSA, it violated the rules. Some in the RUK might say that since Scotland is using RUK's currency, RUK should be able to veto Scotland's budget but not vice versa. This raises the question of the accountability of the OBRSA. This could be handled by having its head appear before the Select Committees of both countries.

4.3.2 Greater Devolution

What are the fiscal issues that arise if Scotland remains within the UK? There may well be a debate about whether more powers, including tax and spending powers, should be devolved. Many of the issues discussed before remain relevant. The UK Treasury has responsibility for the state of the UK's finances and will not want to delegate powers that would lessen its control without ensuring strong safeguards. It will worry, at the macro level, that more autonomy for Scotland might lead to an unsustainable UK fiscal position. And it would worry at the micro level about the harmful tax competition and distortions caused by having different tax and/or benefit rates in different parts of a single currency region. The example of the United States[7] shows there can be different sales and income tax levels in a currency area. At the federal level, there are still large fiscal transfers. These can be sustained as long as the political will remains for the rich states to subsidise the poor ones.

Any major extension of devolution of fiscal powers would almost inevitably raise questions about the Barnett formula. This formula is a classic example of how the *status quo* can be difficult to change. The formula has few defenders, and Lord Barnett himself is not one of them, but there is no consensus yet on how to change it. There would be a strong case for a return to fundamentals and sorting out a new principles-based formula for allocating spending around the UK. An independent commission could be set up to bring forward proposals for a new formula. It is possible that in the period following a Scottish independence referendum, it might suit all parties to reach such an agreement. There could be service-level agreements, for example, for departments such as Work and Pensions, to provide services to Scotland which were different from those in the RUK.

Why would the UK be willing to enter into any of these questions, assuming that the referendum supported the *status quo*? It is in the RUK's interest to have a flourishing Scotland. If, by choosing slightly different tax rates, and allocating spending differently, Scottish growth is higher, then this should also raise UK growth. This assumes the measures do not include ones which simply reallocate spending between Scotland and RUK to minimise tax. In practice, greater devolution, if used wisely, has the capacity to improve performance. But the reason we have a UK Government and do not devolve tax powers to every region in England is that the Treasury believes that the incentive to compete with each other would lead to a 'race to the bottom' and that overall revenues would suffer. While spending has to be financed nationally, there is a lot to be said for treating revenue the same way. The UK Government is highly centralised and the Coalition Government is trying to return more powers to local areas. But it is dangerous to create an imbalance between the degree of localisation of tax and spending. Everyone wants to spend more and tax less, and at the national level that does not add up to a sustainable fiscal policy.

---

7   See the European Monetary Union study by HM Treasury, The United States as a Monetary Union, June 2003: http://webarchive.nationalarchives.gov.uk/+/http://www.hm-treasury.gov.uk/documents/international__issues/the__euro/assessment/studies/euro__assess03__studsussex.cfm

With a shared currency, there would be a single short interest rate set by the Bank of England. This would be set to achieve a UK inflation target and modified as demand-and-supply conditions fluctuate. In a recession the rate is likely to be low to stimulate the economy, and most economists would accept that there is a case for fiscal policy helping in the same way. While 'most' economists might take this view, there are some who would argue that fiscal policy should be set for the medium term and should not be used in demand management at all. A less extreme position would be to allow only the automatic stabilisers – lower tax receipts and higher benefit payments in a downturn – to operate.

An example might help to explain these likely issues. Imagine that Scotland is overheating. The Bank of England's single interest rate is right for the UK as a whole but too low for Scotland. Should the Scottish Government set a tighter fiscal policy to offset the over-lax monetary policy? Many would think it should.

4.5 THE KEY QUESTIONS

Assuming an independent Scotland continuing to use the pound, what are the key fiscal issues for Scotland and the rest of the UK?

THE OBJECTIVES OF FISCAL POLICY

What would be the overriding objective of fiscal policy?

GOOD FISCAL POLICY

How would Scotland define 'good' fiscal policy?

» How would policy be sustainable?
» How would policy support the economy?
» How would policy address the equity challenges?

What would be the size of the state: high taxation and spend or low taxation and spend?

Would an independent Scotland be more willing to forego current consumption to increase its long-term growth rate?

How do both countries ensure the other one has sustainable fiscal policies?

What fiscal rules would each country want to adopt?

- » How is compliance with the rules ensured?
- » What are the sanctions? How do we ensure that the markets view the rules as credible?
- » How are the rules made sufficiently flexible to handle external shocks without reducing the fundamental effectiveness?

Should an 'independent' body be set up to police some agreed rules? How does it get its authority and its legitimacy? What accountability framework is needed?

Would the countries want to agree on harmonisation of key policies to avoid competition harmful to both countries?

FISCAL AND MONETARY COORDINATION

How do you coordinate fiscal and monetary policies to ensure they are not pulling in opposite directions?

REFERENCES

Balls, Ed & O'Donnell, Gus. 2002. *Reforming Britain's Economic and Financial Policy: Towards Greater Economic Stability*, Palgrave.

HM Treasury. 2003. *The United States as a Monetary Union*, June. http://webarchive.nationalarchives.gov.uk/+/http://www.hm-treasury.gov.uk/documents/international__issues/the__euro/assessment/studies/euro__assess03__studsussex.cfm

Mirrlees, J. *et al.* 2010. *Dimensions of Tax Design: The Mirrlees Review.* Oxford University Press: April.

Mirrlees, J. *et al.* 2011. *Tax by Design: The Mirrlees Review.* Oxford University Press: September.

Parker, David. 2009. *The Official History of Privatisation Vol. I. The Formative Years 1970–1987.* January. Routledge

Sandel, Michael. 2012. *What Money Can't Buy: The Moral Limits of Markets.*

Wilkinson, Richard G. & Pickett, Kate. 2009. *The Spirit Level: Why More Equal Societies Almost Always Do Better.* Allen Lane.

CHAPTER 5

The Scottish Financial Structure
Professor Charles Goodhart[1]

This chapter analyses key issues regarding the Scottish financial structure in the light of the ongoing debate about the constitutional future of Scotland. It looks first at official finance and then, more briefly, at private finance.

5.1 OFFICIAL FINANCE

5.1.1 *Introduction*

If Scotland were to move further towards independence, it would at some stage in the process have to take responsibility for managing its own (sovereign) debt, which is currently carried out by the Debt Management Office (DMO) in London. At a further stage in the process, it would also have to take responsibility for monetary and financial management, now carried out in Scotland by the Bank of England.

For debt management, the dividing line, between the present arrangements and responsibility for such management, as set out in the Scotland Act 2012, would seem to come between Devo plus and Devo max. Under Devo plus, a larger assortment of taxes would come under the control of the Scottish Government, but control over the overall Scottish deficit and its associated financing would, it seems, remain unchanged from now; that is, as in the Scotland Act 2012. Under Devo max, modelled to some large extent on the arrangements agreed in Spain for the Basque (and Navarre) region, Scotland would contribute (to an extent to be agreed) to the central finances, but would be able to choose, and would have to finance, its own deficit. Whether in surplus or in deficit it would have to engage in its own debt financing. Although the Basque country has the power to issue its own debt, it is required to agree the arrangements

---

1   Emeritus Professor, London School of Economics, and former Member of the Monetary Policy Committee.

with Madrid. There do not, however, appear to be any cases in which Madrid has refused to accept a Basque proposal. What coordination, if any, of debt management arrangements between Scotland and London might be required remains to be seen.

Even under current arrangements, however, as established under the Scotland Act 2012, there are powers that would 'allow Scottish Ministers to borrow up to a total of £2.7 billion, with a power provided to raise this limit, but never lower it below £2.7 billion',[2] although these powers only extend to borrowing for capital purposes and are fixed at a certain limit each year. The UK Treasury issued a consultation paper in June 2012 which sought responses 'on the costs and benefits to both Scotland and the rest of the UK of Scottish Ministers being granted the power to issue bonds as part of the borrowing powers provided for in the Scotland Act 2012' (ibid, p. 6).[3]

For monetary and financial management, the dividing line would seem to fall between Devo max and (some version of) independence. An autonomous region does not need a Central Bank, whereas, as will be shown below, an independent country within the European Union (EU) *must* have one. So, with Devo max, present monetary and financial arrangements would probably remain essentially unchanged.[4] The implications of independence are discussed further below.

---

2 HM Treasury. June 2012. *The Scottish Act 2012: A Consultation on Bond Issuance by the Scottish Government.* p. 5.

3 Briefly, as discussed further in the main text, the advantage for Scotland of such borrowing would rest in some greater independence, bringing the name of Scotland before a wider public in the market place, and making a limited trial run of independent debt management. The costs would be a higher required yield than on UK gilts because of potentially quite severe liquidity risk problems with an issue of such a relatively small size, and some, uncertain, extra credit risk premium, though both of these might be offset by some local 'patriotic' demand by Scots and Scottish intermediaries. There would also be an operational/managerial cost in Scotland of managing the debt. While the balance of argument might lead Scottish Ministers to ask for such powers, it is harder to see the advantages of this step for the rest of the UK, except to satisfy the wishes of Scottish Ministers. Indeed, recent UK policy has rather been that of the reverse, that is, to concentrate sub-sovereign borrowing through the Public Works Loan Board (PWLB) and National Loans Fund (NLF), primarily to achieve cheaper financing costs.

4 Under Devo max, the Scottish Government might seek to have at least one (external) member of both the MPC and FPC be a Scot. This is not likely to succeed. External members of these Committees are not appointed in a representative capacity.

134

5.1.2 *Debt management*

5.1.2.1 Devo max: the experience of the Basque Country

Since the blueprint for Devo max is to be found in the Statute of Autonomy of the Basque Country, and since under this Statute, Article 45, the Basque Country can, and has, issued its own debt,[5] (with the latest authorisation on 4 May 2012 being for new debt issues of 490 mn euros), it is as well to begin with a brief account of Basque debt financing. The Basque Country is divided into three smaller provinces called *Diputaciones Forales*. These three provinces are Alava, Bizkaia and Gipuzkoa. Each province has a legislative assembly and a government with broad competences such as the collection of direct and indirect taxes and expenditure in education and health areas. The taxes collected by these provinces are sent to the central government of the Basque Country. The Basque Country, therefore, collects all taxes in its area and pays a contribution to the Central Government for common services (for example, defence). The calculation of this contribution is arcane and somewhat contentious. Many outside the Basque Country think it too low. Partly as a result, both the deficit and the debt (see Tables 1 and 2) of the Basque Country have been significantly lower than that of Spain, as a percentage of relevant GDP (see Table 3). The position in the Basque Country has, however, been deteriorating quite rapidly in 2011/12, which the new plan is now seeking to address.[6]

---

5   Under Article 45, such debt issues should be to finance investment (that is, not a deficit on current expenditures), and such issues should be jointly agreed between the Basque regional government and the central authorities. Whether the first limitation will survive the worsening deficit in 2012 in the Basque region is uncertain. There do not seem to be any instances in which the central authorities have blocked a Basque request for debt issuance, but there may have been internal discussions and compromises.

6   See www.minhap.gob.es/es-ES/Areas%20Tematicas/Financiacion%20Autonomica/Paginas/ComisionMixtaPaisVasco.aspx.

TABLE 1. FISCAL DEFICIT, BASQUE COUNTRY AND SPAIN

	Deficit as percentage of GDP	
	Basque Country	Spain
2003	-0.10	-0.35
2004	0.00	-0.11
2005	0.00	1.27
2006	0.07	2.37
2007	0.07	1.92
2008	-1.18	-4.50
2009	-3.89	-11.18
2010	-2.49	-9.34
2011	-2.56	-8.51

Source: Ministry of Finance and Public Administration,
www.minhap.gob.es

TABLE 2. DEBT, BASQUE COUNTRY

Debt as a percentage of GDP			
2000	5.3	2010 Q1	5.1
2001	3.8	Q2	6.0
2002	3.0	Q3	6.3
2003	3.1	Q4	7.8
2004	2.7	2011 Q1	7.6
2005	2.0	Q2	8.1
2006	1.5	Q3	8.1
2007	1.0	Q4	8.3
2008	1.5	2012 Q1	10.2
2009 Q3	2.7	Q2	10.8
Q4	4.0		

Source: Bank of Spain, www.bde.es

TABLE 3. DEBT, BASQUE COUNTRY AND SPAIN

	Spain Debt (as % of GDP)	Basque Country Debt (as % of GDP)
2000	59.4	8.9
2001	55.6	6.8
2002	52.6	5.7
2003	48.8	6.4
2004	46.3	5.8
2005	43.2	4.6
2006	39.7	3.8
2007	36.3	2.8
2008	40.2	3.7
2009	53.9	5.0
2010	61.2	12.7
2011	68.5	12.1

Source: Bank of Spain, www.bde.es

With a higher GDP per capita in the Basque Country than in the rest of Spain and a significantly lower deficit (at least until very recently), the Basque credit rating has been *above* that of Spain by about one notch (see Table 4).

TABLE 4. RATINGS, BASQUE COUNTRY

	S & P (July 2012)	Fitch (June 2012)	Moody's (June 2012)
Paris Vasco	A	A	Baa2
Espana	BBB+	BBB	Baa3

Source: Credit Ratings Agencies

While this latter may appear encouraging for Scotland, it has rested on some conditions (higher GDP per capital, much lower debt ratio, favourable contributions to central financing and, partly hence, lower deficits, until recently, than central government) that are unlikely to get repeated, or at least not to the same extent, in the Scottish case.

But, despite the more favourable credit rating, Basque debt trades at a significantly higher interest rate (yield) than Spanish sovereign debt. Its largest, benchmark debt issue has been the issue of 700 mn euro, maturing 2019, with a coupon of 4.15%. The comparable Spanish debt issue was the one, also maturing 2019, with a coupon of

4.3%. The average (mean and median) spread of Basque over Spanish yields has been slightly over 1%. In earlier years, this was because the market for Basque debt was thin and illiquid, on which see the text below. More recently, as the Bloomberg chart below illustrates for 1 October 2012 (see Figure 1), the spread has widened sharply to almost 4%. This may well be in part connected to fears both about the Basque economy and its enhanced need for debt finance and also to increased concerns about the implications of independence, including possible redenomination risk. At such an elevated yield, the Basque authorities are unlikely to try, or to be able, to access the debt market for new finance.

FIGURE 1. SPREAD OF BASQUE COUNTRY YIELDS OVER SPANISH YIELDS

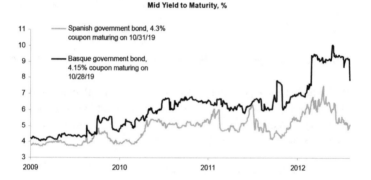

Source: Bloomberg

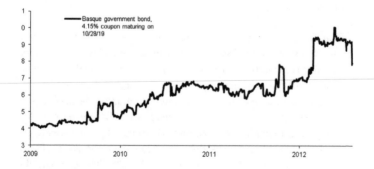

Source: Bloomberg

138

One of the key issues to be resolved would be how large a proportion of the existing UK debt would be allocated to Scotland. For the purpose of this exercise, it is assumed that the share of the UK's public sector net debt (PSND) to be allocated to Scotland in the event of independence would be approximately 8.5%. The scale of UK PSND at that time, say at the end of 2014, is not predictable in advance, of course, but may amount to about £1.5 billion, giving a Scottish share of £120 bn.[7]

What is less clear is the mechanism to be used for transferring the debt once the quantum has been agreed. There are two polar extremes. The first would be for Scotland, having agreed on a net figure, to raise that sum at the outset by issuing new Scottish debt and then transferring that to HMT in London. This would have some advantages. It would wipe the slate clean. It would establish a market for Scottish Government debt at a time when news about Scottish affairs and local patriotism would be most pronounced, thus enabling a better market and lower interest rates than otherwise. Moreover, expectations currently suggest that official interest rates will, *risk premia aside,* remain very low at the end of 2014. So, converting existing debt into new debt could lower the annual interest cost.

But it would also have disadvantages. It would be risky. Trying to sell a large volume of debt of a new government with no track record (and some perceived tendency towards high public sector expenditure) might fail, or only be possible at an unattractively high yield.

The other polar extreme would be to continue (with the agreed percentage) participation in all existing UK debt issues, thereby having to raise new Scottish debt to finance the Scottish deficit, the contribution to UK interest payments and the contribution to UK debt maturities. This would allow the Scottish debt market to be built up more slowly, especially since the average maturity of UK debt is quite long. This would not only be consistent with legal obligations to existing UK debt holders but would also avoid the tricky question of whether what should be apportioned is at book or market value. But it would be a more fiddly process, complex and subject to contention. Moreover, it would leave London at some perceived risk of a Scottish default. This latter issue was raised in the earlier

---

7   See Lesley Hutton's paper for the David Hume Institute, *Issues Facing an Independent Scotland – Scotland's Share of UK Public Debt.* David Hume Institute, Research Paper 1/2012. March 2012.

discussions on Quebec.[8]

Perhaps the best approach would be for some compromise between these two extremes. The Scottish Government could take advice on how large initial issues of its own debt could be. This sum could then be used to retire its participation in a larger number of smaller and/or near maturity gilt issues, leaving just a few larger and longer-dated gilts to be retired as they came due.

So, one key question is the speed with which Scotland would

---

8   John Chant (1991) in Dividing the Debt: Avoiding the Burden wrote:

"The problems of dividing the debt would not end once the division had been made. A schedule would have to be devised for the turnover of Quebec's share. Immediate assumption in one step would increase the existing provincial debt by at least 130 percent. To make the market impact of the new debt more gradual, Boothe and Harris suggest that Quebec assume responsibility for its share according to the maturity of Canada's existing debt." See 'Alternative Divisions of Federal Assets and Liabilities'.

"Delay in transfer would, however, prolong ROC's exposure to risk. Until the debt matured, Canada would bear responsibility for servicing it and would depend on transfers from Quebec for a share of the cost. Moreover, at the maturity, Canada would require substantial transfers from Quebec in order to retire its share. Thus, Canada would have to protect itself against Quebec's failure to meet its obligations.

Such failure cannot be ruled out. Issues surrounding the debt might lead a separate Quebec to feel Canada's actions had imposed costs on it much higher than those it expected. Post-separation policies of the Bank of Canada, over which Quebec had no say, might, for example, force the Canadian dollar to levels higher than anticipated at the time of break-up, reducing Quebec's returns from its exports. It could be tempted to use the debt transfer as a lever to pressure post-separation Canada with respect to these or other policies that worked out to its disadvantage." (Page 88)

"Boothe and Harris suggest that Quebec's posting securities would offer some surety in the bitter atmosphere that might follow separation. Yet many kinds of securities would not offer complete protection. Outsiders might view intergovernmental obligations as different from marketable government securities. Partial default might not face sanctions as large as default on market issues would; as long as Quebec maintained its service of its other debt, it could conceivably stave off (or reduce) the usual market sanctions of lower credit ratings and higher interest rates on new issues.

"Canada could, however, protect itself by specifying the types of securities that it would accept against Quebec's future obligations. It should require securities that:

»   are senior to all existing Quebec provincial debt;
»   are identical in other characteristics to marketable issues of outstanding Quebec debt; and
»   have cleared all regulatory procedures necessary for them to be traded publicly in all markets in which Quebec debt currently trades.

Having such securities lodged with it would protect Canada in two ways. First, it could market them to cover any default in Quebec's payments. Second, any default by Quebec would represent a default on issues that are held by other investors and, like any other default on marketable debt, would lower Quebec's credit rating and raise interest rates on its subsequent issues."

substitute its own debt for that of the UK. The second critical issue is whether Scotland might face an additional risk premium on its own debt, relative to that on gilts, as and when its debt built up. There are two main such forms of risk, liquidity risk and credit risk. Debt issues, which are small and traded relatively infrequently, have larger bid/ask spreads and a smaller order book, therefore a market order imposes a larger adverse price response. The average size of new issue in the UK gilt market in 2011 was many billion pounds. If the Scottish debt management office were to make new issues large enough to enhance the liquidity of each stock, they would then be relatively lumpy and large relative to cash flows. Refinance roll-overs could come at an inopportune time, and between the infrequent large issues, the Scottish Treasury would be increasingly reliant on short dated Treasury Bills.

Liquidity premia can, however, be quite large. A recent paper by Bernoth, von Hagen and Schuknecht, ECB Working Paper 369, June 2004, stated on page 22 that

"Yield differentials across European countries reflect liquidity risk. The liquidity variable shows negative and significant coefficients [see Table 4, p. 23, and Table 5, p. 24] in almost all regressions. An increase of the relative debt size by one percent causes a reduction of the issuer country's interest rate by around 0.7 basis points. An interesting result is that this liquidity effect diminishes or even vanishes with EMU, as shown by the positive and significant coefficients on the Liquidity*EMU variable in most regressions. This is consistent with the notion that financial market integration has become more complete in Europe."

Using their coefficient, and applying that to the Scottish case where the Scottish debt market would be about 8.5% of the size of the UK market, would indicate that Scottish official interest rates could be almost 1% above UK interest rates on liquidity grounds, much the same as used to hold for the Basque Country, though somewhat less than this if the debt office focused on a few large, lumpy issues.

It is worth noting, however, the qualification in the quote above, that by 2004 the market size of the different countries in the euro zone had become less of a factor, because they were then seen as integral parts of a single currency region. Unfortunately by now, confidence in the solvency of some members of the euro zone and belief in the irreversibility of that currency regime has waned badly, with the result that interest rate differentials have sky-rocketed in several cases.

In chapter 3, on the choice of currency regime, it was stated that one prime possibility would be that Scotland remain part of the sterling currency area. In this event, Scotland would inevitably be seen as a small peripheral member of that area. The same would be the case if it chose to join the euro zone. Especially with expectations of continuing fiscal deficits (see chapter 4) and, in the light of the travails of the euro zone periphery, the markets would apply some significant credit risk differential to Scottish debt (whatever the new Scottish Government might say and however unfair that might seem to some). So, like Basque debt, or the debt of the weaker, peripheral members of the euro zone, Scottish debt would probably require a significantly higher interest rate than UK gilts. The present is hardly a propitious moment, from a market standpoint, to choose to become a small, peripheral member of a larger currency union, whether of sterling or the euro, and it is doubtful that this environment will change substantively over the next few years.

What the overall interest cost would be, relative to London, is impossible to predict with any accuracy. But in the present milieu of concern about such currency unions, it could easily be above 1% even if economic events went quite well, potentially spiking far higher, as seen in the euro zone, if economic developments should deteriorate.[9] One of the obvious consequences of this conclusion is that the Scottish Government would be compelled to run a convincingly prudent fiscal position compared to the rest of the UK in order to maintain the confidence of the markets.

5.1.3 *Monetary management*

5.1.3.1 Structure

All separate countries that become members of the European Union are required[10] to have an independent monetary authority and an independent financial supervisor, whether they are new entrants or are, as in the case of Scotland, already members of, or rejoining, the EU by virtue of being part of the UK.

Thus, the general principles on enlargement decided by the European Council in June 1992[11] require as a pre-condition that the

---

9   If Scotland were to choose a currency of its own, the risk premia would tend to be even greater under normal circumstances, since any non-Scottish body buying Scottish debt would also face exchange rate risk.

10 European Communities Commission, Europe and the challenge of enlargement (June 1992). Bulletin of the European Communities Supplement 3/92. See: http://aei.pitt.edu/1573/1/challenge__of__enlargement__June__92.pdf

11 See the reference in footnote 10.

candidate countries have a functioning and competitive economy and an adequate administrative framework in the public and private sectors. In that respect, the existence of an *independent* supervisor and of an independent authority in charge of monetary policy is viewed, by the EC, as essential for the functioning of a competitive market economy

Scotland could, of course, establish its own monetary authority. But there is an unresolved question of whether, if Scotland were to remain within a sterling monetary union and wished to take the Bank of England as its independent monetary authority (assuming the redefined UK were prepared to undertake this role) it would be able to do so. Moreover, it would raise the question of what functions, if any, of a central bank the Scottish Government would need to establish in Scotland. It is unclear whether the EU principles were ever written with the expectation that two countries might wish to share an 'independent' monetary authority. At one extreme, could Scotland come to some agreement with the redefined UK to agree that the Bank of England would be the independent central bank for both countries and fulfil all the necessary EU criteria on behalf of both? It is difficult to assess in advance whether the relevant authorities in London, Brussels and Frankfurt, all of whom would have an effective veto, would agree to this.

Furthermore, if an independent Scotland were to maintain a shared currency with the redefined UK, there is an important question whether it is realistic over the longer term to have separate financial regulation. Europe is apparently seeking to move in the other direction with its proposals for a banking union. One potential solution for Scotland and the redefined UK would be to have the type of framework that the EU authorities are hoping to achieve at some future date in Europe: that is, a banking union, one supervisory body (with potential for some regional variation in application), a common deposit guarantee scheme and a formal process for solving cross-border resolution issues. While this might be a positive outcome for Scotland, at least in the transition phase, there is the question of whether the redefined UK would agree.

On the question of whether a monetary policy authority (the central bank) need be separated from the institution in charge of financial supervision, the answer is that such a separation is not strictly necessary. The model of supervision is left to member-state (MS) decision: every MS can adopt the model they consider the most suitable for their economy/financial system. As regards the *administrative capacity* of the supervisor, this is usually considered as ancillary to the capacity of implementation of the acquis in the specific area and has been clearly set out in the financial service chapter of negotiations for entry into the EU, for example, with Croatia.[12]

In general terms, the independence of the supervisory authority should be based on the Basel Common Principles on Banking Supervision (since there are no common rules on independence of supervisors at EU level).[13] Moreover, this decision could be effected by the ongoing arrangements for the European Central Bank (ECB) to have overall control of banking supervision amongst euro zone countries, as part of the move towards a 'Banking Union', which remains under discussion.

In a relatively small country such as Scotland it might be most sensible to combine the monetary authority (Central Bank), supervisory authority and debt management office into one single institution. While the running costs and staffing levels of such an institution are not negligible (for example, the operational costs of the Icelandic and Finnish Central Banks are equivalent to £16m and £85m respectively, and their staffing numbers are about 150 and 450),[14] they are normally small relative to the seigneurage that Central Banks receive from their note issue. This brings us to the next question, that of the future note issue in Scotland.

5.1.3.2 Note issue

At present, Scotland has a distinctive form of note issue. The three Scottish banks, RBS, BoS and Clydesdale, all issue their own notes. These are, however, backed, once issued, on a one-for-one basis by Bank of England (special) notes. The Scottish banks gain from some advertising benefit and from being able to maintain vault cash (that is, printed but unused notes in their vaults) at no expense (unlike English banks which have to fund their vault cash), while the seigneurage accrues to the Bank of England.

This latter would presumably cease after independence but continue unchanged under either Devo plus or Devo max. The same procedure as before could continue after independence, assuming that Scotland continued to use sterling. The Scottish banks could then transfer their existing holdings of Bank of England (BoE) notes to a Central Bank of Scotland (CBoS), should one be established, which could use them to buy gilts and Scottish Government debt, giving it a balance sheet. Alternatively, the Scottish banks could replace their

---

12 See Croatia, pp. 17 and 32-33, in: http://ec.europa.eu/enlargement/pdf/key_documents/2011/package/hr_rapport_2011_en.pdf

13 Basel Committee on Banking Supervision, *Core Principles for Effective Banking Supervision*, Basel. September 1997.

14 In view of the prior financial problems of Iceland, the size of their Central Bank may be regarded as having been sub-optimally small.

existing notes, as they become returned in payment, by new CBoS notes, transferring the excess BoE notes to CBoS as that happened. The former method would maintain continuity and the existing benefits to the Scottish banks. The latter method, replacing commercial bank notes with Central Bank notes might be seen as more appropriate for a sovereign country. Should Scotland want and be allowed to use the Bank of England as its monetary and supervisory authority, then the seigneurage profits from the issue of Scottish banknotes could be passed back to the Scottish Treasury, less some payment for the use of Bank of England services.

If the decision were taken to join the euro zone, the issue of euro notes would be done in the same way as in other euro zone countries, with seigneurage dependent on the current formula (relating to population and GDP). Again, the banks would transfer BoE notes to the CBoS, which would use them to buy assets to back its new euro liabilities.

The right to seigneurage is valuable. W. Buiter has presented several calculations of how such a valuation can be done.[15] In the estimation of Scotland's share of the UK debt, the transfer of the present value of the seigneurage from the BoE to the CBoS, should it be established, on the existing Scottish note issue would be one, but a minor, element in the overall calculations.

5.1.3.3 Responsibilities of the Central Bank of Scotland

As a small country in a wider currency zone, assuming that Scotland continued to use the pound after independence, the official interest rate would be set in London. However, as already noted in Section 5.1, Scottish debt management can, and should, try to minimise unnecessary interest rate differentials. If the choice was made to join the euro instead, the interest rate would be set by the ECB. There would be no question of establishing a CBoS under Devo plus or Devo max.

---

15 For example, Buiter (2012) section 7.4.

The main banks in Scotland have now become, in effect, head-quartered abroad, with RBS and BoS in London, as discussed below. That would make the redefined UK their home country. The main regulatory powers, particularly on solvency issues, over a cross-border bank lie with the home country.[16, 17] So all the main banks have Scotland as their host country for their Scottish subsidiaries, while other banks, for example, HSBC, Barclays, Santander, would continue to maintain branches in Scotland. The host country is responsible for the maintenance of adequate liquidity in all banks sited therein. Overall liquidity requirements would be primarily determined elsewhere – for example, by Basel, via EC directives and in London – in the form of the liquidity coverage ratio (LCR) and perhaps the net stable funding ratio (NSFR or NSF ratio), but the composition of such liquid assets in Scotland could be problematical. How far, if at all, should the CBoS require financial institutions located in Scotland, including insurance companies and pension funds, to keep their liquid assets in the form of Scottish Government debt, as contrasted with gilts or other countries' sovereign debt? Requiring Scottish financial institutions to hold a proportion of their assets in Scottish Government debt would provide a captive market for the latter, and hence could reduce the thinness of that market and the likely adverse interest differential. But, by the same token, such a requirement could be an extra cost burden on Scottish financial inter-mediaries, albeit usually a relatively small cost, and could reduce the relative competitiveness of Scottish financial intermediation.

Should an independent Scotland wish to join the euro zone, the responsibility for the solvency of the Scottish banks would con-tinue to reside in London. In this case, however, the ECB, under the proposed Banking Union, would also maintain supervisory over-sight over the Scottish subsidiaries of RBS and Lloyds. As before, a CBoS would be responsible for overseeing their local liquidity management.

The Scottish Building Society is the only headquartered build-ing society in Scotland. The CBoS would be responsible for its supervision and resolution if it got into trouble. Given its small size, relative to Scottish GDP, this should not be particularly difficult. In view of the foreign ownership of all the main banks, there may be

---

16 The allocation of responsibilities to home and host countries goes back to the earliest days of the Basel Committee on Banking Supervision. See Charles Goodhart, *The Basel Committee on Banking Supervision: A History of the Early Years, 1974–1997*, Cambridge, Cambridge University Press, 2011.

17 It should be noted that the UK is currently opting out of the initiative to form a 'Banking Union' in the euro zone (and in some other countries in the EU that wish to join).

some public demand, post-independence, for the establishment of a Scottish development bank, whether publicly or privately owned. Such development banks have had a somewhat chequered history in other countries, and the CBoS would have to ensure that it had full independent supervisory powers, free from political pressures, over any such institution.

With all the main banks being headquartered abroad, banking supervision should not be an arduous task. At least Scotland should be spared the kind of banking disaster that befell Iceland and Ireland, since the solvency of RBS, BoS and Clydesdale would remain the responsibility of London, not Edinburgh. Of course, if one of these cross-border banks did fail, the London authorities would no doubt ask the independent Scottish authorities for a contribution to sharing the burden. But any such contribution would be negotiable and limited, since the main regulatory oversight would have remained in London. In other financial fields, for example, life insurance and pensions, general insurance, wealth and asset management, and other financial management, Scotland has a higher share of headquartered (home) institutions, notably in life and pensions business.[18]

This raises the question of whether regulation and supervision of other (non-bank) financial intermediaries headquartered in Scotland should also be done in the CBoS, or in a separate institution. Moreover, the CBoS should not want to get involved in the myriad, often small-scale consumer protection issues that arise in banking. Post-independence, Scotland would have to establish its own separate consumer protection and ombudsman bodies. One possible structure for Scotland could be that the CBoS has overall responsibility for financial stability, macro-prudential issues and the micro-prudential supervision of banks (and building societies), while a separate body (FSA) has responsibility for all other (OFI) micro-prudential matters, including the operation of financial markets, together with all consumer protection issues relating to finance, including those arising from banking. But other structural arrangements would also be possible.

Assuming Scotland remains within a sterling currency union, the present payment system can remain unchanged. There is no case for changing it. If it joined the euro zone, it would immediately become a member of the T2 system.

---

18 See Figure 5 of the Seventh Annual Report on *The Strategy for the Financial Services Industry in Scotland, April 2011–March 2012*. The Scottish Government.

5.1.3.4 Summary

So long as Scotland remains within the sterling currency union (or in the euro zone), with its main banks being headquartered abroad, the CBoS would have relatively little to do, either in setting monetary policy or in maintaining financial stability. Its main role might be in debt management. Should Scottish adherence to that currency union come under question, however, its role would become much more vital, to use its balance sheet, currency reserves and market operations as far as it could to maintain confidence in the maintenance of the currency union, and in the viability and liquidity of the local financial intermediaries; for example, by Emergency Lending Assistance. As a small and newly established independent country with small foreign currency reserves, the power and ability of a CBoS to stem a speculative market attack on its own would be limited. It would need support from the larger members of its currency union or, if it had adopted a separate currency, from the IMF.

As has been shown in the euro zone, lack of confidence in the maintenance of a currency union results in local depositors shifting funds into bank branches in the 'stronger' part of the union. The CBoS would, therefore, be primarily dependent, should confidence slip, on the banks, or in a real crisis the BoE (or ECB), recycling such funds. As with the euro zone now, such recycling would eventually be coupled with conditionality (probably austerity) to try to address the source of such a loss of confidence. If that conditionality was not politically and socially acceptable, the only alternative remaining would be for Scotland to adopt an independent currency. As discussed in chapter 3, there are significant risks in pursuing this policy. It has neither been recommended nor proposed by any major group to date and would be a last resort. But, if that were to happen, the CBoS would then take a much more central role than is currently envisaged.

5.2 PRIVATE SECTOR FINANCE

5.2.1 *Banks*

In the course of the 2008 financial crisis, RBS was recapitalised by the British government, which now owns some 83% of its equity. Halifax Bank of Scotland was merged with Lloyds TSB, and these joint banks were also recapitalised (over 40% of the equity). Both banks are now, and after Scottish independence would remain, owned and headquartered in London.

The cost to Scotland of seeking to buy a majority ownership of either RBS or Lloyds, by issuing more Scottish debt, would, we assume, be prohibitive. The cost of buying those parts of the business of RBS (and/or BoS) located in Scotland would be less astronomical, but having a commercial bank run by the public sector has drawbacks. While the intention might be to eventually sell back to the private sector, this would be a risky exercise, risks that a newly fledged independent government might be wise to avoid.

If Scotland becomes independent, it would seem anomalous to have a bank entitled Royal Bank of Scotland headquartered in London. Perhaps the most likely development would be for the main London bank to change its name (possibly back to The National Westminster?). But those parts of this bank located in Scotland would, almost certainly, retain the name RBS, as would BoS. Both the independent Scottish Government and these banks would want, we would expect, these Scottish parts to be separately capitalised subsidiaries rather than branches; largely because subsidiaries come, at least partially, under the control of the host state whereas branches remain wholly a part of the home bank. If RBS and BoS were to operate in Scotland as branches, not subsidiaries, Scotland would have virtually *no* banks that it could treat as Scottish. The Scottish authorities should have the power to require subsidiarisation in these two instances. There will be other cases of banks headquartered in London doing banking business in Scotland. Whether these should be put under pressure by the authorities to become subsidiaries, or be allowed to remain as branches should they so wish, is partly a question of relative size and could be decided on a case-by-case basis.

5.2.2 *Funding Costs*

As a generality the credit rating of any financial intermediary will be below, and its funding cost above, that of the sovereign state in which that institution is headquartered. For reasons set out in Section 5.1.2 above, and in Chapters 3 and 4, we would expect the credit rating of an independent Scotland probably to be below, and its government debt interest rates above, those in the redefined United Kingdom. The differential might become quite small if the currency union proved successful. But, given the doubts about the continuing success of the euro zone, the differential could be significant at the outset and could increase further sharply if economic events disappointed. This differential in sovereign funding costs would, under normal circumstances, translate into differential funding costs for Scottish financial intermediaries, relative to those in London.

This would be an incentive to relocate headquarters to London, even if the bulk of operations remained physically in Scotland.

Otherwise there would not seem to be any major detrimental (nor on the other hand positive) effects of Scottish independence on the role of financial intermediation in the independent Scotland.

One of the specific claims that has been made is that, under independence, household mortgage payment rates would increase. However, it can be argued that, provided there is a fully integrated financial services sector, where products can be bought across any boundary between Scotland and the redefined UK, and one common interest rate for the sterling zone, this is unlikely to be the case. Financial institutions may be influenced by the relative long-term success of the Scottish economy (and therefore the creditworthiness of households in Scotland) but not the specific differential that may arise in government gilts.

5.2.3 *Summary*

The key problem that independence could bring to the Scottish financial industry would be higher funding costs, as it would suffer in turn from the enhanced risk premia that would, we have argued, face the Scottish sovereign.

5.3 CONCLUSIONS

This chapter has highlighted a range of challenges, depending on the precise nature of any constitutional change that might be considered, that a Scottish Government would face both in the direction of official finance and private finance. In this conclusion, some key questions are identified that arguably should form the centre of the ongoing debate about constitutional change insofar as it relates to the Scottish financial structure.

5.3.1 *Official finance*

Debt management

»   Under the constitutional propositions that entail greater autonomy within the UK, what powers to issue and manage its own debt would be transferred to Scotland from the UK Government? Would the UK Government underwrite the Scottish debt? What agreement might the UK Government seek regarding these powers?
»   If Scotland were to have powers for debt management and for monetary and financial management, what institutional arrangements would it establish for their management?

Debt issuance

» What risk premia might an independent Scottish Government, or a Government with greater debt-raising powers within the UK, face?

» What would be the implications for Scotland of adverse market sentiment on the capacity and the cost premia to issue Scottish debt?

Debt transference with independence

» What share of the prevailing UK debt stock would be transferred to a newly independent Scottish Government?

» Through what mechanism would that transference of debt from the UK to Scotland be effected?

» Over what time horizon would debt be transferred to a Scottish Government?

Monetary institutions

» Under what circumstances would an independent monetary authority, or Central Bank, and an independent financial supervisory capacity be established?

» Would Scotland be able to establish the Bank of England as its independent monetary authority, rather than set up a Central Bank of Scotland, assuming the redefined UK were prepared to undertake this role?

» Would the monetary policy authority be distinct from, or have responsibility for, the financial supervisory authority?

Note issue

» How would the note issue be managed?

» How would the transference of the present value of the seigneurage be determined?

Role of the Central Bank

» How would Scotland exercise its responsibilities as host country in the direction and oversight of the liquidity of the Scottish banking system?

» Would the Scottish Government require Scottish financial institutions to hold liquid assets in the form of Scottish Government debt?

- » Would Scotland seek to establish its own development bank and how might it achieve this?
- » How would Scotland undertake the supervision and regulation of the non-bank financial intermediaries?
- » What role would the Central Bank play if Scotland's position, within either a sterling or a euro monetary union, came under pressure and was called into question?

REFERENCES

Basel Committee on Banking Supervision. 1997. *Core Principles for Effective Banking Supervision*, Basel, September.

Basque Country. 1978. *Statute of Autonomy of the Basque Country.*

Bernoth, Kerstin; von Hagen, Jurgen & Schuknecht, Ludger, 2004. "Sovereign Risk premia in the European Government bond market", European Central Bank Working Paper 369, June.

Buiter, Willem & Rahbari, Ebrahim. 2012. 'Looking into the Deep Pockets of the ECB', *Citi Economics Global Economics View*, 27 February.

Chant, John. 1991. 'Dividing the Debt: Avoiding the Burden', *Closing the Books: Dividing Federal Assets and Debt if Canada Breaks Up.* Toronto: C.D. Howe Institute. The Canada Round: A Series on the Economics of the Break-up of Confederation, no. 8.

European Communities Commission. 1992. *Europe and the Challenge of Enlargement.* Bulletin of the European Communities Supplement 3/92, June. Available at: http://aei. pitt.edu/1573/1/challenge__of__ enlargement__June__92.pdf

Goodhart, Charles. 2011. *The Basel Committee on Banking Supervision: A History of the Early Years, 1974–1997.* Cambridge, Cambridge University Press.

HM Treasury. 2012. *The Scottish Act 2012: A Consultation on Bond Issuance by the Scottish Government*, quote from p. 5. June.

Hutton, Lesley. 2012. *Issues Facing an Independent Scotland: Scotland's Share of UK Public Debt.* David Hume Institute. Research Paper 1/2012. March.

Scottish Government. 2012. Seventh Annual Report on *The Strategy for the Financial Services Industry in Scotland, April 2011–March 2012.*

CHAPTER 6

The Impact of Greater Autonomy on the Growth of the Scottish Economy
Professor Peter G McGregor[1] and Professor J Kim Swales[2]

INTRODUCTION AND BACKGROUND

An important element in the debate on greater fiscal autonomy and independence in Scotland is the potential impact on economic growth. Growth is conventionally measured either as an increase in a country's Gross Domestic Product (GDP) or GDP per head. Scottish GDP measures the value of goods and services produced within Scotland in any particular year. This broadly corresponds to the incomes generated in Scotland by these productive activities. Therefore, as GDP per head rises, average incomes in Scotland should also rise. While there is valid criticism of GDP as a measure of welfare (Stiglitz *et al*, 2009), improvements in the population's material standard of living has been a central plank of the strategy of successive Scottish Governments. The perception is that Scotland's growth performance has lagged behind that of the UK as a whole but there is a debate around whether this performance would be improved if the Scottish Government had a wider range of economic powers.

In section 6.1 of this chapter we consider the evidence on Scottish growth performance in the recent past, in order to get a feel for the size of any problem. In section 6.2 we outline the general sources of economic growth within the context of a small open economy such as Scotland. In this section we do not consider the constitutional position of the economy. In section 6.3 we attempt to evaluate how far the constitutional changes that would occur under greater devolution or independence would affect the primary sources of economic growth and thus the prospects of the Scottish economy. Section 6.4 is a short conclusion, together with some of the critical questions that should shape our future thinking.

---

1   Head of Economics Department, University of Strathclyde.
2   Director of the Fraser of Allander Institute, Department of Economics, University of Strathclyde.

Figure 1 shows that over the last ten years the growth performance of Scotland closely mirrors that of the UK as a whole. Also, Scotland has performed slightly better than a set of comparator small countries used by the present Scottish Government as a benchmark. Over a longer time period, Scotland's growth against the UK is somewhat slower. However, its present GDP per head is very close to that of the UK as a whole, but in so far as this position has been achieved as a result of out-migration, this might be seen as problematic.

It is important to place Scotland's per capita GDP figure performance in context. Perhaps the major fundamental spatial economic issue for the UK is the polarised regional economic performance that has been sustained over many decades (Gardiner *et al*, 2012). For the output per head figures, only London and the South East have values which are above the UK average, by about 40%. All other regions have values below the average. Scotland's performance, at around the UK average, is therefore somewhat atypical. Similar results apply for Gross Disposable Household Income per head, which is a better measure of individual welfare. In Scotland, this is again just below the UK average, with only regions in the English South East having values above the average. Many English regions have very low values, the lowest being the North East, which is 15% below the UK average.

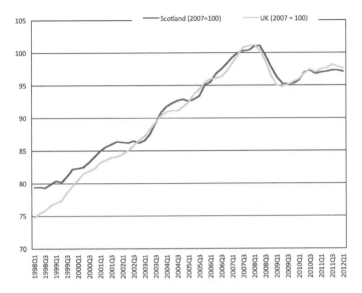

Source: Scottish Government and Office of National Statistics

The key economic issue, therefore, might be framed in the following
way. Are Scotland's economic interests well served within the spatially polarised UK economy, whose general growth performance it
typically tracks? Or would it perform better as an independent country? Of course, rejecting independence does not imply accepting the
status quo. Greater degrees of devolution are possible, and in fact will
be delivered once the Scotland Act (2012) comes into force.

6.2 ECONOMIC GROWTH: KEY DETERMINANTS

The most straightforward way to think about economic growth is
from a supply-side perspective. In very broad-brush terms, output
depends on the quantity of different factors of production employed
and the efficiency with which they operate. Factors of production are
traditionally classified under labour, capital and natural resources.
Efficiency is captured by various measures of productivity. For the
economy to grow, the supply of inputs must be increasing (and be
employed) and/or the productivity with which these resources operate must rise. This can be represented in the expression below.

$$GDP = \left[\frac{GDP}{Employees}\right]\left[\frac{Employees}{Population}\right] Population$$

6.2.1 Population

The population level is a sensitive issue for Scotland. Over the period 1950 to 2000, the Scottish population was very stable, just above the 5 million mark. Up until 1990, although there was positive natural growth in the population (births were greater than deaths), this was matched by positive net out-migration. From 1990 to around 2000, both net migration and natural population growth had values very close to zero. Since 2000, positive net in-migration has dominated a natural population change which remains close to zero. While the present projection for Scotland's future population growth up to 2035 is positive, and higher than the EU as a whole, it is lower than the other countries that make up the UK.[3]

For growth, low population change and, in particular, high levels of net out-migration are potentially problematic. Migration is selective and economic migration is concentrated amongst the young and skilled, so that out-migration is likely to have a detrimental effect on the quality of the labour force, reducing entrepreneurship and economic dynamism. In this respect, in so far as favourable labour market conditions – relatively high wages and low unemployment rates – stimulate in-migration, they improve the quality of the labour force, further improving productivity, generating a potential virtuous circle of growth.

6.2.2 The participation rate

While policy concern often focuses on the growth of GDP, from a welfare (and competitiveness) point of view, increasing per capita GDP is a major goal. It is useful to break this down in the following way. GDP per head can increase through a rise in the average productivity of labour (GDP per employee) or the participation rate (the proportion of the population that is in employment), as is clear from the expression above.

It is most straightforward to outline the participation issues first. The participation rate will depend on a range of factors. The first is demographic. With an ageing population, we expect a higher proportion of the population to be above retirement age. However, as already stated, it is important to stress that Scotland is very open

---

3   It is important to stress that population projections are very sensitive to assumptions on migration, which are simply imposed, not explicitly modelled.

to migration, both from other parts of the UK and also the rest of the EU. Its demographic make-up is therefore not determined solely by natural population change, and variations in migration, which in part depend upon economic activity in Scotland, can have significant impacts.

However, the participation rate might vary for a range of other reasons. First, there are sustained spatial variations in the unemployment rate across the UK: high levels of unemployment reduce GDP per head (as well as having very undesirable social costs). Second, some people of working age might have dropped out of the labour force because they are long-term sick, have family responsibilities or have become 'discouraged' workers. Clearly increasing the participation rate should increase GDP per head and a whole range of welfare, health, childcare, skill and labour demand policies can positively affect this. At present, Scotland has the highest participation rate of all the countries of the UK and is relatively high in international comparisons.

6.2.3 Labour productivity

Labour productivity is typically measured as output per employee.[4] Increases can occur through a number of channels. Perhaps the most straightforward is the contribution of inputs other than labour, primarily capital. This means that the labour productivity within a particular country or region can be strongly affected by its industrial structure. That is to say, a heavy concentration in industries whose technology is capital-intensive will increase measured labour productivity and GDP. Measured productivity can also be influenced by the ownership structure. Foreign direct investment (FDI) typically has higher labour productivity than their domestic rivals. This is likely to reflect both greater capital intensity and greater technical efficiency as measured against local companies.

A second source of productivity variation is the level of human capital in the work force. Extensive econometric studies find persistent wage premia for higher levels of educational qualifications (Psacharopoulos and Patrinos, 2004; Walker and Zhu, 2007). These wage premia are interpreted as reflecting higher labour productivity, so that an important means of increasing GDP is to increase the skill level within the labour force. One way of thinking about attaining higher educational qualifications is as an investment in human

---

4   More theoretically correct measures are output per worker hour and the total factor productivity (TFP). TFP measures output against a composite comprising all the inputs employed. However, data problems mean that it is often difficult to use these alternative measures.

capital. As with physical capital, greater levels of human capital will increase labour productivity. Influencing the level of investment in human capital is clearly a policy variable. For example, Lisenkova *et al* (2010) calculate, from their base year of 2006, that maintaining the existing high levels of university enrolment in Scotland will increase the annual GDP by 6% in the long run.[5]

However, increased human capital is also seen as an important independent facilitator of growth, in that it increases the rate of technical progress and pace of technical change. There are important human capital externalities, so that increasing the skills of one part of the labour force typically benefits the productivity of others. Similarly, the existence of a skilled, educated workforce increases the profitability of developing and using advanced, high-productivity technologies (Acemoglu and Autor, 2012). Policies such as the provision of subsidised or free nursery, school and university places can significantly affect the level of human capital, and all policies to improve skills will fall into this category. In short, while increasing human capital almost certainly also has much wider positive social and personal impacts, it is an important driver of growth.[6]

A third important determinant of labour productivity is the availability of appropriate infrastructure. These are public goods whose provision benefits a wide range of consumers and industries. Their supply would be inadequate if left to private industry alone. These are therefore goods necessarily provided by the state. These include appropriate transport, communications and energy transmission and distribution networks (Stiglitz, 1988). For example, the accessibility of localities by air is increasingly seen as a key element in generating economic growth.

The accumulation of physical, human and infrastructural capital is important for determining the productivity of labour. However, in an open regional economy these stocks of capital are not limited by the region's inherited resources. As has been suggested already, the mobility of factors into the economy can be a source of productivity growth. For example, inward investment and the in-migration of skilled workers can be a key source of physical and human capital. Of course, as we have already noted, regions can lose from the outmigration of skilled workers, and in the past that was Scotland's

---

5   Because the level of educational attainment of the cohorts of workers entering the labour force is much higher than the attainment of those leaving the labour force, the average human capital rises over time until all cohorts in the labour force have benefited from the policy.

6   The notion of human capital also encompasses other human attributes, such as health. High levels of sickness, which can reduce workers' effectiveness or even prevent them working at all, will reduce labour productivity and/or the participation rate.

experience.

However, while all these issues are relevant for a detailed analysis of spatial variations in productivity, there is a strong consensus that the main source of growth in GDP per head in developed countries in the recent past is technical progress: the ability to produce more from less through the development of new methods of production (or new products). This has been one of the central concerns of economics from its very inception as a modern science. Adam Smith's description of the increase in efficiency that specialisation affords, itself generated by the expansion of the market, is a concern with the growth potential of capitalism. The earliest applications of growth accounting, which attempt to identify the contribution made to growth by changes in the stocks of productive inputs, revealed a very large residual (Solow, 1957). This residual has been attributed to technological change and there has been continued interest in identifying its determinants.

One characteristic of the economy which is thought to be crucial in allowing technical change is the institutional arrangements (Acemoglu and Robinson, 2012; Grief, 2006). This applies especially to underdevelopment but is relevant for the performance of all economies. The institutional arrangements should facilitate and reward the adoption of more efficient methods of production and the introduction of new products. Independence is a radical change in the institutional arrangements and many of the arguments for independence concern these issues (Alesina and Spolaore, 2003). Typically, these institutional arrangements cover many areas which are open to government influence. This includes the nature of contracts and property rights, the degree of competition within markets and the financing of technical knowledge. These arrangements have economy-wide scope.

A second set of means by which technical change can be increased relate to the characteristics of individual firms. That is to say, certain types of firm are likely to have an absorptive capacity to develop and adopt new technology. This is strongly linked to research and development activity and the employment of skilled workers. Again, these are areas in which government policy can be active either in providing tax incentives to undertake these activities or other provision of information, encouraging the take-up of new technology.

There is also thought to be interaction between other economic activity and the level of technical change. For example, companies that export typically experience higher levels of technical progress. This is not just because those companies which export are likely to be the most efficient and therefore to be technologically dynamic; rather the process of meeting international competition leads to

efficiency improvements. Similarly, in the urban economics literature, much emphasis is placed on potential spillover effects and
the positive impact of close geographical 'face-to-face' interaction in
driving technical change. There are various sources of these agglom-
eration effects.[7]

In summary, in the modern growth literature a central notion is
that of endogenous growth; that is to say, growth generated by technical change is not something that occurs automatically or randomly.
Rather it is determined by human actions. These include private
decisions, motivated primarily by self-interest but influenced by institutional arrangements and social conventions. However, they also
include a key role for the government in providing important public
goods and intervening where the private market fails. These decisions can have mutually reinforcing effects. For example, an increase
in an individual's human capital will increase their income but can
also increase the income of other workers and the profitability of the
introduction of new technology.

6.3 CONSTITUTIONAL CHANGE AND GROWTH

Independence will increase the formal powers of the Scottish
Government to affect economic behaviour in Scotland. However,
it will reduce the influence of Scottish interests in decisions taken
in the rest of the UK and will introduce an administrative barrier
between the economies of Scotland and the rest of the UK. The
change in the representation of Scotland's interest in international
affairs is difficult to call: Scotland will get its own voice but that
voice will have less weight. Scotland already has a high level of independence in terms of its expenditure and administrative decisions.
However, it has a low level of fiscal revenue devolution and it is in
this area that the major changes introduced by independence would
formally occur.

We will identify the impact of constitutional change on the key
drivers of Scotland's growth potential, as identified in the previous
section. We look at this under four general headings. Two concern
control over fiscal aspects:

» the level of public expenditure in Scotland; and

---

7   A rise in productivity could be linked to increased wages which would stimulate
    in-migration and thereby population change. Alternatively, increased population
    could increase agglomeration that might have positive or negative effects on labour
    productivity.

» the extent and nature of local funding of public expenditure in Scotland.

The final two relate to

» the administration of policy; and
» the impact of the introduction of a border between Scotland and the rest of the UK on Scottish trade.

6.3.1 *Level of government expenditure*

At present, the budget for the Scottish Government comes directly from the UK Government at Westminster and is set by the Barnett formula (Christie and Swales, 2010). This formula is driven by changes in UK public expenditure and Scotland's population share. It is unrelated to the level of taxation raised in Scotland or to a detailed 'needs assessment'. In practice, it has resulted in Scotland's having a public expenditure per head at present 10% higher than the UK average, with the Scottish Government having only limited ability to vary this total. In the devolution referendum of 1997, the Scottish Government were given the power to make a balanced budget variation in the standard rate of income tax within Scotland of three pence in the pound. Curiously, this power has never been used.[8] The Scottish Government has also very limited ability to borrow: it operates under a very tight budget constraint.

It could be the case that in order to stimulate growth the Scottish Government might wish to have a level of public expenditure that differs from that given by the Barnett formula. This would especially be the case if the Scottish and UK Governments differed in their view of the productive use of public expenditure. An example is the change in the financing of higher education in England, away from public funding towards private loans. Through the Barnett formula, this reduction in English public expenditure will produce a corresponding, proportionate reduction in Scottish public expenditure. We have argued that the level of human capital is important for economic growth, and the Scottish Government has decided to maintain a high level of public funding of higher education.[9] However,

---

8   In order for the Scottish Government to implement the Scottish Variable Rate (SVR) of income tax, it had to pay a fee to the Inland Revenue to maintain appropriate records of Scottish tax payers. This was not, in fact, done, so that in practice the SVR could not be implemented at present, even if there was a political will to do so.

9   Of course, there might be other reasons for maintaining a high level of public funding for higher education.

this might now be much more difficult given the reduced revenues coming through Barnett. A linked problem is that the division between current and capital expenditure in Scotland is currently set by the UK Government. This potentially restricts the ability of the Scottish Government to vary the level of public capital investment to improved infrastructure.[10]

There are a number of important points to be made here. First, as we argue in more detail later, the Scottish Government has a high degree of discretion over how it spends its budget. Even if the UK Government decides to reduce the level of expenditure on some activities or transfer them to the private sector, the Scottish Government does not have to follow suit. It can reduce the level of expenditure on other activities within its fixed spending envelope. Secondly, under the Scotland Act (2012), the Scottish Government will be able to vary income tax rates by ten pence in the pound, upwards or downwards. This implies an adjustment, in either direction, of over 10% of the present budget going to the Scottish Government. This means that by adjusting this tax rate the Scottish Government will, in the future, be able to offset any implications for Scotland of the UK Government's changing the aggregate budget within this range. Of course, there will be a corresponding tax differential between Scotland and the rest of the UK. Third, again under the Scotland Act (2012), the Scottish Government will have greater borrowing powers to fund higher public investment.

An argument that in the future a devolved Scotland would have to accept a radically inappropriate level of public expenditure which would hamper the aims of a Scottish Government to stimulate growth seems weak. The Scottish Government will have the powers to make marginal adjustments to the aggregate budget under the new devolved arrangements. However, it is true that under any devolved arrangement, it is unlikely that the Scottish Government will be allowed to operate a fiscal policy that diverges radically from that pursued by the rest of the UK. That is to say, that when the UK is undertaking a fiscal consolidation and attempting to reduce the public sector deficit, Scotland would not be allowed to operate an expansionary fiscal policy, if its debt were implicitly underwritten by HM Treasury. But this is a topic covered more fully in other chapters.

The main ways in which governments in developed countries can influence economic growth is through maintaining a stable macroeconomic environment on the demand side and tackling market and public failures on the supply side. We do not deal with the macroeconomic conditions in any depth here, though they are extremely

---

10 The potential importance of this mix is discussed in Lecca et al (2010b).

important for growth. The level of interest rates and especially expectations about the future stability of the economy are important determinants of the private sector investment which is a key factor in economic growth both directly and as a source of technical change.

6.3.2 *The degree and nature of local funding of public expenditure*

6.3.2.1 The degree of local funding

One issue of debate relates to the extent to which public expenditure in Scotland should be funded from within Scotland. This can be expressed as the country's being able to fully benefit from its own success. That is to say, as the economy grows tax revenues will rise, generating resources to pursue policies to further increase growth. This suggests a benign positive spiral with a symbiotic relationship between private and public sector investment in Scotland.

We begin by outlining the possible costs of a closer linking of Scottish public expenditure to taxes raised within Scotland. This is, of course, a benefit only if Scottish growth is greater than the growth in the rest of the UK. If Scottish growth is lower, then a downward spiral ensues: lower private sector growth will generate lower public sector resources, subsequently reducing growth. Further, the tax base of the smaller Scottish economy would be expected to be more uncertain than that for the more diversified economy of the UK. This is reinforced by the reliance of an independent Scotland, at least initially, on inherently uncertain North Sea oil revenues. Therefore, there are some clear potential downsides to greater fiscal devolution.

However, the key benefit centres on the belief that the more that the public expenditure of a devolved sub-national government is financed directly from taxation generated within its own boundaries, the bigger the incentive for that region's government to become more efficient (Hallwood and McDonald, 2006; Ashcroft *et al*, 2006). The level of local financing in Scotland is at present very low and even with the changes that come from the implementation of the Scotland Act (2012), it will remain small. This efficiency argument has three strands:

» first, it is thought that when a sub-national government has to raise its own taxes to cover expenditure then the opportunity cost of that expenditure is clearer and that this improves the efficiency with which the expenditure is made. This efficiency improvement is thought to be good for growth;
» second, a related argument is that decentralised funding puts the devolved government under a hard budget constraint, while

if it depends on the central government it will be bailed out if it makes policy mistakes. The moral hazard implied in such a situation leads to the sub-national government making risky and inefficient decisions because the decision takers do not bear the full responsibility for their actions;

» finally, where the devolved government's own revenues depend upon the level of taxes raised within its own boundaries, there is an incentive for the devolved government to increase the tax base through increased growth.

It is difficult to judge the strength of these arguments. First, there is no compelling empirical evidence. Attempts to relate the rate of growth in the economy as a whole to the level of devolution of tax-raising powers yield no consistent results. Any relationship that there is relates to the extent of devolution of spending (not taxation) powers, with the optimal choice appearing to be at some intermediate level of devolution which actually corresponds to the position in the UK (Roy, 2006). Even this result is not very strong.

Furthermore, the logic of some of these arguments is also weak. To begin, even where the budget to the sub-national government is absolutely fixed, there is always an opportunity cost to public expenditure in the sense that the revenue could be spent on some other public project. Political parties are competing for votes, therefore there is always pressure for money to be spent efficiently. However, a potential counter-argument is that in devolved governments voters are often confused as to which levels of government actually control which expenditures. Under independence, the responsibility would be much clearer and democratic power might be more effectively exercised.

Second, the notion that the present funding arrangements do not present the Scottish Government with a hard budget constraint is false. The budget must balance from year to year and there is almost no scope for borrowing. In fact, the arrangements under the Scotland Act (2012) seem more suspect on these grounds. Although they will involve a higher coverage of expenditure by local taxation, they also allow a degree of borrowing. The only area where this argument has some traction is that under the present devolved arrangements, welfare transfers are still a central government responsibility. This could reduce the Scottish Government's resolve to reduce unemployment through more rapid growth.

The third argument is rather more robust, from the standpoint of economic theory. This is the notion that the Scottish growth rate would be increased if the Scottish Government received a greater share of any additional taxes raised in Scotland. At present, any increased tax resulting from increased Scottish growth goes to the HM Treasury and Scotland would receive approximately 8% of any subsequent increase in UK Government expenditure. If this were much higher, the argument is that this would provide a greater incentive to pursue growth strategies.

A key point to make is that this incentive argument does not apply to private sector firms. Unless it really dominates the sub-national economy, it is irrelevant to a private sector company which layer of government receives the tax that it pays. Individual firms might have strong preferences concerning the appropriate level at which certain spending decisions are made or about the absolute size of the sub-national budget. However, because each individual firm makes such a small proportionate contribution to the total expenditure on public goods, any incentive effect is also small. However, this incentive argument might be more important for voters and sub-national politicians. In terms of the discussion in section 6.3 these arguments emphasise the extent to which the Scottish Government's commitment to growth can be influenced through the degree of local funding of public expenditure.

Take the voters first. The argument would be that, at present, Scottish voters can choose between different policy programmes presented by the different parties in the Scottish Parliament. They can choose between those that would improve the delivery of current services and those that will improve future growth.[11] With the present Barnett funding arrangements, although Scottish voters receive all the benefits of the current services, some of the benefit of future growth – notably, the increase in the taxes collected in Scotland – primarily accrues to the rest of the UK. These factors would reduce the benefit of growth policies for Scottish voters, as against current public services. For members of the Scottish Government, a similar argument applies. Under present devolved arrangements, policies to stimulate growth do not directly generate increased Scottish revenues. This reduces the desirability of such policies to Scottish politicians.

Of course, voters value growth for the private benefits that it brings. Also, the benefits that increased revenues bring as a result of Scottish political decisions taken now are likely to be felt by politicians not presently in power. Moreover, if the Scottish population rises as a result of growth, then public funding through the Barnett mechanism will rise. Stimulating growth is at the heart of the

---

11 It should be noted that many elements of public expenditure identified as current spending, such as health and education, will, as we have argued already, typically also contribute to economic growth.

present and previous Scottish Government policies. However, there are incentive mechanisms produced by linking more strongly sub-national budgets to taxation raised within their boundaries.

There are clearly countervailing forces on the impact of the extent of sub-national budgets that are funded from taxes collected within their own boundaries. The greater uncertainty generated by a smaller and more specialised tax base, and the lack of automatic stabilis-ers provided by HM Treasury-funded welfare payments under the present arrangements, are likely to make an independent Scottish economy more cyclically unstable and subject to greater external macroeconomic shocks. This would be detrimental to growth. Against this must be set the incentives for voters and local politicians to give greater priority to growth with greater local public sector funding.

6.3.2.2 Tax as a means of directing economic activity

The second set of arguments around taxation concerns not the level of local funding but rather the particular mix of taxes which an inde-pendent country would be able to deploy, as against a devolved region. The idea here is to use taxes as a means of directing eco-nomic activity: to deal with market failure. The argument in principle is that the Scottish Government has better information about the Scottish economy and is more responsive to local demands expressed through the ballot box and local media than is the UK Government. In this sense, the government of an independent nation that had full fiscal control could more accurately target its tax policies to stimu-late growth.

A good example from the Scottish case concerns renewable energy (see chapters 7 and 9). The Scottish Government has tar-geted this industry as a potential growth sector. Many elements of renewable energy are not viable at present. For this sector to play this role requires extensive improvements in technology, particularly in offshore wind and marine. On a broad infant industry argument (reinforced by emissions targets and security of supply consid-erations), substantial subsidies are being paid to these industries. However, these are determined by the UK Government and might not best suit the Scottish economy. On the other hand, in this case, the UK Government is subsidising the UK industry, and the fact that a disproportionate amount of that industry is in Scotland means that Scotland receives a fiscal benefit. Essentially, as far as renewables go, Scotland might be able to get a more appropriate set of subsidies but the Scottish people would have to pay for these subsidies. However, a more central concern for the Scottish Government is the ability to set the rates for more mainstream taxes.

Income tax. As argued already in section 6.3.1, under the Scotland Act (2012) the Scottish Government will be required to determine the rate of income tax that will apply in Scotland, within a wide range of values. If one believes strongly in economic incentives, reducing the rate of income tax should stimulate economic activity. The fall in the tax rate reduces the cost of labour to firms and simultaneously increases labour supply and investment in human capital. However, as Lecca *et al* (2010a) show, the actual impact also depends critically on how the lost tax revenue would have been spent and how workers (and migrants) value the fall in public spending. Also, it is important whether the reduced tax income affects public consumption or capital spending. It is curious that there is little discussion of how this devolved income tax power could be used to stimulate the economy. In point of fact, every devolved government in Scotland has pledged to adhere to the UK income tax rate, so that one of the implications of the arrangements after the implementation of the Scotland Act (2012) is that the Scottish Government will now be forced to exercise this right; that is to say, it will be forced to set an income tax rate, even if that rate simply matches the rest of the UK.

Corporation tax. There was discussion within HM Treasury in 2011 about whether the Northern Ireland Assembly would be given powers to make balanced budget variations in corporation tax, potentially to compete against the lower levels set for this tax in the Republic of Ireland. In the drafting of the Scotland Act (2012), the Scottish Government argued that it should be given control over setting the rate of corporation tax in Scotland. That is to say, even without independence, the Scottish Government would wish to have the power to vary this tax. More specifically, the Scottish Government would wish to lower the tax on profits, in order that the economy can become more competitive, especially for foreign direct investment. Ireland is often taken as a model in this regard.

On the face of it, this is rather curious. First, a reduction in corporation tax would appear to be an inefficient way to stimulate economic activity. In so far as firms benefit from such a reduction, this is rather non-selective. It applies to all firms. It is not targeted towards particular sectors or types of firm. Further, because corporation tax is a tax on capital income, a reduction encourages the adoption of more capital-intensive techniques and benefits more capital-intensive firms and industries. This type of fiscal adjustment is therefore less helpful in stimulating employment, which is typically a key aim of sub-national governments, than a reduction in a tax more closely linked to employment, such as income tax or National Insurance contributions. Why is such a policy regarded so favourably and why is it linked so closely with devolution?

Giving Scotland the power to set its own corporation tax rate presents a key problem within a devolved framework. Corporate income is geographically mobile. There is an incentive, through creative transfer pricing, for multi-plant companies to generate surpluses in locations with low tax rates. If corporation tax varied within the UK, the fear for HM Treasury is that this would produce a loss in tax revenue through UK companies making just such an adjustment. That is to say, in accounting terms, corporate income would accrue in devolved regions with low rates of corporation tax. However, although this would reduce the tax take in the UK as a whole, it could increase the tax receipts in the devolved region with the lower tax rate. If all devolved regions had this power, there would also be the strong possibility of a race-to-the-bottom, with each region attempting to underbid the other regions' tax rates. Potentially all regions could lose in this scenario. Moreover, having by far the biggest existing stock of corporate income, England benefits least from reducing corporation tax because it has to reduce the rate on a bigger initial stock of profits in order to attract the mobile corporate income. As a result, the UK central government is very unlikely to grant this devolved tax power.

Corporation tax and independence. However, if Scotland is independent it can pursue this policy. A key factor is the extent to which a reduction in corporation tax will increase Foreign Direct Investment (FDI). The Scottish Government presented evidence to the Scotland Bill (2012) on the impact of variations in the corporation tax in Scotland, in a devolved context (Scottish Government, 2011; Lecca *et al*, 2012). Specifically, simulation results were presented for a reduction in corporation tax from 23% to 20%. It was assumed that there was no distortion through transfer pricing of UK-based firms. Further, the simulations were performed under the assumption of a balanced budget change in the Scottish public sector. The results show that without an explicit stimulus to FDI, there was a small increase in economic activity, but this had to be set against a reduction in the public services as the total Scottish tax take fell. Where there was an additional increase in FDI, directly attributable to the reduction in tax, then the Laffer curve phenomenon ultimately occurs. That is to say, a reduction in the tax rate led ultimately not only to an increase in activity but also to an expansion in the tax take. Within twenty years GDP increased by 1.4% and employment by 1.1%. This work was done in a static context. Models where growth in productivity is associated with investment give a more dramatic role to the increased FDI.

The stress on corporation tax has in the past often rested on the experience of the Irish economy which had very rapid growth, high levels of FDI and a low corporation tax level. Whether such a policy would be as successful in the case of Scotland is an important question for the independence debate. It is clearly the case that public opinion is moving against multinational companies locating in countries with low corporation tax.[12]

6.3.3 *The administration of policy*

If Scotland were independent, it would be able to administer, control and plan its own economic policies. At present, Scottish Governments have control over a block grant, a fixed budget, from Westminster. However, under full independence, a Scottish Government would also control other elements of public expenditure in Scotland at present reserved to Westminster. In particular, the welfare budget, which makes up around one third of public expenditure in Scotland would be the responsibility of the Scottish Government.

However, most of the expenditure relevant for economic development is already devolved to the Scottish Government. Moreover, there is no ring-fencing. The Scottish Government can impose its own preferences or criteria in spending this budget. It can choose the priority it wishes to give to growth and the most appropriate ways of using the expenditure to increase growth. The budget is not excessively restricted: public expenditure per head is significantly above that in the UK as a whole. Further, as a result of the 1997 referendum vote, the Scottish Government has additional tax-raising powers and these have been significantly extended in the Scotland Act (2012).

Many of the areas of responsibility that are important for growth have been devolved to the Scottish Government: that is to say, policy on human capital formation, such as education, skills and health. Policies on transport and industrial development are similarly devolved. Further, the Scottish Government has a coordinated decision-making process, aided by its own set of civil servants. Such coordination has been an aspect of policy making in Scotland even before devolution, with government activity planned through the Scottish Office and industrial development stimulated through the Scottish Development Agency and the Highlands and Islands Development Board. Devolution has strengthened this. The data for the Scottish economy are much superior to those available to any other UK sub-national government or English region; for example, the construction of disaggregated economic accounts for Scotland

---

12 For example, the Financial Times reports an Australian Government Minister attacking Google for using a tax arrangement known as the 'double Irish Dutch sandwich', involving subsidiary companies in Ireland, the Netherlands and Bermuda to reduce tax paid on advertising occurring in Australia (Hume, 2012, p. 6).

allows a degree of sub-national economic modelling not available elsewhere in the UK. Again, the quality of the data reflects decisions initially made in Scotland pre-devolution, but the situation has improved as a result of increased devolved powers.

Scotland can also formulate its own laws and administrative structures to deliver policy. Scotland retains its own development agencies, Scottish Enterprise and Highland Enterprise, where those in English regions are being wound up as a result of policy determined in Westminster. Similarly, Scotland has its own Council of Economic Advisors. This is an advisory body similar to those employed by other countries, such as the USA, though this institution has not been adopted by the UK Government. Clearly, the Scottish Government already has the power and ability to formulate and coordinate policy to increase growth without independence.

As stated already, there are areas, at present controlled by Westminster, where the Scottish Government would have control over policies which could affect growth. The most straightforward is the welfare budget. It is clearly the case that successive UK Governments have attempted to change the administration of the welfare budget in order to encourage participation in the labour force and therefore increase GDP. It is not clear that Scotland's population has specific characteristics in this regard which would benefit from different rules. Further, the Scottish participation rate is above the UK average at the moment. Of course, having the welfare budget funded from Scottish taxation potentially reduces the power of automatic stabilisers in the Scottish economy which would be detrimental to growth.

There are some policies over which the Scottish Government clearly would like to have greater powers. One is the Crown Estate that owns the seabed around the UK. Policies aimed at maximising the revenues for the HM Treasury might not be those that benefit the development of Scotland's marine resources. Also, there might be policies such as airport or competition policy where what is optimal for the UK as a whole might be to Scotland's detriment. In general, there will be a trade-off between the benefits of having policy specifically tailored for the local economy against the costs and inefficiencies of duplication of institutions and the greater difficulty of coordinating policy. At the moment, the Scottish Government has prioritised growth as a key objective, an objective which is required to be fulfilled in order to facilitate achieving other policy goals. Also, it has already a distinct form of industrial policy.

6.3.4 *The border*

One major difference if Scotland were to become an independent nation, rather than simply a devolved region of the UK, is that a more substantial administrative border would be introduced between Scotland and the Rest of the UK (RUK). What was previously a transaction between two parts of the same country would now be a transaction between different countries. At present, exports from Scotland to the rest of the UK make up 17% of all output in Scotland. Using the conventional approach of tracking the expenditure impact of the purchases of intermediate inputs and labour needed in production, exports to the rest of the UK are estimated to support just under 30% of production in Scotland.

It is difficult to determine the impact of the introduction of a border to trade. This is because a systematic study requires data that identify both the trade between different regions in one country and also the trade between these regions and similar regions in other countries. The most rigorous studies are of trade between Canada and the United States. These studies appear to show a very large border impact. That is to say, trade between two regions in the same country is much greater than trade between similar regions, a similar distance apart, but in different countries. If the border were removed between the US and Canada, Anderson and van Wincoop (2003) estimate that the trade between the two countries would increase by 44%. However, it is not clear what causes these very powerful negative effects (Obstfelt and Rogoff, 2000). Canada and the United States share a common language, are contiguous and have low tariffs. It is argued that additionally nation-specific social or cultural contacts or networks are important (Evans, 2003).

It is difficult to know what role the introduction of a more substantial border between Scotland and the RUK would imply for trade. Scotland and England have the same currency and speak the same language, so this barrier might be very low, and it seems inconceivable that any government of an independent Scotland would not wish to encourage trade with the rest of the UK. Also, as we have outlined, Scotland already has a distinctive set of legal and administrative arrangements. If these institutional differences are generally the source of the negative effects of borders on trade, perhaps the relatively small step to independence will have a small impact on Scotland. However, the possible impact of reduced trade with the RUK is a source of concern and uncertainty that would accompany full independence.

An example would be in the electricity supply industry. At present Scotland exports electricity to the rest of the UK through the interconnector. The Scottish Government's target of having 100% of the electricity used in Scotland supplied by renewable sources by 2020 depends on there being significant exports to the rest of the UK. This would be necessary since the variability in the supply of electricity from renewables requires Scotland to export the surplus renewable electricity when wind, wave, tidal and hydro power are extensive.

However, it is likely that, while the rest of the UK will want trade in electricity with Scotland, for security of supply reasons it is likely to be less reliant on Scottish imports than where Scotland is part of the UK. Similarly, much inter-regional trade is between branches owned by the same firm. In so far as an independent Scotland develops a set of formal and informal institutional arrangements that differs from the rest of the UK, the degree of cross-border branch operations are likely to fall. With this, Scottish exports will fall.

Of course, the more vigorously an independent Scotland wishes to pursue policies that differ from those in the RUK, the more these border effects are likely to operate. One policy which is central to the growth debate in Scotland is migration. Until the recent past, population in Scotland was in secular decline and the birth rate is still below replacement level. Without immigration Scotland's population will decline over the long run with present trends in 'natural' population changing parameters. This is perceived as a problem in itself and is linked to the welfare issues raised by an ageing population. A growing proportion of the population will be above retirement age. In a growth context Scotland's GDP per capita is very similar to that for the UK as a whole, so that the relatively low growth might be thought to reflect low increases in population. Immigration does not seem to be the toxic issue in Scotland that it appears to be in England and a benefit of independence would be the ability to operate a more liberal immigration policy. However, the implementation of a differential immigration policy to that operated by the RUK would require the strengthening of the border between the two countries.

6.4 CONCLUSION

Economic growth is dependent on a set of stable macro-economic conditions and the implementation of a set of appropriate supply-side policies. We have not discussed in any depth in this chapter the macro-stability issues: they were discussed at length in chapters 3 to 5. However, there appears to be a consensus at present that an independent Scotland would be tied closely to the monetary and fiscal policies of the RUK.

On the supply side it could be that there is some psychological 'independence' stimulus that operates through a release of animal spirits. Independence might influence the behaviour of politicians and the perceptions of voters and workers in ways that do encourage growth. However, within the devolved framework that already exists, and will be strengthened after the full introduction of the Scotland Act (2012), many of the policy levers are already in the hands of the Scottish Government. It is important to stress that Scotland has much greater supply-side powers than English regions and that Scotland can already undertake a coordinated growth strategy with appropriately targeted public expenditures and administrative structures.

From a growth perspective, an important potential advantage of independence is that this would give the Scottish Government a greater ability to use tax rates to act as signals and incentives to greater efficiency. Of course, this is only an important power if the appropriate rates required to stimulate growth in Scotland differ from those set by the UK Government. One reason why these optimal rates might differ, and where the UK Government will resist spatial variation in tax rates within a devolved setting, is where there is likely to be tax competition. Corporation tax is one such tax.

Again, from the point of view of stimulating growth, a significant risk is the impact of a national border on trade between Scotland and the rest of the UK. At present, Scottish exports to the rest of the UK make up a large share of the total sales of Scottish goods and services. There is a risk that introducing a border will reduce this trade, and this would impact much more seriously on the Scottish economy than on the economy of the rest of the UK. There are issues here simply of the demand-side effects, but, perhaps more seriously in the longer term, the impact of reduced competition and variety in the Scottish economy.

6.5 SUMMARY OF THE KEY QUESTIONS FOR GROWTH POLICY

This chapter raises some key questions that should shape the ongoing constitutional debate around the enhanced powers that could be transferred to the Scottish Parliament. They are particularly relevant to the propositions based upon an independent Scotland but many are equally appropriate for those models similar to Devo max and Devo plus that allow a lesser degree of autonomy.

Economic growth: key determinants

» are Scotland's economic interests well served within a generally polarised UK economy, whose growth performance it typically tracks, with or without increased devolved powers? Or would it grow faster as an independent country?

» do Scotland's long-term population trends imply an immigration policy that diverges from that for the rest of the UK? Is this achievable within the union?

» in an independent Scotland what would be the main drivers of improved growth?

Constitutional change and growth

» the level of public expenditure in Scotland
  › are the additional fiscal powers given in the Scotland Act (2012) enough to allow future Scottish governments the flexibility to fund the public sector expenditure required for growth?
  › are the fiscal powers under the Scotland Act (2012) too narrowly focused?

» the degree and nature of local funding of public expenditure in Scotland
  › what important elements of growth-generating public sector expenditure are not presently in the hands of the Scottish Government?
  › is a growth strategy built on low corporation tax viable for Scotland?
  › will the income tax powers given in the Scotland Act (2012) allow a devolved Scotland a competitive advantage within a devolved UK?
  › how far could tax and expenditure policies particularly tailored to Scottish circumstances stimulate growth in specific sectors, such as renewable energy?
  › would allowing more of the taxes raised in Scotland to be returned to Scotland increase the incentive to pursue growth strategies? If so, is this enough to offset any increased fiscal instability that this would imply?

» the administration of policy
  › how far do existing institutional arrangements in Scotland favour or hamper Scotland's growth performance, as compared to other English regions?
  › how would independence change the institutional arrangements in Scotland in favour of growth?

» the impact of the introduction of a border between Scotland and the rest of the UK on Scottish trade
  › is the fact that there is uncertainty over the cause of border effects observed in trade between other countries a source of reassurance or concern?

> do cross-border organisations need to be put in place in order to reinforce existing trade links?
> which economic policy differences between an independent Scotland and the rest of the UK are likely to have a negative impact on trade?

Acemoglu, D. & Autor, D. 2012. 'What does human capital do? A review of Goldin and Katz's *The Race between Education and Technology*', *Journal of Economic Literature*, vol. 50, pp. 426–463.

Acemoglu, D. & Robinson, J.A. 2012. *Why Nations Fail*. Profile Books, London.

Alesina, A. & Spolaore, E. 2003. *The Size of Nations*, MIT Press, Cambridge, Massachusetts.

Anderson, J.E. & van Wincoop, C. 2003. 'Gravity with gravitas: a solution to the border puzzle', *American Economic Review*, vol. 93, pp. 170–92.

Ashcroft, B.A., Christie, A. & Swales, J.K. 2006. 'Flaws and myths in the case for Scottish fiscal autonomy', *Fraser of Allander Quarterly Economic Commentary*, vol. 31, no. 1, pp. 33–9.

Christie, A. & Swales, J.K. 2010. 'The Barnett Allocation Mechanism: formula plus influence', *Regional Studies*, vol. 44, pp. 761–76.

Evans, C. 2003. 'The economic significance of national border effects', *American Economic Review*, vol. 93, pp. 1291–1312.

Gardiner, B., Martin, R., Sunley, P. & Tyler, P. 2012. 'Spatially unbalanced growth in the British economy', paper presented at the Regional Studies Association Meeting: 'Smart, Creative, Sustainable, Inclusive: Territorial Development Strategies in the Age of Austerity', London.

Grief, A. 2006. *Institutions and the Path to the Modern Economy: Lessons from Medieval Trade*. Cambridge University Press.

Hallwood, P. & McDonald, R. 2006. 'The economic case for Scottish fiscal autonomy'. Policy Institute, Edinburgh.

Hume, N. 2012. 'Australia cracks down on Google's "double Irish Dutch sandwich" tax move', *Financial Times*, 23 November.

Lecca, P., McGregor, P.G. & Swales, J.K. 2010a. 'Inverted Haavelmo effects in a general equilibrium analysis of the impact of implementing the Scottish variable rate of income tax', *Strathclyde Discussion Papers in Economics*, Department of Economics, University of Strathclyde, pp. 10–13.

Lecca, P., McGregor, P.G. & Swales, J.K. 2010b. 'Balanced budget spending in a small open regional economy', *Strathclyde Discussion Papers in Economics*, Department of Economics, University of Strathclyde, pp. 10–20.

Lecca, P., McGregor, P.G. & Swales, J.K. 2012. 'The impact of devolving corporation tax in Scotland', paper presented at the Conference on International Business Tax, Tax Competition, Common Consolidated Tax Base and Fiscal Autonomy, Graduate School of Business, University of Strathclyde, July 2012.

Oberstfeld, M. & Rogoff, K. 2000. 'The six major puzzles in international macroeconomics: is there a common cause', *NBER Working Paper* 7777. July.

Psacharopoulos, G. & Patrinos, H.A. 2004. 'Human capital and rates of return', *International Handbook on the Economics of Education,* (eds) Johnes, G. & Johnes, J. Edward Elgar, Cheltenham.

Roy, G. 2006. 'Is fiscal decentralisation good for growth?', *Fraser of Allander Quarterly Commentary*, vol. 31, no. 2, pp. 39–49.

The Scotland Act (2012). TSO, London.

Scottish Government. 2011. *Devolving Corporation Tax in the Scotland Bill*. September 2011.

Solow, R.M. 1957. 'Technical change and the aggregate production function', *Review of Economics and Statistics*, vol. 39, pp. 312–20.

Stiglitz, J.E. 1988. *Economics of the Public Sector*. W.W. Norton & Company, New York.

Stiglitz, J.E, Sen, A. & Fitoussi, J-P. 2009. *Report by the Commission on the Measurement of Economic Performance and Social Progress.*

Walker, I & Zhu, Y. 2007. 'The labour market effects of qualifications', *Futureskills Scotland Research Series*. www.scotland.gov.uk/Resource/Doc/919/0065442.pdf.

CHAPTER 7

The Impact of Greater Autonomy on Scottish Climate Change Policy[1]
Professor Peter G McGregor[2] *and Professor J Kim Swales*[3]

7.1 INTRODUCTION AND RATIONALE FOR SCOTTISH CLIMATE CHANGE POLICY

In McGregor *et al* (2011) we provide an introduction to, and overview of, the current Scottish Government's Climate Change policy. In this paper we focus on the likely consequences for Scottish climate change policy in general of the substantial and increasing pressure towards a further move along the spectrum of devolution. This spectrum spans the *status quo*, the implementation of the Scotland Act (2012), the Devo plus and Devo max options, and independence. While these options are defined with varying degrees of precision (see the Introduction to this volume), we direct much of our comment to what currently seem to be the more likely, and certainly less radical, initial outcomes by assuming that the independence option would most likely involve the retention of a permanently fixed exchange rate with the rest of the UK and continued membership of the EU, in line with current SNP policy.[4] However, in view of the long-term perspective of this chapter (and volume), we do not restrict our comments to this case.[5]

In one important sense, climate change policy is effectively already fully devolved to the Scottish Parliament since it was not explicitly reserved to Westminster under the devolution settlement.

---

1   The authors gratefully acknowledge the extensive comments of the Editor on earlier drafts and the support of ClimateXChange, a centre of independent research and knowledge exchange expertise on climate change in Scotland. The Centre is funded by the Scottish Government. Naturally, the views expressed are the sole responsibility of the authors.

2   Head of Economics Department, University of Strathclyde.

3   Director of the Fraser of Allander Institute, Department of Economics, University of Strathclyde.

4   See chapters 1, 2, 9 and 10 in this volume.

5   As noted in chapter 1, the Westminster Parliament could, for example, impose conditions for adopting a permanently fixed exchange rate with sterling that a Scottish Government would find unacceptable. Also, in the longer term, even EU membership cannot be assumed.

The Climate Change (Scotland) Act was passed in 2009, imposing legally binding Scottish greenhouse gas (GHG) emissions in 2050 to be 80% less than their 1990 levels, with an interim target of a 42% reduction by 2020. Of course, the Scottish Government recognises that Scottish emissions are trivial relative to the totality of global emissions but motivates the policy in terms of a moral argument (responsibility for past emissions) and a demonstration effect (that may persuade those currently less committed to tackling climate change). However, while the Scottish Government has the discretion to set its own emissions targets, many of the policies that could be used to achieve these are currently reserved to, and funded by, Westminster, with whom the legal responsibilities for meeting EU targets also lies. Additionally, as we discuss below, Scottish climate change policy is further complicated by being interlinked with what is, in effect, a Scottish industrial policy of stimulating renewables as a 'key sector' in generating sustainable growth.

Climate change policy, like other policies in the context of an economy with liberalised markets, seeks to

» employ the *instruments* of policy to induce firms and households to alter their behaviour in a way that
» achieves the *targets* and ultimate *goals* of policy
» subject to *constraints*, which include all policies and events that are outwith the control of the Scottish Government.

Greater autonomy may influence outcomes, either positively or negatively, through its impact on policy goals, targets, constraints or instruments. We consider each in turn, dealing with policy instruments last, since this is the primary focus of the debate on whether the existing constitutional settlement leaves the Scottish Government with an inadequate set of policy levers.

7.2 THE IMPACT OF GREATER AUTONOMY ON TARGETS AND GOALS

The ultimate objective of climate change policy is to limit *global* warming, which is generated by the accumulation in the atmosphere of greenhouse gases (GHGs).[6] Climate change therefore represents a global externality, which ideally requires a global solution, since Scottish (and indeed UK) emissions are tiny relative to global

---

6   The uncertainties surrounding climate change are such that there are still some sceptics, but the overwhelming consensus is that global warming constitutes a major threat to the future of the planet and that anthropomorphic GHG emissions are the key cause.

emissions of GHGs. In the absence of a global government, international collaboration appears to be the best way forward, and this has been pursued with, for example, Kyoto and the EU Emissions Trading Scheme (EU ETS) reflecting a degree of success, with the Scottish Government fully signed up to these agreements, and indeed pushing for a further tightening of EU policy.[7] It seems very unlikely, given the consensus reflected in the unanimous support for the 2009 Act, that any future Scottish Government would adopt a different view of the importance of limiting GHG emissions, irrespective of the constitutional settlement.[8, 9]

Since climate change policy has been devolved from its inception, with the Scottish Government free to set its own targets, a similar argument could be made for emissions *targets* (and the legal framework in which they are embedded). However, a sharing of the same ultimate objective as the UK Government has not precluded a distinctive approach in target setting. Initially, the Scottish Government's emissions reduction targets were higher than the UK's, though the latter was increased to 80% from 60% on the advice of the Climate Change Committee (CCC). However, although the 80% target is now the same in both jurisdictions, sea and aviation transport emissions are included in the Scottish target but not in the UK's (though these will shortly be part of the EU's emission trading scheme). Second, the Scottish targets are set on an annual basis (with no banking or borrowing), whereas UK targets are set as five-year averages. The legal framework for the target is regarded as providing confidence for the private sector investors in the present (and future) Government's commitment to a low carbon economy.[10]

While the Scottish targets appear more demanding, it is not clear that they are more difficult to achieve than the corresponding Westminster targets, since the cost of abatement may vary between Scotland and the UK (especially given the concentration of renewable

---

7   Of course, the history of the Kyoto and subsequent Copenhagen accords, and EU ETS, also serves to highlight some of the problems of securing agreement, given the attractiveness to individual countries of 'free riding' and avoiding the costs of tackling climate change.

8   Conceivably, public opinion could shift against what is currently a green-ish consensus as energy prices rise, in part reflecting the costs of shifting to a low-carbon economy.

9   At the UK level there is a range of institutions which tie the government into long-run commitments. One issue is whether these would be replicated in Scotland.

10 It is useful to compare the Wales and Northern Ireland approach to emissions here. Will the Welsh Assembly Government be the first to have a legal commitment to sustainable development? Do they currently seek to coordinate emissions targets with Scotland and Westminster? Would such coordination be threatened by independence?

resources in the former).[11] Regardless, while the targets are distinctive relative to the UK's, there seems to be no compelling reason to believe they will become *more* distinctive with growing autonomy of the Scottish Government, since it already enjoys complete discretion over these targets. Perhaps it may be argued that enhanced powers will allow even more ambitious target setting for emissions, but this is unclear.[12]

7.2.1 *The link between Scottish emissions targets and the goal of inhibiting global warming*

If a reduction in the emissions produced in Scotland were to be partially or wholly offset by an increase in emissions elsewhere, then meeting Scottish targets may contribute little or, in the limit, nothing at all, to solving the real problem. While this may seem trivially obvious, there are reasons to believe that this is in fact a very real concern, especially given Scottish Administrations' commitment to EU ETS. In some circumstances, a reduction in Scottish emissions will be compensated for by an increase in emissions elsewhere, so that global emissions, and therefore global warming, is unaffected.

One possible source of such carbon 'leakage' of emissions is through trade (or capital movements), which allows the possibility of reducing the production of emission-intensive goods in Scotland simply to replace them with imports of emission-intensive goods from elsewhere. We return to this point in our subsequent discussion of the constraint imposed by the Scottish economy and of the potential importance of monitoring indicators of the extent of Scotland's 'carbon footprint', an indicator of the total emissions in Scotland that are attributable to consumption in Scotland. So, for example, the carbon content of imports has to be included in such a measure (since these are consumed by those living in Scotland), whereas the carbon content of exports is attributed to consumers in the rest of the world. However, the carbon content of imports is excluded from production-oriented measures of emissions, such as with the present Scottish emission targets and those required by Kyoto, whereas emissions attributable to export production are included.

A second possible source of emissions 'leakage' (from a purely domestic perspective) arises from a striking example of the importance of understanding policy-making under multi-level governance. However, in this case it is the relationship of both the Edinburgh and Westminster Governments to the EU that matters (rather than

---

11 See McDowall et al (2012a, b).
12 In principle, instruments and targets should be chosen jointly, given constraints.

their relationship to each other, which is the main subject matter of this contribution) (Goulder and Stavins, 2011). The EU ETS is a 'cap and trade' scheme that effectively sets the 'cap' or limit for emissions in the EU as a whole for the 'traded' sectors that are covered by the scheme.[13] It was established in 2005 as an instrument to help the EU achieve Kyoto commitments. The scheme allocates pre-determined EU allowances (EUAs) to companies that can then be traded among operators in covered ('traded') sectors. At the end of each year companies must have sufficient allowances to meet all of their emissions or are subject to heavy fines. The traded sectors include energy, ferrous metals, minerals, pulp and paper. Each EUA is equivalent to one ton of CO_2, and all installations within these sectors (of sufficient scale) require a permit to operate. The traded sectors account for around 50% of all EU emissions. While the total of emissions in the EU as a whole is clearly determined by the EU ETS allocation for the particular year, the distribution of actual emissions across the member countries of the EU ETS is not pre-determined, but is an outcome of the trading process. The distribution of actual emissions among member countries should reflect the 'least cost' method of meeting the aggregate of EU emissions.

The Scottish Government has a target of decarbonising the energy supply sector by 2030. It might be thought that this will make a very substantial direct contribution to Scotland's emissions targets, but in fact it contributes nothing directly. Because the energy sector is covered by EU ETS, success in over-achieving this objective (if there is no change in EU allowances) simply induces carbon price changes, as the allowances that are surplus to Scottish requirements are put on the market in the EU ETS, that encourage others to increase their emissions by an exactly offsetting amount (100% 'leakage' from a narrow domestic perspective).[14]

---

13 In the context of regional and macroeconomics 'traded' indicates the extent to which a good is actually traded across regional or national boundaries. While sectors 'covered' by EU ETS might help to avoid confusion, the terminology is so widespread that we continue to use it here.

14 While EU ETS leaves open the opportunity of governments to buy allowances, the present Scottish Government committed itself in 2011 to avoid using this means of satisfying the targets. See the Scottish Government (2012) for detail on assessing progress towards the 2010 emissions target.

The Scottish Government is now clearly aware of this issue, and there are a number of important implications for policy. First, the emissions that are counted in Scottish targets for the traded sector simply reflect its share of the UK's emissions allowable under EU ETS (Scottish Government, 2012).[15] So, within the traded sector *actual* emissions within Scotland do not contribute to the Government's target: that simply reflects Scotland's share of the emissions allocated to the UK through the scheme. Second, the only emissions target that the Scottish Government has the power to choose is effectively that for the 'non-traded' sector,[16] and it can only set an overall emissions target by adjusting the non-traded target appropriately.

Most current proposals for further autonomy envisage Scotland remaining in the EU and therefore continuing to adhere to EU ETS. Proposals that envisage continued participation in EU ETS would have no impact on the basic point that a significant part of Scotland's emissions targets would remain outwith its direct control (as is the case for all members of EU ETS). Nonetheless, it may be that greater devolution, and independence in particular, could alter the mechanism that governs Scotland's share of EU emissions targets, and so influence the EU target for the traded sector to which it would presumably be legally bound.

One major conclusion from this discussion is that the scope for greater autonomy in Scottish climate change policy, even in terms of setting emissions targets, is significantly circumscribed by EU policy in general and EU ETS in particular. As long as there is a commitment to the EU, this will remain true regardless of any shift in powers between Edinburgh and Westminster (although the shift in legal responsibility for its contribution to EU-traded emissions to Edinburgh may have an impact). This may, however, be a good thing: acknowledgement that the fundamental problem here is global in nature and ideally requires a global solution implies a recognition that some issues are most efficiently tackled at higher levels of government in a world characterised by the presence of multi-level governance. However, similar kinds of arguments apply to other dimensions of devolution: the issue is the appropriate allocation of powers across different levels of government. However, in other

---

15 In Scotland the level of emissions in the Net Scottish Emissions Account (NSEA) is compared to the target for emissions. For the traded sector, NSEA counts Scotland's share of the EU wide emissions cap, not the actual emissions of Scottish participants (Scottish Government, 2012).

16 That is, the sectors that are covered by EU ETS but are located elsewhere in Europe. Effectively, this simply alters the geographic distribution of emissions from the covered sectors.

cases the appropriate allocation of responsibility is less clear cut and there is scope for more disagreement.

If Scottish membership of EU ETS were to be discontinued, perhaps because a Scottish Administration ultimately judged the costs of a currency union with sterling and the euro zone to be too high, the constraints of EU ETS on emissions would be eliminated. Scotland would in these circumstances be free to pursue its own climate change policies, subject of course to any continuing constraints, notably being a small, highly open economy (see section 4 below). However, this freedom would come at a price: the motivation for trading schemes is that they provide, at least in principle, the least cost method (from the wider EU perspective) of meeting emissions targets. If EU ETS worked as expected, any break-up or restriction of coverage would imply some efficiency losses at the EU level.

7.3 THE IMPACT OF GREATER AUTONOMY ON THE CONSTRAINTS ON SCOTTISH CLIMATE CHANGE POLICY

Scottish climate change policy does not operate in a vacuum at present, nor will it under any future Scottish Administrations. In particular, it is, and will continue to be, constrained by: the Scottish energy-economy-environmental system and its links with international systems; the other (actual and potential future) goals of successive Administrations; and UK and EU policies. We consider each in turn.

7.3.1 *The Scottish economy*

A key issue is that emissions produced within Scottish borders are driven to a large degree by the level and composition of economic activity here. As economic activity increases, this typically stimulates the demand for energy and the combustion of fossil fuels. Of course, the composition of activity also matters for actual emissions since energy intensities vary dramatically across industries and are particularly high, for example, in the energy supply sector. It is no coincidence that targets have proven easier to meet in the current recession (though Scotland missed its target in 2010 due to the impact of a particularly cold winter on the demand for gas for heating purposes), and future recovery and growth will render emissions targets more challenging. Energy-environment-economy sub-systems are inherently interdependent and policy makers have to deal with this complexity. Few would relish the prospect of meeting emissions targets through limiting economic activity, and the Scottish Government is among them. We discuss the problem that the Scottish Government has with important policy goals other than emissions reductions below.

The Scottish economy is a small, highly open economy with respect to interregional and international trade and financial flows. The labour market is open in terms both of migration flows and, for many workers, wage bargaining systems. Many of the influences on the Scottish economy are therefore not under the direct influence, far less control, of the Scottish Government. Key variables for policy such as the growth of the UK, EU and world economies and the level of the oil price are all exogenous to Scotland. No amount of enhanced autonomy for the Scottish Government can hope to change this to any significant degree. It may be argued that autonomy may enhance the 'voice' of the Scottish Government in international negotiations with the EU, for example (an issue we return to below), but it cannot generally affect external events. (However, policies can, to a degree, influence sensitivity to these events, for example, by reducing dependence on oil imports.)

The highly open nature of the Scottish economy creates a particular problem for climate change policy: the potential for carbon 'leakage' through induced trade (or factor) flows that mitigate, or in the limit, fully offset the impact of policies on domestic targets. The Scottish Government's emissions targets are expressed in terms of the emissions *produced* within its own geographic boundaries. However, it is clear that these targets could be met by reducing domestic production of emissions-intensive goods and importing them from elsewhere, yet this could have no impact or even a negative impact on global emissions. The present Scottish Government is aware of the issue and committed to seeking to avoid such substitution, for example, as would occur through reducing Scotland's livestock while continuing to consume as much beef by importing from elsewhere. Carbon footprint-type measures of emissions, based on consumption rather than production, can be used to monitor this, and the Scottish Government produces such indicators (although this is not straightforward given the complexity of correctly identifying the carbon content of trade flows).

Of course, if *all* countries have emissions targets that they meet, leakage would cease to become problematic. In practice, the concern arises because there is poor compliance with international agreements to reduce emissions, or, in some cases, a refusal to sign up to such agreements.

While leakage is certainly an important consideration in practice for meaningful climate change policy, it is not at all clear that greater autonomy would exert any systematic impact on this.

While the deliberate contraction of the economy to achieve emissions targets is feasible, since it is always possible for a Scottish Government to reduce its expenditure (though this is much easier under Devo max or independence), it would be extremely unpopular. However, the typically direct relationship between economic activity and emissions does provide an example of a trade-off between policy goals. The present Government expresses its overriding objective in terms of *sustainable* economic growth, which is compatible with limited emissions (and equity too). However, stating the objective in this way does not, of course, mitigate the impact of any genuine trade-offs, although it presumably does imply a commitment to seek to do so. It seems very likely that sustainable growth will be a major objective of future Scottish Administrations, so that the trade-off with emissions is likely to remain a significant issue (at least until the power sector is decarbonised – see below).[17]

Of course, sustainable economic growth is not the only objective of the current Scottish Government other than emissions targets (nor will it be for future Administrations). Equity among both households (solidarity) and regions (cohesion) of different income levels are often identified as objectives of policy, with security of supply, affordability and fuel poverty being emphasised in an energy policy context. There is clear potential for further conflict here, but given restrictions on space, we continue to focus on the core trade-off between emissions and growth. While emphases on policy objectives will no doubt vary among future Scottish Administrations, resource constraints ensure that there are always likely to be trade-offs among policy goals.

The existence of trade-offs undoubtedly makes policy much more difficult, and inevitably leads to the search for additional instruments to improve any such trade-offs. Three broad-brush policy areas are currently emphasised in the growth-emissions context and seem virtually certain to continue to be central, irrespective of the degree of autonomy of subsequent Scottish Administrations: establishing a credible carbon price; promoting the adoption of low carbon, including renewable, technologies; and fostering energy efficiency improvements. All of these offer the potential, at least, of 'decoupling' emissions and economic growth to a degree (with possible beneficial impacts in some instances also on security of energy supply and fuel

---

17 All of the major parties are currently committed to growth. If extreme weather events were to lead to increasing fear of global warming, opinion could conceivably shift further towards 'quality of life' arguments and a downgrading of the economic growth objective.

poverty). Many of the major policy instruments under each heading are currently reserved to Westminster (or controlled by the EU), and we consider the likely impact of further devolution of such policies in section 4 below.

There seems to be no reason to believe that greater autonomy would make policy easier by modifying the other goals of the Scottish Administration or by easing the trade-offs among goals. The Scottish Government is already free to adopt its own targets for sustainable growth, for example, as well as for emissions (for the non-traded sector), so it is not clear why further autonomy would be expected to have a significant impact, except if it enhances the portfolio of policy instruments that the Government possesses, a point we discuss in detail in section 7.4 below.

7.3.3 *UK policy*

Bowen and Rydge (2011) review UK climate change policy, drawing attention to the complexity of the policy landscape characterised by numerous policy instruments with overlapping coverage. These policies, including, for example, the Climate Change Levy (CCL), Feed in Tariffs (FiTs), Renewables Obligation Certificates (ROCs), Green Bank, Renewable Heat Incentives, the rolling out of smart meters, and planned Electricity Market Reforms currently apply to Scotland as well as to the RUK. Of course, the Scottish Government can, and does, seek to influence UK climate change policy and may claim some success in this regard. A possible example is the introduction of 'banding' in ROC allocations with a higher subsidy rate for renewable technologies that are currently further from market. However, much of UK climate change policy (and indeed many other aspects of general UK economic, energy and environmental policy) could currently reasonably be considered as broadly exogenous to, and a constraint upon, the Scottish Government. Many of these policies are effectively reserved to Westminster under the current devolution settlement. However, while these policies are not under the control of the Scottish Government, they also do not have to be financed within Scotland, a point we return to below.

A move towards further Scottish autonomy (from Westminster) clearly matters in this context. In the limit, an independent Scotland could reject all UK climate change policies and devise a distinctive set of policies of its own, although we have argued that there is unlikely to be any impact on the goals of future Scottish Administrations. The UK climate change policy landscape is certainly crowded, with many overlapping policies, so it is not difficult to imagine a policy framework that is improved in terms of its focus and transparency.

However, in such circumstances, any Scottish Administration would have to be aware of the highly open nature of the economy and its interdependence with RUK, most especially if the sterling monetary union was maintained (but even if it is not). Any differential green taxes/subsidies *vis-à-vis* RUK would have competitiveness effects that would need to be taken into account in any evaluation of policy distinctiveness. Of course, such taxes/subsidies could be balanced-budget in nature to limit their macroeconomic impacts, but there could still be major effects, both positive and negative. One example of a potential negative impact is the fact that an independent Scotland would have to finance any substitute for the ROC scheme, which is currently funded by the Westminster Government, to encourage renewables development. We consider the impact of greater autonomy on the instruments of climate change policy below.

7.3.4 *EU policy*

As we have seen, the *current* mainstream proposals for greater autonomy relate to autonomy *vis-à-vis* Westminster, not Brussels. In that context we have noted that EU ETS is a major constraint on Scottish (and indeed all member states') climate change policies, and this will not be altered by a shift in powers between Westminster and Edinburgh, except at the margin if the Scottish Government's voice in the EU has greater efficacy. Notice that the current policy stance on the EU implies that the decision on the appropriate degree of autonomy does depend on an implicit cost-benefit analysis of its consequences: 'more' autonomy in the area of climate change is not always judged to be 'better' for Scotland. We return to this issue in section 7.4 below.

We have already noted the fairly radical implications if future Administrations decide to continue membership of EU ETS: any variations in the actual emissions of the covered sector in Scotland result in 100% leakage. The primary focus of the Scottish Government has to be on the non-traded sector, where variations in emissions do impact on targets, though these, of course, remain subject to potential leakage through trade and factor flows. As far as traded sector emissions are concerned, the focus must be on seeking to influence the EU ETS targets and allowances. The current administration is seeking to tighten these perhaps in part to reflect a commitment to decarbonise the electricity generation sector, for example, which has in part been induced by other policies (such as those intended to promote renewable technologies, which we discuss in section 4 below), as well as to reinforce the incentives to decarbonise. Given the nature of global warming, participation in EU ETS is an example of the kind of policy collaboration that should be welcomed. However, the ability of the EU ETS to establish a credible long-term price of carbon remains in doubt. The Scottish and UK Governments have been seeking to exert this influence on EU ETS, to enhance its efficacy. There may be an argument again here that a more autonomous Scottish Government might possess a more powerful and distinctive voice in the EU, though this is not guaranteed (and it is not clear that the Scottish message to the EU would currently differ from that coming from Westminster).

EU policy is not simply about the EU ETS, however. In 2008, the EU introduced its 20-20-20 targets for 2020. These targets require: a 20% reduction in GHG emissions compared to 1990; 20% of energy consumption to be satisfied by renewables; and a 20% reduction in energy consumption through promoting energy efficiency improvements. The EU committed to increasing its emissions reduction to 30% if a successor to Kyoto was agreed and other countries signed up to strict targets. The EU targets are legally binding, and so have impacted on UK and Scottish targets in these areas.[18]

There is some dispute as to the right of a newly independent Scotland to remain within the EU. Furthermore, there may be circumstances in which a future Scottish Administration would choose to leave the EU, even if it had the option of continuing membership. This might arise, for example, if EU membership ultimately required joining the euro zone with constraints on fiscal policy that were judged to be unacceptably restrictive.

Clearly, if an independent Scotland were to leave the EU, the constraints of EU policy would no longer be binding. While such a radical change would necessitate a reconsideration of Scotland's climate change policy, such has been the cross-party agreement in this area that it seems unlikely that the goals of this policy would be significantly impacted. However, there would in these circumstances be a loss of a major policy instrument targeting the price of carbon and of the legally binding commitment to meet the 20-20-20 targets. We consider possible alternatives in our discussion of policy instruments below.

---

18 Note that the EU target for renewables is expressed in terms of energy. To meet this target through electricity generation alone implies a penetration of renewables that is proportionately higher.

Similar considerations would apply if the UK, including Scotland (with a degree of policy autonomy), were to leave the EU. Here, the UK, as well as Scotland, would be freed from the constraints of EU policies, but there is no reason to expect that either Administration's commitment to climate change would be impacted, although the resultant policy instrument vacuum would again need to be addressed.

7.4 THE IMPACT OF GREATER AUTONOMY ON THE INSTRUMENTS OF SCOTTISH CLIMATE CHANGE POLICY

We briefly consider here areas where greater autonomy might be thought to create new opportunities for climate change policy and explore some possibilities. The present Scottish Government has itself indicated a number of areas where it would like to see greater autonomy (from Westminster) allowing: further support for renewables from electricity market reforms (transmission charging, grid investment, access to fossil fuel levy, devolving all offshore licensing (Crown Estates)); enhancing energy efficiency (for example, Green Investment Bank). The Scottish Government understandably wishes to push Scottish interests within the UK, and shaping UK policies at the margin to favour renewables, for example, and offshore renewables in particular, are likely to favour Scottish economic development. However, under Devo max or independence such policies would presumably have to be entirely funded within Scotland.[19]

It is clear that the Scottish Government wishes to see a further hike in the carbon price (through tightening of EU targets on GHG emissions to 30% by 2020 compared to 1990). Clearly, under Devo max or independence options, the Scottish Government would be in a stronger position to manage the Scottish economy, and we briefly consider this as an additional possible climate change policy. We begin, however, with a brief consideration of the Climate Change Act and the likely impact of further autonomy on its provisions.

7.4.1 *Climate Change Act 2009*

This sets the legal framework and is regarded as at least a partial solution to the fact that Governments may be tempted to renege on commitments to emissions reduction for short-term political gain, so that private transactors become reluctant to make the long-term investments required to make the transition to a low

---

19 However, independence would not remove incentives for coordination of policies, although it may make this more difficult to ensure (for example, collaboration between Northern Ireland and ROI on electricity).

carbon economy.[20] However, while the targets embodied in the Act would be expected directly to influence private sector expectations and enhance credibility, the continuation of this impact is crucially dependent on the targets regularly being met. So they cannot legitimately be thought of as an independent instrument of policy. As we have already noted there is no reason to believe that the legal framework or the targets will be affected systematically by further devolution of power from Westminster.[21] However, it would presumably be necessary to establish a Scottish Climate Change Committee under independence (though it may be thought desirable under any of the other options for constitutional change too).

7.4.2 *Aggregate demand management*

Greater fiscal autonomy will undoubtedly enhance the ability of the Scottish Government to manage aggregate demand, and indeed the Scotland Act (2012), which compels the Scottish Government to set a Scottish income tax rate (that can vary by plus or minus 10% from that set by Westminster) and select a corresponding level of government expenditure ensures that this ability will inevitably increase (albeit in the form of balanced budget fiscal changes). Under Devo max or independence, this power would be further enhanced.[22] However, we have already noted that demand management is a very blunt tool in this context and is extremely unlikely ever to be deployed deliberately to meet carbon emission targets.

7.4.3 *Impacts on energy markets and infrastructure*

Current proposals for constitutional change appear to envisage continuing major infrastructural investment in the grid in Scotland and, in particular, its links to RUK. They also envisage the presence of a continuing British-wide integrated market in electricity, and so will be affected by the UK Government's eventual decision on the nature

---

20 See McGregor et al (2012a) for a review of the role and remit of the Climate Change Committee, including a comparison with the Monetary Policy Committee as a mechanism for resolving the 'time inconsistency' problem.

21 This is not to say that modifications are unlikely or undesirable, just that they are not systematically related to the extent of autonomy. Scotland's adoption of annual targets seems problematic, and one such target has already been missed because of the impact of a particularly cold winter on the use of gas for heating. In general, the smaller (and less diversified) the economy the greater the variance we would expect in emissions, and the less sensible annual targets seem.

22 It would, however, still be constrained by the highly open nature of the Scottish economy and by its permanently fixed exchange rate with RUK and the Bank of England's monetary policy. See the Introduction to this volume for further discussion.

of Electricity Market Reform. While there are benefits (and costs) to all residents of the UK from these changes, it is at least conceivable that the RUK Government's position may be different if faced with an independent Scotland. For simplicity, we abstract from the potential problems that would be created by a break-up in British-wide electricity infrastructure and markets.[23]

7.4.4 *The price of carbon*

The EU ETS is widely regarded as having failed to establish a credible long-term price of carbon (due to aspects of the scheme's implementation) that would be sufficient alone to establish a low-carbon economy. The UK is currently planning to introduce a carbon tax to provide a floor to the price of carbon. Among economists, the introduction of a carbon tax is regarded as an effective means of tackling the global warming externality, by seeking to internalise it and making polluters pay.[24]

One option for a Scottish Government under Devo max or independence options would be the introduction of a Scottish carbon tax. If a Scottish Administration were to leave EU ETS, the main instrument to influence the price of carbon currently would no longer apply to Scotland. In these circumstances a carbon tax might be rather more likely, although it could also be implemented under less radical constitutional change.[25, 26] Taxes are unpopular, but here the tax is on a 'bad' and is intended to correct a source of inefficiency. Furthermore, revenues may be recycled either to reduce existing distortionary taxes on 'goods' (for example, employment) or subsidise them (for example, low carbon technologies). We use our model of the Scottish economy to explore the possible consequences of a carbon tax, since we would expect this to have system-wide effects, altering the relative prices of goods and the allocation of production

---

23 In fact, the integrated British electricity market already offers options for interregional coordination within the UK to meet emissions targets. For example, greater electricity production in Scotland might make it easier and less costly to meet UK emissions targets even if it means violating Scottish-specific targets. (See, for example, Anandarajah and McDowall, 2012.)

24 Weitzman (1974) is the classic reference on the conditions under which it is preferable to operate directly on the 'price' of carbon (as under a tax) or its quantity (emissions, as in EU ETS).

25 However, leaving EU ETS would not be costless: the attraction of such schemes is precisely that they should generate a given aggregate emissions target at least cost (in this case, for the EU as a whole). As noted above, this raises the wider issue of the potential gains from the regions of the UK coordinating their responses to climate change to reduce the costs of compliance.

26 A Scottish Administration could presumably legislate for a carbon price to be set equal to that prevailing in EU ETS. However, it would be preferable to impose an equivalent carbon tax and benefit from the associated revenues.

in favour of low-carbon technologies.

Regardless of what happens to the revenues raised by the tax, it always succeeds in cutting emissions substantially, as is apparent from Figure 1, in which percentage reductions in emissions resulting from the imposition of the tax are plotted on the vertical axis, and time is plotted on the horizontal axis. When revenues are in effect not recycled, or recycled 'externally' (that is, absorbed into the Westminster Government's budget), emissions reduction is most rapid, because here there is clearly a contraction in demand in the Scottish economy and economic activity actually falls. Something similar is true of the case when revenues are used to fund general government expenditure, although the decline in activity is less, and so too is the fall in emissions. When revenues are recycled to fund income tax cuts, economic activity actually increases, generating a 'double dividend' (of reduced emissions and increased employment), and so again emissions take longer to fall to the target level.

Of course, in this exploratory exercise, the model does not distinguish traded and non-traded sectors, and identifies the impact on actual emissions, not those that count given a continuing commitment to EU ETS. Furthermore, we have not included here sensitivity of the 'learning rate' of renewables (and endogenous technical change) to the carbon tax, something that would be expected to prove important in the longer term. The interaction of that policy and a carbon tax raises further issues of interdependence under multi-level governance. However, influence on the price of carbon is likely to have substantial impacts.

FIGURE 1. THE IMPACT OF A £50 PER TONNE TAX ON
CO2 EMISSIONS UNDER ALTERNATIVE ASSUMPTIONS
ABOUT FUNDING.

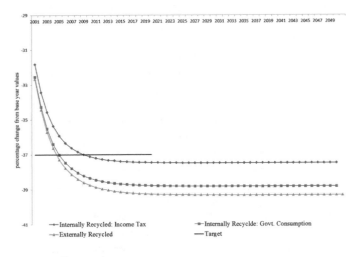

Source: Allan *et al*, 2012.

7.4.5 *Encouraging low carbon technologies*

The extent of successive Scottish Governments' emphasis on renewables and their potential for stimulating economic development,
in particular, has been a distinctive feature of Scottish energy and
climate change policy until now (Allan *et al*, 2010).[27] They appear
to offer the potential for a double or even triple 'dividend': simultaneously stimulating economic activity while reducing emissions
and (probably) enhancing security of supply. Intervention through
effective financial support (for example, ROCs and FiTs) is typically motivated in terms of the external benefits (including spillover
effects to other companies) associated with the development of new
technologies.

However, as we have already noted, given that renewables that
are used to generate electricity are part of the traded sector under
EU ETS, a reduction in Scottish emissions is subject to 100% leakage
and does not directly reduce measured EU emissions (Net Scottish
Emissions Account, NSEA). In the longer term, there are indirect
benefits. First, decarbonisation of energy supply is important to facilitate subsequent reductions in emissions and allow 2050 targets to

---

27 While nuclear is 'low carbon', the current Scottish Government effectively has a
policy of no new nuclear power stations in Scotland.

be met through, for example, electrification of transport and decarbonisation of heat. Second, if EU ETS allowances are tightened significantly as generation is decarbonised, then there will ultimately be an impact on emissions within ETS (though reflecting, rather than generating, a decarbonised energy supply sector).

Ultimately, these policies could decouple the link between economic growth and actual emissions (and measured emissions if EU ETS is tightened appropriately) and so resolve the conflict between (measured and actual) emissions and growth. Certainly, decarbonisation of the energy supply sector by 2030 is a present Scottish Government target, although it does not believe that this target can be met without a significant tightening of EU ETS and a rise in the carbon price with accompanying stimuli to the renewables sector.

Currently, the major policy instrument for encouraging large-scale renewables, ROCs, is under the control of, and funded by, the Westminster Government, though there is now differentiation reflecting a desire to stimulate new technologies at different points in their lifecycle.[28] As we have seen, greater autonomy would allow a Scottish Government, in principle, to reinforce the push to renewables, but full fiscal autonomy, and certainly independence, would imply the Scottish Government having fully to fund renewables policy. While there may be additional sources of revenue accruing to the Government in these circumstances (for example, fuel levy; licensing revenue), it seems inevitable that funding even the existing support for renewables would present a challenge.[29]

We conducted some illustrative simulations using our energy-economy-environment model of Scotland. We used the model to solve for the level of subsidy that would be required to enable the Scottish Government to meet its 80% emissions targets with a target portfolio of a generating mix (based on Anandarajah and McDowall (2012)). A key feature of the portfolio was the huge increase in both onshore (from 0.04 to 2.4 GW) and offshore wind (from 0.0001 to 3.83 GW) necessary over the period 2000–2020 to meet the targets. Our estimates of the extent of the required subsidy proved very sensitive to the assumed 'learning rate' – the rate at which the costs associated with renewable technologies decline – but the scale of subsidy was typically substantial and never less than equivalent to several percentage points on the standard rate of income tax.

---

28 Allan et al (2011) provide estimates of the likely impact on the levelised costs of various renewable technologies.

29 Broadly, we would expect greater revenues from North Sea oil to compensate for currently higher government expenditure per capita in Scotland, so that Scottish-specific renewables policies would have to secure supplementary funding.

The implication is not that greater autonomy will have no ben-eficial impact, rather that, while it may permit the creation of new Scottish-specific instruments of climate change policy, it is inevita-bly not all going to be good news. A number of UK climate change policies that have a significant impact on renewables develop-ment in Scotland (relative to RUK) are currently funded through Westminster, and the more radical devolution proposals (probably with Devo max and certainly with independence) would require the Scottish Government to 'pick up the tab' for Scottish ROCs and FiTs, for example, and fund them either through a hike in income taxation or a reduction in other Scottish Government expenditures (or an increase in debt), or some combination thereof.

7.4.6 *Fostering energy efficiency*

Energy efficiency is often regarded as some form of 'magic bullet', allowing us to do more with less and so perhaps reducing our use of energy. In fact, matters are significantly more complex than this. An improvement in energy efficiency reduces the effective price of a unit of energy, which tends to stimulate the demand for it. Rebound is present if a 5% improvement in energy efficiency generates a less than 5% fall in energy consumption; backfire refers to the case where energy consumption actually rises following an improvement in effi-ciency, perhaps most likely when energy efficiency improvements arise on the production side and so stimulate growth. However, rebound is still possible for households, of course, as when they choose to take part in an improvement in efficiency in heating in the form of a warmer home ('comfort taking'). Hanley *et al* (2009) suggests that rebound and even backfire effects could be important for Scotland. While the impact of rebound and backfire on emis-sions would be mitigated if carbon is appropriately priced, this would reduce the incentives to stimulate activity in response to an improve-ment in energy efficiency.

7.5 CONCLUSIONS

We do not expect greater Scottish Government autonomy to impact substantively on: the ultimate objective of climate change policy, namely to prevent excessive global warming; the legal framework for climate change policy; nor on Scottish emission targets. Scottish climate change policy has been fully devolved since its inception, so there is no compelling reason to expect it to change systematically in the face of greater autonomy (from the Westminster Government, or indeed from the EU). As a practical matter, however, the adoption of annual targets with no banking or borrowing seems an unnecessarily tight constraint, especially for a small open economy, which if frequently breached will undermine the basic framework and its intended impact on the private sector's long-term confidence in its efficacy.[30]

Most proposals for constitutional change currently envisage continuing membership of the EU and participation in EU ETS. This implies that the Scottish Government (like other members) really only has the power to determine the target emissions for the non-traded sector. The EU ETS ensures that any deviation in the actual Scottish emissions in the traded sector from those implied (the given ETS allowance) by the scheme is subject to 100% carbon leakage, and has no impact at all on EU or global emissions or global warming. This is a striking example of the importance of understanding policy making under multi-level governance, though here it is the relationship with Brussels that is key, rather than that with Westminster. The appetite for greater autonomy *vis-à-vis* Westminster does not *currently* extend to Brussels, though this has a huge impact on domestic policy. In effect, there is an apparent acceptance that the appropriate level of government to deal with traded sector emissions is the EU (although the UK Government is proposing to augment this with a carbon price floor), though there is certainly no general acceptance that a similar argument might apply, for other policies, with respect to the UK.

However, there can be no general presumption of a continuing membership of the EU and all that implies, irrespective of the extent of further autonomy of the Edinburgh from the Westminster Government. There may be circumstances in which Scottish membership of the EU is precluded or where a Scottish Administration judges the net cost of continuing membership to be too high. In such circumstances a Scottish Administration would have the greatest freedom to formulate its own package of climate change policies, though even in these circumstances there would have to be appropriate cognisance of interdependence of the Scottish with both the RUK and REU economies.

Climate change policy does not operate in a vacuum but in an interdependent energy-economy-environment system in which a disturbance to any one part of the system has ramifications for the other elements. So the Scottish economy represents a major constraint on climate change policy, since emissions tend to vary directly

---

30 The fact that it is NEAT emissions that matter rather than actual emissions does introduce an element of smoothing, but one that was insufficient to allow the Government to meet its target in 2010, which had a particularly cold winter (and therefore high gas consumption).

with economic activity, indicating a trade-off between the economy and the environment. The link between greater fiscal autonomy and economic growth is the subject of considerable controversy, which we discuss in chapter 6 of this volume. However, to the extent that fiscal autonomy does stimulate economic growth, other things being equal, this makes it *more* difficult for the Government to meet its emissions targets, unless the composition of this growth is skewed towards low carbon technologies and the electricity generating sector is indeed decarbonised, with transport and heat following suit (and EU ETS, if applicable, gradually being tightened). However, greater growth would typically imply greater tax revenues and an ability to further stimulate low carbon technologies and energy efficiency, so that the traditional trade-off between growth and emissions could be altered by appropriate policies. Carbon leakage, either through trade flows or factor movements (for example, outward FDI in emission intensive industries), remains an important issue, however, that could at least partially offset the impact of the Scottish Government on the non-traded sector's emissions on global emissions (or on all emissions in circumstances where Scotland does not remain in EU ETS). Regular monitoring of footprint-type indicators of emissions would alert future Administrations to any significant threats from this source.

While greater fiscal autonomy will undoubtedly give the Scottish Parliament greater influence over aggregate demand, and therefore over the level of economic activity, demand management would be a very blunt instrument to use to meet emissions targets. A much more likely outcome is that greater autonomy would be reflected in attempts to strengthen instruments that more sharply focus on emissions. There are three main areas in which policies seem likely to be concentrated, even over the longer term. First, the Scottish Government could seek to influence the price of carbon. Under Devo max or independence, the Scottish Government would be free to introduce a balanced-budget carbon tax. While we have seen that the likely macroeconomic consequences of this depend on the use to which revenues are put, it always proves an effective means of inducing a reduction in emissions. Of course, in practice there are issues such as interaction with EU ETS (if it remains applicable) and impacts on RUK, but mechanisms by which the Scottish Parliament might influence the Scottish price of carbon seem worthy of further investigation.

A second area where the Scottish Government would be likely to seek to exert greater influence would be in the context of low carbon technologies, particularly CCS and renewables. Policies to subsidise these in some (additional) way can be motivated in terms of R&D externalities, or contributions to security of supply and economic development potential.[31] However, a major issue for Devo max and independence options would be the need to finance existing supports in this area, since these are currently funded by the Westminster Government. Our analysis suggests that major expenditure is required to meet emissions targets through the expansion of renewables, but these constitutional changes would also open up the possibility of new revenue streams (for example, licensing revenues that currently go to the Crown Estate). This is an area that requires careful further study, but the scale of required support will inevitably depend on the speed at which the new technologies are able to reduce their costs, and that in turn will depend to a degree on the credibility of continuing government support.[32]

Finally, there is the idea that promotion of energy efficiency allows us to 'do more with less'. This is not as straightforward a proposition as it seems at first sight, in part because of the interdependence of the energy-economy-environment sub-system. Improvements in energy efficiency should continue to be encouraged, but ensuring beneficial impacts on emissions as well as the economy is likely to depend on getting the price of carbon right (to tackle rebound and backfire effects).

Overall, a movement to greater autonomy of the Edinburgh Government from Westminster need not impinge dramatically on many aspects of Scottish climate change policy, which will remain heavily influenced by EU and UK policies (and by world events). However, it does offer the potential for a wider portfolio of policy instruments, especially if membership of the EU is not continued for whatever reason, but the net effect is extremely difficult to identify. There may be benefits, in terms of the potential for Scottish-specific impacts on the carbon price, renewables and energy efficiency, but such changes typically also involve costs (such as the need to pay for renewables policies that are currently funded by Westminster).

---

31 As we have seen, these policies cannot be motivated in terms of their immediate impact on emissions given membership of EU ETS.

32 The geographic distribution of renewable technologies is clearly uneven, reflecting the scale of the resource and the ease with which it can be accessed at different sites. This clearly could have implications for an autonomous Scottish Government (for example, funding required for PV is much more modest).

This chapter raises some key questions that should shape the ongoing constitutional debate around the enhanced powers that could be transferred to the Scottish Parliament. They are particularly relevant to the propositions based upon an independent Scotland but many are equally appropriate for those models similar to Devo max and Devo plus that allow a lesser degree of autonomy.

Goals and targets of policy

» would a future constitutional arrangement be likely to substantively impact on the present consensus in the Scottish Parliament of the importance of limiting GHG emissions?
  › would it necessitate establishment of a Scottish Climate Change Committee?
» would continuity of vision be likely to imply continuity in target-setting?
» would enhanced powers allow more ambitious target-setting for emissions?
  › if so, what would be the associated costs and benefits?
» would constitutional change encourage a continuing focus on the most appropriate measures of Scottish progress: for example, upon the monitoring of indicators of the extent of Scotland's overall 'carbon footprint', in line with the current Administration's commitment?
» would constitutional change impact on the goal of decarbonising the Scottish energy supply sector, even if the current ETS implied no net benefit to EU emissions or to global warming?
» would a new constitution impact on the emissions goals for the 'non-traded' sector (and therefore for Scotland's overall emissions target) if Scotland remains within the EU?
» how might the EU's current allocation mechanism for allowances among member states be affected? What are the likely implications of more radical constitutional change, specifically:
  › what are the implications for Scotland's approach if an independence model with Scotland's own currency and outwith the EU were to be adopted?
  › what implication would the departure of the UK from the EU have on Scotland's approach, whether Scotland were to remain as part of the UK or become an independent nation?

Constraints on policy

» would Scotland under a new constitutional arrangement accept EU policies (if it remains within the EU)?

» would it agree that the appropriate level of government to deal with traded sector emissions is the EU?

> though ideally a 'World Government' responsibility?

» would greater autonomy enhance the 'voice' of the Scottish Government in international negotiations with the EU?

» would Scotland under a new constitutional arrangement maintain all UK climate change policies or devise a distinctive set of policies of its own?

» will a unified British electricity grid and market be impacted by the more radical alternatives for constitutional change?

» will 'green' policies that lead to higher energy prices (at least initially) risk alienating public support for climate change policies?

» would greater frequency of extreme weather events provide support for tougher climate change policies in Scotland?

Instruments of policy

» which instruments would an Administration with new powers seek to strengthen or introduce?

> would there be a role for a carbon tax (especially if an independent Scotland was no longer a member of EU ETS)

> would there be an opportunity to develop a more focused, transparent and non-overlapping set of climate change policies than currently characterises UK policy?

» would the current emphasis on establishing a credible carbon price, promoting the adoption of low carbon, including renewable, technologies, and fostering energy efficiency improvements be expected to be continued?

> would emphasis on transition to a low carbon economy as a source of sustainable growth retain a key role?

» would Scotland continue to reject the opportunity to buy ETS allowances as a means of satisfying the targets?

» how would a Scottish Government fund any new initiatives, notably with respect to the development of renewables?

> how would it compensate for any loss of subsidy or support from the UK?

> would it find the funding through raising taxation or through a reduction in other Scottish Government expenditures (or an increase in debt, given that this is an option even under

the Scotland Act (2012))?
> revenues from a Scottish-specific carbon tax?
» would a Scottish Administration, in the last resort, manage aggregate demand to meet its emissions targets?

REFERENCES

Allan, G., Lecca, P., McGregor, P. G., Swales, K., Tamba, M. & M. Winning. 2012. 'The impact of the introduction of a carbon tax for Scotland', *Fraser of Allander Economic Commentary*, Special Issue, pp. 13–18.

Allan, G., McDonald, J., McGregor, P & Swales, K. 2008. 'A distinctive energy policy for Scotland?', *Fraser of Allander Economic Commentary*, vol 32, No1, pp. 46–61.

Anandarajah, G. & McDowall, W. 2012. 'What are the costs of Scotland's climate and renewables policies', *Energy Policy*, forthcoming.

Bosquet, B. 2000. 'Environmental tax reform: does it work? A survey of the empirical evidence', *Ecological Economics*, vol. 34, pp. 19–32.

Bowen, A. & Rydge, J. 2011. 'Climate change policy in the United Kingdom', Policy Paper, Centre for Climate Change Policy.

Goulder. L. H. & Stavins, R.N. 2011. 'Challenges from state-federal interactions in US climate change policy', *American Economic Review, Papers and Proceedings*, vol. 101, no. 3, pp. 253–7.

Hanley, N. D., McGregor, P. G., Turner, K. & Swales, J.K. 2009. 'Do increases in resource productivity improve environmental quality? Theory and evidence on "rebound" and "backfire" effects from an energy-economy-environment computable general equilibrium model of Scotland', *Ecological Economics*, vol. 68, pp. 692–709.

McGregor. P. G., Swales, J. K. & Winning, M. 2011. 'Scottish climate change policy: a brief overview', *Fraser of Allander Economic Commentary*, Energy and Pollution Special Issue, pp. 46–61.

McGregor, P. G., Swales, J. K. & Winning, M. 2012 'A review of the role and remit of the Committee on Climate Change', *Energy Policy*, vol. 41, pp. 466–73.

Pearce, D. 1991. 'The role of carbon taxes in adjusting to global warming', *Economic Journal*, vol. 101, pp. 938–48.

Scottish Government. 2012. *The Scottish Greenhouse Gas Emissions Target 2010*. Scottish Government: Edinburgh. www.scotland.gov.uk/resource/0040/00405463.pdf

Weitzman, M. L. 1974. 'Prices vs quantities', *Review of Economic Studies*, vol. 41, no. 4, pp. 477–91.

CHAPTER 8

Economic Development and Skills for the Knowledge Economy: Contribution of Higher Education and R&D

Professor Sir Jim McDonald[1] *and Simon Jennings*[2]

8.1 INTRODUCTION AND CONTEXT

8.1.1 *Objectives*

Scotland's universities, their staff, students and graduates represent a major advantage for Scotland. As economies around the world look to generate competitive advantage in order to secure and retain high-value, high-wage economic activity, Scotland starts from an enviable position. This fact has not been lost on the Scottish Parliament, and our politicians have increasingly looked to our universities to play a critical role in increasing Scotland's human and intellectual capital and, as a result, make increasing contributions to economic recovery and growth.

The introduction to the Scottish Government's December 2010 *Building a Smarter Future* consultation[3] makes clear the sector's strengths:

> "From a country of just five million people, we have five universities in the top 150 in the world. In comparative terms, only England, the USA and China fare better. We also punch above our weight in research: 1.8% of the world's cited research comes from Scotland with just 0.1% of the world's population. This makes Scottish-based research the most cited by GDP in the world."

In short, the strength and scale of Scottish universities' intellectual output is world-leading. In light of this, the question for policy makers is how can this be best harnessed in support of economic growth? That

---

1   Principal of University of Strathclyde and Rolls-Royce Professor of Electrical Power Systems.
2   Director of Strategy and Policy, University of Strathclyde.
3   Building a Smarter Future: Towards a Sustainable Scottish Solution for the Future of Higher Education, Scottish Government, December 2010.

is the primary issue for exploration in this chapter: what are the key factors associated with constitutional change that may have an impact on the effectiveness with which government, university and industry collaborate with the common purpose of stimulating knowledge-based growth in the 'triple helix' model of economic development?

The 'triple helix' reference seeks to characterise the conditions where public, private and academic organisations work together strategically on education, research and knowledge exchange to enhance and accelerate outcomes for high economic impact. For example, in Europe, the Fraunhofer Gesselschaft[4] exemplifies this approach and is seen as a world-leader. Recently, the UK Government has sought to replicate this successful model through the establishment of a series of Catapult Centres[5] in key thematic areas such as High Value Manufacturing, Cell Therapy and Offshore Renewable Energy. Scotland is making a disproportionately high contribution to these entities and the Technology and Innovation Centre (TIC) at the University of Strathclyde is built on such an approach with major industrial partnerships in key sectors.

The breadth and reach of our universities' activities is significant. Reflecting the major role higher education and research will play in shaping Scotland's future, this chapter considers the full range of powers. This extends to economic powers and the underlying economic environment, as well as the growth and performance of the economy. More specifically, we will explore fiscal powers, border controls and immigration, external affairs and specific regulatory powers. In examining each area, we attempt to identify the opportunities and risks of constitutional change as they relate to the sector's contribution to Scotland and consider how these might be respectively maximised and mitigated.

8.1.2 Current policy context in Scotland

Policy interventions intended to enhance the way in which government, industry and universities interact with a view to stimulating economic growth are becoming more common the world over. Scotland is no exception. In return for sustained public investment via the Scottish Government's 2011 Spending Review,[6] the Cabinet Secretary's letter of guidance[7] required that the SFC secure a number of 'improved outcomes' from the higher education sector, namely:

---

4   See www.fraunhofer.de/en.html
5   See www.innovateuk.org/deliveringinnovation/catapults.ashx
6   See http://www.scotland.gov.uk/Resource/Doc/358356/0121130.pdf
7   See www.sfc.ac.uk/web/FILES/About_the_Council/SFC_Letter_of_Guidance_21_September_2011.pdf

» retention;
» articulation from college;
» accelerated degrees, including entry into the second year of the undergraduate degree programme from school;
» access to university for people from the widest possible range of backgrounds;
» international competitiveness in research;
» university/industry collaboration and the exploitation of research;
» the pattern and spread of provision;
» efficiency, both in the learning journey and of institutions; and
» the entrepreneurial and employability skills of graduates.

What is notable about these outcomes is that the overwhelming majority seek in some way to either raise the overall level of skills and entrepreneurial ability of students, or to enhance universities' interactions with industry. Such a focus is well placed given the competitive global context.

Competitor governments around the world are striving to secure economic growth through investing in workforce skills and by harnessing intellectual capital within universities. However, each economy begins from a different position. While it is clear that the intellectual output of Scotland's universities represents a major competitive advantage, Scotland faces significant challenges in maintaining its comparative high-level skills advantage and in securing industry investment in research and development.

OECD's *Education at a Glance (2011)* data indicate that, in 2000, the UK was ranked third amongst OECD nations for the percentage of young people educated to degree level. Analysis of these data makes apparent competitor nations' efforts to secure the economic benefits associated with high-value graduate jobs. Our competitors have increased their investment in human capital with such rapidity that the UK fell to fifteenth in this table in the 2008 figures, below the mean for OECD nations (and Scotland is not an outlier within the UK).

Why is this skills race so important? In examining the global skills needs for 2020, the McKinsey Institute (2012) identifies a potential shortfall of up to 40 million graduate or postgraduate qualified workers and a need for urgent action on the part of policy makers.

We estimate that advanced economies will need to raise the number of young people completing tertiary education 2.5 times as quickly as they are currently doing. They will also need to guide more students to job-relevant training (in the

United States, for example, only 14 per cent of college degrees awarded are in STEM fields).[8]

This is undoubtedly a major challenge for any government seeking to support continued economic growth. Unlike their counterparts elsewhere in the UK, Scotland's policy makers face a challenge of equal magnitude in terms of business investment in R&D. The Scottish Government's latest figures for Business Enterprise R&D (BERD) in Scotland show that expenditure was just 0.52% of Scottish GDP in 2010, compared to 1.09% for the UK and 1.16% for the EU. This low level of investment would position Scotland as the fourth lowest amongst the 26 OECD countries. While it can be argued that this issue is partly compensated for by higher levels of Government (GERD) and Higher Education (HERD) expenditure on R&D – and is likely to reflect the high proportion of SMEs in Scotland's economy – it is clearly not a strong basis for a successful 'triple helix' and an effective clustering approach requiring high degrees of connectivity between the R&D activities in universities and industry.

8.1.3 *The global challenge*

The increasing worldwide policy focus on universities' contribution to economic growth through research, consultancy and graduate skills reflects the mobility of global business and capital investment, especially the R&D spend of global multinationals. This is particularly relevant to Scotland given the relative R&D strength contained within its universities and the high-value employment this supports within related industry, as well as the universities themselves. The OECD has recognised that Multinational Enterprises (or MNEs) play a disproportionately significant role in driving technological advances and the related economic activity within regional and local economies.

> MNEs play a crucial role in the internationalisation of technology, since they develop and transfer proprietary knowledge which gives them a competitive edge. In addition, MNE headquarters largely fund R&D investments of their affiliates abroad, resulting in an increasing share of R&D investments by these foreign affiliates in host countries. In some smaller countries, MNEs account for the majority of R&D investment ... and play an important role in R&D investments across the

---

8   The World at Work: Jobs, Pay and Skills for 3.5 Billion People, McKinsey Institute, 2012.

world: the largest R&D spending MNEs are positioned among the top 10 countries investing in R&D in 2008, and the aggregate spending of the world's eight largest MNEs in 2008 was larger than the R&D investments of all individual countries, except for the United States and Japan ...

Due to these distinctive characteristics, MNEs are responsible for a large share of employment, turnover and value added created in host countries, especially in high-technology industries in manufacturing. However, the benefits of MNEs do not accrue only to host countries but increasingly also to the home countries because of the positive effects of outward foreign direct investment on economies, notably in enabling MNEs to tap into foreign technology and knowledge.[9]

In short, attracting R&D investment from MNEs must be a key consideration in examining the relationship between constitutional change and sustainable economic growth. Delivering the global connectivity, skills base and wider environment needed to grow, attract and retain such companies will be critical to Scotland's overall economic performance. The scale and global significance of MNEs' investment presents a challenge to policy makers looking to retain Scotland's advantage in its research base and to ensure that we derive the maximum possible benefit from this. The OECD makes plain this is not a challenge Scotland faces alone.

MNEs are forceful actors in the current globalisation process, and often limit the effectiveness and success of government policies. Countries need to take this changing reality into account and explore how policies can be designed that benefit both the country and the multinational. Facilitating the location of innovation hubs and decision centres is particularly important, as these centres direct the technology and investment flows within MNEs networks.[10]

At present, Scottish universities' R&D-intensive environment and supportive policy context can claim some success in attracting foreign direct investment, including the R&D facilities and decision centres of multinationals such as the aerospace cluster including Boeing and Rolls-Royce at the University of Strathclyde's Advanced Forming Research Centre and Amazon's Development Centre in Edinburgh. A group of Scotland's universities have also attracted

---

9   Measuring Globalisation: OECD Economic Globalisation Indicators 2010.
10 Ibid.

GSK, Astra Zenica and Novartis to create a major R&D hub in Continuous Manufacturing and Crystallisation (CMAC) on the basis of our collaborative research strengths. Similarly, foreign firms establishing significant activity in Scotland, including Avaloq FMC, State Street and Outplay Entertainment, have cited the quality and skills of Scotland's graduates as critical to their decisions to locate activity in Scotland. Scotland will have to continue to develop policies and approaches in order to sustain a total 'offer' comprising R&D base, skills, employment policies and lifestyle which match, or better, those of competitor countries, whatever the outcome of the constitutional debate.

Policy makers across the world face the same key challenges in seeking to drive economic growth: support for, and investment in, skills skills and innovation. For some nations, this has meant radical government policy interventions, including Brazil's 'Science Without Borders' programme giving 100,000 Brazilian students and researchers – in the STEM fields (science, technology, engineering, mathematics) – up to twelve months of experience at leading universities worldwide. Important also is France's EUR35 billion national loan to fund strategic investments in its universities' capital infrastructure, primarily in support of STEM fields. In China and in India, state investment in universities has been vast. The *Times Higher Education* magazine commented on the rise of Asian universities in the magazine's ranking of leading universities noting that

> Asian nations are investing heavily in high-level skills, innovation and knowledge to stay globally competitive. In contrast, data published last month by the Organisation for Economic Co-operation and Development showed that the US's total spending on tertiary education as a proportion of gross domestic product dropped from 2.8 per cent to 2.6 per cent between 2005 and 2009. The Republic of Korea, notable for strong rises in the rankings this year, has now caught up.
>
> And the UK? Its figure is shameful – 1.3 per cent of GDP, well below the OECD average. As the Russell Group of research-intensive universities has pointed out, UK public investment in higher education, at only 0.6 per cent of GDP, is lower than that of Brazil and Russia, and is on a par with South Africa's. In this context, the fact that the UK has 31 universities in the top 200 is an amazing achievement. Our leading institutions are among the best in the world. But for how much longer?[11]

---

11 'Revealed: for whom the bill tolls', Times Higher Education, 4 October 2012.

Commenting specifically on the fact that the majority of Scottish universities had fallen in the *Times Higher*'s rankings due to improved performance by Asian universities backed by significantly state investment the author, Mr Baty, commented that

> While there are current policies protecting investment in universities, they are unlikely to be enough to meet the challenge posed by massive spending in the East. These disappointing results may resurrect the debate about charging tuition fees in Scotland.[12]

The scale of the challenge should not come as a surprise to policy makers in Scotland, a September 2011 European Commission communiqué on jobs and growth noted that

> the potential of European higher education institutions to fulfil their role in society and contribute to Europe's prosperity remains under-exploited; Europe is no longer setting the pace in the global race for knowledge and talent, while emerging economies are rapidly increasing their investment in higher education. While 35% of all jobs in the EU will require high-level qualifications by 2020, only 26% of the workforce currently has a higher education qualification.[13]

It is in this highly competitive and fast-moving global context, as well as the very particular context of constitutional change, that Scotland's leaders must consider how Scotland's higher education system can be a key driver of economic growth. Chief amongst the challenges of doing so will be increasing the undergraduate and postgraduate capacity to the levels necessary to position Scotland as a high-level skills economy able to compete for knowledge-based inward investment. This will need to be supported by delivery of a policy environment which continues to invest in HE in line with our international competitors and which fosters the production of intellectual capital through encouraging innovative industry/university relationships and capturing mobile business investment in R&D.

---

12 'Scottish seats of learning fall in key rankings', The Herald, 4 October 2012.
13 Supporting Growth and Jobs: An Agenda for the Modernisation of Europe's Higher Education Systems, European Commission, September 2011.

At present, Scottish levels of expenditure on R&D, on higher education and approaches to attracting foreign direct investment are ultimately determined by both the UK and Scottish Parliaments. The underlying economic environment, macroeconomic performance and broad public expenditure levels affect current expenditure on higher education within Scotland.

As such, the current levels of Scottish public expenditure, and for HE programmes in particular, cannot be viewed as completely disconnected to those of the UK as a whole. If the UK reduces spend on HE, as with the recent tuition fees reforms, then the consequential funds for Scotland decline. While there is no direct connection between English HE funding and the levels determined by the Scottish Parliament, the total funds available to Scottish Ministers can decline based on decisions in Westminster and, in such circumstances, continuing to support universities requires the Scottish Parliament to consider expenditure reductions in other areas. Similarly, other Westminster decisions would have consequential effects on potential university funding in Scotland, for example, through Research Councils UK (RCUK) budgets.

When considering in more detail what might be affected by constitutional change, it is important that we first consider the existing powers and the policy context these have delivered. Universities, when their activities are looked at in the round, occupy a somewhat unusual position in the current devolution settlement. While the Scottish Government has responsibility for many of the economic development powers and higher education (that is, the provision of education at undergraduate level and above) and the Scottish Funding Council makes research grants to Scottish universities, the funding of research via the Research Councils UK (RCUK) is reserved to Westminster. The significant levels of such funding Scottish universities win competitively from this source exceeds the allocation it would receive based on population share – approximately 13% of RCUK spend with around 9% of the population.

What further devolution or independence might mean for this funding of circa £330m has, to date, been the primary focus of political debate about universities and constitutional change. However, it can be argued that the overwhelming majority of powers which might be used to enhance skills development or to incentivise R&D investment and economic growth based on intellectual property already rests with Scottish Ministers. They can already put in place policies which enable universities to take on additional undergraduates, do so in specific subject areas and can encourage knowledge exchange through allocations of research funding and incentivising business and universities to work together.

As the above extract from the Cabinet Secretary's 2011 letter of guidance to the Scottish Funding Council makes clear, there can be no doubt that Scottish Ministers are using their existing powers to implement policy with the objective of increasing universities' contribution to economic growth. With the direction and encouragement of Ministers, a range of initiatives are being pursued: Scottish Enterprise works increasingly closely with the Scottish Funding Council and includes the higher education sector amongst its key industry sectors; there are incentives and investments in support of the commercialisation of research made by both the SFC and Scottish Enterprise; the Scottish Government has made additional STEM places available to its universities; the Scottish Government has asked the SFC to increase the engagement between universities and industry by means of a 'single knowledge exchange office'; and recent incentive funding has targetted additional funded places on areas relevant to industry by means of the 'Skills for Growth' initiative. In a similar vein, Skills Development Scotland is engaging effectively with universities, colleges and Scottish Enterprise to develop their strategic, demand-led Skills Investment Plans (SIPs).

In the wider policy sphere, Scotland's Ministers and officials have been active in securing inward investment and Scottish Development International has been extremely supportive of universities' role in this area. As with any policy area, more could be done at the expense of expenditure elsewhere in order to create greater incentives and fund additional STEM places, however, the strong overall support for the university sector from the public purse demonstrates this is clearly an area which the Scottish Government has prioritised.

While Scotland's universities are diverse in terms of their mission and subject focus, there is considerable evidence that universities have embraced the economic aspect of their mission. For some, it represents a continuation of what has always lain at the heart of their mission. At the University of Strathclyde the connection to the Scottish economy is particularly strong. The institution was founded by John Anderson as 'a place of useful learning' – a university whose purpose would be to work for 'the public, for the good of mankind and the improvement of science'. This concept of 'useful learning' still defines the University's purpose and underpins the University's conviction that it has a central role to play in the wider social, cultural and economic life of Scotland.

Over the past three years, this mission has seen the University establish novel modes of engagement with industry such as the Technology and Innovation Centre (TIC), the Advanced Forming

Research Centre (part of the UK High Value Manufacturing Catapult Centre), the Centre for Innovative Manufacturing in Continuous Manufacturing & Crystallisation and the UK Catapult Centre for Offshore Renewable Energy, all of which create a much more integrated working environment in support of collaboration between the University and its industry partners.

In addition to such support, the University has benefited from modest growth in the STEM subject areas with the support of additional places and, more recently, from SFC investment in a significant number of places in support of the University's Engineering Academy. Such initiatives add to Strathclyde's own ambitious targets to increase its postgraduate research student numbers in such fields.

8.3 WHERE MIGHT ADDITIONAL POWERS HAVE AN IMPACT?

As noted above, the overwhelming political focus to date has been on the £330m of funding which Scottish universities win competitively from Research Councils UK. Latterly, a second question, that of the tuition fee regime which would operate in the case of full independence, has arisen. It is suggested that, without action and assuming continued EU membership for an independent Scotland, students from the remaining parts of the UK would be entitled to free tuition at Scottish universities at the expense of the Scottish tax payer. However, despite the fact that these are critical issues, they are far from being the full picture.

Competitively won RCUK funds are undoubtedly critical. They underpin a UK-wide system which provides Scotland with an opportunity to win a disproportionate level of funding for vital research. They also enable collaborative activity focused on problems or 'grand challenges' requiring teams of scale and expertise drawn from across multiple institutions. Attracting such funding also signals the international quality of Scottish research through direct comparison to the leading universities in the rest of the UK. The funding is also 'portable', meaning that individual academics move from one UK university to another taking this project funding with them. Similarly, students from the rest of the UK bring an important diversity to Scotland's university populations. Under the new rest of UK fee regime, their fees also play a key part in funding the Scottish system as a whole. In the case of some smaller undergraduate subject areas, it can be argued that such students play a critical role in sustaining a subject's viability and maintaining the current breadth of subjects available in Scotland.

The political debate is yet to move beyond considerations of the financial 'inputs' required to sustain the research and teaching at

Scotland's universities. To date, there has been little, if any, consideration of the *outcomes* the current system supports and how these might be improved or enhanced through the use of powers which are currently reserved. The potential impact of various constitutional options to either enhance, or to put at risk, a number of areas still requires further exploration. In particular, reference should be made to the sector's UK collaborations, its international connections, the intellectual property our universities contribute to the economy, the single UK market for staff and foreign direct investment. These all require more detailed consideration in the run-up to the 2014 referendum.

In light of the scale of international investment in higher education, three structural questions emerge. Can Scotland match (or surpass) the OECD average for the proportion of GDP invested in higher education? And, if so, what is the balance between public and private investment to be? And in what kind of sector should politicians invest?

The Scottish Government's 2011 Spending Review prioritised investment of public funds in the sector for a three-year period, but the planned investment, boosted by income from fees now paid by rest of UK students, will not come close to putting Scotland amongst the leading nations in terms of percentage of GDP spent on the sector. Even this investment, modest in global terms, has come with significant negative commentary relating to cuts to college budgets over the same period and has seen opposition politicians question the current government's free tuition policy in terms of both affordability and social equity.

Genuine questions of affordability and the political reality of significant disinvestment from other parts of the public sector would undoubtedly arise were the Scottish Parliament to rely solely on public funding to make the much more significant step change in investment required to match the investment of the leading global competitors in this area, as would structural questions about where to concentrate investment in order to achieve maximum economic impact across the sector.

A focus on the outputs or outcomes of the sector in terms of graduates, intellectual property, global connections and the wider economic contribution of the sector is important. It leads to discussion of issues which are currently 'below the political radar' but which are central to our higher education sector's contribution to knowledge-led economic growth and opens up debate about wider powers which may offer Scottish Ministers additional policy levers to further enhance Scottish universities' support for economic growth.

With constitutional change, whether this results in the transference of additional powers to the Scottish Parliament within the UK, a federated structure or the adoption of an independent nation state model, there are specific powers and policies which will play a critical role in determining the future of our universities' higher education and research activity. The locus and use of such powers will therefore also have a related impact on the wider economy and Scotland's ability to attract and retain mobile global corporations and their R&D investment. These areas include:

1. The economic environment and growth performance
2. Attracting talented people
3. Global connectedness
4. Personal and corporate taxation: incentivising philanthropic giving and the generation of intellectual property
5. Regulation of professions and scientific practice

Each of these areas is explored in more detail below.

8.4.1 *The economic environment and growth performance*

In one sense it is obvious that the fundamental economic environment in which Scotland operates is critical to universities. Universities are not only recipients of public funding which can fluctuate in line with overall economic performance but are major employers of individuals who are increasingly mobile. Like employees of any other business, these individuals are interested not only in their remuneration package but the taxation they pay and the welfare, social, cultural, education, transport and physical infrastructure which this supports and their judgement of the relative opportunities this presents to them as individuals and in relation to their families.

While such considerations are factors for any organisation, the connection between the universities' skills base, R&D networks and industry raises a more fundamental question in exploring the likely impact of additional powers or independence. As outlined above, universities play a critical role in capturing mobile global investment in R&D functions through both the supply of skilled employees and the provision of R&D services.

Investment from multinational enterprises is most likely to be made in order to secure resources, access markets or to reduce labour costs. The ability to access the EU single market and to gain access to intellectual property assets and the human capital of a highly educated and skilled Scottish workforce appear likely to act as primary drivers for investment in Scotland. The approach taken in Ireland demonstrates that business tax-based advantages can also attract such investment, but there remain questions about the long-term sustainability of such an approach – even where it can be pursued within the context of supra-national agreements.

This need for demonstrable industry benefit in return for corporate investment in Scotland makes the relationships which universities can support and build with industry and international governments crucial. Such relationships can play a role in attracting high-value employment, but related benefits can accrue: R&D functions often involve senior individuals with responsibility for decision-making at corporate level. Bringing the senior staff of a multinational into a nation, even if the company's initial footprint is small, can be critical to capturing other company activity.

It's important that we also debate the market access which companies may be seeking to secure through investing in an overseas economy. Scotland's own economy is small in global terms, but as part of the UK and the European Union Scotland represents a base from which to access these much more significant markets. Of course, such factors are rarely the sole determinant in a company's decision to invest overseas; it is the combination of access to market, cost and resources which leads a company to invest. Nevertheless, some may argue that the current lack of clarity about Scotland's medium-term position within the UK and uncertainty over a potential requirement to reapply for EU membership, could lead some companies to consider the potential risks that these issues bring. Others will say this is unlikely to be the case. However, the potential for such issues to arise emphasises the benefits if political actors can achieve a much greater level of uncontested clarity about how access to UK markets and the EU single market will be sustained in the event of independence.

8.4.2 *Attracting talented people to Scotland*

Immigration is perhaps the most immediately apparent area where additional powers could see Scotland diverge significantly from current UK practice in support of knowledge-led economic growth. At the most fundamental level, population projections, population density, migrant flows and pressure on public services (whether real or perceived) differ substantively between Scotland and England. This is particularly the case with regard to England's crowded south-east which has been a key determinant of UK immigration policy as a whole.

Immigration policy is a critical issue for universities and for economic development more generally, reflected in the fact that a May 2012 open letter from UK university chancellors calling for students to be removed from the net migration limit included over 70 business leaders amongst its signatories. Universities increasingly compete for staff and students on the global stage, and global corporations expect to be able to transfer key staff between locations around the world. The potential impact of the current, more restrictive visa regime is twofold – Scottish universities' ability to attract the best students from around the world is constrained and there is a potential threat to the income which universities derive from international student fees – currently circa £305m – and the wider economic impact of such students studying in Scotland estimated to be some £300m.

For a brief period prior to the introduction of the current visa restrictions, the Scottish Government secured a competitive advantage in terms of a visa regime which enabled it to offer post-study work. The 'Fresh Talent' initiative had a focus on attracting high quality migrants to Scotland with the twin aim of addressing economic performance and projections of a dwindling population. That this benefit represented a significant competitive advantage is clear in that universities in the rest of the UK successfully lobbied the UK Government to introduce a similar post-study work option across the UK as a whole. What this also makes clear is the ability of competitor nations to erode partly or wholly any advantage based solely on regulatory difference.

With the devolution of immigration powers or through independence, Scottish Ministers would have the option to match or better the offer of competitor recruiters of international students such as Australia, Canada and the USA who offer post-study work and other benefits to attract students, particularly those studying STEM disciplines. However, even in the case of full independence, the UK and Irish Governments may place pressure on an independent Scotland to participate in the Common Travel Area policies which, while not legally binding, were formalised as a signed joint statement in December 2011. While Ireland currently offers some international students the possibility of twelve months of post-study work, any radical departure from the current common approach across Ireland and the UK may come under pressure from those countries with which Scotland shares its borders.

8.4.3 Global connectedness

Just as Scotland's universities have a keen interest in ensuring the continued inflow of students keen to study at our world-leading universities, the wider infrastructure that a fully independent Scotland would introduce to support international relations would be an important element in maintaining our universities' global connectedness. Higher education is a global activity with high levels of staff and student mobility, and, unsurprisingly, universities have their own strong international connections. Nevertheless, government's international infrastructure and intergovernmental relations can be critical to the development of R&D relationships with companies in other countries. Such support has been crucial to a number of Scottish universities' recent success in securing foreign direct investment in Scotland. Examples include Strathclyde University securing its status as the sole European partner for the Korean Government's Ministry of Knowledge and Economics and attracting the Europe's largest contract research spender – Fraunhofer Gesselschaft – to establish its first UK centre in the University's Technology and Innovation Centre.

As these examples make clear, the Scottish Government has invested in this area through SDI and through the provision of support through Ministers' own international engagements. The approach has involved targeting specific markets, but a more detailed exposition of SDI's role in an independent Scotland, as well as the approach to consulates and embassies around the world, is something which will play a vital role in supporting the international engagement of Scotland's universities and business sectors alike. Related to this is a more general question about Scotland's access to networks within the EU and internationally and where we may currently have a route in or established overseas presence via the UK, even if there is no formal or direct link with Scotland. While there is a tangible cost in delivering a sustained overseas presence, and this may be done in a number of different ways, the relationships are not easily costed or replicated, and both can be critical in shaping policy and securing investment.

8.4.4 Personal and corporate taxation: incentivising philanthropic giving and the production of intellectual property

Universities, with the support and encouragement of central and devolved government, are increasingly looking to diversify their income streams and reduce their reliance on the public purse. The Scottish Government's work with Universities Scotland to consider the scale of the 'funding gap' examined this issue, and subsequent consultations on the reform of post-16 education also referenced this opportunity. Within Holyrood's existing powers there are incentives which the Scottish Government could put in place to enhance philanthropic giving and develop universities' fundraising capacity. For example, the Higher Education Funding Council for England put in place a capacity-building, time-limited, fixed-pot funding scheme from 2008 to 2011 in order to support voluntary giving. The evaluation of the scheme judged it to be successful, but there has been no such equivalent Scottish scheme, although the Scottish professional grouping of university development directors are proposing a modified version of such a scheme to Scottish Ministers.

Looking ahead to potential devolved powers, the debate about tax relief on major donations, sparked by George Osborne's March 2012 proposals to substantially withdraw such reliefs, has made clear the importance of incentivising such donations in support of the charitable and educational sectors, particularly in relation to major capital initiatives in the research arena. Scottish universities received strong support from the Scottish Government in joining charities and universities across the UK to successfully lobby against the proposed changes. Clearly, with the devolution of the relevant tax powers, or through full independence, Scotland's Ministers could choose to create a tax relief regime or other fiscal incentives which would provide greater encouragement for individuals' philanthropic support for universities or provide state support which enabled Scottish universities to build up their endowment funding, invest in the creation of knowledge, support student scholarships and reduce long-term dependence on the tax payer.

A further possible area where additional taxation powers could be deployed to provide a competitive advantage to Scotland's universities is in relation to intellectual property (IP). This is an area which the UK Government is already progressing by means of its 'Patent Box' proposals. Essentially, this is a preferential regime for profits arising from patents, which is just one element in Westminster's stated aim of creating 'the most competitive corporate tax system in the G20'. The proposals are to be phased in over five years from April 2013, from which date companies in the UK will pay a reduced 10% rate of corporation tax. This reduced rate will apply to all profits attributed to UK and EU patents, with worldwide income and existing IP to be included in the scheme. The question which arises in the case of Scotland acquiring powers over corporation tax is: will Scotland continue to match this important incentive in support of the knowledge economy (or perhaps even better it)?

Beyond the importance of tax incentives to address Scotland's low levels of R&D investment, the overall taxation regime of a federal or independent Scotland would be a significant factor in its economic prosperity. Providing a corporation tax regime which is attractive in comparison to key competitor economies could be critical in attracting inward investment from global companies. In recent years Scotland has been able to harness its relative size and strong international connections to achieve some significant success in this regard.

There are, however, examples where nations have put in place specific incentives to attract companies' R&D activity to their shores. The most obvious example of such support for R&D investment by business is that of Ireland which, in addition to a low overall rate of corporation tax, provides a 25% R&D tax credit linked to university research. The scheme also offers companies further reliefs in relation to key staff working in R&D. New companies, establishing an R&D operation in the country, are eligible for this credit on all qualifying R&D expenditure. Is this something Scotland could replicate? At present this is unclear. In a situation where Scotland were to achieve additional powers within the UK, the Westminster Government would be unlikely to countenance significant variation in corporation tax which might leach investment from northern England. In the case of independence, EU state aid rules would be a critical factor, assuming continued EU membership.

Finally, in the area of taxation, the use of additional powers in relation to personal taxation and pensions regime will be a critical element in attracting and retaining skilled human capital in Scotland. The way such powers are used to deliver policy objectives and any deviation from UK arrangements has the potential to impact positively or negatively on individual academics' decisions to live and work in Scotland rather than another part of the UK – something which is not the case at present. The fact that a consistent approach currently exists across the UK means that universities, in common with all employers, will be affected by such changes and will take a keen interest in proposed approaches in this area.

8.4.5 *Regulation of professions and scientific practice*

Universities are subject to a wide range of regulation by professional bodies. The UK Higher Education Better Regulation Group identified 60 regulatory bodies which accredit universities activities, many of which function at the UK level and a number of which set standards for professional entry, or higher-level employment within a given sector. Over and above this, there is a raft of regulatory oversight of scientific procedures which cover clinical trials, use of human tissue, embryology, animal testing and the use of hazardous substances, to name but a few.

Such regulations can be important for individuals by enabling them to work across the NHS UK-wide or to practise as a professional anywhere in the UK. The regulation of scientific procedures is perhaps not an area where Scotland would wish to see more permissive regulation in order to gain competitive advantage (and EU regulation may not allow it), but a more restrictive regime could be a threat to the strong relations Scotland enjoys with the pharmaceutical industry, or to its indigenous bio-technology industry. Given that any uncertainty in this area could have an impact on international investment, proponents of constitutional change should look to provide clarity in such areas as soon as possible.

8.5 CONCLUSION – KEY QUESTIONS

Given the central role in economic development now attributed to universities around the world and their relative importance in attracting inward investment and projecting Scotland overseas, a number of critical questions arise in relation to constitutional change. These questions are not currently raised in political debate, which has yet to address universities' role in enhancing Scotland's global competitiveness in the context of the challenges and threats in the global economy. To date, the debate has focused too narrowly around inputs to the sector and not addressed those outcomes the sector delivers for Scotland. As the constitutional debate continues, we need the discussion to extend beyond research council funding and the student flow around the UK (important though these are) and to focus on what will be critical factors for Scotland as a whole and not just universities themselves.

The central question for all those engaged in the constitutional debate is how can the higher education and research activity carried out within Scotland's universities continue to contribute to the nation's sustainable economic growth? At a more detailed level this leads to a number of related questions:

» The major levers of power over higher education and research are already devolved to the Scottish Parliament. Are these currently constrained, or could we already be doing more with these powers to increase the rates of our young people's participation at university and the level of GDP investment in the sector to match those of our international competitors?

» How would further powers or independence enable us to better address these resourcing issues in order to ensure Scotland's skills base and intellectual property can maximise the attraction of inward investment?

» If enhanced powers can enable additional investment in the sector, should this be by means of public funding or to what extent should such investment come from private funding, supported by either regulatory or taxation changes?

» How will enhanced powers or independence help Scotland address the major resource challenges of competing globally by increasing the fundamental strength of economic performance, protecting against the loss of Barnett consequentials if the UK reduces HE expenditure, addressing the issue of research council funding and tackling the issue of Scotland paying for EU (and potentially English) students' tuition costs being met from the Scottish public purse?

» Could further powers enable us to create a favourable regulatory environment in support of universities' role in delivering economic growth? And, if so, how would we protect ourselves against our competitors' response?

» Where would a transnational approach be required or offer benefit? This possibility has already been raised in relation to research council funding, but should this be considered in other areas?

» Can key actors in the debate offer greater clarity on the way in which key policies will function within remaining UK structures and/or overarching European Union regulation?

The role of higher education and research in Scotland's future should not be underestimated, and, as such, the debate concerning these critical points needs to move higher up the agenda of all those involved in the debate about Scotland's constitutional future.

REFERENCES

European Commission. 2011. *Supporting Growth and Jobs: An Agenda for the Modernisation of Europe's Higher Education Systems*. September.

The Herald. 2012. 'Scottish seats of learning fall in key rankings'. 4 October.

McKinsey Institute. 2012. *The World at Work: Jobs, Pay and Skills for 3.5 Billion People*. www.mckinsey.com/˜/media/McKinsey/dotcom/Insights%20and%20pubs/MGI/Research/Labor%20Markets/The%20world%20at%20work/MGI-Global__labor__Full__Report__June__2012.ashx

OECD. 2011. *Education at a Glance*.

OECD. 2010. *Measuring Globalisation: Economic Globalisation Indicators 2010*.

Scottish Government. 2010. *Building a Smarter Future: Towards a Sustainable Scottish Solution for the Future of Higher Education*. December.

Scottish Government. 2011. Spending Review 2011 and Draft Budget 2012–13. www.scotland.gov.uk/Resource/Doc/358356/0121130.pdf

Scottish Government. 2012. *Cabinet Secretary's letter of guidance*. www.sfc.ac.uk/web/FILES/About__the__Council/SFC__Letter__of__Guidance__21__September__2011.pdf

Times Higher Education. 2012. 'Revealed: for whom the bill tolls'. 4 October.

CHAPTER 9

Energy and Constitutional Change
Jamie Carstairs[1]

9.1 INTRODUCTION

Scotland has high expectations of job creation through the growth of the renewable energy sector. By mid-2012 Scotland had over 5.4 GW of renewable generation capacity with nearly 12 GW consented or in planning.[2] While existing and near-term capacity is dominated by onshore wind, Scotland also has a potential of up to 206 GW of generating capacity that could be recovered from offshore wind, tidal and wave energy.[3]

The offshore wind resource accounts for 25% of the European resource and 40% of the UK resource, and wave power for around 10% of the European resource. Scotland also has significant levels of onshore wind plants and large reservoirs for storing CO_2 if carbon capture and storage becomes widely deployed.

If over time this resource can be developed at reasonable cost, Scotland would not just benefit from the export of power generated from these low carbon sources but could also use them to develop and export research, design and innovation capability, manufacturing knowledge, operational know-how, finance and investment expertise and skills more broadly. The decline of economic activity based on hydrocarbon could be offset by the rise of activity based on low carbon energy sources.

Independence will not alter the nature of the renewable resources or the substantial challenges in moving them to feasibility. However, independence will have an important impact on *how* Scotland

---

1   Head of Linnfall Consulting. I am grateful to many academic and industry experts in Scotland in this area of study for their considerable insights and contributions. I have sought to reflect their views objectively and accurately in order to enhance the value of this chapter.

2   Source: www.scottishrenewables.com/scottish-renewable-energy-statistics-glance/#chart2.

3   House of Commons Scottish Affairs Committee written evidence available at: www.publications.parliament.uk/pa/cm201012/cmselect/cmscotaf/1117/1117we16.htm.

pursues its ambitions to transform power generation. That is the issue addressed in this chapter.

A useful starting point is to consider what is needed to meet Scotland's ambitions and how delivery may be affected by the Scottish constitutional position.

Scotland's renewable resource ranges from relatively mature technologies such as onshore wind to marine technologies which have yet to be demonstrated at scale. All are high-cost relative to fossil fuel generation. There is a need to accelerate the development of technologies and have them demonstrated and deployed at scale with significant capital and operational cost reductions.

New power generation is likely to continue to be privately owned. Revenues need to be high enough to attract the investment required to meet Scotland's ambitions. Revenues are likely to come from subsidies, ultimately funded by electricity consumers and from power sales.[4]

The framework for subsidy to renewable generators is likely to be affected by independence. Currently, the main subsidy is through the renewable obligation. The obligation is imposed by UK Government legislation with Scottish regulations setting the level of the obligation for suppliers in Scotland and of revenues[5] to renewable generators in Scotland. This is being replaced by a more centralised mechanism, the award of contracts for difference to renewable generators.

One of our main topics below is how that framework has been evolving and how it might change in future. The key issues are how Scottish objectives are reflected in the framework for subsidy to low carbon generation, who bears the costs and how that might change with independence.

The power market needs to perform effectively as Scotland transforms its generation mix. Other countries have functioning power markets with near 100% hydro and with much higher wind penetration than in Great Britain. However, no power market has as yet managed Scotland's target of the equivalent of 100% of energy consumption from a variable renewable generation mix.

It seems likely that Great Britain would continue as an integrated power market if Scotland became independent. Our second topic is how the market rules will evolve to accommodate Scotland's

---

4   The renewable obligation has been the main source of subsidy. Revenues are additional to revenues from the sale of power. The new subsidy mechanism being developed by the UK Government, a feed-in tariff based on contracts for difference, would still leave revenue dependent on output but substantially reduce any link between power prices and the prices received by renewable generators.

5   To be more precise, Scotland can set banding which determines the number of Renewable Obligation Certificates issued for each MWh generated by different technologies.

generation mix and the governance arrangements for continued market evolution.

Scotland will need to export surplus renewable energy to get to market. It will also benefit from integration with other systems to provide back-up reserve and short-term balancing.

Scotland's green ambitions will require a much higher degree of interconnection. Initially, this requires higher-capacity connections to England and Wales, and, in the longer term, with other European countries, potentially providing interconnection with hydro storages in Scandinavia and Switzerland. Intermittent wind and hydro with storage make particularly good partners; for example, pumped-storage hydro schemes can both store energy at times of surplus output and provide back-up at times of low output.

There is discussion and some progress on a new, sub-sea grid that enhances connection between the Scottish system and the rest of the UK (the east and west coast 'boot-straps') and could link to northern mainland Europe. However, the approach to transmission interconnection is strongly affected by EU Directives, by the role of independent regulators and by existing arrangements for coordinated planning. Our third topic is how independence could affect this framework for transmission links.

Finally, the current governance arrangements for the sector include an economic regulator accountable to the UK Parliament and a single system operator integrated with the transmission business in England and Wales. Our fourth topic is the implications of Scottish independence for the institutional framework in the sector.

To sum up, the issues most affected by Scotland's constitutional position include arrangements for subsidising renewable generation, the framework for evolving the national electricity market, Scottish representation in decisions on interconnection, and the institutional framework for regulation and system operation. These topics are considered in turn below. Before doing so, we summarise what the objectives and targets are at UK and Scottish level.

9.2 OBJECTIVES AND TARGETS

The UK and Scottish Governments have similar and reasonably consistent objectives. Both aim to reduce greenhouse gas emissions, ensure security of supply and minimise costs to ensure affordability. Both have ambitions to develop new industries based on renewables.

The UK and Scottish Governments have both introduced climate change Acts. Both require 2050 emissions to be 80% below 1990 levels. Both Governments are also subject to interim targets. For the UK this requires 34% abatement by 2020. Scotland has set a higher target of 42% abatement by 2020 and with a wider coverage. Both use the Committee on Climate Change as an independent arbiter on progress.

The renewables target flows from the EU Renewables Directive.[6] This requires the UK to meet 15% of its energy from renewable sources by 2020 with around 30% of electricity to be from renewable sources. The Scottish Government is not independently subject to the Directive. It has set its own target of the equivalent of 100% of electricity consumption in Scotland to be from renewable sources by 2020.[7]

How would this alter with constitutional change? The legislated abatement target for Scotland and the renewables target would remain in place. The Renewable Directive applies at member-state level and would need to be amended if Scotland became an independent member-state.[8]

Historically, targets have been set to reflect the initial starting position and the challenge in reaching the target. We assume this would lead to a higher target for Scotland and a lower target for the rest of the UK (RUK) than the aggregate target which currently applies to the UK. However, this is speculation. There is no precedent for modifying country obligations under the Directive.

A final question is which of these targets is binding. Analysis by UCL[9] suggests that Scotland's abatement targets are consistent with what could be expected from Scotland in meeting the UK abatement target. However, the target for renewables in 2020 is well above Scotland's contribution to least cost delivery of the UK's renewables target.

This suggests that any requirement for the share of renewables established under the Renewables Directive is likely to be lower than the targets set by the Scottish Government.[10] Assuming the Scottish renewables targets remain in place this will be the key driver in increasing the share of renewable generation.

---

6   Directive 2009/28/EC.
7   A fuller description of the complex interaction between EU, UK and Scottish targets is set out in McGregor, P., Swales, J.K. & Winning, M., 2011. Scottish Climate Change Policy: An Overview. Fraser of Allander Economic Commentary.
8   If Scotland does not become a member-state we assume it would continue to set its own domestic targets, which in practice are likely to prove more demanding than being subject to the Renewables Directive.
9   Anandarajah, G., McDowall, W. 'What are the costs of Scotland's climate and renewable policies? Energy Policy (2012). http://dx.doi.org/10.1016/j.enpol.2012.08.027.
10   The Renewables Directive relates to the share of renewables in energy while the Scottish Government renewables target relates to the share of renewables in electricity. As the UK target is based on the expected cost-effective contribution from electricity in meeting the overall target for the share of renewables in energy, the conclusion is likely to remain.

Reasonable questions for any policy are: what does it cost? who is going to pay? and where is the money going to come from? The answers to date have been that the UK requires around £200 billion investment in gas and electricity up to 2020[11] with agreement that some of this is attributable to renewables policy but a heated debate about how much; consumers across the country are going to pick up a share of the costs for supporting renewables proportional to their electricity consumption; and the money to pay for generation and networks is expected to come from private investors and to be paid back over time.

The total cost may not be strongly affected by independence and the reliance on private finance is likely to stay in place – although qualifiers to these conclusions are discussed below. However, the allocation of costs could well change.

We start by outlining how the framework for funding support to renewables has been changing. Currently, renewables are not viable against electricity revenues. The wholesale electricity price is roughly £50/MWh. The cost of renewables[12] is roughly £94/MWh for onshore wind[13] and lower in Scotland, and £140–180/MWh for offshore wind, and probably at the high end in Scotland given offshore conditions. Illustrative figures for wave and tidal technologies are £350–400/MWh and £200–300/MWh[14] respectively while recognising that neither has yet been demonstrated at scale.[15] Scotland has a leading international position in the testing and demonstration of marine technologies, particularly through the facilities at the European Marine Energy Centre (EMEC) in Orkney.

Onshore wind has been the dominant source of renewable generation in Scotland to date.[16] It has the lowest costs and the best

---

11 Ofgem Project Discovery at: www.ofgem.gov.uk/Markets/WhlMkts/monitoring-energy-security/Discovery/Pages/ProjectDiscovery.aspx.

12 As with other numbers quoted, this is a levelled cost at generator level and does not allow for any variation in network, reserve or system balancing costs as the generation mix changes.

13 Mott MacDonald. 'UK electricity generation costs update' (June 2010) at: www.decc.gov.uk/assets/decc/statistics/projections/71-uk-electricity-generation-costs-update-.pdf.

14 DECC. Technology Needs Assessment for Offshore Wind Power and Marine Energy at: www.decc.gov.uk/en/content/cms/funding/funding_ops/innovation/tinas/tinas.aspx.

15 Tidal barrage is relatively mature; tidal stream much less so.

16 Ofgem's annual report on the renewable obligation for 2010/11 states that onshore wind accounted for 62% of the Renewable Obligation Certificates issued to generators in Scotland, compared with 11% in England and Wales. The share of ROCs is similar but not identical to the share of energy from different renewable sources.

prospects of viability without subsidy. However, to meet its long-term ambitions Scotland is also planning to develop offshore wind, wave and tidal generation. These technologies will require long-term subsidy.

Under section 36 of the Electricity Act, new generation requires consent. These powers have been transferred to Scottish Ministers with respect to the mainland and offshore deployments.[17] Devolved planning powers give further control.

These powers enable Scotland to prevent certain types of generation investment in Scotland or impose conditions as a basis for their consent. However, no one would suggest that Scotland's ambitions for investment in low carbon generation will be achieved by refusing to give consent to other generation. Financial support to renewable generation will be needed.

The largest subsidy to renewable generation comes from the Renewable Obligation (RO). This imposes an obligation on suppliers to source a share of energy from renewables and creates an additional revenue source for eligible generators from the sale of Renewable Obligation Certificates (ROCs).

The support to the renewables industry from the RO has risen in nominal terms from £232 million in 2002 to an expected £2.2 billion in 2012/13. Payments depend on the location of renewable generation. Funding is from suppliers and spread across all consumers in the UK. Scotland's renewable resources both benefit from this – with Scottish generators receiving 35% of the ROCs issued in 2010/11 – and assist in reducing the total costs to the UK.[18]

The supplier obligation is established through UK Government legislation. Secondary legislation establishing the level of the obligation and the banding for different technologies is implemented through Scottish regulation and similar instruments in England, Wales and Northern Ireland.

Scotland has used these powers to establish differences in the ROCs awarded to renewable generators based in Scotland. The level of the supplier obligation has been uniform between Scotland and England and Wales.

Under the UK Government's electricity market reforms and the Energy Bill[19] introduced into Parliament in November 2012 support

---

17 www.legislation.gov.uk/uksi/2006/1040/memorandum/contents gives the explanatory Memorandum on Transfer of Functions.

18 Net transfers to Scotland also apply for the second largest subsidy, feed-in tariffs for renewable generators of less than 5 MW. Scotland had around 20% of installed capacity in 2010/11, and unlike RUK had a high share of wind and low share of solar photovoltaic, with consequent higher output per MW installed.

19 www.publications.parliament.uk/pa/bills/cbill/2012-2013/0100/130100.pdf provides the Bill.

for new low carbon generation will be from Contracts for Difference (CfDs). Support to existing renewables will continue to 2037 but the use of the RO for new generation will cease from 2017.

The CfDs will set a price to be paid for each MWh of output (known as the strike price). A reference price such as the cost of electricity in contract markets will be compared with the strike price. Generators will receive a payment when the strike price is above the reference price and make a payment when the strike price is below. The instrument will be close to a fixed tariff per MWh. Costs will be recovered through a supplier levy.

The CfDs are still under development but are likely to differ significantly from the ROCs. Nuclear power will also be eligible to participate under this mechanism. The existing supplier obligation will be removed. This could create some problems in contracting intermittent generation although market liquidity is to be kept under review.

Decisions on the quantity and price of contracts will be made centrally rather than relying on decisions by suppliers. The strike price will be set initially through administrative processes (similar to those used under the Renewable Obligation) and in time be set through competition. The Government has powers to introduce a capacity mechanism if it concludes that existing market mechanisms will not ensure sufficient firm capacity to meet peak demand, and the Energy Bill suggests early use will be made of this new power.

The UK Government envisages that National Grid will act as the delivery body. National Grid will plan and help to deliver the CfD programme and will advise on the capacity mechanism. Final decisions will be taken by Government. The Government may also negotiate some CfDs itself.

The impact of independence (or not) depends on how the new arrangements will work or change in both scenarios.

9.3.1 *If Scotland remains within the UK*

The existing subsidy arrangements have three attractions for Scotland: it receives a high share of the subsidy paid by all UK consumers; the payments are higher for the less mature, high-cost technologies which Scotland is starting to develop; and it has devolved powers.

If Scotland's constitutional position remains unchanged, the new subsidy arrangements through CfDs may bring some of the same advantages. Scottish generators are likely to continue to receive a high share of payments and costs will be recovered across the UK. But at least three issues would need to be resolved.

1. If the delivery body is planning a CfD programme, what objectives is it seeking to meet? Scottish and UK objectives differ. Scotland is seeking higher levels of renewables and requires higher levels of support per MWh for some of its less mature technologies.
2. If the CfD programme addresses Scotland's higher ambitions for the share of renewable energy, how will those additional costs be recovered from Scottish and consumers in the rest of the UK? Those consumers could draw on Scottish renewables to minimise the costs of meeting the Renewable Directive but may baulk at paying the additional cost of a specifically Scottish target. On the other hand, they may get additional benefits from security of supply, spillover benefits from industry development and faster abatement.
3. How will the decisions be made? Decisions on the CfD programme will be taken by the Secretary of State based on advice by the delivery body. Supporting documents to the Energy Bill confirm that energy, generation and supply are reserved matters but also recognise the split of powers is not a clear one. There will be a statutory consultative role for the Scottish Government on design and delivery of the CfDs and institutional arrangements but the details are as yet thin.

Scotland's ambitions of meeting the equivalent of 100% of electricity consumption from renewables will require sufficient firm capacity to provide back-up when renewables output is low, and to provide balancing as renewables output varies. It may well be efficient for a higher share of renewables to come from Scotland and more of the reserve and balancing to come from RUK. As yet, it is unclear how Scotland will be reassured that the CfD programme – and any decisions by the Secretary of State to institute a capacity mechanism – will meet its requirements.

9.3.2 *If Scotland were independent*

If Scotland became independent it seems likely that it would be subject to its own target under the Renewables Directive and that target would be higher than the targets for RUK. As an independent state, Scotland could form its own views on the mechanism to be used. It could revert to the Renewable Obligation, adopt CfDs or a modified version of them or use some other framework.

It seems unavoidable that independence would in time lead to separate targets for Scotland and RUK. Sovereign states cannot be held accountable for the performance of other states. However, it is possible that Scotland and RUK could use joint arrangements for meeting their separate obligations. For example, Norway and Sweden use certificates which allow trading in certificates (similar to the ROCs in the UK) produced in either country.

The UK Government has indicated that it expects to meet its targets through domestic action but is open to joint projects where electricity is imported into the UK from external sources. It has also said that it might award CfDs to generators outside the UK. If these policies continued they might apply to surplus Scottish energy. Scotland would have an advantage through its existing interconnection.

It may be questionable whether RUK would pay the full costs for developing Scotland's relatively high-cost offshore wind and marine technologies. Lower-cost joint projects may be available in other countries. On the other hand, generation in Scotland may be seen as contributing more to RUK's security of supply and industry development objectives.

The Renewables Directive also allows for statistical transfers. These do not require interconnection or the actual flow of energy. Scotland could use this mechanism to benefit from renewable generation surplus to its requirements under the Renewables Directive to countries by providing this to countries other than RUK.

Scotland is likely to be a price-taker in these statistical transfers. Ten countries have reported a potential surplus against their 2020 obligations.[20] A few have reported a shortfall – although the numbers may rise as we approach 2020. Those countries that realise a surplus are all potential sources for countries in deficit. The marginal supply of renewable energy is likely to be biomass heat or renewable energy from heat pumps. The price established by these technologies is likely to be insufficient to cover the subsidy required for Scotland's offshore wind, wave or tidal generation. It could provide some additional revenue.

9.3.3 *Financing*

The three questions we raised on renewables policy were: what does it cost? who is going to pay? and where is the money going to come from? The key question discussed above is the allocation of costs. The total cost is likely to stay reasonably constant through constitutional change. However, how do we address the question about where the money is going to come from?

---

20 ERCN. Preliminary Assessment of Renewable Energy Surplus in EU Member States, December 2011.

The general expectation is that private investors will finance the upfront investments and recover the costs from future revenues. Finance for generation investment to date has largely relied on equity funded from utility balance sheets and to a lesser extent from equipment manufacturers. This is supported by debt with ultimate recourse to the balance sheet of the equity investors. The ability to sell down equity share post-construction, once risk is reduced, increases the finance available.

There are limits to this financing approach. The need to maintain strong credit ratings limits the investment which can be supported from energy balance sheets[21] and the available finance needs to be allocated across European markets, not just Great Britain.

This financing model will struggle with the scale of investment required, and efforts are being made to attract additional sources of finance, generally with a lower appetite for risk.

This is an important topic for Scotland's ambitions. It may not be heavily affected by independence. Equity investors and debt providers will be sensitive to the impact of independence on funding support, market design and regulation – all issues discussed in this chapter. However, they generally operate in several European countries and are likely to be less sensitive to constitutional change, provided these issues are well managed, including the transparency and clarity of transition to future arrangements.

9.4 ELECTRICITY MARKET

Great Britain is likely to remain a single electricity market managed through a common set of rules (or 'Codes') regardless of Scotland's constitutional position. This section considers the need for market evolution to meet Scotland's ambitions and the impact of independence on market evolution.

The market design in Great Britain has changed radically over the last twenty years. The changes include geographical coverage with the integration of Scotland in 2005; the role of the market which shifted from a pool covering 100% of electricity to a balancing mechanism covering only a few per cent; and the existence of a capacity payment,[22] which was in the original market design, removed in 2001 and is likely to be reinstated. There have also been changes

---

21 2010 estimates of the investment which could be supported by the Big 6 energy businesses in the UK plus GDF Suez are given in a KPMG report at: www.kpmg. com/UK/en/IssuesAndInsights/ArticlesPublications/Documents/PDF/Market%20 Sector/Power__and__Utilities/Securing-investment-in-Nuclear.pdf.

22 That is, a payment per MW for being available to meet peak demand rather than a payment per MWh for generating.

to secondary legislation governing the renewable obligation nearly every year.

It seems likely the rules for this market will continue to evolve. The existing market arrangements are already under some stress:

» High wind penetration is likely to lead to high price volatility. An example of a possible future for Scotland is seen in South Australia, a region within a wider integrated market. Wind accounted for 26.7% of energy in the region in 2011. Prices were negative for the equivalent of three days and peaked at over £7,000/MWh. This extreme volatility may be desirable since it can create price signals for back-up generation which may be required to run very few hours or not at all, but it is also hard to manage.

» Once renewables and other generation technologies are connected to the network they need to be compensated if they cannot operate as desired due to network capacity. Recent policy changes have been successful in ensuring renewable generation gets connected to the grid more quickly. However, congestion costs have risen sharply; mainly due to transmission constraints within Scotland, and from Scotland South.

» The market design needs to ensure sufficient reserve and sufficient short-term balancing. This becomes more challenging as the share of intermittent renewable generation increases.

These are not intractable problems. It should be perfectly possible to evolve the market to cope with this prospective major change in generation mix. Other electricity markets have worked successfully with near 100% hydro and with much higher wind penetration than the current British electricity market has.

However, running an electricity market with renewables from a variable mix with output equivalent to 100% of energy demand is untested. The challenge is to ensure that the necessary market evolution is done effectively and in an open and transparent manner.

A final driver for change comes from Europe. The European Commission also has powers to establish network codes applying in the UK following consultation.[23] This may sound like an arcane issue but it could result in the creation of a new price zone for Scotland.[24] If that happened, Scottish wholesale electricity prices would drop to low levels when transmission lines south were congested. Price separation between Scottish generators and suppliers in the RUK would create contracting and hedging risks. The impact on Scottish ambitions needs careful consideration – although these issues are successfully managed in many other markets.

These complex issues cannot be adequately covered in a short chapter. They are also partly addressed by the electricity market reforms in the Energy Bill. The CfDs will reduce the exposure of wind generators to low prices and the capacity mechanism will address security of supply. But, the point is that market design matters to Scotland's ambitions and needs to keep evolving. So who is in charge?

Unfortunately, the answer is not straightforward. Much of the framework for the market dates back to the New Electricity Trading Arrangements (NETA) reforms around 2000. The mind-set was strongly liberal – that is, markets were best left to businesses and any government intervention should be kept to a minimum. The market rules are embedded in a set of Codes. Code change is under industry control with a requirement for regulatory approval of changes.

This may be the theory. In practice Government and regulators are driving the major changes. The UK Government has used legislation to impose major change to the market design once every four to five years on average and has also used legislative powers to amend Codes and Licences to implement more minor changes. The current electricity market reforms are embedding longer-term government powers to modify the market through introducing a capacity mechanism.

---

23 http://ec.europa.eu/energy/gas—electricity/codes/codes—en.htm describes the process.

24 www.ofgem.gov.uk/Europe/Documents1/EU%20Target%20Model%20open%20 letter.pdf Ofgem's letter on implementing the target model states: An example of a binding requirement is a mandate on National Grid to propose, and Ofgem to consider, the merits of separate price zones to manage internal constraints in GB more efficiently. The document makes clear Scotland could be such a price zone.

The regulator has always had power to veto industry-led changes. It has also sought to broker agreement. However, until recently it has not had powers to impose changes. In 2010 Ofgem introduced new powers to undertake Significant Code Reviews and accelerate industry reform. These also enable the regulator to implement changes required by the European target model.[25]

9.4.1 *If Scotland remains within the UK*

If Scotland remains within the United Kingdom, market evolution may continue as at present. Some elements may be determined by EU Directives; minor change managed by industry and Ofgem; and major changes imposed by the UK Government every few years. The UK Government will also have new discretionary powers to introduce a capacity mechanism.

Scotland is the most exposed to this issue given the need for market rules to work well with the transformation of its generation mix. It may have a statutory consultative role as set out in the Energy Bill but will have little control over changes to the market rules or decisions on the exercise of central powers to award CfDs and introduce a capacity mechanism.

9.4.2 *If Scotland were independent*

We assume that if Scotland were independent a single electricity market with one set of market rules would continue to operate across Great Britain. There are plenty of precedents for unified markets with one set of rules and involvement of two or more regulators.

This single electricity market would need to resolve what processes apply to market evolution. The choices could include:

» industry-managed code change with regulatory approval – this appears unlikely to work any better than it has to date in managing major change;
» major change driven by government and implemented through legislation as at present – this would require coordination between the two governments and coordinated changes to legislation;
» major change managed by the regulators, similar to Ofgem's powers under significant code reviews – assuming there were

---

25 Ofgem's consultation of March 2012 provides background on the model and its implications for Scotland, at: www.ofgem.gov.uk/Europe/Documents1/EU%20Target%20Model%20open%20letter.pdf.

two regulators this would require coordination between the regulators (and possibly the governments) to agree what to review and how; and

» a single independent commission with powers to review and modify the rules subject to compliance with due process – this could be combined with two separate regulators for the economic regulation of networks.

The way in which the market evolved might also differ. A market with two independent countries might be more inclined to longer-term integration with other markets (for example, the Irish Single Electricity Market). The integration of National Grid, the current system operator with English but not Scottish transmission networks might encourage a shift towards an independent system operator following independence. However, while the likelihood of these changes might be affected, they are not dependent on Scottish independence.

9.5 ELECTRICITY NETWORKS

If Scotland's very large renewable resource does move to viability over time, it will have surplus electricity which it will need to export. It will also benefit from integration with other systems to provide back-up reserve and short-term balancing.

Scotland's green business and low-carbon economy ambitions will require a much higher degree of grid interconnection. Initially, this requires higher-capacity transmission connections to England and Wales, and, in the longer term, with other European countries. Intermittent wind and hydro with storage make particularly good partners, since the pumped-storage hydro can both store energy from wind generation at times of high output and provide back-up generation to the power system at times of low wind output. The benefits of such network expansion need to be assessed against the substantial costs of major interconnection, so investment could be delayed.

Network arrangements are heavily influenced by European policies and by regulatory determinations. We consider below: the key issues of concern to Scotland; how they are managed; and how that could change with independence.

One long-running concern has been the availability and rapid provision of grid connection for renewable generators. The historical approach has been to defer connection until work to upgrade the transmission network had been undertaken. A new policy called 'Connect and Manage' has enabled around 26 GW of connections – including 20.7 GW of renewables – to be advanced by five to nine years. Around half the renewable projects concerned are in Scotland.

This has helped solve one problem but worsened another. Once connected, generators have firm access rights and have to be compensated if they cannot operate due to transmission constraints. These costs are rising as a result of the Connect and Manage approach. They could rise further if Scotland develops a large surplus – or fall if transmission capacity rises sufficiently. There is no consensus on how high they may go.

A large share of the costs arises in Scotland from constraints in the Scottish network and in exporting electrical energy south. These costs are spread across all UK consumers. Major congestion and persistent congestion could form an argument for creating a separate price zone for Scotland. As noted above, this might reduce electricity prices and conversely push up subsidy costs.

Part of the problem is the incentive for some generators to increase the costs of constraints, either by their generating decisions or by the prices they offer to National Grid to reduce their output and so help balance the system. The UK Government has used legislative power to amend licence conditions to limit behaviour which pushes up constraint costs. It remains to be seen whether this will work.

Connection is not sufficient unless networks are upgraded. A substantial investment programme is under way. This will include strengthening of interconnection with England and Wales up to around 4 GW and at least one HVDC subsea link. The investment programme, which has had its share of controversy in Scotland, is being managed through normal regulatory processes bolstered by substantial joint planning between the transmission companies concerned.

A third area of conflict has been around transmission charging. Transmission charges in the UK include a component related to the incremental costs. The result is higher charges for generators in the North of Scotland and lower charges for generators nearer load centres in the south of England. A review by the regulator has made minor adjustments to the charging regime rather than the shift to a simple per MWh charge advocated by some in Scotland.

There are other distinctive Scottish features. One has been long-term support to offset the high per capita costs of distribution networks in parts of Scotland, funded by a small levy on all consumers. The total level of charging may rise, if this 'smearing' of the costs did not continue after independence.[26]

---

26 See the review of the Hydro Benefit replacement scheme on DECC's website and a submission covering the issue at: www.publications.parliament.uk/pa/cm201012/cmselect/cmenergy/writev/1912/sco12.htm

Enhanced grid connection to England and Wales can help Scotland export its low carbon generation. It can also help power system operations by ensuring sufficient reserves and sufficient generating capacity that is able to respond quickly when renewable generation reduces or increases its output.

However, in the long term a very large increase in Scotland's low carbon generating capacity may require greater interconnection to Europe. This would connect renewable generation from Scotland and the North Sea to demand centres in Europe. It could also assist with reserves and balancing by interconnecting renewables with hydro-based storage in the Nordic region and Switzerland.

The trend for interconnections under the EU Third Package[27] is towards open-access regulated interconnectors. This will require: coordination around Europe; new models to overcome the complexity of different regulatory regimes in the countries to be interconnected; and major investment and access to large amounts of finance. The institutions are gradually gearing up and include the Commission itself; groupings of the relevant countries, in the case of the North Sea through the North Sea Countries Offshore Grids Initiative (NSCOGI); the Transmission System Operators (TSOs) in the countries concerned; and the regulators.

9.5.1 If Scotland remains within the UK

To date, the Scottish Government has had limited direct powers and mainly relied on advocacy to influence the regulator's decisions. The Scottish Government and businesses successfully made the case for accelerated connections; a major investment programme is proceeding although inevitably with differing views as to scale and priorities; and the case advanced by some commentators for less cost-reflective transmission charges was largely lost.

9.5.2 If Scotland were independent

This would change if there were a change in Scotland's constitutional position, but only a little. The role of regulators in setting price controls for the network industries is well established; regulatory independence has the backing of the EU Third Package; and this model is familiar to financiers and keeps costs down. Scotland could have its own regulator[28] but the Government would not be able to

---

27 A package of two directives and three regulations relating to electricity and gas markets.

28 Like other relatively small countries, it might establish a multi-sector regulator to minimise costs.

impose regulatory decisions. And existing arrangements for coordinated planning between the three transmission companies should also remain largely unchanged.

A simplistic view that independence would give the Scottish Government greatly increased power to advance its agenda for networks may not be accurate. However, there are less direct ways in which arrangements could improve. Ofgem is accountable to the UK Parliament against objectives largely set in UK legislation. Appointment is by the Secretary of State in the UK Government. As an additional measure, DECC intends to introduce a statement of strategy and policy to which the regulator has to have regard.

This accountability framework is entirely at UK Government level. But Scotland differs in its objectives, might make different appointments and might have different content in the strategy set for the regulator. It will also face distinctive regulatory challenges such as the greater concentration of the supply market in Scotland and its possible impact on the effectiveness of retail competition. So, while regulatory independence will remain in place there may be scope to improve accountability and governance arrangements and areas of regulatory focus in ways that better reflect Scottish interests.

The impact on the European scene is also likely to be limited. The power sector agenda has taken years if not decades to develop. It is unlikely to be influenced quickly. However, Scotland could boost its representation in bodies such as NSCOGI.

9.6 INSTITUTIONS

Ofgem is currently the National Regulatory Authority for Great Britain. This gives it four main roles. It issues licences[29] to conduct activities such as power generation or power transmission and enforces licence conditions. Ofgem undertakes price reviews to establish the revenues for the monopoly transmission and distribution networks. It has final approval of Code changes proposed by industry and, as noted above, has recently acquired more powers to initiate code reviews.

Ofgem also represents the UK in a pan-European body, the Agency for the Co-operation of Regulators (ACER), which is developing Codes to apply to congestion management and electricity balancing. Much of the focus of this work is the harmonisation of market arrangements to allow trade within regions of Europe. Since 2006 Ofgem has been working with the French and Irish regulators to push this forward.

---

29 To be precise, the Secretary of State issues licences following Ofgem advice.

As discussed above, Ofgem is required to have regulatory independence and has powers to impose Code changes developed by ACER. Ofgem is accountable to the UK Parliament and will shortly be subject to a statement of strategic priorities to be issued by the UK Government.

The arrangements for power system operation are distinctive to the UK. Three companies own onshore transmission networks: Scottish Hydro Electricity Transmission (SHETL) and Scottish Power (SPTL) in the north and south of Scotland and National Grid Electricity Transmission (NGET) in England and Wales. A wider range of companies is involved in offshore transmission.

Since 2005 NGET has been the system operator for Great Britain. It manages the real-time operation of the power system, including in Scotland, as well as generator and consumer access to the network. NGET manages generator and consumer requests to connect, with obligations on SHETL and SPTL to give dates and costs for the work required, and is responsible for collecting user charges on behalf of the two Scottish companies. NGET also bears the cost of constraints, that is, the costs when transmission lines cannot meet the desired output by generators.

SHETL and SPTL both maintain their networks. A coordinated approach is taken to investment planning with NGET responsible for a seven-year statement across the whole of the transmission network in Great Britain. All three companies are represented at ENTSO-E, a body made up of all the TSOs in Europe and charged with developing the network Codes.

All three companies are also subject to price regulation by Ofgem, which determines the revenues allowed from their transmission charges based on an assessment of capital and operating costs. A separate price control provides for NGET's costs as system operator. This exposes NGET to some financial risk if costs differ from forecast but major cost divergence is borne by consumers.

An independent Scotland may have its own regulator accountable to the Scottish Parliament. This regulator could issue licences, conduct price controls for the network businesses and represent Scottish interests in Europe. A regulator for England and Wales could play the same role.

As noted, the Scottish and English regulators could not unilaterally modify market rules within a single electricity market, and a framework for coordinated decision making would be required. Alternatively, a single commission could regulate rules for the market.

Independence would also require consideration of the future arrangements for power system operations. It might be desirable to maintain NGET as the system operator for the network as a whole. This could be done with a single price control or, possibly, with separate price controls for the System Operator (SO) functions in Scotland and England and Wales.

Under the UK electricity market reforms[30] National Grid will be playing a very major role in advising the Government on the award of contracts to support low carbon generation. Several commentators have pointed out potential conflicts in advising on an investment programme which materially affects the transmission network. A further possibility may be that the system operator role is discharged through an independent system operator rather than being undertaken by a transmission company and that this independent system operator is common across Great Britain.

9.7 ISSUES FOR DEBATE

» Scotland's renewable generators will require subsidy:
  › how will this support be provided if Scotland remains within the UK?
  › if Scotland becomes independent, would joint arrangements for meeting renewables targets be put in place and, if so, what form would they take?
» what is the expected impact on costs for Scottish households compared with current arrangements?
» assuming a single market stays in place across Great Britain:
  › how will the evolution of market design be managed to ensure it works effectively for Scotland's generation mix?
» what difference would independence make to Scottish representation in key decision-making bodies in Europe?
  › what changes would Scotland argue for and what level of influence can realistically be expected?
» at what point is it likely to be viable to finance major new transmission to interconnect Scotland's increasingly renewable-based power network with thermal and hydroelectric grids in Europe and Scandinavia?
  › what difference will the constitutional arrangements make?
» if an independent Scotland has its own regulator:
  › what coordination would be required with England and Wales, given the single market?
  › who would act as system operator?

---

30 The Energy Bill at www.publications.parliament.uk/pa/bills/ cbill/2012-2013/0100/130100.pdf provides details of the proposed electricity market reforms, as does the Department of Energy and Climate Change at www.decc.gov. uk/en/content/cms/meeting_energy/markets/electricity/electricity.aspx.

REFERENCES

Anandarajah, G. & McDowall, W. 2012. *What are the Costs of Scotland's Climate and Renewable Policies?* Energy Policy.

Department of Energy and Climate Change. 2012. *Electricity Market Reform Policy Overview.*

Department of Energy and Climate Change. 2012. *Capacity Market Design and Implementation.*

Energy Research Centre of the Netherlands. 2011. *Preliminary Assessment of Renewable Energy Surplus in EU Member States based on Projections in their National Renewable Energy Action Plans.*

House of Commons Select Committee on Energy and Climate Change. 2012. *The Impact of Potential Scottish Independence on Energy and Climate Change.*

KPMG. 2010. *Securing Investment in Nuclear in the Context of Low Carbon Generation.*

McGregor, P., Swales, J.K. & Winning, M. 2011. *Scottish Climate Change Policy: An Overview.* Fraser of Allander Economic Commentary.

Mott McDonald. 2010. *UK Electricity Generation Costs Update.* Department of Energy and Climate Change.

Ofgem. 2010. *Project Discovery: Options for Delivering Secure and Sustainable Energy Supplies.*

Scottish Government. 2012. *Draft Energy Policy Statement.*

Scottish Government. 2011. *2020 Routemap for Renewable Energy in Scotland.*

Scottish Government. 2010. *A Low Carbon Economic Development Strategy for Scotland.*

CHAPTER 10

North Sea Oil and Gas
Professor Alex Kemp[1]

10.1 INTRODUCTION

It is arguable that the development of the North Sea oil and gas industry has been one of the most important events in the post-World War II period of British and Scottish economic history. The contribution of the sector to the overall output of the economy, the balance of payments and the public finances has been very substantial. For financial year 2011–2012, total tax receipts were £11.2 billion. The technological achievement has also been very noteworthy. In turn, this has produced a supply chain which is now internationally competitive on an increasing scale.

The impact effects have been most visible in Scotland, particularly the region centred on Aberdeen which has grown from being the operations centre for the UK Continental Shelf (UKCS) to the 'Oil Capital of Europe'. Estimates of employment generated by the industry made by Experian and Oil and Gas UK indicate that, for the UK as a whole, direct plus indirect employment in 2010 totalled 239,000 with induced employment adding another 100,000. For Scotland, the direct plus indirect employment was estimated at 151,000 with induced employment at 41,000. In addition to the above total, export-related employment was estimated at 100,000 for the UK and 45,000 for Scotland. Around 45% of the turnover of the supply chain based in Scotland is now from exports. In 2011, total field development expenditures in the UKCS were £8.5 billion, with operating expenditures totalling £7 billion. These were responsible for generating most of the employment.

Given the importance of the industry the possibility of radical constitutional change in Scotland has implications not only for the industry itself but for the public finances and balance of payments of both Scotland and the rest of the UK. These implications are explored

---

1 Professor of Petroleum Economics and Director of the Aberdeen Centre for Research in Energy Economics and Finance, Aberdeen University.

in this chapter. Given the forthcoming referendum on independence particular attention is given to that eventuality.

10.2 THE BOUNDARY ISSUE

In the event of Scottish independence, a priority subject is the division of the UKCS between the Scottish and rest of the UK jurisdictions. This would initially be determined by negotiation between the two governments, following the precedents set by other delimitations not only among the neighbouring countries with Continental Shelves in the North Sea, but also in the Irish Sea and Atlantic Ocean. Following the practice in these negotiations, there is a presumption that the median line extending the boundary to the north of Berwick between Scotland and England would form the initial basis of the negotiations. Importantly, the median line has been employed for purposes of the demarcation of Fisheries Management responsibilities between the Scottish and UK Governments since 1999. This line is shown in Figure 1 below. It should be noted that departures from the median line principle have occurred in various settlements around the world, including rulings made by the International Court. An example is the judgement made in 1969 with respect to the lines of delimitation between West Germany, Denmark and the Netherlands.

FIGURE 1. SCOTTISH MARITIME BOUNDARIES

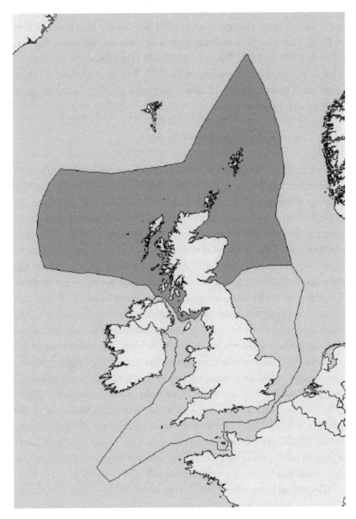

Source: Marine Scotland

While an agreement between Scotland and the rest of the UK is obviously the most important boundary issue to be resolved, it is not the only one. Currently, a Treaty between the UK and Norwegian Governments governs the delimitation line in the North Sea based on the median line. In the event of Scottish independence, the status of the provisions of the Treaty regarding the boundary between Scotland and Norway would have to be resolved. An agreement would have to be reached between the two governments. While acceptance of the existing line is the obvious solution, it should be recalled that the use of the median line provoked much controversy in the past, though mostly after the Treaty had been signed in 1965. There are other delimitation agreements between the UK Government and the Danish and Irish Governments relating to what are currently other parts of the UKCS to the west and north of Scotland. Their status could also require clarification in the event of Scottish independence.

10.3 TRANSITIONAL LICENSING ISSUE

Currently, there are many oil companies holding large numbers of production licences awarded by the UK Department of Energy and Climate Change (DECC) on behalf of the UK Government for the exploitation of hydrocarbons from the UKCS. Several transitional issues arise were there to be Scottish independence. Thus, the status of these contracts, many of which are very valuable and have many years to run before expiry, will require clarification. To prevent the emergence of major uncertainties, the obvious reaction of a Scottish Government could be to honour these existing licences. While that should be relatively easy to implement, effective licensing raises some more difficult issues. Licensing includes the assessment of new applications, awards to successful bidders, the monitoring of the performance of licensees throughout the duration of their licences, assessment of and approving new field development plans and drilling of all wells, and assessment of field decommissioning plans. Other licence-related roles of DECC include the monitoring of the fallow block/field initiative and the stewardship initiative on mature fields. DECC also has an important role with respect to third party access to offshore infrastructure. Yet another increasingly important duty relates to the environmental impact of operations in the UKCS.

Clearly, all these roles require considerable expertise. This would have to be rapidly acquired by a Scottish Government which would have to establish a licensing authority or Department of Energy. Efficient licensing also requires the availability of very large amounts of data relating to seismic surveys and wells (exploration, appraisal and development) to assess prospects, including for future licence rounds. Furthermore, large amounts of data relating to field development plans are required to efficiently assess the performance of licensees. All this would require the transfer of huge amounts of information from DECC to the Scottish licensing authority. In this context, it should be noted that DECC currently has an office in Aberdeen dealing with many licensing issues, including environmental impact and decommissioning.

A special tax system applies to the UKCS. There are three elements: namely, Corporation Tax (CT) at 30% rate, Supplementary Charge (SC) at 32% and Petroleum Revenue Tax (PRT) at 50%. The whole system is very complex. Thus, SC now contains a series of field allowances relating to small fields, HP/HT fields, heavy oil fields, remote gas fields, large deep-water fields, large, shallow-water gas fields, and high-cost brownfield projects. PRT is levied on a field basis, also with complex allowances. For this tax, there should be no major problem in establishing the costs, revenues, and tax allowances attributable to the fields in the Scottish and rest of UK sectors. When decommissioning time comes, field losses are clawed back against PRT paid in earlier years. Hence, information going back many years is required to calculate the tax refund. A potential complication is that the period of loss clawback could well extend back from a period post-Scottish independence to a date before independence.

CT and SC are levied on the basis of a ring fence covering all of the UKCS (and onshore upstream activities). This means that allowances relating to eligible expenditures in one field can be set against income in other fields for tax purposes. This can mean that an allowance emanating from expenditure in what would become the rest of the UK sector can currently be offset against income arising from within the Scottish sector. After independence, there would be a need to separate the activities pertaining to the Scottish and rest of UK sectors for purposes of calculating taxable income and tax payments for CT and SC.

To undertake this work effectively, much knowledge and data would be required of the accumulated tax allowances, and other information would be required to calculate taxable income in the Scottish sector. Much exchange of information between the relevant UK and Scottish authorities would be necessary to produce an efficient system. A considerable expertise in this tax area would have to be developed within the Scottish Government. Other more specialised tax issues would arise with independence. For example, currently gas is exported from fields in pipelines in what would become the Scottish sector to Teesside and Bacton in England. The pipelines cross what would become the Scottish–rest of UK boundary line. The tax status of the pipelines would require clarification. Fortunately, there exists UK legislation dealing with exports by pipeline. For example, there are exports from the Markham field to Dunkirk, and UK legislation exists to deal with the tax and other issues.

A specific tax issue relates to decommissioning relief. As noted above, for PRT the rules are that decommissioning losses in a field are clawed back indefinitely against earlier PRT field profits and tax refunds made, while for CT and SC clawback is permitted to 2002. A complex situation arises when decommissioning takes place after Scottish independence but the claw back period extends to a pre-independence date. The allocation of the relief between the new and former tax jurisdiction offers ample scope for complexity, confusion and disagreement. Over the next thirty years, the total decommissioning costs could well be in the £30–£35 billion range at today's prices, and the average tax relief will exceed 50% of the total. Further, the great majority of the decommissioning expenditures will be incurred in what would become the Scottish sector.

The decommissioning issue will be of major interest to the oil and gas operators for another reason. In 2011 the UK Government increased the SC from 20% to 32% but retained decommissioning relief at 20% (or 50% rather than 62% for CT and SC combined). This produced vigorous protests from the industry. From their viewpoint, it is clear that SC is a profits tax and decommissioning costs are a legitimate business cost and should therefore be deductible at the full relevant tax rate. The issue has resulted in a substantial consultation between the UK Treasury and the industry with a view to the introduction of guaranteed tax reliefs for decommissioning through a contractual arrangement. Details are expected in Budget 2013. The industry is extremely concerned that effective relief is obtained, and much depends on the detail as well as the general principle. It is argued that effective guaranteed relief would facilitate the acceptance of letters of credit/ bank guarantee relating to the financial liability for the decommissioning work to be based on post-tax costs rather than gross values. Because letters of credit have to be noted in company accounts and have the effect of reducing borrowing capacity, the effects of assured relief are potentially significant in terms of increased investment spending and the facilitation of mature field asset transfers. Given all this, it would be important for investors to be assured that a Scottish Government would provide decommissioning relief guarantees, particularly as the expensive work would take place in what would become Scottish waters.

Efficient tax policy would require North Sea investors to designate establishments with central management and control based in Scotland to ensure that effective taxation could be levied on the activities in the Scottish sector. There could be a possible need for a tax treaty between Scotland and the rest of the UK, and possibly with other countries, such as the USA and Canada, which are the source of important investors in the North Sea.

The possibility of Scottish independence has generated much interest in the likely size of the tax revenues which could accrue to a Scottish Government. Using financial simulation modelling and a high quality field database, Kemp and Stephen (1999, 2008) have made estimates of the hypothetical share of the revenues which would have accrued to Scotland in the past had it been independent. The estimates have been updated to financial year 2011–2012 for the purposes of this chapter. The modelling incorporated all the elements of the changing tax system over the years. The data relating to individual fields were segregated into the Scottish and rest of UK sectors using the median line as the boundary in the North Sea. Allocations of exploration and appraisal expenditures, R&D and overhead costs were made between the two sectors. Estimates had to be made of the relevant R&D costs and allowable overheads for tax purposes. The results of the modelling in terms of absolute tax revenues (at 2009–2010 prices) are shown in Figure 2.

FIGURE 2. HYPOTHETICAL SCOTTISH ROYALTY AND TAX
REVENUES FROM THE UKCS (£M. AT 2009/10 PRICES)

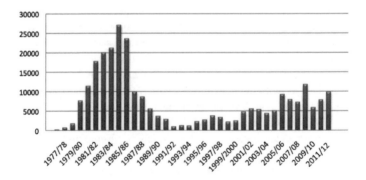

Source: Kemp and Stephen (1999) and (2008) plus updated estimates

The obvious features of the results in Figure 2 are: 1) the substantial absolute sums for many of the years; and 2) the volatility of the amounts raised. To a large extent, the volatility relates to the major fluctuations in oil prices over the years, though there are other causes such as the frequent changes to the tax rates, production increases and decreases and the irregularity of capital allowances. The latter is a consequence of the lumpiness of capital investment which has been a characteristic feature over much of the period. To give a perspective on the recent position, the modelling indicated that in 2010 the Scottish share of total oil production in the UKCS was over 95%, while for gas it was 58%. The Scottish share of total hydrocarbon production (including NGLs) was 80% and the Scottish tax share exceeded 90%. This reflects the much higher value of oil compared to gas. For 2011 the Scottish share of gas production fell to 52% due to production problems, and the share of total hydrocarbon production fell to 78%. But the tax share increased to nearly 94% reflecting the much higher value of the oil. To indicate the difficulty in estimating even short-term tax revenues from the UKCS, in Budget 2011 the OBR estimated receipts at £13.4 billion for year 2011–2012, but in Budget 2012 this was reduced to £11.2 billion.

10.6 FUTURE PROSPECTS

Kemp and Stephen (2012) have conducted extensive economic modelling of the future prospects for the UKCS. This involved financial simulation to project future oil and gas production, field investment, operating and decommissioning expenditures. The Monte Carlo technique was used to forecast future discoveries. The exploration effort and success rates were based on experience over the last decade. A high quality field database, incorporating key data for sanctioned fields and those currently under consideration for development (probable and possible fields), and validated by the relevant licensees, was available for the study. In the results presented below, the future price scenario of $90 per barrel and 55 pence per therm in real terms (with inflation at 2.5% rate) was used. Reflecting some capital rationing, an investment hurdle of post-tax NPV at 10%/pre-tax I at 10% > 0.3 was employed. The present (late 2012) tax system was assumed to continue. For full details see Kemp and Stephen (2012). In the study, activity levels have been broken down into five regions. They are close to the division according to the median line between Scotland and the rest of the UK. The Southern North Sea (SNS) and Irish Sea (IS) are wholly in the rest of the UK sector, while the Northern North Sea (NNS), West of Shetlands (WoS), and most of the Central North Sea/Moray Firth (CNS/MF) are in the Scottish sector. A few fields in the CNS/MF (with modest production) are in the rest of the UK sector. The modelling showed results for activity levels over the period to 2042.

The results for prospective production under the price scenario of $90 per barrel and 55 pence per therm in constant real terms are shown in Figures 3, 4 and 5. Total oil production over the thirty years is 11.1 billion barrels (bn bbls) of which 10.97 bn comes from the Scottish sector. For gas, the total for the whole of the UKCS is 5.3 bn boe of which 3.19 bn boe (60%) comes from the Scottish sector. Total hydrocarbon production (including NGLs) from the UKCS amounts to 16.75 bn boe over the thirty years of which 14.54 bn boe (86.8%) comes from the Scottish sector. Cumulative hydrocarbon production to 2050 is 17.5 bn boe for all the UKCS with 15.2 bn boe (86.8%) coming from the Scottish sector. Production continues beyond 2050. It should be noted that the achievement of these production levels depends on several other important factors, such as the absence of major unplanned shutdowns and the continued availability of infrastructure.

FIGURE 3. POTENTIAL OIL PRODUCTION

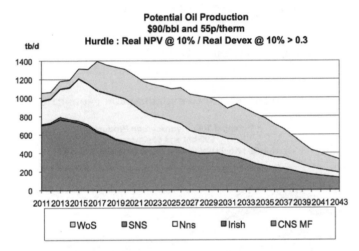

Source: Kemp and Stephen (2012)

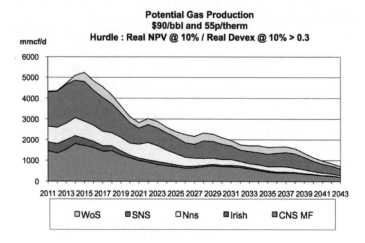

Source: Kemp and Stephen (2012)

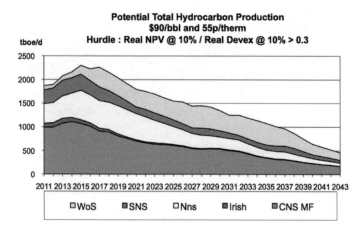

Source: Kemp and Stephen (2012)

The above projections for the next thirty years may be compared with the most recent official estimates made by DECC of the ultimate potential from the UKCS. Their central estimate is 19.7 bn boe with a low estimate of 10.3 bn boe and a high one of 33 bn boe. There is no time period attached to these estimates. Total hydrocarbon depletion to date (since production commenced in 1967) is around 41 bn boe.

The prospective expenditures of the North Sea oil industry are also of major importance to the Scottish and UK economies. Over the last few years, the continued growth of the offshore supply chain (for both UK and foreign markets) has been the major success story in the stagnating Scottish economy. The economic modelling conducted by Kemp and Stephen (2012) produced projections for the next thirty years for expenditures on field development, operating activities and decommissioning. These are shown in Figures 6, 7 and 8 respectively, according to the five main geographic regions of the UKCS.

In Figure 6 it is seen that field development expenditures are expected to exceed the remarkably high levels of £10 billion per year in the near term. This is due to the coincident development of several very large, expensive fields and projects, all of which are in the Scottish sector. The subsequent fall still leaves development activity at relatively high levels compared to historic periods. Thus, in 2009 development expenditures were £4.9 billion, in 2010 £6 billion and in 2011 £8.5 billion. It is seen that over the whole period to 2042 investment relating to the Scottish sector dominates the total. Thus cumulative total investment in the UKCS is £134.5 billion (at 2012 prices) of which £123 billion (91.5%) is in the Scottish sector.

FIGURE 6: POTENTIAL DEVELOPMENT EXPENDITURE

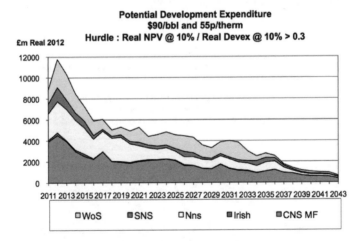

Source: Kemp and Stephen (2012)

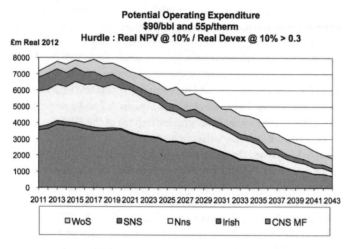

Source: Kemp and Stephen (2012)

In Figure 7 it is seen that operating expenditures increase somewhat over the next few years, reflecting the growing total number of fields in production. At their peak they total nearly £8 billion per year (at 2012 prices). Over the period to 2042, they total £173.1 billion of which £156 billion (96%) relates to the Scottish sector. Over time, the share attributable to the Scottish sector increases.

FIGURE 8: POTENTIAL DECOMMISSIONING EXPENDITURE

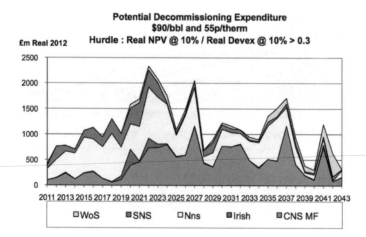

Source: Kemp and Stephen (2012)

In Figure 8 it is seen that decommissioning expenditures become increasingly significant from around 2015 with large amounts being spent in the subsequent years to around 2028. The pattern of expenditure exhibits major peaks and troughs, with the peak periods reflecting the coincident decommissioning of some very large installations. Over the whole period, aggregate expenditures total £36.7 billion (at 2012 prices) of which £31.6 billion (86.1%) is attributable to the Scottish sector. Over the period, 604 fields are decommissioned. In the next decade, many are in the SNS but, given the shallow water depth and small size of platforms, the decommissioning costs are relatively low. In the NNS, there are some very large platforms which will be expensive to decommission. In the CNS/MF region, there are many fields, some with large platforms.

10.7 PROSPECTIVE TAX REVENUES

The tax revenues which will emanate from the Scottish sector in the future depend on the behaviour of oil and gas prices, production, investment, operating and decommissioning costs. All these costs are allowable deductions. A considerable amount of detailed research work would be required to produce fully informed estimates. An educated guesstimate is that over the next decade the annual values attributable to the Scottish sector could be in the £5 billion to £10 billion range (at 2012 period). In the near term, the very high investment levels mean that allowable deductions are also very high, as reliefs are on 100% first year basis. It can safely be concluded that substantial revenues from the upstream oil and gas sector would become available to a Scottish Government, with a strong probability that they would fluctuate over the years. In the long run, they will also decrease as production falls, but, as the results of our modelling above show, there could be substantial production for many years ahead.

10.8 PETROLEUM POLICIES WITH INDEPENDENCE

Independence gives the Scottish Government the opportunity of developing its own policies towards North Sea oil and gas exploitation. These should be seen in the context of the prospects for the industry as detailed above. Policy initiatives can come principally in the areas of licensing and taxation.

The taxation system has been changed substantially in recent years with the increase in the SC rate followed by a series of field allowances to encourage new investment. The twin objectives of raising revenues and encouraging investment would both obtain the priority attention of a Scottish Government for whom both the tax revenues and supply chain involvement would clearly be very important. Because the oil and gas cluster is relatively more important to the Scottish economy than to the UK one, it is arguable that more attention would be given to it by a Scottish Government. But the tax revenue needs would also be very important, and the familiar balancing act problem between current receipts and incentives is likely to continue.

The likelihood that tax receipts will be large but volatile poses special problems, particularly if they are used as part of general macroeconomic policy where the receipts are treated no differently from other taxation revenues such as from income tax and VAT. Full reliance of the oil revenues in this manner could readily introduce instability into the public finances. It is for this reason that there is a case for treating oil tax revenues separately.

Fundamentally, tax revenues from oil and gas production are conceptually different from other taxes such as income tax and VAT because they emanate from the depletion of part of the nation's capital stock. Oil and gas reserves form an important part of the UK's capital stock and their depletion constitutes a diminution of that stock. In order to mitigate this undesirable outcome, it is arguable that the economic rents from oil production should be invested with the objective of maintaining the nation's overall capital stock. If the revenues were invested in an Oil Fund, the capital stock could be kept intact and annual benefits could be taken in the form of the income received from the invested monies. The nation could thereby receive benefits in perpetuity from the oil windfall. In retrospect, it is arguably regrettable that successive UK Governments did not establish an Oil Fund. It could have ensured that the oil revenues were not employed for normal macroeconomic budget purposes but were invested to maintain the nation's capital stock and produce a yearly permanent flow of income.

The benefits of such schemes have become increasingly recognised around the world. The many existing schemes have different rules. In the Alaska Permanent Fund 25% of bonus bids and royalties are paid into the Fund and the Government does not have access to the capital. The Fund has a manager and every year a dividend is paid to the permanent residents of Alaska. In Norway there is also a Fund manager who invests the oil monies in securities of various types, generally outside the country. The investments of the large existing Funds around the world are to a considerable extent in financial assets, but investments in real assets are also made. For example, the long established Fund set up by Shetland Islands Council has announced its intention to invest (along with SSE) in the proposed Viking wind farm. (It may be noted that in recent years pension funds have also become investors in real assets, including energy utility distribution schemes.)

When the debate on the utilisation of oil revenues took place in the UK in the late 1970s and early 1980s, the argument which prevailed was that the revenues would cut the budget deficit, interest rates would thereby be reduced, investment would increase, and current and future generations would benefit as a consequence. Unfortunately, the investment ratio did not increase and the oil revenues were to a large extent used to maintain public consumption in the face of large unemployment. Thus, the revenues were essentially employed as part of regular departmental spending programmes. The Scottish Government indicated in 2009 that a Scottish Oil Fund was desirable, essentially on the grounds noted above. But there are likely to be temptations to use the revenues for departmental spending programmes. This is likely to be sub-optimal. To indicate the nature and extent of the issue the ONS in its regular publications on the UK Environmental Accounts produces oil and gas monetary balance sheets. For the year 2010 the estimated negative value to the UK balance sheet from oil and gas production was £11.6 billion.

While great attention is given to the tax receipts from North Sea oil, it should be noted that the economic rents procured from the exploitation of the revenues also include the post-tax profits of the licensees. It is the sum of the two which is relevant from the viewpoint of reinvestment to maintain the nation's overall capital stock. Thus policies which encourage reinvestment by the licensees are also relevant.

10.8.2 *Policy for the economic recovery of oil and gas*

A Scottish Government would also have to deal with several non-tax, licence-related issues, some of which relate to the problems of a mature petroleum basin. Such problems have been examined on an ongoing basis by the UK Government and the industry, often through the medium of PILOT, the joint government/industry consultative body (which also has representation from the current Scottish Government). For some years, there has been a problem of fallow acreage/fields whereby exploration acreage has remained unworked for some years and undeveloped discoveries not fully appraised but not relinquished. Currently, the government initiative on this subject, whereby licensees were incentivised to work the fallow acreage or trade or surrender it, has borne fruit, and the problem is now much reduced. But it could re-emerge, and the Government should ensure that, when it is clearly important that North Sea acreage is worked as expeditiously as possible, incentives in the form of both carrots and sticks should be available and used.

In mature producing fields, a problem in recent years has been the growth of unplanned downtime on platforms, resulting in deferral of substantial production volumes. This was a main cause of the dramatic fall in production in 2011 and 2012. The projections of production shown above reflect planned but not unplanned downtime, and, if the experience of the last two years were to continue, the production decline rates would be significantly faster than those shown. Currently, DECC has a stewardship initiative whereby operators in mature fields can be quizzed on their performance and have to satisfy the department that all reasonable measures are being taken to maximise economic recovery. Sanctions are available if DECC is not satisfied, including, as a last resort, obligations on the licensees to sell or relinquish the assets in question. The problem results, at least in part, from the age of the installations. Thus, over 15% of platforms are more than forty years old and 33% are more than thirty years old. The subject of asset integrity from a production as well as safety perspective is likely to become increasingly important as the North Sea matures. Hence, an effective policy to deal with the problem also becomes a greater priority. In this context, it is noteworthy that the ever increasing interconnectedness of producing fields in the North Sea increases the size of the potential knock-on effect of disruption to one element of the production, processing and transportation chain.

Third party access to infrastructure is another increasingly important issue in the North Sea, given the typical small sizes of new fields which depend on utilising existing infrastructure to render them economically viable. Very often new, small fields are discovered and developed by medium and small players in the North Sea who do not own the infrastructure (it tends to be in the hands of the majors). Access refers not only to the tariffs payable but other possible terms and conditions. The conclusion of negotiated agreements has often been a very time consuming and even fraught affair. The development of the Industry Code of Practice (ICOP) has helped, but problems remain. Historically, DECC has preferred to play a watchful but, until recently, passive or very limited interventionist role, though since 1975 it has had the powers to determine tariffs if requested. Recently, it has been given powers to proactively intervene if negotiations are unduly slow. Despite much recent effort by the industry an efficient scheme remains to be put in place, whether led by industry or through full government regulation. This problem would certainly have to be faced by a Scottish Government. A related issue is the need to ensure that the infrastructure of pipelines and processing platform hubs is reinforced to accommodate the small fields in the post-2020 era. Without this, the long-term production profile noted above would be put in jeopardy.

10.9 ENHANCED DEVOLUTION AND NORTH SEA OIL

It is possible that enhanced devolution rather than independence will eventually emerge as the constitutional arrangement for Scotland and the UK. The possible position of North Sea oil and gas then becomes an issue, and many of the considerations and challenges raised in the previous sections of this chapter in the context of a constitutional arrangement that entailed independence would, of course, be equally relevant and important to the constitutional arrangements that embrace enhanced devolution.

There are several possible ways in which the North Sea might be managed. One would be a sharing mechanism whereby the tax revenues are shared between the Scottish and UK Governments, but the legal rights and policy continue to rest with the UK Government. There are plenty of precedents for this around the world in oil-producing countries. Generally, they are in countries where there are multi-tier governments, particularly federal ones. The underlying rationale is the derivation principle. Regions which are endowed with oil resources bring the associated benefits to the whole country and should receive some recognition for this. In the case of Scotland it could be argued that, when Scotland joined the Union in 1707, she brought with it what subsequently became a large and productive part of the UKCS. In essence, this concept was recognised by the UK Government in 1968 when a limited sharing of revenues from licence fees and royalties with the Governments of the Isle of Man and Northern Ireland was introduced on a per capita basis. The UK Continental Shelf was larger because of the existence of the Isle of Man and Northern Ireland. The UK Government subsequently became less keen on such sharing arrangements (for example, with the Governments of the Channel Islands) when the large scale of the oil resources became apparent. In the Scottish case, sharing on a per capita basis would, of course, be very much less valuable than sharing on a geographic basis such as that indicated in Figure 1. The case for the latter rests on the geographic basis of the resource endowment brought to the UK.

Sharing the tax revenues on a geographic basis produces an odd result in that the policy-making government would end up receiving only around 10% of the revenues for which it had policy and collection responsibilities. There would be grounds for wondering whether in these circumstances adequate attention would be given to the policy complexities involved.

This leads to the proposition that, in these circumstances, devolution of policy responsibilities for the Scottish share of North Sea oil and gas is more appropriate. As with sharing, this would be part of a wider devolution settlement between the two governments. Thus, how devolution of responsibilities for oil and gas affected the overall public finances of the Scottish Government would depend on all the other elements in the devolution package. The derivation principle would be one element in the debate. Property is generally regarded as a suitable tax base for devolved/local governments because of its immobility, and this argument could apply to North Sea oil and gas. It should be recognised, however, that, while the petroleum reserves are not generally mobile, the capital necessary to produce the oil certainly is, and policies have to acknowledge this fact.

It is arguable that devolving responsibilities for oil taxation policy in the Scottish sector of the North Sea without devolving the licensing arrangements would be very odd. The two policy areas should operate in tandem. This leads to the view that licensing should also be devolved. In this context, it is noteworthy that petroleum licensing has been devolved in Northern Ireland for very many years for onshore activities. Currently, some licences are issued. Responsibility for petroleum royalties is also devolved to the Northern Ireland Government.

But it should not be thought that devolution of North Sea oil and gas to a Scottish Government would constitute an unambiguous bounty. This would depend on the overall balance of the enhanced devolution settlement. As well as the transitional problems discussed above, there is the problem of reliance on a major source of revenue which is subject to large and relatively unpredictable volatility. If a Scottish Government were substantially reliant on oil revenues for its normal budget requirements, there would be a need for borrowing powers to deal with the situation when these revenues were unexpectedly low. There is also a clear case for a contingency fund. The arguments in favour of an Oil Fund as discussed above remain compelling, but in the likely circumstances of the next few years, a Scottish Government might feel it necessary to utilise the revenues for normal departmental spending programmes. As discussed above, this could be sub-optimal.

Constitutional change resulting in Scottish independence would be likely to result in a Scottish Government gaining control over a large share of the current UKCS, including the areas which contain the great majority of oil reserves, current production and most of the tax revenues. There are several significant transitional issues which would have to be resolved expeditiously if the investment uncertainties were to be minimised. These relate particularly to the complex taxation system and several licensing and licensing-related issues. Relevant expertise in these areas would need to be developed. Effective taxation and licensing also depends on the availability of very large amounts of data and other information currently with DECC and HMRC. New legislation would be required to ensure that taxation and licensing were effective. Some extra costs would fall on investors and there would be some restrictions on their ability to utilise tax allowances compared to the current situation.

The remaining potential from the UKCS remains very substantial and the Scottish share would constitute the dominant element of revenues, investment, operating and decommissioning expenditures. The Scottish Government would also continue to receive substantial tax revenues. Historically these revenues have been large but volatile, and it is most likely that this will prevail in the future. Oil production is likely to revive above its recent levels but will later enter long-term decline. While tax revenues will also eventually decline, their behaviour in the short and medium terms depends on other factors as well, particularly the behaviour of oil prices. If they rise, they can counter the effects of a decline in production for some time.

An independent Scottish Government would have to pursue policies which determine the delicate balance between revenue-raising and incentivising investments in both new field developments and incremental projects in mature fields. Incentivising enhanced oil recovery (EOR), including the use of CO_2 injection as one of the technologies, could become a big issue over the coming years. The case for an Oil Fund remains strong, but claims on the oil revenues to meet the needs of departmental spending programmes may inhibit its establishment on a substantial scale.

A Scottish Government would have to deal with several other policy issues relating to the maturing offshore oil and gas industry. These relate to third party access to infrastructure, asset integrity (relating both to safety and production), fallow acreage and the longer-term need to maintain the infrastructure capacity. The current level of exploration is very low in relation to that required to discover the reserves which DECC believes could ultimately be found within the time period when the offshore infrastructure can remain economically viable.

If enhanced devolution, rather than independence, were the outcome of the constitutional debate, a Scottish Government could have devolved powers relating to offshore oil and gas. Similar issues to those discussed above would then arise. Another possible constitutional outcome is that a revenue-sharing arrangement with respect to the UKCS would be established. If the revenue-sharing were on a geographic basis, this situation would in practice be very odd and potentially unhelpful to sound policy.

10.11 SUMMARY OF KEY QUESTIONS

Boundary issues

» according to what criteria should the division of the UKCS between the Scottish and rest of the UK jurisdictions be effected?
» would there be a requirement for Treaties or other agreements regarding the boundary between Scotland and Norway and other countries, particularly Denmark and Ireland, and what would be their provisions?

Transitional licensing issues

» what would be the status of the production licences currently held by the oil companies, which were awarded by the UK Government for the exploitation of hydrocarbons from the UKCS?
» would Scotland need to set up its own licensing authority and what would be its role and responsibilities?
» how would the significant transfer of information from DECC to a Scottish authority be agreed?

Transitional taxation issues

» since the period of decommissioning loss clawback could well extend back from a period post-Scottish independence to a date before independence. How would this be handled?
» how would the activities pertaining to the Scottish and rest of UK sectors be separated for purposes of calculating taxable income and tax payments for CT and SC?
» how would the necessary and considerable expertise in this tax

area be developed?

» what would be the tax status of the pipelines exporting oil and gas from the Scottish sector to the rest of the UK?

» how would the allocation of the relief between the new and former tax jurisdiction be managed?

» would guaranteed tax reliefs for decommissioning be introduced through a contractual arrangement?

» how would investors be assured that a Scottish Government would provide decommissioning relief guarantees?

» would there be a need for a tax treaty between Scotland and the rest of the UK, and possibly with other countries, such as the USA and Canada?

Future output and tax revenue prospects

» what assumptions should underpin the estimation of the future prospects of the North Sea oil and gas?

» what policies should be assumed?

» how sensitive are the estimated prospects to these assumptions?

Petroleum policy with independence

» how would policy uphold the critical twin objectives of raising revenues and incentivising investment?

» how would the anticipated volatility of tax receipts be managed?

» should oil tax revenues be treated separately in the fiscal accounts?

» should an Oil Fund be established?

» how is the economic recovery of oil and gas incentivised and secured to ensure maximum recovery?

» how are the other key policy areas handled, notably with respect to third party access to infrastructure, asset integrity (relating both to safety and production), fallow acreage and the longer-term need to maintain the infrastructure capacity and integrity?

Enhanced devolution

If enhanced devolution were extended to Scotland, which of the issues raised above would be equally relevant and important?

» what would be the nature of that devolution?

  › would there be a sharing mechanism, whereby the tax revenues are shared between the Scottish and UK

Government, but the legal rights and policy continue to rest with the UK Government?

> would this option create policy confusion and suggest that the devolution of policy responsibilities for the Scottish share of North Sea oil and gas, too, would be more appropriate?

> should devolving responsibilities for oil taxation in the Scottish sector of the North Sea also be accompanied by the devolution of the licensing arrangements?

» how would the problem of the reliance on a major source of revenue, which is subject to large and relatively unpredictable volatility, be handled?

» is there a case for a contingency Oil Fund?

> is it realistic for Scotland to accumulate an Oil Fund in the light of the foreseeable fiscal constraints over the coming decade?

POSTSCRIPT

The above chapter was written before the publication of the Autumn Statement (Cm8480) in December 2012. In that document the OBR forecasts a substantial decline in tax revenues from the UKCS over the period to 2017-18. This emanates from a combination of falling market prices for both oil and gas (to $92 per barrel and 47.4 pence per therm respectively in 2017-18), and continuous declines in oil and gas production. The production data are based on projections made by DECC (see http://og.decc.gov.uk/assets/og/data-maps/chapters/production/projections.pdf). It should be noted that the DECC projections "applied very significant negative contingencies to the aggregate figures" supplied by the industry and reflecting their plans. The net effect is that the OBR tax estimates are very pessimistic.

REFERENCES

Kemp, A.G. & Stephen, L. 1999.
*Expenditures in and Revenues
from the UKCS: Estimating the
Hypothetical Scottish Shares
1970–2003*. University of Aberdeen,
Department of Economics, North
Sea Study Occasional Paper, no. 70,
January 1999, pp. 1–24, www.abdn.
ac.uk/ ̃pec144/acreef.

Kemp, A.G. & Stephen, L. 2008. *The
Hypothetical Scottish Share of
Revenues and Expenditures from the
UK Continental Shelf 2000–2013*,
2008, p. 38. www.scotland.
gov.uk/Publications/2008/06/
UKContinentalShelfRevenue

Kemp, A.G. & Stephen, L. 2011. *The
Short and Long-Term Prospects for
Activity in the UK Continental Shelf:
The 2011 Perspective*. University
of Aberdeen, Department of
Economics, North Sea Study
Occasional Paper, no. 121, August
2011, pp. 1–61. www.abdn.
ac.uk/ ̃pec144/acreef.

Kemp, A.G. 2011. 'The Great North
Sea Oil Saga: All Done or Still
Unfinished?', *in* Mackay, Donald
(ed.), *Scotland's Economic Future*.
Reform Scotland, October 2011, pp.
119–34.

Kemp, A.G. & Stephen, L. 2012.
*Prospects for Activity in the UK
Continental Shelf after Recent Tax
Changes: The 2012 Perspective*.
University of Aberdeen, Department
of Economics, North Sea Study
Occasional Paper, no. 125, October
2012, pp. 1–82. www.abdn.
ac.uk/ ̃pec144/acreef

Natural Resource Tax and Scottish
Devolution. 2009. Evidence from the
Independent Expert Group to the
Commission on Scottish Devolution,
June 2009, pp 1–28. www.
commissiononscottishdevolution.org.
uk/uploads/2009-06-06-ieg-natural-
resource-taxation-1.pdf

CHAPTER 11

Governance and the Institutional Framework
Sir John Elvidge[1]

The first thing to make clear about this chapter is that there are no essential changes to governance arrangements in Scotland which have to be made in order to accommodate any changes in the constitutional settlement which fall short of independence; and very few which meet the test of absolute necessity, if Scotland becomes independent. The institutional framework which exists in Scotland and the relationships which exist between the component parts of that framework would be serviceable in relation to the possible changes in the constitutional settlement between Scotland and the rest of the United Kingdom. It is reasonable to ask, however, whether grafting a set of governance arrangements designed for one constitutional settlement onto a substantially different set of constitutional arrangements would maximise the probability of good governance. A parallel question is whether, at a time when other major aspects of Scotland's constitutional arrangement are being given fresh consideration, there is any reason to exempt governance arrangements from that consideration.

11.1 GOVERNANCE AS A SYSTEM

It is important to understand governance arrangements as a system rather than a series of separate parts. Although each part must be fit for purpose, it is the relationships between the parts which are the stronger determining factor in the overall nature and quality of governance. It is commonplace in discussion of systems of governance to speak about 'checks and balances', which highlights the importance attached to the issue of relationships between the constituent parts of the system.

Without attempting an exhaustive listing of the desired characteristics of an effective system of governance, within the context of a constitutional democracy, it is useful to set out some of these

---

1   Former Permanent Secretary to the Scottish Government.

characteristics. The most central is achieving a balance between the ability to conduct the business of government effectively and the limitation of the executive power of government in order to avoid abuse of power or loss of democratic consent. Closely related to this is clarity of accountability and of responsibilities. A third desired characteristic observable across a range of governance systems is to achieve a balance between representativeness of society and the availability of high levels of expertise in the matters with which government is concerned.

Scotland, along with Wales and Northern Ireland, differs from the UK in having a governance system which was designed as a whole and is embodied in legislation, as the approximate equivalent of a written constitution. In any of the possible variations on the devolution settlement, the existence of a statutory basis approximating to a written constitution would remain. In the case of independence, this would no longer be so. The Parliament of Scotland would decide for itself which aspects of Scotland's governance system should have a statutory basis.

11.2 GOVERNANCE WITHIN AN INDEPENDENT SCOTLAND

Although the decisions which the Parliament of an independent Scotland would take are inevitably subject to varying degrees of uncertainty, one consequence of a move away from the statutory framework provided by the Scotland Acts which seems certain is that the present position whereby all the requirements of EU legislation are effectively imported into domestic law in Scotland, by section 57(2) of the Scotland Act 1998, would cease. This provision, which is intended to protect the UK as the member state within the EU from the potential consequences of action by the Scottish Government which is contrary to EU legislation, would serve no purpose irrespective of whether or not an independent Scotland retains EU membership. This change in governance, which changes the risk calculation involved in acting upon interpretations of EU legislation which might be at odds with the intention of the legislation, would have particularly interesting consequences in relation to the use of economic and fiscal powers.

The general topic of an independent Scotland's relationship with other countries, either individually or through treaty-based organisations, has other dimensions. The question whether a member state should be able to agree to changes in treaty arrangements without some particular form of Parliamentary consent, such as a two thirds majority vote, or extra Parliamentary process, such as a referendum, is one which we have seen argued through in various other countries. The question of NATO membership has become topical and one can see that there could be debate about whether the power of the Government to commit to military action should be subject to some form of legally based restriction, such as a requirement for Parliamentary consent.

A different dimension of this topic would be whether new institutions would be required in the context of Scotland's relationship with the remainder of the UK. The British–Irish Council already exists, with a standing secretariat based in Scotland, and it might be an adequate forum for managing relationships with Scotland on the same basis that it operates at present in relation to the UK and Ireland. As is touched upon in other chapters, however, there are connections postulated between Scotland and the remainder of the UK which differ from those between the UK and Ireland, and it would be a natural subject of discussion to ask whether this required more specialised institutional arrangements than the British–Irish Council provides. This discussion would have to take account of the limited use which has been made of the Council to date and the effect of its large and heterogeneous membership, embracing Jersey, Guernsey and the Isle of Man. An extension of this question is to ask whether there would need to be treaty arrangements between Scotland and the remainder of the UK to provide a framework for the operation of any specialised institutional arrangements which might be required, to augment the framework provided by the Belfast Agreement for the establishment and operation of the British–Irish Council.

A much larger question prompted by a move away from the statutory framework provided by the Scotland Acts would be whether it would be desirable for Scotland to have a written constitution. It is not my purpose here to debate the merits and demerits of written constitutions. For the purpose of my discussion of governance, I wish simply to draw out that a written constitution, like the statutory framework for devolution, places the domestic courts in a more significant position within the overall governance structures than would be otherwise the case. An illustration of this can be found in the impact of the incorporation of the European Convention of Human Rights into UK and Scottish domestic law and the several high-profile instances of the courts taking decisions which differed from those which had been taken by governments or Parliaments and had been challenged by those affected. As with the effect of the incorporation of EU legislation into the Scotland Acts at present, it is possible to envisage circumstances where the use of economic and fiscal powers in an independent Scotland might be circumscribed by the contents of a written constitution.

Courts are, of course, arbiters of the interpretation of a constitution, not the authors. Irrespective of the actual authorship, the ratification of a constitution and the power to amend it would rest with the Parliament of an independent Scotland. This is one way into a question which must be central to any consideration of future governance: the nature of the Parliament. This question arises under any version of an independent Scotland, irrespective of whether it might have a written constitution, and is worth addressing even in the context of a devolution settlement with further significant extensions to economic and fiscal powers.

At present, Scotland has a unicameral Parliament, which sits within a broad governance framework which also embraces the UK Parliament. The UK Parliament by no means fulfils the functions which a second chamber fulfils in bicameral parliaments. At the same time, its presence can be argued to be part of the rationale for the adoption of unicameral structures in Scotland, Wales and Northern Ireland. There is a commonality in this respect with many other countries with both national and sub-national legislatures: Australia, Belgium, Canada, Germany, Italy and Spain.

About half the world's sovereign states are unicameral, including several which are often taken as comparators for Scotland: Denmark, Finland, Iceland, Norway and Sweden. Ireland is the most obvious exception among those customary comparators but, in general, population size appears to be a factor. The larger European nations are bicameral, with the divide falling at around a population size of 11 million. One argument sometimes advanced for the existence of a correlation between population size and the choice between unicameral and bicameral parliaments is that the larger the size of a country's population the more likely it is that the population embraces diversities, whether geographical or arising from other forms of shared identity, which can be better represented in a bicameral system than through the operation of majority governments in a unicameral system. It is interesting, in the context of that argument, that there is a longstanding perception within Scotland of significant diversity between the Central Belt and the Highlands and Islands, which was the focus of much discussion in the constitutional discussions which preceded devolution.

Clearly, on the basis of international comparisons, there is no basis for asserting any necessary relationship between the future constitutional changes made in relation to Scotland and the composition of the Parliament. There is, however, an interrelationship with another aspect of the Parliament, the electoral system. In a unicameral Parliament, all the criteria to be fulfilled by an electoral system must be accommodated within one set of arrangements even if those arrangements contain the type of hybridity which the current electoral system for the Scottish Parliament exhibits.

At present, the combination of 72 constituency seats elected on a first-past-the-post basis and 57 seats elected on the basis of a second vote and the application of the De Honte method to eight regional lists is designed to give a measure of political balance between the main parties, create a route for representation of smaller parties or independent candidates and recognise Scotland's regional diversity. These may all remain objectives which command support. It has also been the generally accepted view that this electoral system renders a single party majority a very difficult thing to achieve, notwithstanding the Scottish National Party's success in achieving a majority in the 2011 elections. It is an obvious question whether this tendency to render a single party majority less probable than other outcomes would remain desirable in the context of a devolution settlement which included substantial economic and fiscal powers or of an independent Scotland. Although there is now greater experience of coalition government, at both the Scotland and UK levels (and in Wales and, in a very specialised form, in Northern Ireland), than there was when the Scotland Act 1998 was passed, it is not clear that it has become generally preferred to single party government.

11.4 EXPERTISE AND GOVERNANCE

One merit sometimes claimed for coalition government is that it broadens the talent pool available to serve in Ministerial posts. In pursuit of that same objective, many governance systems have a route to Ministerial office for non-elected individuals. At the UK level, this is one of the functions served by the House of Lords and the ability of the Prime Minister to arrange for a peerage to be conferred on someone whom it is wished to bring into a Ministerial role or to assist the government in some other way. In some other countries, it is not the case that members of governments must be drawn from the legislature: so, individuals with the capacity to hold Ministerial office can be co-opted into that role. It is often argued that the nature of political careers in the UK in recent decades has precluded politicians from acquiring any depth of expertise, for example, in economic matters. In the context of any substantial widening of the economic and fiscal powers of the Scottish Parliament, this might be an aspect of governance arrangements which attracts increased interest.

Consideration of sources of expertise within government inevitably leads to consideration of two other components of the governance system: the Civil Service and public bodies (the Non-Departmental Public Bodies or NDPBs in current terminology, quangos in earlier terminology and often in current usage).

11.5 NATURE OF THE CIVIL SERVICE

Scotland, like Wales and Northern Ireland, currently shares with the UK a set of common principles about the nature of the Civil Service. Except for in Northern Ireland, which has had a separate Civil Service (NICS) for close to a century, this is currently reflected in common membership of the Home Civil Service. There is also a common legislative framework established by Part 1 of the Constitutional Reform and Governance Act 2010, after decades of debate about whether a statutory basis for the Civil Service would be beneficial.

There has been consistently a body of opinion arguing that there should be a separate Scottish Civil Service within the devolution settlement and, clearly, an independent Scotland would have a separate Civil Service. In the context of the devolution settlement, the debate has been, in essence, between an argument of principle and arguments of pragmatism. The argument in principle is that the absence of a separate Scottish Civil Service raises questions about the ultimate loyalty and accountability of the Civil Service. The arguments of pragmatism are that it is sensible to share some common services, for example, the design and administration of pension schemes, and that it is desirable to preserve the facility for interchange between civil servants working in different parts of Great Britain. One of the consequences of a separate NICS is that members of the Home Civil Service may not be employed in posts serving the Northern Ireland Assembly Government (without applying for employment on the same terms as anyone else and resigning from the Home Civil Service) and members of the NICS may not be employed in posts serving the UK Government, Scottish Government or Welsh Assembly Government. This is a consequence of decisions taken by the two sets of independent Civil Service Commissioners, one for the Home Civil Service and one for the NICS, which are the arbiters of the rules for the admission to posts within the relevant administrations.

Within the devolution settlement, one of the consequences of the transfer of more areas of responsibility within the jurisdiction of the Scottish Parliament would be that the Scottish Government would require separate expertise in areas where it currently depends upon the pool of expertise within Whitehall. In several of the possible areas of responsibility for transfer, such as fiscal and macroeconomic management or the design and operation of the pensions and social security systems, relevant expertise is scarce in the labour market. It could, of course, be developed over time but there would be some degree of transitional challenge. The existing facility for interchange within the Civil Service is one potential means of addressing that challenge. The evidence of the post-devolution era is that there is a variety of reasons which lead some individual civil servants to have a preference for working in Scotland rather than Whitehall. The evidence that Whitehall Departments value experience of working in the devolved administrations is less clear; so those choosing to work in Scotland have to accept the risk that it may be, in practice, a one-way street. This runs contrary to the intended position in principle, however, and is not therefore incapable of resolution, if those making appointments in Whitehall Departments had the will to resolve it.

It is possible that transfer of fiscal powers could breathe fresh life into the arguments about ultimate loyalty and accountability of civil servants working for the Scottish Government. It is perhaps worth saying therefore that those arguments often appear to rest on a misunderstanding of the constitutional position, which is that civil servants owe their loyalty to the Crown and that the authority of the Crown is vested, for this purpose, in the Ministers of the various governments which employ individual civil servants. One source of evidence that this misunderstanding may have receded is that political debate in Scotland in recent years has been more likely to feature arguments from members of Opposition parties that civil servants employed by the Scottish Government should selectively withhold their services from Ministers on particular topics than arguments alleging that civil servants are displaying improper loyalty towards anyone other than those Ministers.

As there is no strong evidence that increased transfer of responsibilities within the devolution settlement would have any necessary impact on the debate about the status of the Civil Service, it is sensible to focus on the potential relationship between independence and the options relating to the Civil Service.

11.6 INDEPENDENCE AND THE CIVIL SERVICE

Independence constitutes an opportunity, on this as on other aspects of governance, to consider from first principles the nature of parts of the system and the relationships between them. Since the Northcote–Trevelyan reforms of 1855 onwards, the nature and constitutional position of the Civil Service have been remarkably stable, in the context of a period during which the UK has been subject to substantial constitutional changes. For example, there have been the various changes since 1911 affecting the House of Lords, as well as successive developments in Ireland and, most recently, devolution in Scotland, Wales and Northern Ireland, as well as the changes in the scope and nature of the government process involved in the emergence and development of the modern state. Although there has been considerable evolution within the Civil Service, and periodic discussion of what is usually called Civil Service reform has become a staple of the political agenda, the fundamentals of the place of the Civil Service in our overall system of governance are largely unchanged.

It is worth reminding ourselves, therefore, that international comparisons reveal some significant variations from the UK model. The most obvious concerns appointments to the most senior posts. While it is general practice in the developed world to apply the core principle of the Northcote–Trevelyan reforms, appointment on merit rather than through patronage, to the generality of Civil Service posts, this is not the case with the most senior posts in a large number of countries. The best known example of this is the United States, where the number of senior posts which are appointed for the duration of a Presidency by an incoming President is so large that it can take up to two years of a four-year Presidency to complete the appointments process, but there are variations on this in many countries. These range from the application of the same principle of appointments from any source but to a smaller number of posts than in the US (as is the case in Finland, for example) to Ministerial choice between candidates who are existing civil servants but on the basis of criteria which may explicitly include declared political sympathies or party membership. Our UK arrangements for giving senior Ministers a right of veto over individual candidates who have been selected on merit, under the auspices of the independent Civil Service Commissioner, and input to the setting of criteria for appointments are further along the spectrum. The possibility of giving Ministers a greater role in senior appointments is one of the proposals which the current UK Government has included in the latest iteration of consideration of Civil Service reform.

It is reasonable to assume that within an independent Scotland there would be some consideration of this issue. In principle, one would expect this to embrace the related question of whether those who are already employed within government through direct appointments by Ministers – special advisers – should have the power to give direction to 'normal' civil servants. At present, after Mr Blair's Government experimented with the removal for a small number of special advisers of the previous prohibition on that, the position has reverted to a general prohibition.

All these variations on the way in which positions of authority over the day-to-day working of civil servants are filled interact with questions about the powers of government and, in particular, powers which involve public money through another distinctive feature of our present arrangements within central government across the UK: the concept of the Accounting Officer or Accountable Officer. It is a good illustration of the point that governance arrangements need to be seen as systems rather than individual components. The role of Accounting or Accountable Officer can only be understood in the context of a system in which Parliaments and Assemblies control expenditure by voting supply (that is, budget allocations) to a government and Ministers have very broad authority to direct expenditure within the vote or budget framework. The Accounting or Accountable Officer role closes the loop by making an individual senior civil servant (usually the Permanent Secretary for the relevant Government or Department within the UK Government or Northern Ireland Assembly Government) personally and directly responsible to the Parliament or Assembly for the propriety of the expenditure.

One of the functions this is intended to serve is to provide the Parliament or Assembly with assistance in preventing abuse of Ministerial power in relation to public money. It is, self-evidently, a mechanism which fits into a system in which the holder of the Accounting and Accountable Officer role does not hold the post to which it is attached at the discretion of the Minister whose power over public money is the focus of the role. If one wished to increase the role of Ministers in senior appointments, it might be a corollary that one should consider balancing adjustments in the system for control of public expenditure. An enhanced role for independent audit would be one obvious option, although it would be difficult for such arrangements to operate before the event, as the Accounting or Accountable Officer system does, rather than after the event.

Another option would be to move to a more rigid basis of control over authority to spend than is a feature of current arrangements across central governments within the UK. International comparisons illustrate the possibility of requirements for much more explicit authority for specific spending activities. None of the possible alternatives to the Accounting or Accountable Officer system could be expected to emulate its fine-grained nature, in which scrutiny can often be brought to bear on a few thousands of pounds within overall budget responsibilities of tens of billions. There are balancing arguments of proportionality, but one observes that many issues related to public money which attract high public concern and prolonged debate concern relatively small sums of money.

The substantive point in relation to this set of issues is that there is a complex discussion to be had about the balance which should be struck between flexibility and control and about acceptable levels of risk.

11.8 ACCOUNTABILITY FOR DELIVERY AND OUTCOMES

Accountability for outcomes, or delivery of particular services, is distinct from financial accountability, although some of the underlying issues are similar. In both cases, the authority over high-level decisions is unambiguously with Ministers. It was once the orthodox view of Ministerial accountability that it extended from those high-level decisions down to actions taken by those acting on their behalf of which they had no knowledge but, in current practice, there is a greater tendency to seek to locate accountability closer to the person taking detailed decisions.

In relation to financial accountability, the Accountable Officer function transfers accountability for the propriety of financial actions away from a Minister to the Principal Accountable Officer, who may further delegate it to subordinate Accountable Officers. There is a comparable formal transfer of accountability for operational delivery where a function falls within the remit of an Executive Agency, in which case the accountability rests with the chief executive of the relevant Agency, but there is no similar arrangement across the remainder of central government activity. This often leads to the transfer of accountability to Agency chief executives being overlooked in the context of Parliamentary debate. There are examples beyond the UK, most notably in New Zealand, of attempts to transfer accountability for delivery formally to civil servants across the generality of government activity. This requires the transfer of authority to take operational decisions, as is the case with Agency chief executives in the UK – at least in theory. Attempts have been made elsewhere to formalise this into a form of contract, or series of contracts, between Ministers and civil servants under which Ministers specify the resources they are willing to make available and civil servants specify what they commit to deliver on the basis of those resources. It is an obvious question therefore whether some such innovative approach to accountability might be explored in Scotland in the context of further constitutional change.

Any such developments would have to take account of the separate question of the difficulty of locating accountability for delivery or the achievement of outcomes exclusively within central government, given the tendency in the current governance system in Scotland to locate delivery responsibilities with arm's-length public bodies or local authorities, and the growing recognition that progress towards outcomes is rarely within the control of individual organisations acting alone. The outcomes-based approach to government adopted in Scotland since 2007 has led also to recognition of the need for accountability to be held jointly by those in several organisations and, often, partly by those who are not part of the public sector. It also creates a basis for further scepticism about models of Ministerial accountability which extend beyond the actions of civil servants to embrace the actions of those not employed by central government. Fresh thinking about forms of accountability across the public sector for progress towards desired outcomes might build on the changes to responsibilities and accountabilities already made within the Scottish Government, as part of the abolition of the Departmental structure of the Scottish Government in 2007.

11.9 THE SCOPE OF THE CIVIL SERVICE

Another issue highlighted by international comparisons relating to the place of a Civil Service in governance systems is the nature of the activities included within the scope of a Civil Service. Some countries adopt wide definitions, embracing schoolteachers, for example; others, such as the Nordic countries, adopt very narrow definitions related to those functions directly related to Ministerial work, in a context where operational activities are located with bodies separate from central government. Rationally, the nature of a Civil Service, and the principles within which it operates, should relate to the nature of the functions which it carries out. This is related, in turn, to the question of which functions are organised nationally rather than locally and, of those organised nationally, the degree of direct Ministerial control which is appropriate.

Leaving until later the issue of national and local organisation of public services within Scotland, it is appropriate, in the context of a general focus on enhanced devolution or independence to focus first on functions which might move from the UK level to the Scottish level or, more challengingly, which the Scottish Government might choose to develop but which do not currently exist at the UK level.

In general, over the past few decades, there has been, at the UK level, a tendency to place outside the boundaries of government a number of functions which were previously exercised within government. This has been particularly marked in relation to activities which have a high potential impact on the functioning of the market economy. The transfer to the Bank of England of responsibility for setting interest rates is the totemic example, of course. The regulation of sectors of the economy, particularly those moved from the public sector to the private sector during the 1980s and 1990s, is another example relevant to economic management. One might also argue that the creation of the Office of National Statistics as a non-Ministerial Department and the creation of an independent Statistics Commission fit this pattern, given the significance for the market of some of the data which the ONS assembles and publishes. Even where functions remain within government, we have seen the creation of new independent bodies designed to provide assurance, arguably more to the market than to the electorate, about the conduct of those functions. The Office of Budget Responsibility is the obvious example.

In relation to existing devolved functions, practice in Scotland has been mixed. There is an independent regulator for the water industry, despite the fact that it remains in government ownership. On the other hand, there is no equivalent to the Office of Budget Responsibility at the Scottish level; nor, despite some debate on the desirability of such a change, an institutional framework in relation to government statistics which distances the activity from Ministerial intervention, although the inclusion of the Scottish Government within the remit of the Statistics Commission could be seen as a half-way house. In a different area of interaction with the market economy, the pre-devolution design of the Scottish Enterprise network as business-led and decentralised has been modified post-devolution to correspond more closely to the more centralised and Ministerial-influenced model characteristic of the generality of Non-Departmental Public Bodies.

One might argue that these differences are related to an absence of significant market impact from decisions taken within the current range of devolved functions. Looking to the future such judgements might be related to the extent to which the Scottish economy functioned separately from the economy elsewhere in the UK and the extent to which any additional powers exercisable by the Scottish Government might have greater market impacts, either alone or in combination with present powers, than present powers alone.

11.10 CHALLENGE FUNCTION

Discussion of potential changes in institutional arrangements which would involve a greater role for bodies outside government is linked partly to discussion of the importance of a challenge function. While there has been some discussion of the desirability of a stronger challenge function inside government (usually revolving around the assertion that a Scottish Treasury would be beneficial, which seems to me to betray a lack of understanding of the attempt to develop a more effective model within the Scottish Government), there has been relatively little discussion of external challenge.

At present, the responsibility within our system of governance for challenge to the financial proposals put forward by government, and to policy and delivery generally, rests with the Scottish Parliament. The emphasis placed on the Committee system in the design of the functioning of the Parliament was intended to enhance the capacity of the Parliament to fulfil that function, among other purposes. While the Committee system has delivered some important benefits, the effective scrutiny of the draft annual Budgets presented by successive governments, and the exercise of the scope to present alternative proposals, could not be judged to be among them. If the economic and fiscal powers of government are to increase, this raises the question whether the Parliament would be better supported in the challenge function by a more specialised and expert body, along the lines of an Office of Budget Responsibility, than by the present reliance on the Parliament's own staff and, indirectly and unsystematically, Audit Scotland. Similar questions might arise if powers in relation to the social security system were to be transferred from the UK Government to the Scottish Government. The existence of such a transfer in relation to Northern Ireland does not offer much assistance in considering this question because no use has been made there of the power to vary the system. We can observe, however, that, for the UK excluding Northern Ireland, the Social Security Advisory Committee is an interesting example of a ministerially appointed expert body with an independent function, which offers advice and challenge within government but whose independent expertise also appears to be of value to the relevant Committee within the UK Parliament.

The point is that one should be cautious about making presumptions about the institutional arrangements which would accompany additional powers, particularly fiscal and economic powers, for the Scottish Government. It is possible that a future Scottish Government would look elsewhere than London for models for organisational arrangements related to these functions. It is possible that political attitudes to the relationship between the state and the market might be less close to what some of our EU partners call the 'Anglo-Saxon model'. Movement in the direction of a more interventionist role for the state in the functioning of the economy might imply the development of new institutional structures, for example, building on the current First Minister's initiative to establish a Council of Economic Advisers. One possibility would be the creation of independent bodies involving the business and trades union sectors, of a kind which are observable in the past arrangements at UK and Scottish levels and are in current use in some other European countries which give prominence to what is sometimes called social partnership. If new institutional structures were to emerge, the question of their degree of independence from government would be an obvious key point for decision, as well as the extent to which such institutions might have functions which extended beyond a purely advisory role.

11.11 PUBLIC BODIES AND GOVERNANCE

In addition to questions about the impact of potential new powers on the governance system in Scotland, there are questions about the penumbra of public bodies which surrounds central government at present. In the post-devolution era, we have had two high-profile exercises to reduce the number of such bodies, and the number has reduced as a consequence. Some of this has involved the elimination of functions and much of it has involved the amalgamation of bodies without substantive change in functions. There has been much less use of the option to bring within central government functions that were previously undertaken 'at arm's length' by Non-Departmental Public Bodies, although there are examples such as the abolition of Scottish Homes.

As a consequence, the model in Scotland remains one in which relatively little operational activity is conducted within central government, with the Scottish Prison Service as the largest exception, and both detailed policy and operational delivery are carried out either by local government or by Non-Departmental Public Bodies. It is interesting to contrast this with the post-devolution approach in Wales, where there has been a tendency to bring functions within central government, particularly including key economic development bodies such as the former Welsh Development Agency and Welsh Tourist Board.

This set of decisions is already within the control of the Scottish Government and, where legislation is involved, the Scottish Parliament. So, in a narrow sense, it would be affected by any extension of responsibilities only to the extent of the need already discussed about the location within the organisational framework of the new responsibilities.

There is, however, another dynamic. On the basis of the set of devolved responsibilities which predated the Scotland Act 2012, the approach to accountability of Scottish Ministers to the Scottish Parliament which has evolved has tended to treat Ministers as accountable even for matters which are formally delegated to Non-Departmental Public Bodies or, within central government itself, to Executive Agencies. This is most striking in relation to the operational decisions and performance of Health Boards but it extends to the actions of many other bodies. This approach to accountability, unless it is to be robustly resisted, creates a driver towards centralisation.

One possible hypothesis is that this approach to accountability evolved as a response to the dominance of social policy responsibilities over fiscal and economic policy responsibilities in the original devolution settlement. If so, the approach to accountability might change as fiscal and economic responsibilities increase, through the Scotland Act 2012 and possible future changes. One way of expressing this is that the approach to accountability might move closer to that applied at the UK level, and in other countries, to government and away from an approach which appears to have more in common with the UK experience of that applied to a local authority.

If the approach to accountability were to change, a wider range of options involving bodies at arm's length from central government might emerge. This range of options would include the model observable in the Nordic countries, in which responsibility and accountability for operational policy and delivery is located with bodies at arm's length from government as a clear organising principle across public sector functions. It is interesting to observe that this can be reinforced by robust barriers to selective Ministerial intervention, which can otherwise blur responsibility and accountability. One consequence of this approach is to encourage focus by central government on fiscal and economic responsibilities, and this might impact, in turn, on decisions about whether to locate functions relevant to those responsibilities within central government itself or in independent or arm's length bodies.

11.12 LOCAL GOVERNMENT AND GOVERNANCE

These broad issues also have some implications for local government. Scotland has already explored a distinctive approach to the relationship between central and local government built around the set of principles set out in the 2008 Concordat, the National Performance Framework and the Single Outcome Agreements. Further change is already within the powers of the Scottish Government and, to the extent that legislation is required, the Scottish Parliament. It is possible, however, that a further increase in fiscal powers or a transition to independence would make available a wider range of options for such further change.

One might expect there to be pressure for such change on the basis of arguments that the devolution of power should be a continuum, based on the principle of subsidiarity, so that any function of government would be carried out at the most decentralised level at which it could be discharged effectively.

An aspect of the relationship between central and local government which might be likely to be the subject of future consideration, particularly in a changed context of power over fiscal matters at the Scottish level, is the very high proportion of local authority expenditure funded through grant payments from central government. This stands at over 80% and it is often argued that this weakens the case for greater autonomy for local authorities. Although arrangements in Scotland since 2008 have involved a substantial reduction in the proportion of central government grant which is hypothecated to specific uses and an increase in local authority autonomy over priorities and service design, there is scope for discussion of further changes.

There has been for several years discussion of the scope for a reversion to discretion at the level of individual local authorities in setting the poundage for business rates, allied to the retention by individual authorities of the revenues for business rates levied in their area, in place of the present arrangements whereby the revenues from a standard poundage across Scotland for business rates are pooled and redistributed between local authorities by central government. It is argued that current arrangements deprive individual local authorities of a potential fiscal incentive to locate economic activity in their areas and weakens their incentive to minimise potential adverse effects on the viability of individual businesses from the activities of the local authority. If central government had additional sources of fiscal revenue which could be used to equalise the availability of resources relative to expenditure needs across local authorities, it seems likely that this would change the context for consideration of the competing arguments on the business rates regime.

It is also possible that the existence of additional fiscal powers at the Scotland level might lead to consideration of subsidiarity in the use of these powers. Comparisons with countries outside the UK provide illustrations of possibilities such as local sales taxes or tourism taxes. Adoption of new revenue-raising mechanisms at local authority level could change local authorities' degree of reliance on central government grant, and, by foregoing the revenue which might have been raised by the same mechanisms at national level, central government would also reduce the potential aggregate resources out of which it could fund grant payments to local authorities.

The other means of changing the proportion of local authority expenditure funded by central government grant would be to remove some functions which give rise to expenditure from within the responsibilities of local authorities, although this would create an obvious tension with the principle of subsidiarity. To make a substantial change in the proportion, the functions removed would have to be substantial. The possibility discussed most frequently in the past has been school education. Transfer of that function, either to central government or to new single-purpose public bodies, would reduce local authority aggregate expenditure to a level at which locally raised revenue would exceed 50% of the aggregate.

11.13 SECURING BETTER OUTCOMES

Consideration of options of this kind raises public policy issues, for example, about the coordination of different forms of support and intervention in the lives of young people and their families, which are particularly relevant to the wider discussions which already take place in Scotland about the contribution of governance systems to the design and delivery of public policy to maximise achievement of the desired results. In this respect, the discussion of future options in relation to the functions of local authorities is of a piece with the same discussion in relation to the division of functions between central government and public bodies operating at a national level.

In both contexts, the first order question is how best to maximise the effectiveness of the public sector as a whole in supporting the realisation of desirable economic and social outcomes. In Scotland, since 2007, there has been radical innovation in the framework for achieving this, based on the creation of a set of National Outcomes. These provide a shared focus for all parts of the public sector and emphasise integrated working between parts of the public sector to achieve progress towards those common objectives, with considerable scope for local variation. This displaced the emphasis on centrally determined input or process targets within individual organisations or sub-sectors of the public sector, which had dominated thinking about the pursuit of improved results from public sector activity for the preceding two decades or more and which has been an important factor in the trend towards centralisation in government and away from localism. There is no necessary reason why this should change as a consequence of further constitutional change, as is apparent from the consideration currently being given to emulation of these changes in some European countries of broadly comparable size to Scotland. This does not guarantee, of course, that change would not occur. It would be ironic if the transfer of more political power away from the UK Government to the Scottish Government resulted in a greater degree of emulation of the governance framework observable within the UK Government and the loss of the innovation demonstrated by the Scottish Government.

An important second order question is that of capacity in different parts of the governance system. Changes in the responsibilities of central government raise questions about the creation of additional capacity at that level, which are likely to have consequential implications across the complex network of public organisations which make up the governance framework. These issues about capacity connect back to wider policy questions about aggregate supply within the labour market in Scotland. At present, Scotland faces growing competition between the public and private sectors for a gradually diminishing population of working age, in which it seems probable that the public sector will be unable to match the ability of the private sector to use increased financial rewards as a source of competitive advantage. Whether further fiscal and political changes would alter demographic trends is a question which provides another point of connection to other chapters in this book.

11.14 CONCLUSIONS

This chapter has sought to draw out the very wide range of choices about a future governance system which it would be possible to explore in the context of further changes to devolution or of independence. It is illustrative, rather than attempting to be definitive, because of the very broad range of possible changes which exist. The central argument is that change in governance systems cannot be considered piecemeal and that change in one aspect would have implications for the way in which other parts of the system operate. So, although I list below some of the individual questions which I have touched upon, that should not distract from the proposition that any change should involve systems thinking:

GOVERNANCE

» should Scotland, were a substantially different constitutional arrangement to be favoured, give fresh consideration to its governance arrangements?
» does any new system of governance that might be proposed uphold the desired characteristics of an effective system? (See section 12.1.)
» would it be desirable for Scotland to have a written constitution?
» would new institutions be required to facilitate Scotland's relationship with the remainder of the UK?

» would an independent Scotland need to establish treaty arrangements with the remainder of the UK?

PARLIAMENT

» what would define the most effective Parliament?
» is a unicameral Parliament optimal?
» is an electoral system that tends to disfavour single party majorities appropriate?
» how might Parliament ensure access to the highest quality of expertise?
» should Ministers be drawn only from the elected members of the legislature?

CIVIL SERVICE

» should the Civil Service be separate from that of the rest of the UK?
» how would a Scotland, with a significant extension of powers, secure the necessary expertise to effectively conduct government?
» should the Civil Service in Scotland continue to be based on the principle of political impartiality, particularly at the most senior levels?
» what is the most effective institutional mechanism for ensuring financial accountability and responsibility?
» what scope for the Civil Service is preferable, and according to what underlying rationale should it be determined?

CHALLENGE FUNCTION

» would the Scottish Parliament be better supported by more specialised and expert bodies?
» should any such new institutions be independent from government?

PUBLIC BODIES

» what model of governance in relation to public bodies would be most effective?
» how is accountability secured with a structure of public bodies?

» what formal or informal relationship between the local and central tiers of government is most effective in securing desired outcomes?
» how should local government resourcing be established to uphold the principle of local accountability?

OUTCOMES

» how best can the effectiveness of the public sector as a whole be maximised in supporting the realisation of desirable economic and social outcomes?
» is there the necessary capacity in different parts of the governance system to secure the desired outcomes?

A Note on Welfare Policy and the Distributional Objectives of Economic Policy
Compiled by Professor Andrew Goudie[1]

The future of welfare policy is a key element of many proposals for constitutional change. Moreover, welfare expenditure plays a pivotal role in the economic system. It is an important component in the macroeconomic framework and in aggregate public expenditure, in particular, and contributes directly to both the short-term goals of economic stabilisation and to the long-term goals and performance of the economy. At the microeconomic level, as is explored in more detail here, it is a primary driver of economic incentives and the wellbeing of individuals. Social security expenditure accounts for a significant element of total welfare expenditure and is the primary focus here.

This appendix sets out some of the history and current experience that would form the context for any transference of welfare powers to Scotland. It then looks at some of the basic principles that would need to be taken into account in the design of any new system, including the trade-offs and choices that would be faced.

The summary of these issues in this appendix is based on many detailed discussions with experts in this field, to whom I am most grateful for sharing their expertise.

A.1 INTRODUCTION

In order to understand the factors which might influence the structure of the social security system that an independent Scotland, or one with much greater autonomy, might adopt, it is helpful to begin by discussing the general aims and constraints on social security. This appendix begins with these and then proceeds to discuss the particular influence that Scotland's circumstances might have on these.

Social security systems have traditionally fulfilled three functions, as:

---

1   Visiting Professor and Special Adviser to the Principal, University of Strathclyde; former Chief Economic Adviser to the Scottish Government.

1. *a means of redistribution of resources*, along with the tax system, towards those whose lifetime earning power is, for one reason or another, low;
2. *a safety net*, providing incomes to people in particular circumstances: notably, to those whose incomes are temporarily low but, perhaps because of youth, have not had the opportunity to build up the sort of buffer of precautionary saving which would allow them to support themselves in such circumstances; and
3. *a means of transferring resources between different stages in people's lives*, offering an alternative to saving as a means of providing for old age. Moreover, because they have often been implemented across the population as a whole and with a less than full contributory basis, they have unwittingly served as a means of transferring resources from future generations to people currently alive, with much the same consequences as national debt.

In practice, of course, the distinction between these different aims is not clear cut. Historically, unemployment risk has been higher for low wage earners than for high wage earners; thus, people with low lifetime incomes are more exposed to the risk of unemployment and are probably less likely to have built up the reserves which could support them during unemployment. Support in periods when earnings are low is, therefore, likely also to be a means of alleviating inequalities to lifetime income.

Any social security system, however, affects the way in which people respond to their economic circumstances. If people can derive an adequate income without working, then those who do not enjoy their work may conclude that work is something which could be avoided. The provision of benefits as a safety net for people who become unemployed reduces the pressure people would otherwise feel to build up precautionary balances. Similarly, the provision of State Pensions reduces the need people feel to save for their retirement.

These income effects are present whatever the terms on which benefits are available. But a separate issue arises from the need to pay for any social security system. Its costs, one way or another, have to be met out of taxation. Not surprisingly, a social security system which provides significant benefits to a significant number of people faces a greater financing problem than one that is less generous. The rates of tax needed to support such a system might turn out to be politically unacceptable. High tax rates have the effect of narrowing the tax base and it is possible that some apparently attractive schemes would require a share of national income higher than that which could be raised through taxation, even if there were no political problems associated with high tax rates.

A.2.1 *Need and affordability*

Two means have traditionally been adopted in the UK as a way of addressing the affordability problem with social security:

» *circumstances*: the social security system has tried to identify people who need help the most, notably on the basis of their circumstances, rather than their income. Circumstances may be closely correlated with income but, provided circumstances are the consequence of exogenous influences rather than choice, restricting benefits to people in particular circumstances mitigates the incentive effects. This principle lay behind the system as it was proposed by Beveridge in 1942. It was assumed that the adult wage for someone in full-time employment provided a socially acceptable level of support for a couple with no more than one child. Thus, benefits were payable only to those with more than one child (through Family Allowances), to those who were unemployed or sick and to women aged sixty and over and men aged sixty-five and over;
» *contributions*: entitlement to benefits depended on a history of National Insurance contributions. The contributions were flat-rate, rather than earnings-related, and the benefits similarly were independent of earnings history. The scheme thus maintained the form of a contributory scheme.

The system was, however, never introduced on the scale proposed by Beveridge. Given that the levels of support it offered were inadequate and that not everyone had the required contribution history, the question then arose of how to provide an adequate safety net as cheaply as possible. The solution adopted was to introduce an additional element through the provision of:

» *a separate means-tested benefit*, originally known as National Assistance, an arrangement which had its roots in the provision of means-tested unemployment benefits during the 1930s. National Assistance was available both to people of working age not covered by National Insurance, such as disabled people and single mothers, and elderly people who required other benefits in addition to the State Pension to reach a subsistence level. It included an allowance for rent, normally equal to the rent actually paid, and this delivered an element of regional variation which matched the regional variation in rent. This component has mutated into housing and council tax benefits.

A.2.2 *Effectiveness and incentives*

In the years since 1948 the view gained ground that earnings were not necessarily adequate to provide a socially acceptable standard of living even for small families. Benefits were therefore introduced which were payable even to households with at least one spouse in full-time work. These were, of course, also mean-tested.

This expansion of the scope of the system had the effect of worsening the incentive effects associated with it. As the range of means-tested benefits increased, so the risk of being exposed to very high withdrawal or 'taper' rates increased. And, as the living standards which could be sustained on benefits rose, relative to the wages available relatively low down on the income distribution, so too the disincentives to work increased.

Between the 1960s and the 1980s benefits became more generous in most advanced countries.[2] Since the 1980s replacement ratios – that is, the ratio of benefits received by people not working to the earnings they might typically receive were they working – have become less generous in the United Kingdom, Belgium and Ireland, but continued to become more generous in some other countries. Studies[3] suggest that benefit levels and the length of time for which they are available have an important effect on unemployment rates, notwithstanding that they are, of course, also strongly influenced by aggregate demand. A belief that benefits affected unemployment was almost certainly one of the factors behind the reduced generosity of the benefit system from the 1980s onward in the United Kingdom.

The provision of benefits for old people has been subject to a different dynamic. Historically, State Pensions were linked to earnings rather than to prices, with, in normal economic circumstances, wages rising faster than prices. Concerned by the costs of this as the population aged, the UK Government decided, in 1979, to link pensions to prices rather than earnings. The expectation was that people would, in anticipation of this change, build up their savings while of working age, so that living standards could be sustained after retirement. But the policy did not have the intended effects. First of all,

2   See Nickell, Nunziata and Ochel (2005).
3   For example, again see Nickell, Nunziata and Ochel (2005).

those who retired around the time of the change had little scope for building up their savings. Many of these people were still alive by the mid-1990s and they could reasonably argue that the social security system had not delivered what they had been led to expect from it. Second, despite the announced change, saving, at least at an aggregate level, did not increase. Those reaching retirement more recently have also protested about pensioner poverty. In 1997 the government introduced an additional means-tested benefit for people aged sixty or over; the basis on which this was paid was linked to wages rather than prices, and more recently there has been a general drift back to wage linkage.

A.2.3 *Public opinion and politics*

Benefit arrangements both for people of working age and those who are retired generate considerable and continuing public debate, largely focused on the incentive effects or their consequences. Thus, people who have saved for their retirement – and feel that having done so, they are little better off than others of the same age who did not do so – may press for an extension of benefits or an easing of the means test. Similarly, those who work – and who find their incomes are not much higher than those of people in comparable circumstances who do not work – argue that they receive little reward for working. The political equilibrium of the benefit system is likely to depend heavily on the attitudes of those who currently do not receive benefits and see themselves as financing the system, and how they regard the payment of benefits to others. This will be in addition to any view of the magnitude of the actual incentive effects that the system creates. This is very likely to be as true in Scotland as in the United Kingdom as a whole.

There is a separate point, very relevant to the situation in which Scotland might find itself were it given the powers to develop its own social security system, whether within the current UK or with one of the independence models. Any change to the tax structure, while revenue is maintained, results in winners and losers. Consequently, the political costs associated with creating a body of losers may be substantial. Much the same point applies to any rearrangement of state benefits. People who have organised their affairs in the expectation of the continuance of one particular state benefit regime would probably find their voice if any rearrangement to the regime led to them noticeably losing out. A Scottish welfare system would be bound to carry a large legacy associated with people who had planned on the assumption that key aspects of the system would remain much as they are at present. This could pose a substantial political obstacle to change, even if Scotland were to have the powers to amend the system to better meet its preferences. It would not, of course, prevent change – as would be entirely legitimate and, indeed, anticipated with such a constitutional change – but it would suggest that transformation of the welfare system would be both a delicate process and one that might be expected to span many decades.

A.3 WELFARE ARRANGEMENTS FOR PEOPLE OF WORKING AGE

The welfare arrangements in the UK for people of working age are due for substantial reform in 2013/14. The core of the new proposals is that there should be a single Universal Credit replacing the current range of benefits, and that there should be a single taper rate attached to this. The UK Department of Work and Pensions (2010) sets out, in a White Paper, the arrangements proposed.

As far as the numbers of people facing high withdrawal rates are concerned, these arrangements should lead to marked reductions compared to the pre-2013 system. The DWP estimate[4] that there are currently around 200,000 people in work who lose at least 80p in taxes paid and benefits withdrawn for each extra pound of income from employment. In contrast to this withdrawal rate of 80%, under the new system there will be a single withdrawal rate of 65% for those earning less than the income tax threshold and of 76% for those paying tax at the basic rate. The DWP also suggest that, under the pre-2013 arrangements, about 1.4 million people in workless households would currently face withdrawal rates of 70% or more if they were to work for ten or fewer hours per week; this would fall to around 200,000 after the reform. The Department's assessment is that the reform benefits people in the bottom half of the income distribution, with costs borne predominantly by those in the seventh decile.

The White Paper expected modest increases in overall costs, compared with present arrangements, but with some of these offset by reductions to administrative costs. As always, however, such effects cannot be assessed with certainty, and it is possible that costs may be higher or lower than was estimated. It is also, of course, the case that these taper rates would remain much higher than those faced elsewhere in the tax-benefit system.

Such analysis of the impact on incentives and costs clearly addresses only these two dimensions of the reform: it does not address the other objectives of a social security system that were set out at the start of this appendix.

---

4   DWP White Paper (2010), p. 54.

The main benefit available to people of State Pension age and above is the long-standing State Pension. The full State Pension is available to anyone who has paid National Insurance contributions for thirty years or more, with reductions *pro rata* for those with incomplete contribution records but with a minimum contribution of seven and a half years required. In addition, the State Second Pension is an earnings-related benefit available to those who have not contracted out,[5] and was intended to provide earnings-related benefits to people who are not otherwise able to undertake retirement savings. On top of these benefits, people above the State Pension age can also benefit from the Pension Credit. This is a means-tested benefit with a withdrawal rate of 40% designed to deliver in 2012–13 an income of at least £142.70 for a single pensioner and £217.90 for a pensioner couple.

However, the Turner Report[6] recommended major changes to the pension system designed to address, on the one hand, the fact that high charges were a barrier to retirement saving by people on relatively low incomes and, on the other hand, that a substantial number of pensioners received means-tested benefits. It recommended, first, setting up a new saving scheme, a recommendation which has led to the establishment of NEST (the National Employment Savings Scheme) and, second, that the State Pension and the State Second Pension should be merged. Contracting out was abolished from 2012, except for those with access to defined benefit pension schemes and, from 2016, the State Second Pension will be merged with the State Pension to give a single flat-rate pension for an individual. It is intended that the long-term costs of the State Pension will be kept in check by raising the State Pension age in line with life expectancy. This is likely to mean that, by 2050, the State Pension age may be over seventy. A White Paper setting out the proposals in full had been expected in Autumn 2012, but this has been delayed.

A.5 THE LEGAL FRAMEWORK: THE BASIC POLITICAL AND
ECONOMIC CHOICE

Under the constitutional arrangements that were established in 1999, most powers over welfare policy and social protection are reserved to the UK Government, except in the areas of housing and social

---

5 Employees have to be members of other pension schemes to be able to contract out.
6 Turner (2005).

inclusion. Over recent years, however, as the debate over Scotland's future constitutional status has developed, more attention has focused on both the revenue and expenditure elements of fiscal policy, including the appropriateness of welfare policy remaining as a reserved policy. As a set of policy instruments that are crucial to many government objectives, the importance of this debate is self-evident. The location of welfare powers is equally critical to broader issues of fiscal management, accounting as it does for around one third of total expenditure in Scotland in 2009–10.[7]

A.5.1 *UK-based constitutional models*

Of the primary strands of current constitutional thinking – as are outlined in more detail in chapter 1 – most address the future of welfare policy in the UK. Of the models based on the maintaining of the present United Kingdom, the model founded on the most recent Scotland Act (2012) retains the current set of reserved and devolved expenditure responsibilities. However, the other two primary models that have been proposed which take the continuance of the Union as a basic premise, Devo plus and Devo max, both assert the benefit of transferring welfare expenditure powers to the Scottish Parliament. Devo plus, for example, proposes that all the major welfare benefits – with the exception of State Pensions and Sickness and Maternity Pay – move to Holyrood. Underlying these policy propositions is the assertion that this would 'achieve a more coherent and effective approach to the alleviation of poverty' and that 'the Scottish Government can make no concerted attempt to address poverty without the necessary tools and that requires welfare provision to be devolved'.[8] The transfer of such powers would necessitate a negotiated agreement between the Scottish and UK Governments on the appropriate transfer of expenditure to finance the implementation of policy under those powers.

The Devo max model remains relatively poorly explained but appears to imply the full transfer of all expenditure powers to Scotland, including, therefore, those related to welfare support and distribution policy. Payments would be made by the Scottish Government to the UK Government for any services provided by the

---

7   Total expenditure in Scotland by the Scottish and UK Governments is estimated at £61.63bn in 2010-11, of which social protection accounted for £21.05bn. Of this, £15.89bn was accounted for in the UK Government accounts, £5.16bn in Scottish Local Government and Scottish Government accounts. (See *Government Expenditure and Revenue, Scotland 2010-11*, Scottish Government, 2012).

8   *Devolution Plus: Reform Scotland's Evidence to the Scottish Parliament's Bill Committee.* Reform Scotland. September 2011.

UK for Scotland (as, for example, might be the case were the Scottish Government to contract with the UK Government for the latter to continue providing welfare support to Scotland) or provided collectively for the benefit of the UK as a whole including Scotland (as, for example, with UK defence or UK overseas services).

It is unknown at this time precisely which elements of welfare policy would be transferred to the Scottish Parliament under either Devo plus or Devo max – or indeed any variant of these – were such powers to be granted in principle. It is possible that a UK Government might limit the transfer or limit the use of the transferred powers if it considered that they might be detrimental to the UK interest. For example, maintaining significantly different welfare policy north and south of the border might be expected to have potential implications for the behavioural response of individuals and, therefore, for the implementation and, possibly, the sustainability of the two systems. It would certainly raise practical questions of residence that would require resolution, but these would not be insurmountable.

A.5.2 *Independence-based constitutional models*

With all the independence models that have been proposed, powers over all expenditure decisions would transfer to the Scottish Parliament. Consequently, the definition of all welfare policy would be the responsibility of the Parliament. This would not, of course, preclude the Parliament from deciding to continue with any existing UK policy or from contracting with the UK to continue to provide a welfare service to the newly independent nation.

A.6 TRADE-OFFS IN WELFARE SYSTEMS

This section illustrates the nature of some of the important trade-offs that are inherent within any welfare system and which must be addressed explicitly in the design of any new or reformulated set of programmes.

A.6.1 *Incentives and benefit withdrawal*

The earlier discussion has highlighted the problem of paying for a welfare system and the obvious fact that efforts to reduce its costs by means of tapering benefits have adverse incentive effects. This issue was discussed by Mirrlees (1971). He considered the problem faced by a state which wanted to maximise some function of the welfare of its people by redistributing labour income but was aware of the possible role of taxes and taper rates as a disincentive to work. When those disincentive effects are large, redistribution is less desirable than when those disincentive effects are small. It is therefore necessary to trade off the perceived benefits of redistribution against the deadweight costs of taxes and withdrawal rates leading to a narrowing of the income base.

The Universal Credit is designed with this in mind. It was noted above that it is designed to have withdrawal rates lower than those built in to the current system, with the belief that expenditure will be reduced because incentives to work will be increased. To the extent that this is successful – and there is necessarily an important demand-side perspective in whether the labour market can absorb additional labour supply at the relevant time – the costs would be expected to decline. But, to the extent that welfare payments are reduced and individuals remain with no or very low earned income, public expenditure need not fall by the anticipated amount. The burden may be passed on – or partly so – to different public services if the loss or reduction of one benefit automatically increases the individual's eligibility for other state benefits or services. This would clearly have a consequent associated cost, with the burden potentially falling to a different part of the public sector. This could involve a different UK DWP welfare benefit or a different UK Government department, but, equally, could be an additional cost falling to the Scottish Government or local authority.

It is also important to take account of the fact that most individuals have two key choices: whether to work or not (the extensive margin) and how much to work (the intensive margin). To the extent that people may have greater choice about the former than the latter, the use of differential withdrawal rates associated with those who earn, compared to those who do not, needs to be taken into account insofar as they impact on work incentives. Determining these withdrawal rates is therefore a key decision. The social security system must also take into account the fact that high withdrawal rates might simply put people off working all together.

A.6.2 *Simplicity and flexibility*

On top of these issues, a further important trade-off involves striking an appropriate balance between simplicity and flexibility. While few would dispute the value of a simple, well-defined and transparent system, there is also a significant benefit from a system that has the capacity to respond effectively to the very diverse circumstances and needs of the population.

The growth and the development of an immensely complex UK welfare system since its birth does, to a large extent, reflect a continuous process of attempting to target particular groupings in what was perceived to be a fair and more cost-effective manner, given the policy priorities and distributional objectives of the government of the day. The cumulative impact of decades of such development inevitably has led to a massively complex and opaque system. Consequently, the current system appears to incorporate a very significant degree of irrationality – or, at best, reflect an improbable series of social preferences – in the selection of which services are universal or selective, which are free or charged, which are subject to a means test, and which are the subject of other forms of targeting and rationing. In addition, the implementation of the system, in practice, has introduced huge complexity too, inducing confusion and, in some cases, low take-up rates, often as a result of the interaction between benefits and the complexity of eligibility criteria.

One of the primary motives underlying the UK's current programme of proposed welfare reform is precisely, therefore, to reduce this complexity and increase the rationality with the introduction of the Universal Credit.

One of the key risks, however, that is inherent in the current reforms and in establishing any new system, is that the system will fail to discriminate adequately between different groupings in society, deemed worthy of support, in the interests of a much needed simplicity.

A.6.3 *Incentives, costs and poverty*

Significant attention has focused on the UK programme of reforms and particularly the key objectives of achieving both a sustainable and affordable system and one that provides positive incentives to individuals to work.

Many observers have, however, questioned the extent to which the reforms address all three functions of social security set out in section A.1. While recognising the tension between, on the one hand, providing adequate incomes and maintaining reasonable living standards – however these might be ultimately defined – and, on the other hand, addressing issues of financial cost and economic disincentives, it has been argued that too little attention has been brought to bear on both poverty and inequality. Prolonged periods of economic recession and poor employment opportunities[9] necessarily exacerbate the problem, as the pressure on incomes increases sharply and can coincide – as has certainly been the case in recent years – with significant reductions in public expenditure levels and thus in the affordability of benefit programmes. In this regard, the growth in the numbers in employment receiving benefits has been cited as one clear contributor to the overall challenge within the current system.

There has typically, however, been a lack of clarity surrounding what constitutes poverty and inequality and around the objectives of policy in these regards and, consequently, about how policy should be designed from these perspectives. In moving to a new UK system or in designing any new welfare system under a new constitutional arrangement, it is clearly legitimate – and some would argue necessary – to rethink a wide range of the elements of the system: to reconsider both the extent to which poverty is addressed and the minimum levels of income that are seen as appropriate by society; to determine what specific goals society wishes to pursue with respect to any move to a more equal society or not, looking to address the challenges at both the lower end and the top end of the income distribution, as well as at the ability of individuals to contribute to society from both income and wealth; to consider the interaction with the labour market and wage levels, and address the questions that have been raised around minimum acceptable wage levels and the *living wage* level; to revisit whether the circumstances that make individuals eligible to receive benefits – and those circumstances that do not – are indeed reflecting the views of the majority in society; to enhance the take-up of benefits, once their role and value are established, founded on clear eligibility criteria; to ensure the fairness with which the eligibility of individuals for specific benefits is assessed and determined; and, finally, to enhance public understanding of the value of the welfare system and, in particular, remove the stigmatisation of benefit recipients.

As with any public service, these challenges can only be resolved in the context of what expenditure resources are available in total and for these specific services, in particular, and with a comprehensive

---

9   The present appearance of relatively strong (headcount) employment rates, of course, masks the significant pressure on full-time equivalent employment and on the quality of employment, both of which have the effect of reducing incomes even for those in employment. Lower economic activity rates can equally mask the real employment problem.

understanding of the wider implications of policy for economic incentives and behaviours.

What all these trade-offs demonstrate is the inadequacy of any welfare system that does not have a clear vision of what the system is intended to achieve with respect to *all* the objectives upon which it bears. Determining the balance between the objectives is obviously a hugely political question, not least when resources are under greatest pressure, but the neglect of any one objective is a serious weakness in any welfare system design.

A.7 A DIFFERENT WELFARE SYSTEM?

Why might Scotland want a benefit system different from that in the rest of the United Kingdom? There are a number of possible reasons:

» the first is that it is possible that the benefit system in the UK – or rather that which will be in place following the introduction of Universal Credit – is simply regarded as misconceived by the majority of the population in Scotland, either because of its fundamental objectives or its perceived technical shortcomings or due to the concerns over the feasibility of its implementation;

» a second is that the way in which people in Scotland react to the effects of the social security system on incentives to work and save is different from the way in which people in the rest of the United Kingdom react;

» a third possibility is that views on the redistribution of resources between rich and poor people are different in Scotland from those in the rest of the country;

» a fourth is that Scotland's capacity to pay may be different from that elsewhere. In other words, if the tax base in Scotland is either higher or lower than in the rest of the United Kingdom, it would be natural to expect a social security system to be either more or less generous; and

» finally, it was noted above that a feature of the way in which social security has developed is that resources are transferred from future generations to people currently alive. Thus, any differences in the demographic pattern between Scotland and the rest of the United Kingdom would suggest differences in the long-term affordability of social security. This would have implications either for the long-term structure of social security or for the tax rates needed to finance it.

Are the views of Scots on redistribution and support for people with limited incomes markedly different from those in the rest of the UK? And have these disparities been a consistent feature for many decades? From a practical point of view, this question may be explored by means of social attitude surveys.[10]

The evidence from the 2010 British Social Attitudes Survey provides a snapshot and suggests that the Scots may be more supportive of redistribution than are people in England and Wales. Table 1 shows the responses people give to statements about redistribution and the welfare system, with the first three statements (A, B and C) being supportive of the welfare system and the remaining two (D and E) being critical of it. This Table alone, of course, tells us nothing of the stability of these views over time or of the statistical significance of the differences between the nations.

These data suggest that more people agree with the supportive statements in Scotland than in England and Wales, while more people agree with the critical statements in England and Wales than in Scotland. A reasonable conclusion from this is that, providing individual preferences are relatively stable, the political process is likely to be more supportive of a generous welfare system in Scotland than in the whole of the United Kingdom, and that, given the opportunity offered by either independence or one of the UK-based enhanced devolution models, Scotland is likely to aspire to benefits and taxes being higher than those in England and Wales.

While the message from the British Social Attitudes Survey is suggestive, it is, however, an incomplete analysis and an inadequate basis for welfare reform. The survey is only a snapshot at one moment in time and, additionally, it takes no account of the fact that people's views are time inconsistent. That is when young, they may be keen to be protected from the risk of unemployment by means of generous unemployment benefits while, when retired, they may think that benefits paid to people of working age encourage economic inactivity. Equally, these same people may consider that it is unfair that, because they have worked and saved while young, they do not receive the full range of benefits available to some old people.

---

10   See Alt, Preston and Sibieta (2010).

	A	B	C	D	E
England and Wales					
Agree Strongly	4.3%	9.0%	7.9%	7.6%	13.1%
Agree	26.2%	26.8%	35.0%	29.0%	43.5%
Neither Agree nor Disagree	31.7%	27.9%	31.8%	34.8%	23.0%
Disagree	32.1%	29.9%	22.4%	24.7%	16.8%
Disagree Strongly	5.7%	6.4%	2.9%	3.9%	3.6%
Scotland					
Agree Strongly	5.6%	7.9%	8.6%	5.6%	9.7%
Agree	33.1%	35.2%	38.1%	26.2%	35.2%
Neither Agree nor Disagree	25.7%	26.2%	31.0%	33.3%	27.0%
Disagree	29.4%	26.6%	19.0%	30.3%	22.1%
Disagree Strongly	6.3%	4.1%	3.4%	4.5%	6.0%

Key	Statements
A	The Government should spend more on welfare benefits for the poor
B	The Government should redistribute income
C	Cutting welfare benefits would damage too many people's lives
D	Many people who get social security don't really deserve any help
E	If welfare benefits weren't so generous people would learn to stand on their own feet.

Source: British Social Attitudes Survey 2010

One logical way to design a social security system would be to ask the question: what structure would appeal most to young people who do not know how their lives are going to turn out but do expect to live out those lives with that same social security system and incur the tax burden that the system implies? Such an analysis is, unfortunately, very complex, making this a difficult proposition to pursue, but it is likely to lead to a different outcome from that which a poll of everyone of working and pensionable age today would favour.

Indeed, recent UK experience may confirm that this is more than a risk. Since the current government came to power, benefits available to some people of working age have been reduced while those available to old people have tended to be protected or enhanced. It is much easier to see this outcome reflecting the preferences of people currently alive – especially the highly influential 'grey' interest groups – than those of a notional cohort of young people who do not yet know how life will treat them. Similarly, this difference between the interests of young people expecting to live the whole of their lives in a given benefit regime and the interests of the entire current population probably explains why there has been a move away from means-testing of retirement benefits.

Thus, there is a strong case for any reforms to the welfare system to be assessed against the background of whether individuals would be likely to be happy if they lived in any reformed system for the whole of their lives. It is not enough simply that reform responds predominantly to the short-term preferences.

A.9 SCOTTISH POPULATION STRUCTURE AND THE AFFORDABILITY OF SOCIAL SECURITY

Over and above the issue discussed in the previous section, the government of the day would need to make a judgement about what aggregate expenditure level could be financed and what share of that expenditure could be deployed in its welfare system.[11] Clearly, even with a stable welfare system, the welfare cost will vary significantly over time, not least due to the inherent automatic stabiliser role that welfare expenditure would typically play. It will also vary according to the underlying determinants of the demand for welfare support. The most striking example of this, which would be expected to dominate the thinking around welfare policy over coming decades, is the increased demand resulting from the anticipated demographic trends and their implications for welfare support amongst the elderly.

In addition, the provision of universal and free benefits is a key issue here, with any preferences for universality and the absence of charging necessarily being shaped by the affordability of the targeted welfare programmes. Some observers[12, 13] have drawn attention to the deadweight costs that typically accompany such policy instruments and the associated cost of provision, depending of course on the generosity of the policy. Moreover, to the extent that the policy interacts with growing demand pressures – as sharply demonstrated by the provision of universal services to the rapidly increasing elderly

---

11 As a historical benchmark, estimates for the Scottish budget suggest that total expenditure on social protection expenditure in Scotland in 2010-11 was 34.2% of total Scottish expenditure. See *Government Expenditure and Revenue, Scotland, 2010-11*, Scottish Government (March 2012).

12 Crawford Beveridge, Neil McIntosh, Robert Wilson. *Independent Budget Review: The Report of Scotland's Independent Budget Review Panel* (July 2010).

13 For a valuable summary of many of the key issues here, see Bell (2010).

population – the potential resource burden would grow rapidly and bring the sustainability of the policy into question. Whether universal provision contributes unambiguously and cost-effectively to a specific economic, distributional or environmental outcome is critical: if not, it is likely to prove an unsustainable burden in this context.[14]

The affordability of welfare expenditure will therefore be an integral part of the overall expenditure decision and one that reflects the tax and borrowing capacity that is judged to prevail over the medium to long term.

The history of social security in the United Kingdom is that, as the system has expanded, a cohort of old people has tended to receive more in benefits than it had contributed when young to meet the costs. This is a problem in itself. But it becomes much more of a difficulty if the proportion of old people in the economy rises relative to that of young people. There are two factors behind a demographic change of this type. First of all, as the large cohort of people born in the baby boom of the 1960s passes into retirement, the proportion of old people tends to rise relative to that of young people. Second, longevity is rising in a way that has no historical precedent; this too increases the proportion of old people in the population. The United Kingdom is planning to primarily address the cost implications of this issue by means of increases in the State Pension age over the next fifty years or so.

Official forecasts of population structure, as illustrated in Figure 1, suggest that the ratio of people aged sixty-five and over will increase somewhat more in Scotland than in the UK as a whole. This means that, other things being equal, a Scotland with its own welfare powers will face more of a problem in paying benefits to old people than will the remainder of the United Kingdom.

One study,[15] carried out for the United Kingdom, identified considerable fiscal pressures that are likely to come from demographic change. These are associated with other forms of age-related spending such as health spending, as well as spending on state benefits for old people. For the spending plans as set out in the Budget of June 2010 to be maintained, tax increases of around six per cent of GDP were thought to be necessary. The analysis does not investigate how the change to Universal Credit affects this, but there is little reason to think it has a substantial influence on the effects of demographic

---

14 It should be noted that UK Universal Credit is not, despite its name, a universal benefit in the sense that it is paid to everyone independent of their circumstances. The reason for this is clear. Universality tends to place a heavy cost on the system. If entitlement to benefits is not made contingent either on income or other criteria, then a high rate of tax is inevitably needed to pay for it.

15 McCarthy, Sefton and Weale (2011).

change: it certainly was not designed with that in mind.

A reasonable conclusion is that the affordability problem may be more severe in Scotland because demographic change is expected to be more marked. This, combined with the earlier observations about the time inconsistency of individuals' preferences, would be expected to set a limit to a substantially more generous benefit system, and especially so if that involves net transfers to old people.

FIGURE 1: THE POPULATION AGED SIXTY-FIVE AND OVER AS A PERCENTAGE OF THAT AGED 20–64 IN SCOTLAND AND IN THE UNITED KINGDOM

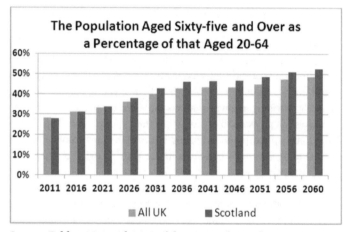

Source: Tables A3-1 and A3-6 of the National Population Projections ONS, 23rd November 2011

A.10 RISKS IN WELFARE TRANSFORMATION

In the event of Scotland assuming responsibility for welfare powers, whether within one of the UK-based models or one of the independence-based models, one of the key considerations would be the risks to the welfare system of transformation to any new constitutional arrangement. Here, several areas are identified where risk identification and management would be critical.

» the first issue is *continuity* of service provision. Arguably, in the short, or, indeed, medium term, the primary objective would be continuity and ensuring the resilience of the system through a major constitutional change. The loss of key services and the failure to pay legitimate benefits at any time – and for any length of time – would clearly be potentially catastrophic for individuals or groups of individuals, and no doubt additionally result in major political damage. Providing an uninterrupted service would, therefore, be of paramount importance. In time, no doubt, once the new governance surrounding the welfare system was embedded and proven to be robust, systemic change would be feasible and would, of course, be totally legitimate to reflect the political objectives of the governing administration.

» second, the experience of *systemic change* in other parts of the public services in recent decades has demonstrated the serious obstacles to effectively and seamlessly moving from one established system to another, while upholding the quality of the service provision, not least when it incorporates – and, especially, when it depends heavily or, indeed, totally upon – a major information technology element. The failure to undertake a meaningful pilot study of such a transformation over an appropriate period of time, often several years, prior to confirming the wisdom of the proposed change and attempting the roll out of the full service, has been at the root of some of the dramatic failures seen in the past. Thus, while the risk in implementation is very substantial, the capacity to mitigate the risks through the highest quality project management and through the avoidance of excessively rapid phasing does exist. Clearly, this has the potential to be a major factor in the first risk outlined above. In the event of a more, rather than a less, ambitious change, either in the policy environment or in the event of seeking to deliver services through newly determined mechanisms, the risks would rise sharply.

» third, there is the matter of *system design*. This chapter has focused heavily on the challenges of welfare system design and has highlighted the critical considerations surrounding the impact of system design on individual behaviours and, specifically, the incentives to work, save and consume, both for those of working age and for those who are retired. The implications of poor policy, therefore, for economic development and for the other distributional objectives of government are profound. These risks are further highlighted in the conclusions below.

» additionally, designing a new *institutional framework* for the management, implementation and delivery of welfare policy would be a huge and challenging task. The organisational risk in a context where there is currently little practical experience of such implementation would be very significant. Closely associated with this, of course, would be the need to find the appropriate administrative capacity. The assumption of welfare powers in Scotland would bring with it a significant need for specific administrative and technical skills, not only with the adoption of major changes to welfare policy and delivery, but also in the event that there were to be little substantive change in the system itself. With the imperative of continuity in mind, the risks can, of course, be reduced if service provision is contracted out to experienced current providers, but, with accountability resting with the Scottish Parliament, the organisational direction would necessarily be a high priority.

» in addition to these risks, there are different types of risk in needing to design systems that generate highly *efficient delivery*: for example, around the means of extracting the greatest economies of scale in service provision and in defining the optimal spatial unit for the organisation of delivery. Similarly, optimising the coherence of service provision and the quality of the outcomes, while maximising the efficiency of the system, is a key challenge.

» a separate critical risk is, as noted earlier, the *affordability* of either an inherited welfare system, with its existing set of policies, or, equally importantly, any redesigned set of policies. This appendix has flagged up the considerable risks associated with the design of policy and with the inherent generosity embedded within a system, together with the manner in which service delivery is organised and implemented. The identification of the anticipated costs for any proposed future welfare system is therefore critical to its integrity and credibility. Moreover, these costs would not necessarily all fall to central government. Indeed, as with the present UK reforms, a far greater burden may be redirected to local government, and their capacity to find the necessary financial and skilled resources would similarly be crucial.

» finally, there is a risk that a new system fails to satisfy all the *objectives of government* to at least the minimum required degree. As was noted earlier, for example, the trade-off between simplicity and the distributional objectives is a case in point. By over-emphasising one, albeit worthy objective, the capacity to meaningfully meet others may be lost.

A.11 CONCLUSIONS

This appendix has not sought to provide a blueprint for a future welfare system. It has focused on the identification of the critical issues that might helpfully steer the debate around any proposal for welfare powers to be assumed by the Scottish Parliament, irrespective of the precise form of constitutional arrangement. It has, moreover, particularly stressed the key parameters in welfare system design and their potential implications for the incentive structures that determine the behaviour of individuals within the economy more broadly. It has highlighted the central questions of design that must be addressed from this perspective and also from the perspective of affordability. It has, moreover, drawn out the tensions between objectives, notably between the incentives and costs of a system and distributional objectives.

The following section summarises those critical challenges that must be addressed. Some of them would not apply immediately if the proposition were heavily biased towards the continuity of the prevailing system, but, in time, in the light of the underlying rationale for the transference of such powers, any system redesign would need to face these questions.

These challenges are, notably, not focused upon any one vision or objective of a single administration: rather, they focus on defining a system that can be responsive to a range of objectives over the long term and has the capacity to respond flexibly as circumstances and objectives change. These are summarised below.

BASIC OBJECTIVES IN WELFARE SYSTEM DESIGN

Objectives

What are the fundamental objectives and circumstances that the welfare system seeks to address?

How are societal preferences most effectively identified?

Design

What design of welfare system facilitates the attainment of these basic objectives of government?

What are:

» the key components of the system to meet the basic objectives;
» the primary choices to be made: particularly as regards the trade-offs between individual wellbeing, economic incentives, affordability, simplicity and flexibility;
» the value and costs of universal and free welfare support systems and of mechanisms of means-testing and the targeting of support, and the balance to be struck here;

» the key design elements of the contributory element;
» the mechanisms of adjustment and revaluation.

Economic incentives

What are the objectives of the system for the key economic incentives and for the behaviour of individuals both of working age and of retirement age?

» notably, for
  › the incentive to work;
  › the incentive to work more;
  › the incentive to save;
» and for
  › the replacement ratio;
  › the withdrawal or taper rate;
  › the power of the automatic stabiliser function.

Poverty and inequality

What are the poverty and inequality objectives of the welfare system?

» what high-level objectives does society wish to pursue with respect to poverty and inequality?
» what does welfare policy seek to achieve with respect to poverty and minimum income/benefit levels?
» does it consider the interaction with the labour market and wage levels, and address the questions that have been raised around minimum acceptable wage levels and the *living wage* level?
» do the circumstances that make individuals eligible to receive benefits – and those circumstances that do not – reflect the views of the majority in society?
» is the system fair in determining and assessing the eligibility of individuals for specific benefits?

AFFORDABILITY OF THE SYSTEM

» Over the short and medium term is the inherent generosity of the system financially sustainable, given a realistic assessment of the associated costs and resource availability?
» Over the long term is the system sufficiently flexibly designed to adjust to significant changes in affordability? What are the drivers of long-term costs?

» With the UK-based models of devolution, what agreement would be struck with the UK regarding the transfers of resources to support the welfare programme?

DEMOGRAPHIC TRENDS AND THE RETIREMENT CHALLENGE

» What are the primary objectives of welfare support for the elderly?
  › what are the primary scenarios for future demographic trends and their implications for the ratio of the number of people of working age to the rest of the population?
  › what are the costed implications of these trends for the alternative welfare system options?
» Are there basic questions about the appropriateness of the personal lifetime savings profile, especially in the light of the expectations of future life expectancy?
  › do individuals make sufficient preparation for an unknown period of retirement?
  › how might the system incentivise such behaviour?
» How does the system manage this challenge without distorting work and savings incentives?

ISSUES OF TRANSITION

» What are the inheritance and current degrees of freedom in designing any new system?
» How would a transition to a new system be managed?
» What is the direct distributional impact of moving from the current welfare system to a new system: the winner and losers from change?

INSTITUTIONAL CHALLENGES

» What are the logistical, human capital and administrative design challenges for the establishment of a new system?
» What are the administrative costs associated with the options of welfare system? Are there economies of scale in the provision of such a system and an optimal spatial unit for its organisation, in order to maximise the coherence of service provision, the quality of the outcomes and efficiency of the system?
» What are primary options for the delivery of a welfare system? What are the internal or out-sourcing options?

How are the key risks identified and managed, notably in the areas of

- » the continuity of service provision;
- » system transformation;
- » system design;
- » the institutional framework;
- » human capital and skill requirements;
- » affordability;
- » the fulfilment of objectives.

OTHER QUESTIONS

- » What are the other key elements of demand for welfare support that need to be analysed?
- » What are the implications of there being a distinctive welfare system in Scotland compared to the rest of the UK?

Alt, J., Preston, I. & Sibieta, L. 2010. 'The Political Economy of Tax Policy', chapter 13, *Dimensions of Tax Design*, pp. 90–173. Oxford University Press. Oxford. Pp. 1204-1279.

Bell, David. 2010. *Meeting the Challenge of Budget Cuts in Scotland: Can Universalism Survive?* Paper for the Scottish Parliament Finance Committee, Scottish Parliament, April.

Beveridge, Crawford, McIntosh, Neil & Wilson, Robert. 2010. *Independent Budget Review: The Report of Scotland's Independent Budget Review Panel.* July.

Beveridge, W. 1942. 'Social Insurance and Allied Services'. CM6404. HMSO. London.

Department of Work and Pensions. 2010. 'Universal Credit: Welfare that Works'. Cm7957

McCarthy, D., Sefton, J. & Weale, M.R. 2011. 'Generational Accounts for the United Kingdom'. *National Institute Discussion Paper* No. 377. www.niesr.ac.uk/pdf/150311__171852.pdf.

Mirrlees, J.A. 1971. 'An Exploration in the Theory of Optimum Income Taxation'. *Review of Economic Studies.* Vol 38, pp. 175–208.

Nickell, S., Nunziata, L. & Ochel, W. 2005. 'Unemployment in the OECD since the 1960s. What do we Know?'. *Economic Journal.* Vol 115, pp. 1–27.

Reform Scotland. 2011. *Devolution Plus: Reform Scotland's Evidence to the Scottish Parliament's Bill Committee.* September 2011.

Scottish Government. 2012. *Government Expenditure and Revenue, Scotland, 2010–11,* March.

Turner, A. 2005. *A New Pension Settlement for the Twenty-first Century: The Second Report of the Pensions Commission.* www.webarchive.org.uk/pan/16806/20070717/www.pensionscommission.org.uk/www.pensionscommission.org.uk/publications/2005/annrep/main-report.pdf